BEFORE THE COMPUTER

PRINCETON STUDIES IN
BUSINESS AND TECHNOLOGY
David Hounshell, Series Editor

BEFORE THE COMPUTER

IBM, NCR, BURROUGHS, AND
REMINGTON RAND AND THE INDUSTRY
THEY CREATED, 1865–1956

James W. Cortada

PRINCETON UNIVERSITY PRESS   PRINCETON, NEW JERSEY

Library of Congress Cataloging-in-Publication Data
Cortada, James W.
Before the computer : IBM, NCR, Burroughs, and
Remington Rand and the industry they created,
1865–1956 / James W. Cortada.
p.   cm. — (Princeton studies in business and technology)
Includes bibliographical references and index.
ISBN 0-691-04807-X
1. Office equipment and supplies industry—United States—
History.   2. Electronic office machine industry—
United States—History.   I. Title.   II. Series.
HD9801.U542C67   1993
338.4′768—dc20   92-25399   CIP

This book has been composed in Linotron Times Roman

Princeton University Press books are printed
on acid-free paper and meet the guidelines
for permanence and durability of the Committee
on Production Guidelines for Book Longevity
of the Council on Library Resources

Printed in the United States of America

10   9   8   7   6   5   4   3   2

To Dora

Contents

List of Illustrations

Following Part Three, page 287

List of Figures

List of Tables

Preface

Each office within the skyscraper is a segment
of the enormous file, a part of the symbol factory
that produces the billion slips of paper that gear
modern society into its daily shape.
  (*C. Wright Mills, 1951*)

THE NOTED American sociologist, C. Wright Mills, saw the extent to which American society had become an information world. The data-processing industry, with its most visible symbol—the computer—stands out as one of the obvious features of the late twentieth-century world. Yet this industry has only recently come under the scrutiny of historians, the period before its advent—scarcely at all.

The problem largely has been one of time. The computer-based phase of the data-processing industry is barely forty years old, little time for historians to focus on it. The industry, if viewed as a collection of services based on the manufacture and use of mechanical tools for the control and use of information, has, in fact, been around as a distinct economic sector for more than one hundred years. As with many other industries, its pedigree is characterized by evolution from one base of technologies and customers to others. Yet one's vision of data processing has been influenced by commentators interested only in the present. The vast literature on information processing has been written either by journalists or by members of the industry, all of whom have been influenced profoundly by the immediacy of events rather than by patterns of long-term developments within the economy that fostered the industry and by specific occurrences in the industry itself.

Depending on whose definition is used, the data-processing industry in the United States (where it was conceived and grew to its most significant form) by the late 1980s represented approximately 5 percent of the gross national product (GNP). Worldwide, it appreciated to more than $300 billion for products and services. User expenses brought the total closer to $900 billion. Thus, by any measurement, a quantitative discussion of the industry represents a sizable issue.

The purpose of this book is to review the evolution of data processing in the United States from its nineteenth-century inception down to the period when the computer became the most important technology influencing the scope and nature of the industry. I have set patterns of behavior and major events in this industry in context with the American economy as I added comparative material on activities in other countries. The focus remains primarily on business issues. This is not a technical treatise, yet technology is not ignored because it is the basis for much that happened in this industry. It offered new levels of productivity and, thus, illustrated one conclusion that the use of data processing is very price sensitive. Contrary to what marketing members of the industry would argue, the cheaper technology-based products became to buy and use, the more they were adopted as substitutes for older, often more expensive alternatives.

Historians of this industry take various points of view on why and how this industry developed. Most have not focused sufficiently on specific reasons why data processing was accepted and used or for what purposes. Many have been tempted to view the industry at 35,000 feet from an imaginary airplane. At that level, topographical features blend into strings of mountain ranges—a useful perspective but obviously misleading. What I propose is to drop altitude metaphorically to define and characterize each mountain in the range. It then becomes possible to answer precisely basic questions about the American data-processing industry's evolution and to characterize the features of that portion of the economy known as the office appliance or equipment industry, the ancestor of the modern information processing industry. Ultimately, it allows me to generalize but with the support of a more detailed background.

How did the industry develop? What constituted the industry? Why did people acquire its technology? How did they use it? What influence did technology have on economic patterns of behavior? How were uses justified? In what ways did this industry respond to the demand for data-processing equipment and services? Answers to many basic questions allow one to understand the interrelationship of technology and economics—a cause and effect marriage that will obviously continue to influence everyone's life for the foreseeable future—while suggesting the future role of information processing. Importantly, it emphasizes how past events and practices remained evident in the industry after the advent of the computer.

This book is largely traditional business history. The industry is constantly redefined from one era to another. I measure size by volumes of items sold, log annual sales of major vendors, and review forms of manufacture and distribution. I also pay attention to customers. I discuss major institutions within the industry and their actions from an almost Whiggish perspective as meaningful case studies, windows into the industry. Snapshots of technological innovations and their effects on vendors and customers play critical roles in this study.

This is also the story of an industry peopled by entrepreneurs equipped with outstanding technical backgrounds, facing obvious and sometimes less-than-obvious economic opportunities. The "power of one," often remarked by the founder of International Business Machines (IBM), Thomas J. Watson, Sr., was a factor in the huge success of this industry. Scientists and spies, engineers and customers, military personnel and sales staffs, government officials and eccentric dilettantes, all worked to create what so many like to call the Age of the Computer or, as James R. Beniger and so many have named it, the Information Society.

To look primarily at the American experience is a necessary first step in understanding the total influence that this economic sector had on the societies of the industrialized world. Over the years it became obvious to me, even after completing this book, that more unanswered questions than not were facing historians of early data processing. Many of the company archives that would have to be studied to review the industry thoroughly remain closed or poorly stocked. Too little is known about how office appliances were acquired by customers. Biographies of key inventors and users remain unwritten. But enough information is available to begin a general history of this industry's earliest days.

To accomplish a history, I relied heavily on published primary and secondary materials because in many ways the industry was open, its achievements and failures were subject to constant public discussion. The literature on this industry is vast, and a great deal of it is useful. Company histories and popular magazine articles and brochures describe products sold while technical journals detail the technologies involved. Lawsuits make boardroom decisions public. When published sources failed to address a critical issue, such as the size of the adding and calculating machine market before World War I, I turned to archival materials, especially those of Burroughs, IBM, and the U.S. government.

Chronological chapters reflect convenient (if arbitrarily established) epochs in the industry's history. For each era I deal with the technological underpinnings of the industry because they led to the specific marketable products and incentives that were necessary preconditions for the use of dataprocessing equipment. I described major vendors when they either reflected or dominated the activities of the industry. Thus, on the one hand, one learns about the National Cash Register Company (NCR) of the late 1800s and about IBM in the 1940s, but on the other hand, something concerning the Powers Accounting Machine Company of the 1910s. My primary concern is to describe common patterns of behavior within the industry that defined it and helped explain why it became such an important element within the economy.

No history of an industry would be complete without a round of measurements of its business volumes, profitability, application of products, and major events. These, in turn, must be set within the broader context of economic history. I have presented these various elements within as broad a perspective as possible. However, because this industry generally continued to grow in both good and bad times, it had its own internal economic features that need to be identified.

I have organized much of the material by specific devices rather than by functions. The nature of available machines usually dictated what mechanical aids to information processing could be used. Equipment was often the focal point of users and vendors and, in their minds, represented either classes of tools or market segments. In short, it was a convenient way to organize material. The book is highly selective. I have studied only those devices that (1) were mechanical means of handling data that otherwise would appear just on paper and (2) were precursors to the modern computer and its applications. Thus detailed discussions of paper-filing systems, both the telegraph and telephone, and dozens of other management, clerical, and mechanical methods are absent despite the fact that these, too, were important aspects of American business history. I contend that threading through mechanical aids to data handling offers a more convenient approach to the study of the interrelationship of technology, function, and marketing in the new industry that ultimately became the information-processing industry.

I focus on how products came to market and why, who bought them and why, and what they were used for. I have taken corporate politics seriously and paid homage to lone achievers. I have dealt also with such concepts as the role of feedback in controlling purposeful economic behavior and what the literature of the industry teaches the interested observer.

Because this book is an attempt to write a detailed history of the early decades of the industry, it avoids elegant theoretical structures and debates with other historians and focuses more on narrative descriptions of major events and patterns of behavior. It is bound to have errors of fact and judgment, but I hope that future historians will write the company histories and biographies that are needed, formulate a better conceptual basis for defining the industry, and study the effects of these machines and their industry on society. Let this book be a step in the right direction.

Acknowledgments _____

THIS BOOK required the support of many individuals and organizations for more than one decade. In particular, Anne Frantilla at the Unisys Archives, home of the Burroughs Papers before they moved to the Charles Babbage Institute (CBI), shared all the information with me. Robert E. Pokorak, late head of the IBM Archives, was equally generous. Nancy Y. McGovern at the U.S. National Archives along with associates at the National Museum of American History and at the NCR Archives provided critical support. CBI's collections are a must for any student of this industry, and individuals at CBI were helpful at every turn, particularly in advising on how to conduct the research. The Computer Museum in Boston and the Smithsonian Institution helped me understand the benefits of various machines as I studied their exhibits.

I owe an intellectual debt to Alfred D. Chandler who taught me a great deal through his books on business history. Bill Aspray read the manuscript and offered many suggestions for improvements. David A. Hounshell provided the same kind of support and led me to the Princeton University Press.

Princeton University Press made me feel as if everyone there was working on my book to make it the best. Jack Repcheck navigated the manuscript through the acceptance process, strongly supporting my work. Molan Chun Goldstein and the production department produced a beautiful book. I want to extend a special thanks to Virginia M. Barker, the copyeditor on this project, for work well done and for her enthusiastic involvement with the book. I also want to acknowledge the faith shown in my work by Princeton's readers and the editorial board.

A special thanks is also due my family, who made it possible for me to write this book. This volume is bound to have errors of fact and judgment that are my failings, and I take responsibility for them.

Part One

ORIGINS OF A NEW INDUSTRY, 1865–1920

1

From Opportunities to Typewriters

BEFORE COMPUTERS were available, mechanical aids for computing and managing data existed. These products represented a broad range of mechanisms that supported data input (typewriters and tabulating machines), calculation (adding machines and calculators), communications (telegraph and telephone), and dozens of other devices to increase the ability of office and manufacturing personnel to manage their firms more effectively, to increase control over their jobs, and to improve their ability to make better decisions. All of these tools were in use before 1900 and collectively constituted a recognizable part of the American business scene by the 1920s—five decades before the first useful digital computers. These early tools shaped many features of the modern office and helped make possible large manufacturing facilities. By coming in an age of increased reliance on the results of technology and the mechanization of work, these devices and their users collectively formed a new industry that, by the late 1880s or early 1890s, was recognizable as an office products or, in the parlance of the day, an "office appliance" industry complete with companies, customers, products, associations, publications, and business conventions. That cluster of organizations and events (with the exception of the telephone) emerged in the 1950s as the data-processing industry.

The central issue of part one is the early development of the office appliance industry in the period from the end of the American Civil War to the start of the 1920s. In this period, various technologies emerged to address the needs of offices and plants but without the cohesion that "systems" of products offered later. The amount of activity, variety of products, and extent of their use, both in the United States and in Europe, far exceeded what previous historians have noted. NCR cash registers appeared on all continents, tabulating gear was used from Russia to California, adding machines were sold by the thousands, and nearly one hundred firms were active. Before World War I, patterns of behavior and a sense of industry identification existed. Publications of the period identified a new industrial sector while its volume of activity made typewriters and telephones common items in many offices. The need for more control, the ability to manage ever-growing amounts of paper and information, and competitive pressures made it obvious that it was no accident that a large, important office equipment market would exist in the 1920s.

Many of the practices of this industry in the 1920s–1930s and later, in the era of the data-processing industry, were worked out in the years before World War I. Practices at NCR in the 1880s and 1890s were carried over into the IBM of the 1920s and beyond by its founder and former NCR executive, Thomas J. Watson. Hardware leasing and sale of supplies by computer firms in the 1950s points to similar practices by Herman Hollerith, who sold tabulating equipment before the turn of the century. Antitrust problems emerged before World War I at NCR, in the 1930s and 1940s at IBM and Remington Rand, and in the 1950s at AT&T—all before the computer was widely available. Although the technology upon which the data-processing industry was based changed and always gave off an image of newness, the industry's business practices were always very conservative.

Historical issues evident in the 1865–1930 period mimic those faced by students in the 1950s to 1970s. How does one define the industry? Too often the student perspective of this industry was narrower than the facts suggested. There are those who see the industry as comprising just equipment manufacturers[1] and others who see the industry through company histories, particularly as extensions of IBM.[2] To some, it includes telecommunications[3] whereas to others it does not.[4] They have defined the industry variously as the "computer industry,"[5] the "semiconductor industry,"[6] as part of the "electronics industry,"[7] and the "knowledge industry."[8] All definitions either left out the largest element of the industry—users such as the typists of the 1890s or programmers in the 1980s—or minimized their roles. Vendors never did; they called them customers. One needs to see them as part of the new industry in some cases.

Similar definition problems exist for the earliest period in the history of data processing. But to appreciate fully the significance of office technology, one must broaden the definition of what constituted the industry in the late 1800s. It included vendors, engineers and mechanics who developed products, and equipment users.

Many disparate lines of development that preceded 1920, superficially at least, did not seem connected. Various lines of activity included, for example, the invention, marketing, and acceptance of the typewriter and, to an important corollary extent, the telegraph. Another thread involved the evolution of the cash register. A third concerned adding machines and calculators. Other miscellaneous devices dotted the office to a lesser extent, offering possible confusion. The one aspect of development that enjoyed much attention—Hollerith's equipment—must be set within the broader context of the industry; his was not the only or the largest portion of the new industry in its formative stages.[9] The development and use of typewriters, cash registers, adding machines, calculators, and tabulating equipment provided a collection constituting the origins and early makeup of the modern data-processing industry. Technologies applicable to one set of products lent themselves to other types of devices (e.g., keyboards). In many cases, they were sold to the same set of customers. Most types of devices were marketed by the same companies. Thus the NCR of the 1880s was, by the late 1920s, also selling adding and calculating machines. The same was true of Burroughs, IBM, and Remington Rand.

How does one measure industry activities? One defines industry size and documents its financial performance, given the fact that much hard data is not available; narrates what products were introduced and why; and represents their users. In the first four chapters, I devote attention to each of these elements, arguing that the industry existed much earlier and was larger and more significant than previously thought, and that many of the features of the modern office can be attributed to the robustness and nature of this new industry. By the end of chapter 4, those who work within the information-processing industry in the 1990s should recognize much that is familiar in the work of their predecessors in the 1890s. Finally, the effects on a broad range of organizations evident in the years before World War II are later seen in the 1960s–1990s again looking for control and purposeful activity and using this technology and its industry for support.[10]

Economic Preconditions and Influences

The development of new technology and products was no accident. Nor was it by chance that these items were bought, sold, and used and, thereby, made possible the inception of the data-processing industry. New technology to help manage information developed and emerged in response to perceived needs, not as an uncontrolled or accidental by-product of the pursuit of science and engineering. Reaction was to a real need to manage larger amounts of information (data) in shorter periods. The earliest and most fundamental impetus for modern data processing came from the positive economic conditions that prevailed in the United States for so many decades.

Individual events in this industry were either the result of some specific issue or were changed by longer-term and less obvious economic and technological trends. Most students of technology and mechanization have recognized the interrelationship of the problem. Those who do, understand that as technologies advance and create new jobs, economic impact may not be predictable when, for instance, jobs are simultaneously lost with little advance warning of the number or types that will be affected.[11] Historians have recognized the correlation between the shift in employment from agricultural to manufacturing sectors as a direct and obvious element that influences the rise of data processing.[12] Corporations as new economic elements after the Civil

War, with their increasing ability to control production and distribution of goods and services, highlighted the variety of influences that affected all industries, including the fledgling office equipment suppliers.[13]

The industry began most intensely first in the United States and second in Europe. First and more frequently in the United States, individuals and their firms spotted opportunities and exercised good inventive engineering and effective marketing. But economic conditions contributed mightily as well. Modernization of the American economy, with its broad move to industrialization, led to a "takeoff" in the 1840s that lasted until long after the introduction of computers. This move ensued despite civil war in the 1860s, financial panic in the 1870s, and a severe depression in the 1890s. The fundamental circumstance of long-term growth of the economy promoted confidence in bold ventures to, for example, the developers of railroads and, later, to large steel and chemical companies.

Total output of commodities rose at 4.6 percent before the Civil War and then at 4.4 percent between 1870 and 1900. Manufacturing share over agriculture grew proportionately as well.[14] Manufacturing value added expanded at about 6 percent per year from 1870 to 1900 while that portion attributed to durable goods hovered at 42.5 percent. Per capita output grew rapidly too, averaging annual rates of 21.1 percent (compared to 1.45 percent between 1840 and 1860).[15]

The size of the American market was very important as a critical factor that made possible economic expansion in the late 1800s. Alfred Chandler commented that during "the second part of the nineteenth century the American domestic market was the largest . . . and fastest growing market in the world." He noted that in 1880 American national income and population were 1.5 times larger than Great Britain's, twice that of the British in 1900, and three times theirs by 1920.[16] The population of the United States grew dramatically in the late 1800s too, but it was the rate of growth that provided such striking evidence of the dynamism in this national economy. Rates of growth of 25 percent between 1869 and 1878 and 1889 to 1898 were not uncommon. Such rates of growth in population and in national product exceeded those of all other industrialized nations. Other technologically advanced countries, such as Germany and Britain and, to a lesser extent, France, also were shifting to larger and more industrialized economies.[17] A more homogeneous income distribution in the United States hastened adoption of new technologies while encouraging mass production, mass marketing, and mass distribution.[18]

Conversely, those who studied Europe's economic modernization for the same period have argued that largeness of population and national economy gave Britain an initial edge over other European states in starting her industrial revolution in the 1700s but later served as a barrier to expansion on the continent, which was dotted with so many smaller national economies. These states imposed tariff barriers, practiced protectionism too frequently, and had smaller populations to support economic transactions. As economies of scale presented problems, so too did the smaller economy upon which a nation depended for infusions of capital.[19]

The most obvious ways that largeness could influence an industrializing economy were through availability and productivity of labor. Between 1870 and 1960, productivity of American workers more than quadrupled. Employment jumped sixfold to more than 65 million; 12.5 million U.S. workers in 1870 expanded to 45.3 million in 1920. During the same period, the percentage of workers in industry increased from 32 percent in 1870 to 32 percent in 1920 while the absolute number of workers also rose. The service sector rose from 16.2 percent in 1870 to 25.1 percent in 1900, then dropped to 17.7 to 17.8 percent until the 1920s.[20]

Office appliance customers came from outside the agricultural sector until very late in the twentieth century; thus the expansion of the manufacturing and service sectors proved critical to the success of this new industry. The industrial sector included about 25 percent of the U.S. labor force from the late 1800s to World War II and closer to 40 percent during the war years of the 1940s. Another sector, illustrated by James R. Beniger's work, grew from negligible numbers before 1865 to significant proportions by 1917. Frequently labeled the information sector (a phrase coined in hindsight), it consisted of that portion of the work force who handled data (bookkeepers, teachers, professors, statisticians, etc.). That community grew to 4.8 percent in 1870, jumped to 6.5 percent in 1880, then to 12.4 percent in 1890. The depression in the 1890s probably restrained this sector to 12.8 percent in 1900, but it grew to 17.7 percent by the end of 1920.[21]

Increasingly, expanding organizations managed more people, who, if in the information sector, handled more information. By the 1860s, the volume of data being handled was rising. The trend accelerated in subsequent years, contributed to the ascendancy of office management, and increased bureaucratization—seedbeds of motivation and need for those who wanted to mechanize data handling. A by-product was the increase in American clerks from 1 to 2 percent of the work force in 1870 to more than 10 percent by 1940.[22] The growth trend continued into the era of the microcomputer in the late 1970s.

For organizations that needed to handle greater amounts of information, reliance on the availability of people and technology became pressing. The availability of people to handle information provided one reason for data processing's success. This result is as true today as it was in the 1870s or 1880s. These clerks, accountants, and other "knowledge workers" became the most important general economic input for the new industry. The economic value of what they added to a product or service influenced directly the justification for information-handling technologies. Individuals, dramatic in

TABLE 1.1

Gross National Product for the United States, 1869–1921
(dollars in billions)

Years[a]	GNP	Years[a]	GNP
1869–1871	9.1	1897–1901	34.4
1872–1876	11.2	1902–1906	45.0
1877–1881	16.1	1907–1911	52.5
1882–1886	20.7	1912–1916	59.7
1887–1891	24.0	1917–1921	67.7
1892–1896	28.3		

Source: U.S. Bureau of the Census, *Historical Statistics of the United States, Colonial Times to 1957* (Washington, D.C.: Government Printing Office, 1960), 144.

[a] Figures given for each five-year period are annual averages.

their singleness, influenced events too by inventing products and selling them through corporations thereby giving truth to Watson's idea that the "power of one" was, indeed, significant.

Labor productivity in this period was impressive and a closely related element. The GNP per capita grew steadily in general terms from the 1870s to the 1990s despite the panic of 1873, the depressions of the 1890s and 1930s, and the recessions that dotted American economic life after World War II. These rates of growth usually exceeded those of labor in Britain and in Europe. More importantly, however, anybody working in the American economy could have concluded that increases in productivity and, hence, standard of living and output were made possible by using new technologies. Real product per capita rose throughout the century. Growth in the early 1900s came despite economic fluctuations before 1917. The bottom line is that by 1870 the American economy had a full head of steam and was fed further between 1870 and 1910 by expansion across industrial America in steel, electricity, other forms of technology, and so forth, some of which was to make up the new data-processing industry in the twentieth century.[23]

The GNP also rose in absolute dollar volumes, doubling in almost every decade before World War I (see table 1.1). In short, a nation that had 9.6 million workers in 1870 had, in the process of more than doubling these by World War I, increased its output per capita and the overall volume of goods and services and experienced dramatic shifts from agriculture to manufacturing. In turn, these trends heralded a postwar period in which the American economy could scarcely operate without the aid of corporate and governmental bureaucracies, all of which used information technology.

One vital economic precondition for the use of better information-handling machines was the pattern of behavior that led to larger corporations, distinct and often new industries, the manufacture of larger quantities of goods, equally greater consumption of raw materials and labor, and the flow of goods through distributors to large retail or mail order enterprises. Transportation, distribution, merchandizing, and financing of these activities were obvious elements. Chandler contends that as the 1800s passed, control was such that the economy reacted purposefully to the new mandarins of industry— business managers—and made possible features of the twentieth-century economy. He argues that the remolding of the American economy into corporate form had been completed by the 1920s and that subsequent activities extended features already evident by that time. Others, such as Beniger, add the biological analogy of all living things wanting to "control" their environments, extending in their own ways Chandler's position. In essence, the argument is that no large organization can function successfully unless it controls its affairs. Control requires "feedback" mechanisms for information provided by the brain and nervous system, which handle vast quantities of information rapidly and accurately so that the organism can respond advantageously to changing conditions in a timely manner.[24]

Chandler noted that the "modern business enterprise took the place of market mechanisms in coordinating the activities of the economy and allocating its resources. In many sectors of the economy the visible hand of management replaced what Adam Smith referred to as the invisible hand of market forces." The market still generated demand but the modern corporation assumed responsibility for producing, delivering, and selling goods and services. The size of large organizations came to dominate the economy and its managers, therefore, creating "managerial capitalism."[25] Modern American governments and corporations became the largest customers of data-processing equipment.

Chandler identified railroad companies as the first prototype of the modern organization. They had to move large amounts of goods across the very large land mass of the United States, control thousands of miles of tracks, millions of tons of cargo and rolling stock, employees scattered across many states, and safety. Railroads used every information-handling technology as it appeared. They began with telegraph systems, then acquired typewriters, tabulators, adding machines and calculators, often adopting such devices before any other industry did. Railroads were among the first commercial users of the U.S. postal service on an expanded basis. Key to large organizations was the ability to gather vast sums of information and send it to many points quickly while providing responsible and responsive accounting.[26] As with other industries, Chandler found that "technology of production was certainly the critical determinant in the growth of the firm" between 1880 and 1920. Companies developed technologies when the maintenance of high-volume output required precise scheduling of flows of finished goods to customers. That could not be done without advancing beyond the pen and book ledger techniques of the early 1800s.[27] "Where administration coordination provided competitive advantages, integration brought concentration" (even before 1900) encouraging larger institutions often with vertical integration from production through sales and distribution.[28]

New technologies could only be marketed if their developers made significant investments, in Chandler's words, in "production facilities large enough to exploit a technology's potential economies of scale and scope." A similarly significant investment had to be made in distribution (e.g., a national sales force) "so that the volume of sales might keep pace with the new volume of production." A third investment in management took advantage of the first two. Those who made all three investments first within an industry typically came to dominate it. They gained significant competitive advantages and often became oligopolistic. Vendors of technology-based products could market more through functional and strategic effectiveness than through price.[29] This is exactly what happened in the proto–data-processing industry before 1956.

This pattern was evident among cash register vendors; a high concentration of market share was in the hands of NCR by the turn of the century. All tabulating business was controlled by C-T-R (Hollerith's old firm reconfigured with additional companies in 1911) and the Powers Accounting Machine Company (later part of Remington Rand). Typewriter production by hundreds of companies was concentrated in a few firms by the 1920s. The process continued into later decades with the evolution of vertically integrated manufacturers of digital computers (such as IBM and Sperry Rand by the late 1950s).

The need for efficient and effective resource management on a much broader scale than before led many potential users of data-processing equipment to become oligopolies more frequently than monopolies and was reflected in the development of the integrated corporation. Oligopolies took advantage of resources, by-products of new wares, and market positions in competitive battles with each other. It was the U.S. government's practice to enforce legislation against monopolies but by discouraging formation of oligopolies, which made the process all that much more possible.[30] C. Wright Mills, in his classic study of American business workers, documented the result of big business and—by implication—information handling: "The organizational reason for the expansion of the white-collar occupations is the rise of big business and big government, and the consequent trend of modern social structure, the steady growth of bureaucracy." In turn, this created "elaborate specializations" generating "the need for many men and women to plan, co-ordinate, and administer new routines for others" and requiring more clerks and people reporting to other people.[31] What he described for the midtwentieth century applied to earlier decades as well. It was already evident as early as 1870 that bureaucracy was rapidly creating new opportunities for products, different careers, and a greater reliance on technology. In short, information management and its dependent technologies appeared when complex and large organizations needed them.

Beniger took Chandler's discoveries further by arguing that control could only come by using information technology, perhaps energetically overstating the case somewhat. Nonetheless, he documented the emergence of the typewriter, telephone, and accounting and tabulating equipment in response to control. JoAnne Yates studied several cases of control through filing systems and paper-based communications for this period too, reinforcing the extensiveness of the effort.[32] Managers thought equipment could control costs or enable them to do more with existing resources (dollars, staff, and office facilities). Without information-handling tools, the economy could not have controlled the increases in speed provided by innovations in transportation, production, and enhanced communications. Beniger argued that a "crisis of control" had developed by the mid-1880s that was resolved, for all intents and purposes, by the end of the century.[33] Both Beniger and Yates saw the economic response as both the rise of bureaucracy and the systemization of office functions, noting that the modern office of the 1870s could use telegraphs, telephones, a complex postal system, delivery services, newsletters, and subscriptions to directories. The office of 1890 could add typewriters, phonographs, and cash registers, reflecting "a trend toward integration of informational goods and services, media and control."[34]

There are some obvious pitfuls, however, to avoid. Although Beniger illustrated that information technology began to emerge simultaneously with the rise of bureaucracies observed by Chandler and others, the absolute assumption was that the handling of information did too. Exactly how much more paperwork existed in the period immediately following the Civil War than for the years subsequent to World War I is not known.[35] The paucity of data on business sales volumes of many information-processing equipment manufacturers of the late 1800s precludes an assumption about the influence of such technology. However, as I will note later, many specific pieces of evidence suggest that sales were high (e.g., for typewriters) and that the number of cash registers expanded fiscal controls outside the office in stores. But the picture is incomplete. That information management was a new and crucial element in late nineteenth-century organizations cannot be questioned. But was it as important then as in the years following World War II? The question remains unanswered despite a strong urge to say no. One can point to post–World War II expenditures for data-handling devices as a percentage of an organization's total budget and come up with figures ranging from 1 to 5 percent[36] but still cannot do the same for the period 1870–1900 or for the 1920s to 1930s. For the earlier years, all evidence gathered so far is impressionistic.

The growing demand for information-handling technologies as they developed is obvious. As time passed, demand increased sharply for such equipment. Demand was identified by individuals such as inventors and sellers:

William S. Burroughs saw the need for an adding machine; John Henry Patterson and James and John Ritty identified the requirement for the cash register, as did Christopher L. Sholes for typewriters.[37] Always, the economic basis for justification and the means to market existed. Inventors and manufacturers worked in a society characterized by an expanding economy stocked with a considerable and growing population, blessed with an abundance of raw materials, and evolving organizational structures to manage its enormous volume of rapidly used inputs and outputs.

Inventors and Vendors on Opportunity

But did the creators of data-processing's products and market concur with the analysis of an economy sufficiently full of opportunity to warrant invention? Could a market then be developed for new products for which few or no precedents possibly existed? Although evidence to answer these questions for the period before 1900 remains severely limited and most early "pioneers" of data processing did not write memoirs or even record motivational comments, one, however, can suspect that they too subscribed to the notion that theirs was an era of opportunity.

NCR's founder, John H. Patterson, who developed so many of the business practices later evident in the data-processing industry, especially at IBM, saw clearly the value of cash registers in what was an expanding retail market during the 1880s.[38] E. Remington and Sons (long-time manufacturers of rifles and pistols), during the 1870s, identified a market for typewriters after the idea of manufacturing them was brought to their attention. In the early 1880s, they expanded their marketing of this product as a result of quick initial success with it.[39] Even before Hollerith began constructing tabulating equipment in the 1880s, at the U.S. Bureau of the Census in the 1870s an employee, Charles W. Seaton, expressed optimism about the possible uses of punched card equipment after constructing the Seaton Tabulating Machine.[40] Those who helped either what eventually became the Burroughs Corporation by selling adding machines or were early executives of the firm recalled the optimism their technology posed.[41] In the late 1860s or early to mid-1870s, other, lesser-known members of the industry also identified the potential of data handling. For example, John C. Wilson conceived and patented the mechanical time stamp in 1871. Harlow Bundy created the Bundy Key Recorder in 1888. His firm eventually joined other small companies to form C-T-R in 1911, the precursor of IBM.[42]

Even outside the inventor's workshop the mood reflected growing faith that problems could be solved with the aid of machines despite the fact that each inventor and almost every early "high-tech" firm initially experienced slow sales. Dorr E. Felt, successful vendor of adding machines that rivaled those of the Arithmometer Company (predecessor to Burroughs) in the 1880s and 1890s, commented that increased demand for statistics and accounting was "turning men into veritable machines" while Oliver Wendell Holmes called forth the benefits of a mechanical solution. Charles W. Eliot, president of Harvard College and an outspoken proponent of technology, stated the position, "A man ought not to be employed at a task which a machine could perform."[43] In reality, the optimism, although warranted and fulfilled, did not come immediately or without the normal difficulties of any capital-hungry start-up business. But Americans lived in an era in which, the astute British observer James Bryce noted, the individual wanted "to be let alone, to do as he pleases, indulge his impulses, follow out his projects."[44]

Development of the Typewriter

Of all the pre–World War I direct antecedents to modern data processing in America none has received more attention than the typewriter. Yet equally true, none has been so obviously ignored as an ancestor of the new industry.[45] Interest in the typewriter is relatively easy to explain. As a "stand-alone" instrument, it is small, usually convenient to move about and, once its modern form became available by the end of the 1890s, simple to use. In time, its expense dropped to a price that almost anybody could afford. It became a convenience that appeared almost simultaneously in government agencies, in the hands of writers, and in business offices. Tens of thousands were built in the single generation between the early 1870s and the dawn of the new century. Millions of additional machines made it almost as commonplace as the telephone throughout the twentieth century.[46] Just two years after the Spanish-American War, roughly one typewriter was available for every 640 Americans. One simply could write more words faster on a typewriter than by hand. A second reason for historical interest in the machine was the collection of social implications contributed by the device. In a period when office populations were rising in both the United States and Europe, it opened another socially acceptable career path for women and, thus, went far to explain the rise of the female secretary.[47] By the 1890s, women not only had invaded the office but were also operating typewriters, not just telephones as more traditional studies of women suggest (see fig. 1).

Although these various causes of interest in typewriters are important, particularly for the history of women and of organizations in business and government, by themselves they miss the fact that typewriters were also an antecedent of data processing and its technologies. Typewriter manufacturers became builders of other data-processing equipment. Without the profits of the typewriter busines, some might not have had as much incentive to market other office appliances in the 1920s as they did. The typewriter also gave

1.1 An office of the 1890s with "typewriter girls" in what appears to be an early typing pool (courtesy IBM Archives).

firms the courage and experience to market high technology–based products in the office market, which, at least in the 1880s and 1890s, was a relatively new and changing world but one well understood by the early 1920s. These companies could transfer their knowledge of office customers to other technologies as well, applying what they learned with typewriters to other, new office equipment. Thus they could apply keyboards to calculators and accounting machines. The manufacturing processes for typewriters or accounting machines were very similar, calling on the same economies of scale, methods of production, and materials and management skills.[48] Thus for a combination of reasons, the story of the typewriter represents an important, if early, step toward the data-processing world and the use of computers.

The evolution of the typewriter, as with other technology-based devices, predates the Industrial Revolution as the machine gained enough effectiveness and momentum to become a widely marketable item. At least twenty significant milestones in its development occurred before 1867, dating back to 1714. Sixteen came in America; the rest originated in Europe before a practical "Type-Writer" could pass into the American lexicon.[49]

Many of the key milestones have been described by historians and need not detain one here. However, some facts are crucial to the modern American experience. "Writing machines" had been under development since at least the early 1700s, but the first American patent went to William Austin Burt in 1829 for his "typographer." Nearly two dozen patents were issued on both sides of the Atlantic Ocean during the 1830s and 1840s, none of which were exploited effectively as products. Historians credited Christopher Latham Sholes of Milwaukee, Wisconsin, as developer of the first important machine because his became commercially successfully and made possible wide introduction of the device. He worked extensively on the machine between 1867 and 1873, when it became ready for mass production.[50] How Sholes took his invention from idea to product reflected a pattern evident continuously throughout the history of American data processing.

Sholes built on experiences of earlier developers, most notably on John Pratt's machine of the 1860s. Improving upon earlier designs, he worked on his own in the 1860s and 1870s when a large number of technologies were being applied to office functions. When Sholes finally had what he perceived to be a marketable device, he sought financial backing from James Densmore, a successful lawyer, businessman, and newspaper editor. Densmore, functioning like a late twentieth-century capitalist, sought a manufacturer to produce the device and found E. Remington and Sons of Ilion, New York. Remington had simultaneously taken the initiative to find a similar product. As the often-told story goes, in February 1873, Harry Harper Benedict at Remington saw a typed letter that caused him to suggest that the company look at the typewriter as a possible product.

Remington had prospered during the Civil War as an arms manufacturer. Following the end of the conflict it sought new diversified product lines, initially electing farm equipment, which proved a failure. Yet the company's great strength lay in its ability to mass produce equipment and parts—a critical requirement to manufacture typewriters. Remington could manufacture the quantity needed to be profitable, could facilitate the production process with interchangeable standard parts, which any vendor would want to be able to interchange among models, and could adopt existing technologies and processes within manufacturing. Such capabilities could reduce manufacturing costs per unit.

Thus the marriage of Sholes's invention to Remington's manufacturing capability seemed a strong union and was formalized with a contact signed March 1, 1873. It called for the production of at least one thousand units and up to twenty-four thousand, if needed. The first machines appeared in 1874 and were named the Remington No. 1. They were primitive, looked more like

TABLE 1.2
Major Developments of the Typewriter, 1868–1896, Selected Years

1868	"Type-writer" developed	C. L. Sholes
1872	Spring-seated keys and carry type introduced	Various inventors
1874	First commercial machine	Remington
1876	Remington No. 1 (capitals only)	Remington
1878	Remington No. 2 (capitals and lowercase, first shift)	Remington
1878	"Caligraph" with capitals and lowercase with keyboard	Yost-Wagner
1878	Type on ends lever	Various inventors
1881	Plastic type plate	Various inventors
1884	Oscillating type segment and hammer patented	Various inventors
1890	First portable introduced	G. C. Blickensderfer
1896	Ford typewriter introduced	Various vendors
1896	First automatic ribbon reverse	Remington
1896	First "noiseless" typewriter	W. P. Kidder-C. C. Colby

Sources: George N. Engler, "The Typewriter Industry: The Impact of a Significant Technological Innovation" (Ph.D. diss., University of California at Los Angeles, 1969), 16–17; Carroll H. Blanchard, Jr., *The Early Word Processors*, Research Report 3 (Farmingdale, N.Y.: State University at Farmingdale, Educators Project 4, 1981): E1–E211.

sewing machines (upon which some of the design was based) than typewriters, and could only type uppercase letters. With the Remington No. 2 in 1878 came lowercase letters as well.[51]

Between July and December 1874, some four hundred machines were built and sold at between $25 and $50 each. Others soon saw ways to improve on these machines, and throughout the 1870s and 1880s, dozens of changes were made outside Remington by manufacturers marketing their own products. By the 1890s, however, the essentially modern manual typewriter was available. It had upper- and lowercases and a space bar, and the keyboard faced the typist, which meant that the text being typed could be seen. To accomplish these changes a number of technical features had to come together: from movable type, from piano and sewing machinery, from the telegraph, and, finally, from the machining skills used to make clocks. Some of the major events that made the typewriter of the 1890s possible are listed in table 1.2.

Fairbanks and Company, a well-known scale manufacturer, to market the Remington machines in 1878 after Remington's earlier efforts had failed to generate sales large enough to cover the manufacturing plan. Some four thousand copies of the machine sold between 1874 and the end of 1878. The original market targeted for the Remington No. 1 consisted of reporters, lawyers, editors, authors, and clergymen, all of whom were seen as logical users. Businesses were not at first viewed as a significant market. Why is not clear.

Were they not seen as handlers of data and correspondence in large enough quantities? Obviously, with what was then an expensive piece of equipment, high usage was essential to cost justification. But by the turn of the century, businesses and governments were large users of typewriters.

Competitors emerged quickly in the typewriter market. In 1879, for example, the American Writing Machine Company came into existence and began selling a machine in 1881. By then, Remington No. 2 was on the market, selling for $100 each while the No. 1 was repriced at $80. The American Writing Machine Company sold its devices for less in response to Remington. Remington reacted by acquiring the marketing services of Wyckoff, Seamans and Benedict in 1881, which sold 1,200 machines that first year. How many machines were sold subsequently can be gleaned from the royalty payments to Densmore, who held patent rights on Remington equipment: in 1880 he was paid on 610 machines; in 1881, on 1,170 machines; in 1882, on 2,273. He enjoyed similar sizable increases in sales volume throughout the decade. By 1884, however, a buyer could acquire a machine from Remington, the American Writing Machine Company, Hammong, Crandall, or Hall—all based on patents owned by others than Densmore.[52] Thus in less than ten years there was a thriving typewriter industry in the United States complete with industry leaders, competition, and market conditions defined by function, cost, and rivalry. Inventions and innovations came, manufacturing was ongoing, and distribution and marketing were active. Small as it might have been, an industry existed. Most surprising is the speed with which the typewriter business came alive, which supports Beniger's thesis that control was a necessary and critical element in Chandler's purposeful economy.

Competition was a significant feature even in the industry's earliest days. It was sufficient to cause the larger vendor—Remington—to respond by lowering prices through its agent Wyckoff, Seamans and Benedict. Thus the No. 2, which sold for $100 in 1883, by 1885 retailed for $95, while the No. 1 went from $80 to $75. Although there is no evidence of discounting, it would not be surprising to find it because it was practiced already in other industries. Despite competitive pressures, Remington's devices remained the most popular. Demand increased in the 1880s to support substantial growth in business volumes for most vendors.[53] Yet volumes did not reach the levels Remington wanted, and thus in 1886, the firm sold the typewriter business to Densmore for $186,000 ($10,000 down), which satisfied some 90 percent of the company's debts. Densmore kept the same marketing arrangement as before and retained the name Remington in his product's title. His new organization was called the Remington Standard Typewriter Company. It was not related to the old Remington firm that had sold off the typewriter business.

With hindsight, it is easy to see that selling the business was an error because the market continued to grow. In 1886, some fifty thousand machines were sold by all vendors. In 1888 alone, the Remington Standard Typewriter

Company produced about fifteen hundred machines monthly and still could not keep up with demand. A U.S. government census of the typewriter business estimated that there were thirty firms in the young industry with a total capitalization of $1,421,783. These companies employed 1,735 people, who earned wages of just over $1 million. The industry produced products valued at $3.6 million. And during the late 1880s, the Remington No. 3 was introduced quietly into the British market and had become a significant element by 1890.[54]

One should note that as with other technological introductions, despite growth acceptance of the typewriter was not always smooth. Early on, some people were insulted if they received a typed letter rather than a handwritten note and complained about the impersonal quality of the communication. This attitude might explain why the initial customers targeted by Remington did not include businesses, which were far more sensitive to customer satisfaction than were other professions. The business potential for typewriters was not obvious and, perhaps, at first simply did not exist. In the 1880s, a typewriter cost between $70 and $100, when a good meal could be had for a nickel and a fine pen for 10 cents.[55] Historians like to quote Mark Twain, who called it a "curiosity-breeding little joker"; but he also became the first major American author to write book-length manuscripts with it. By 1930, no book manufacturing plant in the United States wanted to accept manuscripts for typesetting that had not been typed.[56]

A second obstacle to overcome was the lack of trained operators to use the machines. Was one machine easier to use than another? Men, but not women, were thought to be strong enough to use them at first. The YMCA in New York City decided to find out, so it bought six Remingtons, found eight "strong women," and set out to prove that they could type by running the first typing school in the United States. The YMCA school was successful, and soon after, no vendor of any size operated without training schools for young ladies. Within a half-century more than two million women were typing in the United States.[57]

The story of Remington and the typewriter provides some important lessons on marketing office equipment, particularly in start-up stages. The most obvious lesson is the need to have an extensive, well-trained marketing organization to sell the product—a requirement lacking at the old Remington arms firm and a lesson that was learned by the founders of NCR. The key to profitability was then to sell in volume, and Remington failed to do that, hence its perceived need to sell the business. Clearly, Remington had the manufacturing prowess to produce in quantity, but that was not enough. Those who marketed Remington's typewriters did well when they bought the rights, set up the Remington Typewriter Company, and focused on marketing, not just on manufacturing. Consequently, they were successful, as were the Singer

Sewing Machine Company and NCR.[58] Chandler defined the case for marketing high-technology products of the late 1800s to early 1900s: "They could sell in volume only if they created a massive, multiunit marketing organization. All their products were new, all were relatively complicated to operate and maintain, and all relatively costly. No marketer knew the product as well as the manufacturer. None had the facilities to provide after-sales service and repair."[59] This passage could have read as a description of events in the computer industry of the 1950s or 1990s.

The Typewriter Industry between 1890 and 1920

The years between 1890 and 1920 were marked by extensive growth in this industry and characterized by new entrants, more competition, and evolving technologies. Collectively, these elements fostered a broad demand for typewriters, which, in turn, led to large volumes of sales. Although volumes would continue to grow after 1920, the industry rapidly matured in many ways as demand became more defined. Technological developments—although significant with the sale of portable and, later, electric models—were less dramatic than before. Importantly, by consolidation and mergers, firms became sublimated within the larger office equipment industry and lost their separate identities.

As in other American industries during the 1890s, companies consolidated to react to the depression of the decade. In 1893—the year of the depression and financial panic—the largest volume of consolidations took place. Remington Typewriter Company behaved typically, combining with an organization of four Smith brothers to form the Union Typewriter Company of America as a reaction to a growing number of competitors.

In the typewriter business, however, such tactics did not stop new entrants. For example, John T. Underwood and his father, John Underwood, acquired the Wagner machine and in 1895 established a factory in Hartford, Connecticut, to build the Underwood Model 5. It was functionally superior to many rival models because it was the first widely distributed machine with the front-strike technology so characteristic of all typewriters since then. Prior designs for typewriters included typebars that made it nearly impossible for users to see what they were typing. Yet relative technological superiority for the moment did not help sales because the firm failed to take full marketing advantage. Thus in 1903, the four Smith brothers broke away from the Union Typewriter Company to form the L. C. Smith and Brothers Typewriter Company (later the Smith part of the Smith-Corona Company in 1926 and the SCM Corporation in 1958) to exploit these easier to use innovations.

Technology spurred others on as well. Edward B. Rees developed a machine to address four problems: the large number of knobs that blocked a user's view of what was being typed, the inadequate quality of presswork, the need to lower machine cost through better design, and the demand for additional ease of use. In time, he earned 140 typewriter patents for his work, and his machine became one of the most advanced, lightweight devices on the market. It led to the creation of the Royal Typewriter Company in 1904. Thus by 1904–1905, the industry's four largest vendors were the old Remington firm (the Union Typewriter Company), Underwood, L. C. Smith, and Royal. In 1904, some one hundred firms were spread across the industry in the United States. By 1909, failures and consolidations had reduced these to eighty-nine, almost all of which had been formed since 1905. Most companies also had active marketing programs in Europe that usually employed agents.[60]

By 1900 alone, more than 100,000 machines had been sold, and the industry was manufacturing some 20,000 units per year. As machining and manufacturing costs dropped, these devices became more affordable, which, in turn, generated more sales. This early example of commodity marketing in the office products industry presaged a similar situation with microcomputers in the 1980s. Price elasticity influenced a high-technology product at a very early date. Of course, typewriters became very price sensitive at a time when the number of people working in offices was climbing sharply, confusing any discussion of direct cause and effect. Obviously, more workers meant more possible customers for typewriters (increased demand) yet prices dropped, possibly in reaction to known increases in competition from new entrants into the market.[61]

The role of technology was clearly impressive as it influenced the new industry. As noted, Royal came into existence because of technological innovation. Remington had enjoyed several years of relative sales freedom (1870s) because of its technical superiority. By the start of the 1880s, technological rivalry posed two directions: (1) toward touch typing methods using a single keyboard and shift key or (2) toward devices that employed numerous methods on double keyboards. The issue of which track to follow was settled dramatically by a contest in July 1885 in Cincinnati, Ohio. A Mr. McGurrin on a touch machine and a Mr. Traub on a dual keyboard competed. Mr. McGurrin typed faster by a significant margin. The Paul Bunyon-like contest ended as it did for the mythical tree cutter: the more modern technology won.

After the contest, which was a symbol of a trend already evident, manufactureers increasingly standardized technology throughout the 1890s and early 1900s. By 1900, most of the technical features of the manual typewriter had been introduced. In the 1920s came the noiseless version. The third and last phase before the advent of word processors was the electric typewriter (with initial models as early as pre–World War I), buttressing office sales seriously after World War II. But more germane to the early years of the twentieth century was the standardization of technology and its consequence, similar manufacturing processes, which made consolidations of products and companies easier to implement than in many other industries.[62]

Technological developments, especially from 1886 to about 1915, heated up competition. Remington Typewriter's slow response to change cut deeply into its sales when, for example, L. C. Smith introduced better machines that required fewer repairs and were lighter and better priced. Underwood did the same and enjoyed a long run deep into the 1920s of benefits from technological superiority combined with good advertising. In 1920, for instance, its sales equaled those of all other vendors combined, primarily because of the Model 5.[63]

No evidence suggests, however, that consolidations made these firms take better advantage of technology to drive up profits. Consolidations reflected a widespread pattern: local companies with small markets became regional or national in size. Unlike in other industries, new entrants ensured that none of the large vendors could relax and remain confident of holding market share. It was a market that one could enter relatively easily. The nearly one hundred entrants made that obvious. All tried to use some technological edge or gimmick for marketing, usually subcontracted manufacturing, and employed agents who represented multiple vendors. But the major approach to sustain market presence appeared to be technological innovation, differentiation that yielded some 6,200 patents for typewriters in the United States by 1910. One historian estimated that sales in the United States that year reached $2 million, the work of eighty-seven U.S. firms and twenty-two foreign companies operating in North America.[64] Unfortunately, sales data on typewriters marketed in Europe are not available; evidence for European activity generally remains scanty. If, however, one assumes that foreign sales made up the same proportion of revenues for typewriter companies as for cash register firms (about which more data are available), then one could assume that foreign sales contributed between 25 and 40 percent of American revenues by World War I. Similar relationships of sales can be documented for Hollerith-type equipment, but not for adding machines and calculators (the data are terribly scattered); the latter two were strong products in Europe's office market.

However, there is evidence of an active typewriter industry in Europe. By 1910, twenty-two firms marketed the machines in the United States and, obviously, operated from some base of strength in Europe. From Germany they included Adler, AEG, Ideal, Kappel, Mercedes, Mignon, Regina, Saxonia, Titania, Torpedo, and Urania—almost all of which did not survive the early decades of the twentieth century. Italian firms—Heperia, Vittoria, and Olivetti—had greater longevity but not without some casualties. One each from Switzerland, Canada, and Japan (Japy) entered the American market and

TABLE 1.3
Early U.S. Typewriter Firms, circa 1900–1917

Acme[a]	Dollar	Keystone	Rex
Alexander	Duplex	McCall	Royal
Allen	Edland	Manograph	Schiesari
American	Elliott-Fisher	Merritt	Secor
Atlas	Ellis	Molle	Sholes Visible
Barlock	Emerson	Monarch	L. C. Smith
Bennett	Essex	Moon-Hopkins	Smith Premier
Bennington	Fay-Sholes	Morris	Stearns
Blake	Federal	Munson	Sterling
Brooks	Ford	National	Sun
Century	Fountain	Nickerson	Taylor
Chicago	Fox	Noiseless	Triumph
Commercial	Franklin	Odell	Type-Adder
Corona	Garbell	Official	Underwood
Cram	Hammond	Oliver	Victor Visigraph
Crandall	Harris	People's	Walker
Crown	Hartford	Pittsburgh	Williams
Darling	Hooven	Postal	Woodstock
Daugherty	Jackson	Rapid	World
Demountable	Jewett	Reliance	Yost
Densmore	Junion	Remington	Yu Ess

Source: George N. Engler, "The Typewriter Industry: The Impact of a Significant Technological Innovation" (Ph.D. diss., University of California at Los Angeles, 1969), 29.

[a] The purpose of listing so many firms is to point out that so many machines were named after their inventors or were identified with a region; very few had machinelike names and very few existed after the 1920s.

were joined by three from Britain and two from France. In table 1.3, I list some of the U.S major firms that they competed against in Europe in the years before World War I.[65]

The result of nearly fifty years of activity was an active and still-growing typewriter industry in the United States. An expanding work force used these machines in increasing quantities each year. Between 1870 and 1885, various technological paths began to merge, leading the industry into fifteen years of product and technological standardization. Next, prices dropped leading to a de facto commodity market, which made it possible to refer to these and other office machines as "appliances" by the end of World War I. The typewriters had led also to consolidations early in the industry's history in attempts to control market share, to shore up profits, and to take advantage of manufacturing economies of scale. Chandler noted a similar pattern in other industries in the same period.[66]

The organizational and sociological impact of the typewriter, although difficult to define, was nonetheless present. One account of these early years presented the typewriter as part of a larger contribution by technology to American society:

> In the reform came efficient division of labor, machine bookkeeping, systematic filing, indexing, multigraphing and revolution in circularization which became, eventually, a business in itself. The machine's collateral relatives, if not its immediate legitimate progeny, were checkmakers, addressographs, mimeographs, and calculating machines in a variety defying the briefest inventory.[67]

In the final analysis, to what extent did the typewriter influence American society? It is a question more readily answered in the period following World War II when almost every piece of business correspondence and, increasingly, personal letters were typed. But not so for the period 1870–1920 when the temptation to exaggerate the typewriter's significance is great but unjustified. Evidence is too meager, which leads one to conclude that the device's impact was embryonic, rippling with potential but still waiting for its day.

Daniel Boorstin came closest, perhaps, to providing an answer both reasonable and applicable to the early period of the typewriter. In discussing the much broader problem of how to make duplicate copies of information—a concern dating back to ancient times—he viewed the development of the typewriter as a small step toward solving the problem. He noted that by 1845 Samuel F. B. Morse and partner were using a keyboard of sorts to send messages and that later, Sholes, himself a printer, was at work on the problem. He recorded that the earliest models were like sewing machines or piano mechanisms and were not convenient until the turn of the century. Yet he observed that with typewriters came more standardized mail. The size of typewriters contributed to the standardization of the size and shape of correspondence paper and envelopes, which was reinforced after World War II with various postal regulations. Typewriters also provided additional employment opportunities outside the home, farm, or factory. Handwriting declined as typing spread, and with it, the personal distinctiveness that had actually grown with literacy during the nineteenth century was lost.[68]

Boorstin argued that in the attack on the problem of copies, "few inventions were as important as carbon paper."[69] An early patent for carbon paper in the United States was issued when the first typewriters were produced in 1869. It was originally intended to copy handwriting, but in 1872, another patent was issued for carbon paper designed for use with typewriters. Close on its heels came a mimeographic paper (to *mime* the original text) and a company formed by A. B. Dick to manufacture paper and machinery for that purpose. His products, even more than the typewriter, increased a person's ability to duplicate quickly and conveniently without typesetting. Not until the photocopy machines of the 1960s would such an invention be so convenient. A. B. Dick's products, like those of successful typewriter vendors were accepted because they were well conceived and built; he also carefully retained good sales personnel, invested in manufacturing, and established a network of agencies to represent his products.[70]

The typewriter was essentially the first of many new technologies that in time merged to form the office equipment industry; a new level of mechanical sophistication had been reached in the office. Its success simply confirmed the wisdom of attempting to produce other types of equipment for the office worker. Without the typewriter, it would be difficult to envision the origins of the new industry before the late 1880s.

2

Adding and Calculating Machines

THE INTRODUCTION of these new types of machines as commercially viable products, either almost simultaneously with the typewriter or rapidly within a few years, added a whole new dimension to mechanical handling of information. Their arrival gave considerable definition to the emerging office equipment industry. They made possible more sophisticated data handling than that afforded by a typewriter. Yet these machines were close enough to the typewriter in the kind of manufacturing, marketing, and distribution required, and, in some instances, in price to make them logical cohabitants of the new market or at least attractive "add-ons" for companies already in the typwriter business.

The history of adding machines and calculators dates back hundreds of years, especially in Europe where mathematicians and others long had sought mechanical aids to calculations.[1] Most writers focus on the technology, and their texts are descriptive, leaving unanswered many questions about machine use. Nowhere is this more obvious than for those machines that came in the years following the American Civil War.[2] My concern is primarily the late 1800s when a new era in mechanical computing opened, one that made such devices possible on a broad and significant scale. In the postwar period, such devices played an important role in the modernization of the American office. By introducing the capability to handle larger amounts of information in new ways, these machines provided additional support for the development of larger entities—bureaucracies—than had been realistically or profitably possible before. They joined a plethora of new technologies that supported organizations—telephones, cash registers, bookkeeping equipment, and faster printing machinery in the office—and provided more efficient transportation and logistics controls for railroads and automobiles as well as electrical devices of vast variety.

Like typewriters, adding and calculating machines became permanent fixtures in organizations of any size. They also came closer than the typewriter to fitting the image of a precursor for the modern computer because they computed and handled numeric and, later, alphabetic data. These devices were the direct ancestors of computers. Their evolution led to the creation of computers capable of work that could not be done by calculators. In short, adding machines and calculators contributed to the foundation of the American data-processing industry while they introduced thousands of office workers and scientists to the possibilities presented by mechanical aids to data calculation and handling.

The history of such equipment is complicated because of the variety of devices available between roughly 1885 and 1930. Adding machines only added and subtracted. Calculators also multiplied and divided, whereas specialized machines became available for specialized applications, such as billing. Devices were classified by their engineering designs with manual and, later, electrical versions. The field became more crowded as various manufacturers sold individual versions of such equipment. Burroughs Adding Machine Company battled with Felt & Tarrant as the two largest vendors at the turn of the century, but other, less visible firms also operated. These products enjoyed similar popularity in Europe where the same process of modernization was evident replete with industrialization and the rise of large organizations.

Like typewriters, adding and calculating machines required precise engineering and machining. They were also sold to the same kind of customer. All borrowed technology heavily from each other. For instance, data entry keyboards and printer mechanisms were similar on typewriters, adding machines, and calculators. The variety, volumes, and uses to which these machines were put were astounding. Acceptance of adding machines and calculators came far more rapidly than historians have acknowledged. Clearly, therefore, many patterns in the evolution and use of typewriters were concurrently at work in the evolution of calculating devices. The one important exception was that calculating devices were more varied in design and could be used in a broader range of applications than the typewriter, which, after all, could only record data not generate it in the form of answers.

The nature of demand suggests why these machines were well received. Unlike the typewriter, which was at first not intended for business, adding and calculating machines targeted business even more than science and engineering. No concern existed about the perceptions of insensitivity or lack of personal touch that greeted typewriters. John S. Coleman, president of Burroughs Corporation in the late 1940s, described the environment his company's founders encountered: "Bookkeeping, before the advent of the adding machine, was not an occupation for the flagging spirit or the wandering mind." Further, "It required in extraordinary degree, capacity for sustained concentration, attention to detail, and a passion for accuracy."[3] This pressure to perform precisely increased at a time of rapid expansion by industry and, hence, by bureaucracies with attendant needs to obtain more information faster. This was especially the case with accounting data, which, in turn, highlighted the limits of the functional capabilities and speed of the old "pen-and-ink accountant." That development created sufficient demand for mechanical aids to calculation.

One writer described the office at the turn of the century as a place of "long hours and slow, tortuous business progress." He continued: "Record-keeping was done by hand in ponderous bound volumes. Trial balances appeared at historic intervals, and departmental digests and comparison reports were almost unheard of." Reliance on instruments led to "a complete revolution in office methods—the substitution of machines for hand-work, and, to a large extent, for brain-work."[4]

In the late twentieth century it is easy to superimpose a vision of offices that is contrary to the reality of the 1800s. Despite the introduction of equipment and old photographs that depict desks and chairs similar to modern versions, and events and men's suits essentially the same as those worn today, times were different. One who lived then said:

> The sheer necessity of keeping office work abreast of the extraordinary expansion of business during the last quarter-century, of course, was the dynamic force behind the quest for simplified, improved methods of carrying on office routine and solving office problems, but it was the exchange of ideas among business men that brought about similarity of methods and made possible the mechanical handling of office work.[5]

In such a manual environment, days had to be long because the only other way to increase productivity would have been simply to add faster. Companies employed "lightning calculators," people who could add long, wide columns of numbers rapidly and even entertained with this skill. With every stage of technological development on the brink of entirely new ways of doing work, existing methods were stretched to their limits as individuals tried to squeeze the last bit of increased efficiency out of them. Thus it was no surprise to learn that the Académie des Sciences in France appointed a committee in the 1880s to study "lightning calculators" in hopes of learning how to transfer these people's skills to accountants in general. Dorr E. Felt, one of the more important producers of adding machines, accused manual accounting practices of "turning men into veritable machines," while Oliver Wendell Holmes commented that "calculating power alone should seem to be the least human of qualities."[6] Times were right for the new technology.

The history of mechanical calculating machines went through two phases before the introduction of the electronic computer. During the seventeenth century, strides were taken in the development of mechanical devices by Wilhelm Schickard (1623), Blaise Pascal (1642), Rene Grillet (1670s), and Gottfried Wilhelm von Leibniz (1674). That flurry of activity represented the first phase, one characterized by limited demand for such machines and plagued by inadequate machining capability. This phase is not a concern in the discussion of computing aids; the second is.

It began in the early 1800s and can be dated to 1820 when a French inven-

tor, Charles Xavier Thomas de Colmar, built a calculator called the Arithmometer. It was a landmark development because his machine became a
commercial success in Europe, selling possibly several hundred over the next
three to four decades.[7] That success called attention to the need for calculators, particularly in scientific circles. It exposed scientists, mathematicians,
and even a few accountants to such technology, encouraging some to design
their own machines during the 1840s–1860s, including Charles Babbage who
began work at the same time as Colmar. The Arithmometer sold for the same
reasons that later computers might sell over rivals: good marketing and better
technology. Better technology was, perhaps, more important in the 1820s
because it opened doors to many possibilities. It resulted in a machine that
was more reliable than its predecessors (seventeenth-century designs), so
much so that a variety of arithmometers from several vendors came onto the
market by the late 1800s. Colmar's machines remained in use down to World
War I, when smaller devices, often with more functions, finally displaced
them.[8] Colmar's machine was, however, a hint of things to come. New developments occurred throughout the 1840s and 1850s, and, then, beginning in
the 1860s many new machines began to appear. By the 1870s, a market had
emerged on both sides of the Atlantic Ocean complete with vendors, competition, and customers.

Various interpretations attempt to explain the sudden wave of new products
that appeared after midcentury. The two main arguments tout either technological causes or focus on demand and changes in the business climate. The
technological proponents argue that a breakthrough in both design and production methods of such machines permitted replacement of cumbersome
Leibnitz stepped-drum designs with one far more compact and light. A
stepped-drum gear was a "device which would allow the result register to be
turned through a variable number of positions (0 to 9) depending on the set-up
mechanism which held the number being manipulated." A leading historian
of this technology argued that "in effect the Leibnitz drum provided a gear
with a variable number of teeth, the number of teeth in use being determined
by the position along the drum of the next gear being driven off this shaft."[9]
The result was a bulky machine. Accountants and mathematicians wanted a
small, variable-toothed gear device, and that did not become possible until
materials and machining had improved sufficiently.

The first successful attempt came almost simultaneously in the United
States and in Russia from Frank S. Baldwin (American) and T. Odhner
(Swede). It was called the Baldwin Machine in the United States and the
Odhner Machine throughout Europe. Baldwin and Odhner developed a round
disk with movable pins that could be extended beyond the outer edge of the
disk; a lever controlled the number that protruded. Input was a function of
which and how many pins protruded.[10] In comparison to earlier devices, these
newer machines were easier to use, proved more reliable, and could be made

out of thin, flat disklike plates. Other technical improvements included spring-loaded keyboards, and listing and printing models. When mounted sideways on a shaft, these devices take on the image of the modern calculator with only the keyboard to follow later. The Baldwin-Odhner machine took up only a portion of a desk's surface instead of all of it as did the Thomas Arithmometer. Brunsviga, a major 'nineteenth century vendor, sold over twenty thousand Baldwin-Odhner machines between 1885 and 1912, which suggests their popularity.[11] Yet some of the old Arithmometers were still in use during World War I.

A second school of thought suggests that the need for such equipment, especially in accounting and in science, created the necessary economic incentives to develop it. Such machines, to use Beniger's phrase, reflected part of the "Control Revolution," in which technology was employed to support the flow of greater amounts of information in ever-larger organizations.[12] Most contemporary writers and historians lean toward the economic interpretation of the development of adding and calculating machines.[13]

As organizations evolved in size and were characterized by multiple layers of management or locations, such structures provided economic incentives to generate cost-effective, useful information. Statistical reports and numerical data, in particular, made it possible for middle and upper management to carry out one of their most vital functions: to inspect performance. The information-handling process directly contributed to the expansion of the managerial class that Chandler called the new mandarins of the economy.

Both camps cite impressionistic evidence of sales volumes from Brunsviga, lists of office applications, and a variety of machines to buttress their arguments. Although circumstantial, this evidence is impressive. The existence of so many essentially similar machines in the late 1800s that served a growing market successfully supports a strong argument that the time was right for such products and that the convergence of technological capabilities simply made these products possible. The number of manufacturers also shows a lack of barriers to market entry in the early stages of development comparable to the situation in the microcomputer era of the 1970s and 1980s. Thus a combination of interests came together. As I will show, especially with Burroughs, the more accurate view is to observe both technological and economic factors at work, with the business case more compelling, particularly after the technology became available.

One other innovation, however, was necessary to make these products attractive to a wide range of customers. Neither Baldwin nor Odhner had quite resolved the problem of how to speed up the setup of the levers to register amounts. Missing was the capability to enter data quickly using a keyboard much like a typewriter's. That development—a known requirement at the time—would speed data entry, make the equipment easier to use, while borrowing manufacturing know-how from typewriter suppliers. Attention fo-

TABLE 2.1
Innovations in Adding and Calculating Machinery, 1820–1939

1820[a]	Arithmometer invented
1850	First key-driven adding machine
1875	Baldwin/Odhner variable tooth calculators
1885	Brunsviga calculator
1886	Add-subtract calculator (Felt Comptometer)
1887	Direct multiplication calculator (Leon Bollee)
1889	First practical adding and listing machine
1890	Multiplier calculator
1893	Four-function calculator marketed (Millionaire)
1905	Motor-driven, keyboard, self-stepping carriage combined (Ensign)
1908	Printing calculator (Trinks-Arithmotype)
1910	Automatic division on calculator
1911	First commercial keyboard rotary machine
1920	Electric arithmometer demonstrated (Torres y Quevedo)
1924	Electric printing calculator introduced
1928	Multiple-register cumulating calculator marketed
1939	Electronic calculator available

Sources: James R. Beninger, *The Control Revolution* (Cambridge, Mass.: Harvard University Press, 1986), 400–401; Robert H. Gregory and Richard L. Van Horn, *Automatic Data-Processing Systems* (San Francisco: Wadsworth, 1960), 624–26.
[a] Experts do not agree on dates for "firsts"; above is a composite view.

cused on developing key-driven machines at about the same time as typewriter inventors were moving to front-strike keyboards. With the key-driven innovation, adding and calculating machines could be sold for a variety of uses, such as adding up invoice amounts for billing or doing normal accounting and mathematics. Development of a key-driven machine was an important event, highly ergonomic. Dorr E. Felt's popular Comptometer, for example, might not have sold without that feature. As it turned out, his Comptometer and Burroughs's products were the two most popular sets of devices available in the United States at the turn of the century. They remained marketable in various models to the end of World War II.[14]

Table 2.1 is a list of milestones in the evolution of such machines. Changes continued in both Europe and the United States, sometimes independently of each other or as reactions to earlier developments known to the inventor. Because many of the developments were publicized, one is led to believe that they built on each other. More importantly, no history of computing technology in the late 1800s or in the early years of the 1900s can be segregated by nationality; the technology was a true international development taking place throughout the industrializing nations.[15]

Such developments received attention in the scientific press of the day. By looking at the information journals published on computing, one could conclude that interest in the subject was broader than it is today or, as seems closer to the truth, that early publications were not as market-focused as those in the 1960s or 1970s. In the late twentieth century, specialized journals aimed at subsets of the computer science community by carrying news of developments; in the nineteenth century, the most widely read scientific publications broadcast the word, which suggests perhaps, a wider significance. Yet like their twentieth-century counterparts, these descriptions were usually penned (or typed?) by their developers or members of the vendor organization. Although technological evolution continued until adding machines and calculators were replaced largely by digital hand-held calculators in the 1970s, these earlier gadgets had most of their features by the end of the decade preceding World War I.[16] In the following years, they were sometimes electrified, always repackaged, and shrunk in size. Additional minor improvements were always touted by several thousand salespeople in the United States, operating out of hundreds of storefronts and branch offices. The fundamental technological innovations, as with manual typewriters, had become available after less than thirty years of evolution and appeared concurrently.[17]

The Burroughs Adding Machine Company

The Burroughs Adding Machine Company provides a window into the American office appliance market of the late 1800s and early 1900s. This important vendor's products and marketing typified the available technology and practices of the industry. However, it was not the only vendor and experienced considerable competition from its earliest days.

The firm was formed by William S. Burroughs (1855–1898), a one-time bank clerk who, like his peers, calculated figures by hand at the cost of very long workdays. His career as a business machine supplier resulted from his desire to automate an accounting clerk's function. Although many others were also developing mechanical aids to calculation at the time, his work led ultimately to the creation of a company that dominated the market. He built a practical adding machine and, unlike many other inventors, had the business skills to manufacture profitably and to market effectively his products. In retrospect, the ability to manufacture and distribute his products cost-effectively ultimately accounted for the company's success over less-efficient rivals with equally good products. By the early 1900s, the Burroughs Adding and Listing Machine was one of the most popular devices available. It enabled clerks to add many times faster and more accurately than by hand. A less well-paid clerk could do more work with an adding machine than a better-paid accountant working by hand. A consequence, however, was that some skills were no longer needed because some of their tasks could be shifted to machines, such as adding totals.[18] As a result, in years to come less-skilled employees were used.

With these machines, banks kept current records; insurance companies developed and maintained necessary files; and railroad companies monitored vast operations. A partial list of the uses to which these machines were put in the early 1920s suggests the broad applicability to basic business functions: daily postings, daily ledger balances, daily cash balances, deposit slip preparation in duplicate, daily recapitulation of sales—cash, credit, and so forth, checking invoices and freight bills, figuring discounts, computing commissions, summarizing a day's receipts and disbursements, figuring estimates, listing and adding yardage, feet, or weight of goods packed, received, or shipped, listing and adding hours, minutes, tons, hundredweights, feet, inches, fractions, and other compound numbers, and posting perpetual inventory records.[19] Many of these applications had not been done before mechanical aids to calculation came along because people could not handle the volumes of numbers involved in a timely, convenient, and cost-effective manner. These tasks also were performed later on tabulating equipment and ultimately on computers. Thus if someone asks when many of these functions first emerged, one could easily point to humble adding and calculating machines.

One exuberant writer suggested what life was like after these devices became available, largely thanks to Burroughs:

> In the future, it is safe to say, the history of accounting will be the history of adding and calculating machines. For these machines are today [1920s] the chief factor in the development of better bookkeeping practice. Their greatest service lies in giving the world a way of controlling business by figures. Adding and calculating machines are not only adapted to current bookkeeping practice, but they are teaching men the value of business records.[20]

But all that was still in the future when Burroughs and many others first tangled with the thorny problem of how to mechanize calculation.

Burroughs, like so many others who experimented with office machinery, was no stranger to engines. He was the son of a mechanic, and he worked with machines while growing up. His first employment was as a clerk in a bank where long hours of adding numbers diminished his health, forcing him at the age of twenty-four to leave his job. Burroughs next took up his father's profession and at the same time sought to develop a device that banks could use for calculating and tabulating numbers. In 1880, he had plans for a machine and a company. By 1885, he had established the Arithmometer Company. He constantly refined his machine throughout the 1880s and 1890s. Burroughs was a driven man, who, as his co-worker Joseph Boyer later recalled, would sit at his workbench all night to be found "still there in the morning."[21] Burroughs filed for his first patent in 1885, and his initial machines sold for $475 each. By 1889, he had built fifty boxy units that were difficult to use and that required redesign. Yet during the 1890s, his product achieved some acceptance, and by 1898—the year of his death—the company had its own factory in the United States and another in Britain. It had an office staff of sixty-five in the United States and assets valued at $300,000. In 1895, he began marketing overseas through the Burroughs Adding and Registering Company Limited, headquartered in Nottingham, England. By the end of 1897, on both sides of the Atlantic, his firm's product line consisted of four device types.[22]

The American Arithmometer Company began to pick up momentum in the last five years of the nineteenth century, shipping increasing numbers of machines and raising prices per copy. Increases in demand are reflected in the sales summarized in table 2.2. In the 1895 to 1900 period, sales grew from $63,700 to $322,934, or by more than sixfold. That growth was equal to and often ahead of increases in many high-growth firms of the 1960s in the data-processing industry even though some started from different size bases. The population of machines expanded by some five times. Those figures suggested growth in market demand for such technology and probably reflected the kind of growth competitors enjoyed too. This demand was unaffected by the Spanish-American War of 1898.

Momentum was maintained in the early years of the 1900s. As illustrated in table 2.3, the number of units built and sold in the last years of the American Arithmometer Company (before it became Burroughs) was impressive. Volumes sold increased by 30 percent between January 1901 and January 1902 and by 49 percent by the end of 1902. Inventories, which had obviously been building up, were used to advantage with sales rising by over 40 percent in 1903 and settling to a "mere" 13 percent more in 1904. It was a profitable business. Even conservative auditors for the firm could comment concerning 1903, "The results for the year show a very substantial improvement over those for the preceding year" with a reduction in the cost per unit resulting from increases in economy of scale in production. All of that made this a very profitable business. To illustrate this point, the auditors noted, "profit for the year [1903] . . . amounted to $684,087.86, as compared with $474,168.88 for the year 1902."[23] In the decade before World War I, the market grew for those who could run a profitable business, which included Burroughs, a company now with many years' experience in the new industry.

Examining Burroughs by how many machines they sold does not tell the full story. Annual sales data for the decade before World War I clarifies more about the vagaries and size of market demand (see table 2.4). Growth, particularly after 1895, experienced few ups and downs from momentary market circumstances or features of the economy at large. The impressive performance is the growth from nearly $5 million (eightfold) in 1905 to nearly $40 million in 1916, which far exceeded the GNP rate of growth in the U.S. economy. The performance also evidences the growing importance of the control Americans and Europeans wanted over the flow of data and of its

TABLE 2.2
Adding and Calculating Machines Sold by
American Arithmometer Company, 1895–1900

Year	Number Made	Number Sold	Average Price Received (Dollars)	Sales ($000s)
1895	225	286	222.74	63.7
1896	544	418	212.98	89.0
1897	565	498	218.35	108.7
1898	804	729	224.29	163.5
1899	962	972	227.18	220.8
1900	1,676	1,399	230.83	322.9

Source: From annual audits of the firm by Audit Company of
New York, American Arithmometer Company Records, Burroughs Papers.

TABLE 2.3
Total Machines Built and Sold, American
Arithmometer Company, 1901–1904

Year	Number Built	Number Sold
1901	2,667	2,122
1902	3,470	3,163
1903	Flat[a]	4,446
1904	4,504	5,008

Source: Drawn from annual audits by Price,
Waterhouse and Co., American Arithmometer
Company Records, Burroughs Papers.
[a] No hard numbers are available on how
many were built, but it appears that volumes
were the same because the cost of manufacture
of machines sold in 1903 was $242.7M and in
1904, $241.4M.

value in terms of the calculations required to get that information for use
across the entire economy.

It suggests what was happening to Felt & Tarrant and other firms in the
same market. Demand appeared to be almost insatiable. In 1909, admittedly
a boom year for Burroughs, the firm sold 15,763 machines or twice what
William Burroughs thought back in 1885 could ever be sold worldwide. Volumes achieved in 1909 represented a more than threefold increase in shipments over the past five years (since 1904), a pattern repeated by other firms
in the information business in subsequent decades.

TABLE 2.4
Total Annual Sales, American Arithmometer Company and
Burroughs Adding Machine Company, 1905–1916 (dollars in millions)

Year	Dollar Sales	Year	Dollar Sales	Year	Dollar Sales
1905	4,923	1909	16,030	1913	23,720
1906	7,835	1910	15,300	1914	19,077
1907	14,777	1911	18,020	1915	22,152
1908	13,776	1912	22,559	1916	39,858

Source: Minutes of both firms, Burroughs Papers.

However, growth initially was slow. During the 1880s, Burroughs had to develop a practical, patentable device, find financial backers with good business skills to help manage manufacture, distribution, and sales of products in a market that had to be taught to use this machine and then to accept it. Burroughs's time in the sun did not come until the late 1890s, at the end of his life; but sales volumes achieved levels contrary to what some have characterized in biographical treatments of the inventor. The great takeoff came after 1895, following fifteen years of work, nearly ten within the framework of a company. In 1885, when only 286 machines had been placed, the firm could only afford three agents. The following year more representatives were hired, and sales grew to 418 machines. Finally, in 1898, the climb to 729 led an executive in the firm to comment that "the machine was taking hold."[24] "As late as the turn of the century it had not yet been absorbed, so to speak, into the blood stream of business. It was, at best, an appendage."[25]

Members of the firm saw the need for such devices "but there was a very natural reluctance to see in this startling machine the answer to that need. It took years of pushing, cajoling, wheedling, the most inspired moments of dozens of pioneer salesmen, and the ever-rising flood of figure work lapping at the threshold of business before the jump was made from pen to machine."[26] As with typewriters and, later, computers, it was not enough to see need, it had to be sold. Burroughs began with banks—customers Burroughs knew best—and only later did he and fellow officers of the firm realize that there were needs outside of banking that could be satisfied with his machines.

The key to selling them was their practicality; both Burroughs and competitors harped upon it to customers. Gradually, these machines became easier to use; the keys responded increasingly to a lighter touch; they became smaller and cost competitive with manual processing. As machines improved, they were sold to support accounting for payrolls, purchasing records, inventory management, overhead allocations, and shipping costs. New data became available to managers so they could make better decisions earlier based on more facts. Sales analyses could be daily, weekly, or monthly and could be sorted conveniently by marketing representative, territory, or product type.[27] In 1914, one commentator on the American office could argue that "bookkeeping today is largely a matter of machinery. Formerly it was necessary for a bookkeeper to make separate entries in bound books" but "with the introduction of card and loose-leaf records and billing machines it is now possible to make fifteen or more different records at one writing and to prove their accuracy almost automatically."[28] "Figure work" increased, thanks to more complex and extensive applications, larger organizations that increasingly had to rely on statistical data to operate, and the arrival of cost accounting as a standard business practice.

The income tax law of 1913 was a harbinger of the kinds of records New Deal legislation of the 1930s would force American users of data processing to keep.[29] The new tax law called for more citizens to pay taxes based on progressive rates. Therefore, more people had to file income and tax data and document that information. Corporate taxes were expanded during World War I, which also generated more paperwork. The concept of withholding was introduced with the law of 1913. By 1939, over four million Americans were withholding; by 1945, forty-three million. Incomes had to be tracked continuously, causing associated record keeping to expand. Thus the idea that it was possible to do so was well ingrained by the time New Deal legislation expanded tax and income records and payments. As indicated by the volume of articles published in the literature of the day, the use of information-handling equipment for payroll alone entered a golden age of popularity.

The Burroughs organization reflected the growing need for such equipment. In 1903, the American Arithmometer Company outgrew its plant in St. Louis and moved to new facilities in Detroit, source of a larger supply of labor. The new plant opened in 1904. During that year, the firm was renamed in honor of its founder and reincorporated in Michigan as the Burroughs Adding Machine Company with $5 million in capitalization. The following year, the company had 148 marketing representatives selling the product directly; they obtained orders for 7,804 machines.[30]

The Burroughs Adding Machine Company did not have a free hand to sell at will although the market appeared to be larger than its sales suggested; it was able to sell increasing numbers of products at higher unit prices. A crowded field of inventors also found manufacturing facilities, venture capital backing, and marketing agents or established direct sales forces to move their products. Beside Burroughs machines were Baldwin and Odhner devices and those of Felt & Tarrant, as others applied for patents and went to market for the first time. Newcomers included A. C. Ludlum in 1888 with an adding and writing machine; Felt, who applied for his first important patent in the same year; Frank C. Rinche in 1901 with an electric motor-driven adding-listing device; Felt again in 1902 with a machine that could cross-tabulate (thus "horizontal adding and recording could be accomplished as well as vertical"); and in 1904, H. C. Peters with an automatic nonadding mechanism for cross-tabulation. To make it easier to use electrical devices, the Pike machine came out in 1905.[31]

The frenzy of activity is indicated by the rapidity and quantity of improvements that continued to arrive until World War I. C. W. Gooch developed the split keyboard in 1906, and in the following year, Felt was back with a patent for a flexible or self-correcting keyboard that rectified mistakes in depressing keys "instantly, simply by depressing the correct key or keys." William E. Swalm obtained a patent in 1908 for a totalizer, which could sum all totals of a footed column and print it. In 1912, Jessie G. Vincent produced a nonadd symbol printer, and, the following year, out came a shuttle carriage for the Pike machine. The number of other, less important developments, continued to increase.[32] By World War I, it was possible to use an adding machine to total accurately fifty amounts containing six figures each or a bill of a dozen items extended and proved in thirty seconds. Many machines were "also capable of dividing and substracting with similar rapidity."[33]

The number of these developments suggests the level of activity. Developments also point out a feature of the market that would be evident in a continuum to the present: when technological improvements appeared, either an established vendor had to offer them on his products quickly or be superceded by other, usually new, upstart firms, most of which had a single product or technology to sell. Burroughs's management understood these rules of the market and survived with other companies. By World War I, a buyer could acquire a Burroughs or shop around for a Wales, Dalton, or for devices with such names as Comptometer, Ensign, Millionaire, or Brunsviga. One could choose products from Elliott-Fisher, Moon-Hopkins, and Underwood—vendors also of typewriters—who were beginning to diversity their product lines and expand from regional to national markets.[34] Although Burroughs had considerable name brand recognition, one does not know exactly what its market share was; one can surmise that it was more than that of any other vendor by World War I. What is known is that the commitment to dominance required 115 sales offices in the United States and 6 in Canada by 1911, not an insignificant investment of resources and efforts.[35]

Non-U.S. Sales of Adding and Calculating Machines

Burroughs, like most competitors, sought to broaden its market through sales outside the United States. European producers competed in the U.S. market, although on a far smaller scale. The Ensign and the Brunsviga were, perhaps, the two most formidable foreign rivals in the U.S. market. In the decade before World War I, trade was international in adding and calculating machines with the largest non-U.S. market emerging in Europe. Burroughs was in Britain in 1895; its first non-U.S. plant was constructed in 1898 at Notting-

TABLE 2.5
Exhibitors and Products at Napier Tercentenary Celebration, July 24–27, 1914

Product	Vendor
Archimedes	Glashutter
Colt's Calculator	Teetzmann
Brical Adding Machine	British Calculators, Ltd.
Brunsviga Calculating Machine	Grimme, Natalis & Co., Ltd.
Burroughs Adding and Listing Machine	Burroughs Adding Machine Ltd.
Comptometer	Felt & Tarrant Manufacturing Co.
Layton's Improved Arithmometer	Charles & Edwin Layton
Hamann's "Mercedes-Euklid" Arithmometer	O. Sust, Kgl Landmesser
"Millionaire" Calculating Machine	O. Steiger
Thomas de Colmar Arithmometer	Multiple vendors/secondhand dealers
H. M. Nautical Almanac Office Anti-Differencing Machine	No vendor (one-of-a-kind)
Barrett Adding and Computing Machine	Barrett Adding and Computing Machine Company, Ltd.
Monarch Wahl Adding and Subtracting Typewriter	No vendor listed
T. I. M. Single Slide Calculating Machine	No vendor listed
Unitas Double Slide Calculating Machine	No vendor listed

Source: E. M. Horsburgh, ed., *Handbook of the Napier Tercentenary Celebration* (Edinburgh: Bell and Sons, and Royal Society of Edinburgh, 1914; reprint, Tomash Publishers, Los Angeles, 1982), 69–136.

ham, England. In 1900, a Canadian company was established, and, by the early 1920s, the American firm owned more than twenty-five marketing subsidiaries around the world. These contributed to a record of some forty years of continuous profitability from 1890 to the end of the 1920s, with minor exceptions.[36] It was a crowded market too.[37] One senses who participated by looking at the vendors and products represented at a conference celebrating the 300th anniversary of John Napier's invention of logarithms, held in Edinburgh in 1914. In table 2.5, I catalog the vendors there and the products they exhibited and, most likely, demonstrated.

One U.S. government survey of the office appliance industry proudly declared in 1914 that "the United States stands preeminent in the marketing and exportation of labor-saving devices for office use."[38] In 1913, American manufacturers of typewriters, for example, shipped products valued at over $11 million or approximately five times the office products exported to the U.S. from Germany and sixty times those from Britain. That same year, American firms shipped overseas adding and calculating machines valued at $1.37 million, whereas Germany, the second largest exporter of office equipment worldwide, shipped products worth slightly less than $500,000. U.S.

exports of cash registers amounted to $4,535,000 compared to Germany's $103,000. French exports of all three types of products reached $444,000, whereas other European nations fell far below that figure as a group.[39] Clearly, the data suggests that market performance had not emerged in one or two years but was the result of steadily climbing business sought overseas. One U.S. government analyst estimated that nearly two-thirds of the office equipment produced in the United States in 1913 was shipped out of the country.[40] The experiences of Burroughs and NCR, however, suggest that for the entire data-processing industry, truer figures probably approached 30 to 40 percent. The data, nonetheless, suggests first an active market worldwide under development and second, that American firms were leading the charge in creating the market they came to dominate. Although protectionist tariffs helped national firms, "with few exceptions, American exporters of office appliances compete[d] on equal terms with shippers from other countries."[41] Trade barriers were minimal in France but somewhat higher in Canada and Germany, whereas in Britain, goods were admitted duty free.[42]

The Felt & Tarrant Manufacturing Company

Felt & Tarrant, another vendor of adding and calculating machines, rivaled Burroughs in popularity and proved significant because of its size. Less information is available about its operations, but enough exists to reconstruct its activities. It was the second most important vendor during the early days of the twentieth century, with the possible exception of Brunsviga in Europe, whether measured strictly by its activities in the United States or on the broader scale of world demand. Felt & Tarrant's significance illustrates how high-technology firms of the period came into being and suggests what, why, and how products were sold. Like Burroughs, it operated globally from its earliest days and for the same reasons. Like Burroughs, its history represents another window through which one can view the early phases of modern data processing.

The power of one individual's dream and actions was at work at this company as well. Dorr Eugene Felt (1862–1930) invented one of the first key-operated calculating machines and, like William Burroughs's, it was one of the first practical adding and listing machines, both of which became popular in the last years of the nineteenth century. Felt was born and raised in the Midwest and, like Burroughs, had his own firm in 1886 to sell the initial invention. In addition to a growing collection of patents, his primary asset was a manufacturing facility in Chicago. He also served as president of the firm until his death on August 7, 1930. Financial backing came initially from Robert Tarrant. Felt argued that adding long columns of numbers was turning accountants into veritable machines. In short, he saw the need for a solution to that problem and to the growing volumes of work that could not be handled manually anymore. He approached the problem as did Burroughs, seeking relief with mechanics. The most important machine produced by Felt's firm was the Comptometer, which was introduced in 1890. Along with the Burroughs Adding and Listing Machine, it became one of the most popular accounting devices in the United States.[43]

Felt's initial Comptometer was a black box with keys that represented numbers, much like the adding machines of the next century. The Comptometer simultaneously entered a number and added it to a results register. That function increased the speed of mechanical addition by orders of magnitude over that of competitive devices.[44] Felt began to develop the earliest version on Thanksgiving Day, 1884. Historians never fail to tell how he built his initial device on the kitchen table in his home using a wooden macaroni box, metal staples, rubber bands, and meat skewers to create a key-driven machine. For his effort he won patent protection in 1887. The moral of the story was that he identified a need and developed a solution using existing materials—a strategy that continues to be employed to introduce new and more useful processing products. Like others, he too added innovations to initial technology. Revisions of the design resulted in more patents for him personally and others for individuals he employed throughout the 1890s and during the early 1900s. Many years after his invention was marketed, he would recall that the only way such devices could be successful was if they worked faster than accountants; that is, machines had to work faster and more accurately than an individual who could add simultaneously four columns of numbers. Although he did not mention it, he must have kept a close eye on his competitor's products and noted technical deficiencies as potential opportunities to create a marketing edge. He also protected his many innovations with his relatively large number of patents. For him, technology was a marketing tool. He never diversified, electing to sell to a niche market for adding/calculating machines only.

Felt's machine was so successful that Burroughs momentarily had a difficult time when, in the early stages of establishing significant market share, both of their machines competed well. In fact, from about 1887 until roughly 1902, the Comptometer was probably the most popular desktop calculator. Burroughs's sales indicate that a significant takeoff did not occur until the early 1900s, which confirms indirectly that Felt's hardware was popular. But by 1902, Burroughs had finally developed a solid product line, strong enough in function and backed by sufficient marketing and manufacturing capability to maximize sales and to take advantage of perceived demand while going after Felt's market share. In time, Burroughs's machine won the preeminent position in the market. From the beginning, Felt sold his machines to railroad companies, banks, and insurance firms. Later, primarily through agents operating their own retail outlets, Felt made his products available to smaller businesses. Both Burroughs and Felt & Tarrant found a ready market in government agencies, which included the U.S. Treasury, the U.S. Navy (which, for over two decades, standardized on the Comptometer the mathematics required to design warships), and the New York Weather Bureau—all of which calculated enormous amounts of data by the standards of the day. Thus applications were both commercial and scientific. As with Burroughs's machines, users of Felt's products found more applications for them than the inventors originally envisioned. As a result, each firm began to compete more through technological advances than price. For instance, the original Comptometer could not record calculation results, so Burroughs reacted with a machine that printed all numbers entered and the results in a grand total. In turn, that innovation caused Felt and others to offer similar enhancements.[45]

Developments in Europe

Perhaps because of language and market similarities, American producers moved quickly and early to be first into the British and Canadian sectors with calculators, typewriters, and cash registers.[46] Activity generated in Europe seemed foremost in Germany, although marketing occurred in each European nation. In Germany, the economy was more industrialized than elsewhere in the late 1800s, which, in turn, created increased demand for control over office and factory processes. More responsive data was required to run a business, for example, than ever before. Germany was, therefore, more appropriately positioned to accept the aids to calculation offered by the new technologies. In Germany, the adding and calculating machine industry dates to 1878 when Arthur Burkhardt began manufacturing and selling the Thomas-like machine called the Arithmometer. Historians resist pegging a date for the start of any trend, but 1878 is as good a symbolic peg as one can find. In that year, at least one person thought enough of the market and of the demand for such technology to commit fame, fortune, and time to the endeavor. The Odhner class machine, developed originally in Russia, quickly spread throughout Europe, appearing first in Germany. By 1918, the Odhner type had even made it to Sweden where the Facit Company offered it as its primary product and became a major source of such devices during the first two decades of the new century.[47]

Lest one be led astray by northern European marketing initiatives, the vital market remained German. The most important of the early German firms was Grimme, Natalis & Company, better known by the name of its product, the Brunsviga Calculating Machine. The company came into existence in 1892 with the introduction of the Brunsviga calculator. The product remained essentially the same, with some modifications, throughout the first twenty years of the firm's existence. Its market, which remained overwhelmingly European, absorbed some twenty thousand machines by March 1912. Odhner's original patent was issued in 1891. In March 1892, Natalis acquired rights to the machine, which it then manufactured at its facility in Braunschweig. Between 1892 and 1912, as a result of technological improvements and marketing pressures, the firm obtained 130 German patents, another 300 in other countries, and 220 registered designs in Germany.[48] These machines were usually pitted against Baldwin-like devices, such as those sold by Felt & Tarrant or Burroughs. Brunsviga products also faced other German competitors. By World War I, the Mercedes-Euklid Arithmometer, designed by Herr Ch. Hamann, of Friedenau, Berlin, was also popular.[49] Equally available were, of course, the Millionaire and other, lesser-known machines.

The British market had its own indigenous vendors, who competed against American, German, and French companies. In the early 1900s, British Calculators, Ltd. offered a little device that looked like a round dish and used pegs instead of a typewriterlike keyboard—the Brical Adding Machine. The Charles & Edwin Layton Company sold the Layton's Improved Arithmometer in the same period. The original device became available in 1883 as an early British arithmometer and, hence, descended from Colmar's technology.[50] As with other vendors, this firm improved the machine, reduced its size, and made it easier to use. Thus by 1914, its model sold with emphasis on its small size (half the weight of its predecessors) and quiet performance.

The American presence in European markets for office equipment reflected what was happening with other light machinery products. Indigenous German and British firms in the office appliance market, like other light machinery vendors (e.g., of sewing machines), failed to survive the rapid American invasion. U.S. first movers established dominance quickly, making it difficult for European rivals to become significant threats.

In Britain, for example, in 1919, no British manufacturers of typewriters, cash registers, adding or mimeograph machines were among the top two hundred corporations; yet several U.S. firms were in the top tier.[51] U.S. manufacturing plants were rapidly reaching high levels of efficiency by the early 1900s, and entrants from Europe faced a difficult situation in all classes of office equipment.

German suppliers simply moved out of the office equipment market into other products (e.g., bicycles and automobiles) despite the competition from U.S. products manufactured in the United States and exported, marketed, and serviced on a highly competitive basis.[52]

However, the uses to which these machines were put in Europe were the same as in the United States. By World War I, the Millionaire and Brunsviga machines supported applications ranging from bills of lading, factory orders, and purchase orders in factories to traditional accounting procedures.[53] The Millionaire, because it did direct multiplication, proved especially useful in more complex applications. Between 1895 and 1898 alone, some one thousand were sold. The firm marketing the Millionaire was taken over by Hans W. Egli of Zurich, Switzerland, in 1915, making the Swiss an important supplier of calculating equipment. The two companies combined sold 4,600 machines between 1894 and 1935.[54] A contemporaneous commentator surveyed an increasingly cluttered market and concluded that "in almost every field of human endeavor the accounting and tabulating machines have become indispensable for the ascertaining of actual facts."[55]

Summary

Calculating devices were widely available by the 1890s. Contrary to the conventional belief that calculators had not penetrated the business world of the late 1800s,[56] they had, in fact, made impressive gains. More than one dozen vendors operated during the 1890s, whereas all the basic inventions had been patented during the previous decade. Hundreds of innovations emerged between 1890 and 1914 in the United States and across Europe, even in Italy and Spain—the two largest European nations to be the least industrialized in that period. Basic applications were understood and machines applied to them in accounting, engineering, and science, and inside manufacturing and offices. The active, competitive market that existed by 1914 was the largest in the United States with major suppliers including the Felt & Tarrant, Burroughs Adding Machine, Marchant Calculating Machine, Monroe Calculating Machine, and Ensign companies. These firms played a significant role in the rapidly expanding office appliance market of the 1920s.

Another emerging pattern was the demise of small start-up firms before World War I as pressure to manufacture cost effectively and to distribute nationally forced out under capitalized or poorly managed rivals, as in other industries such as light manufacturing. The pattern was also evident in the automotive market, which Henry Ford came to dominate because he too used a direct sales force and nationally based marketing and applied effective manufacturing technology. Mergers in the automotive world, as in office equipment, and sewing and agricultural machinery, occurred to enhance product lines not to centralize operations. Internal expansion was more the norm, however, by the end of World War I.

3

Hollerith and the Development of Punched Card Tabulation

A THIRD LEG in the data-processing industry, and the one that most clearly originated in its modern form within the United States, was the punched card tabulating business. It is also the early source of data processing most cited by those who write about the infant days of the computer business.[1] Although it developed in response to specific needs to gather and manipulate large volumes of numerical and, later, alphabetic data, its development occurred concurrently and as part of a more complicated response to industrialized society's requirements for aids to calculation.

Thus in concert with the typewriter and the adding and calculating machinery of the 1880s and beyond, tabulating equipment made up one more component of the young office appliance industry. Nonetheless, it was just a small contributor before the 1920s. By the 1930s, however, its importance was more widely realized because of its enormous capacity for processing data, which created the demand and the mind set that largely motivated organizations to want what eventually became known as the computer. This situation held particularly for businesses and industries with large or data-intensive calculating needs. For those reasons, tabulating gear has always been the heart of data processing's precomputer history and is the computer's most direct ancestor.

The reason was simple. Unlike typewriters or calculating machines, which were single units of equipment that handled small amounts of information in a restricted fashion, tabulating gear operated on thousands, even millions of pieces of data. Full use of tabulating equipment meant implementing a series of devices ranging from key punches to verifiers and sorters to tabulators in which data entered the system in machine-readable form, was processed, and output obtained. The important difference between this technology and others was that it dealt with a *system* that processed information quickly and in high volume.

Reliance on such equipment by a large number of organizations laid the foundation for computers because the first users of computers were primarily those who had experience with punched card tabulating gear. This was particularly the case during the first twenty years of computer use both in government and business. As a group, these users had already stretched to the limit the capabilities of tabulating machines to calculate and manipulate data and, thus, needed faster, greater capacity. They required computers and made their acceptance possible. An intermediate step, begun in the 1930s and continued through the 1940s, was the merger of calculating machine technology with tabulating equipment technology. Systems combined punched card and expanded calculating functions in large volumes of calculations or in more varied forms. Most commands from humans were entered with typewriterlike keyboards or with knobs. The effect was lasting, perhaps one of the great constants of data processing. Even as late as the end of the 1970s, a common device to input data to computers was the ubiquitous 80-column card that had been developed originally for tabulating equipment in the late 1920s to replace earlier Hollerith designs.

The configuration for tabulating equipment bolsters the argument that these devices came closer than any other to being predecessors of computers. It also hints at the cohesive and synergistic quality of technologies that borrowed from one another to form a new one that became a basis for the modern data-processing industry. Although the number and variety of equipment could be mixed in response to needs or because of products available, they all essentially performed the same functions. Vendors usually had several models of a machine that operated at different speeds, handled more or less data, or had more registers that could be linked mechanically to each other, were printing or nonprinting, and so forth. Over time the machines acquired more functions, most of which either sped up processes or further automated tasks that people used to perform.

Unlike previously discussed equipment and technologies, one must now think of a variety of machines working in concert rather than as single devices. With systems, users could process more data faster by reducing human intervention; which lowered the odds of human error while driving down the costs of data manipulation. Fewer skilled operators were needed to perform a series of data-handling tasks. That was very important for organizations that had large data-handling requirements.

Thus the idea of a *system* represented an important step toward the computer system, which also had many component machines. Individual units of hardware comprising a system or, to use modern data-processing jargon, *configuration*, had input, processing, and output elements. The operating process could be relatively more continuous than before: while cards were being manipulated by some equipment, other elements could be absorbing new data (input) or disgorging results (output). Output could be an end product, such as a card or report readable by humans, or be stored for future use in machine-readable form (cards). Initially all such equipment operated independently but were linked in a series of steps that humans performed, such as carrying freshly punched cards to a sorter or to some other machine. As vendors gained experience in how customers needed to process data and in how that could be done, enhanced products, and reacted to demands of their customers, some of the functions previously performed on separate machines were combined into fewer devices, or various independent machines were linked through electrical circuits. These developments allowed information to pass from one part of the system to another automatically, hence more quickly.

The medium used was a card, and to quote from an early twentieth-century Hollerith sales manuel, "Data appearing on order blanks, bills, time cards or forms of any kind, are transferred by means of the punching machines to cards, one card being used for each item of separate classification." It continued, "These cards are then sorted by the automatic electric sorting machine into the desired classifications, and are then passed through the electric tabulating machine, which automatically adds the amounts or value of these classes upon one or more counters."[2]

The card punch (also known as a keypunch) was used to punch holes in cards to represent data. Initially portable devices, in which one moved hole punches over cards, in time they became like typewriters with cards fed through them. Verifiers were used to check punching of data on cards and were used like keypunches. If a key went through the card where a hole was, the data was correct, so it served as a mechanical proofreader. Sorters (called counting sorters at the time) shuffled decks of cards into groups according to classes of information punched on the cards. It dropped sorted cards into hoppers by subject (as predetermined by an operator); the number of hoppers varied from machine to machine and over time and by vendor.

Tabulators, in essence, were rapid adding machines that read numbers to be added and processed in volume quickly. In time they acquired printing capability, allowing them to print numbers being added and results generated while the machine produced result cards. They also acquired mathematical functions during the 1920s and 1930s and could be construed as very primitive computerlike processors. A multiplying punch could read two numbers from a single card, determine their product, and punch the result on the same card. The interpreter simply typed on the top of the card the information represented on it by the holes. The reproducer transferred data from one card to another faster than either a duplicator function on a keypunch or a human could retype. A collator (the last major type of equipment to join the family of tabulating gear) could be used to insert or remove cards from a deck, much like a human clerk removed files from a filing cabinet. There was other specialized equipment and variations on the ones just mentioned, but the key elements of any full configuration were those described.[3]

This technology came into modern use thanks to the inventive efforts of Herman Hollerith (1860–1929). He was initially a clerk at the U.S. Bureau of the Census and later the founder of his own firm that built and sold the equipment. The idea of punching holes in cards or rolls of paper was not a new one when he began tinkering with them in the 1880s; their only successful and wide use previously was to control the operation of thousands of looms that wove cloth in Europe.[4] From the Napoleonic Wars until Hollerith's day, various individuals had worked with the concept but with no significant results such as a full system that could be marketed.[5]

One minor exception was the work done by Charles W. Seaton, chief clerk of the U.S. Bureau of the Census, who, in the 1870s, tackled the problem of how to manipulate the large quantities of raw data gathered and then analyzed by his agency. His response was the Seaton Tabulating Machine, built with the encouragement of his superiors. It was made of wood and comprised a hand-operated box armed with rollers over which blank paper unwound. The operator entered columns of figures on that paper, advancing it before entering each set of data. He believed such a system would reduce eye strain and bring together six to eight types of data.[6] Although not sophisticated, in the minds of the bureau's management the machine created the thought that mechanical means might be refined—a critical conclusion because it would be this agency that later encouraged Hollerith to go beyond Seaton's efforts. Without that encouragement, one might speculate that someone other than Hollerith would, perhaps later, have developed some sort of punched card system.

Dr. Walter F. Wilcox, who worked for the Bureau of the Census in 1900, recalled that "while the returns of the Tenth (1880) Census were being tabulated at Washington, John Shaw Billings," director of the Division of Vital Statistics, "was walking with a companion through the office in which hundreds of clerks were engaged in laboriously transferring data from schedules to record sheets by the slow and heartbreaking method of hand tallying. As they were watching the clerks he said to his companion, 'there ought to be some mechanical way of doing this job, something on the principle of the Jacquard loom.'"[7] Hollerith confirmed the story, adding that Billings had "said to me there ought to be a machine for doing the purely mechanical work of tabulating population and similar statistics."[8] It was a singular moment in the history of data processing, one historians could reasonably point to and say that things had changed because of it. It stirred Hollerith's imagination and ultimately his achievements.

Clearly the power of one was at work again. Upon graduating from Columbia University in 1879, Hollerith had taken a job at the U.S. Bureau of the Census working for Billings. In 1881, Billings remarked on the potential of using machines to trap and manipulate data. In 1882, Hollerith taught mechanical engineering at the new Massachusetts Institute of Technology (MIT) while developing tabulating equipment for the bureau. The following year he returned to Washington, D.C., to continue work on his "census machine" while employed at the Patent Office. On September 23, 1884, he applied for his first patent. By the late 1880s, he had built a device that could tabulate and handle aggregates using cards and electrical sensing. By aggregates he meant that a hole in one card could help represent more than one piece of information. For example, in census data, a hole could define a man; the same hole in combination with another, that he was a farmer. He demonstrated his machine in Baltimore and later in New York. When both cities tested its capabilities with vital statistics, he was able to start selling his machine's services. During the 1880s, his device also changed from a simple card reader into a full system that could punch, read, and tabulate. It was made of oak, looked like a desk and box with rows of clocklike counters, each of which could count up to ten thousand occurences. He also developed an electric sorter for grouping cards by predesignated types.[9]

Hollerith's first major U.S. government contract came in 1889 with the Army Surgeon's Office to handle statistics. Following a pattern easily identifiable in the 1930s and 1940s, government agencies were frequently first to install new data-processing technology and to encourage development of new computing devices. This trend was evident in the 1880s too; the only fundamental difference between then and later was that the government did not fund any of the R & D in the beginning. That changed by the early 1900s, when the Bureau of the Census began to develop machines at its own expense. The major early event for Hollerith was when the bureau awarded him a contract to help support the census of 1890. This was the first national census to use data-processing equipment on a wide scale, and it was that event that enabled Hollerith to convince other governments to do the same in Austria, Canada, Italy, Norway and Russia before World War I.[10]

The U.S. Census of 1890 represented more than the single most important event of Hollerith's early career. It was a milestone in the history of modern data processing. It occurred independently of the maturation of calculating and adding machine technologies. No other occurrence so clearly symbolized the start of the age of mechanized data handling. The census measured a large country and a greater variety of issues than ever before. Hollerith's machines were seen as one of many contemporary symbols of progress. With these one person could count thousands of people a day, keypunching data captured by thousands of census takers. Thousands of families were tabulated daily; each day, between 10,000 and 15,000 were counted. Before the end of that year, his machines had tabulated all 62,622,250 souls in the United States. Use of his machines saved the bureau $5 million over manual methods while cutting sharply the time to do the job. Additional analysis of other variables with his machines meant that the Census of 1890 could be completed within two years, as opposed to nearly ten years taken for fewer data variables and a smaller population in the previous census.[11] With that success, Hollerith and his technology were recognized as important features on America's technological landscape.

Tabulating Equipment Uses and Market, 1890–World War I

Hollerith was at the center of his technology from 1890 to World War I. Afterward, others took control of his enterprise, and competitors were active. However, in the first quarter-century of tabulating, Hollerith, like his contemporaries Burroughs, Felt, and others, saw a need, applied his skills, and possessed sufficient creativity to produce practical solutions. He also had the ability to convince managers to adopt his equipment and to find the wherewithall to manufacture and distribute them. It was a slow process initially.

Hollerith first convinced the city of Baltimore to use his machines in 1886. He used what became a common expediency in the data-processing industry: he demonstrated how his equipment worked and benchmarked the system against manual methods to show that his performed better and faster. For Baltimore, he recorded deaths as a hole in a card with a train conductor's punch at the rate of one thousand per day. The use of his cards—in addition to making the Baltimore project the first use of such technology—clarified in his mind the benefits of cards over punched continuous feed paper.[12] By departing from Seaton's use of rolled paper, he was able to develop a standardized, interchangeable, and portable medium. Cards could be reshuffled into any order as often as necessary to process and extract every piece of data. It was the single most critical step taken in the late 1800s by any inventor working on the concept of data management by machine. Although it looks obvious and simple in hindsight, it was new for the period and, when enhanced by using electricity, made the Jacquard concept practical.[13]

Besides dealing with Baltimore, Hollerith offered his services around Washington, D.C. At the Surgeon General's Office at the War Department, he rented his system for $1,000 per year to capture information on the health of soldiers. Types of disease, whether admitted to sick report, if illness was contracted while on duty, and other data, were recorded on cards beginning in December 1888. By July 1889, the army's file had grown to fifty thousand cards, making it dependent on the system to perform routine record keeping.[14] In 1889, Hollerith cast an eye on Europe and exhibited his equipment at the Paris Universal Exposition, the same event for which Alexandre-Gustave Eiffel built his famous tower. For his work Hollerith received a gold model.[15] In the 1890s, business picked up as his approach gained acceptance. In 1891, Austria used his machines for its census as did Canada and Norway.[16] In 1893, the U.S. government used his devices to conduct an agricultural census.[17] The biggest project was the Russian census of 1897, which involved 129 million citizens, 900,000 enumerators, and 2,000 census analyzers working on fourteen categories of data.[18]

Hollerith also turned his attention to commercial users, realizing that they too had large volumes of data to manipulate. His biographer noted that Hollerith "clearly recognized that steady employment of his tabulating machines by commercial customers was preferable to their intermittent use in the census."[19] He went after railroads because they were very large enterprises with data-processing needs that he believed his machines could satisfy. Yet even at first he was hesitant, concerned that "I did not know the first damned thing about railroad accounts."[20] In 1895, the New York Central Railroad agreed to use his equipment to process nearly four million freight waybills per year, weekly rather than monthly as before. The speed-up made it possible for the railway to increase control of what was moving while beginning to solve the problem of its "blizzard of paper." Hollerith modified his equipment to meet its need to start a pilot project by mid-1896. On September 28, he won the order to provide rental equipment and to sell cards to support the application. Cards were sold at $1.00 per 100 cards. He sold the same application and other accounting uses to additional railroads while offering new services to his original customer. These services included passenger and car accounts. He received some indirect help in 1902 when the Interstate Commerce Commission ordered railroads to report more statistics. The New York Central said these demands would pose no problems; other lines protested the expense of (manually) tabulating the data. After others saw the New York Central using Hollerith's equipment to do the job, they fell in line and began renting his equipment.[21]

Between 1900 and 1917, companies in other industries began to use his equipment, most notably insurance firms.[22] Manufacturing and process companies began next. The Pennsylvania Steel Company opened the door for Hollerith's equipment in heavy industry, using it for cost accounting of parts and labor.[23] In 1902, Marshall Field, the important Chicago retailer, decided to use his machines and quickly became a reference account for his Tabulating Machine Company. Firms used his equipment for purchase records, inventory management, overhead allocation, payroll analysis, shipping costs, sales projections, and market forecasting, all before World War I.[24] Retailing by large organizations had become increasingly mechanized. As mass-produced goods were widely distributed, which led to increased use of data to manage business, technology became more obviously useful and was incorporated into the strategic imperatives of Hollerith's customers. The cash register became a critical component of data gathering at the store level, and calculators and adding machines tabulated information, all of which increased pressure to analyze sales quickly. Hollerith's equipment was perfect for the job because it could sort and tabulate by topics, which is why his first order from Marshall Field was unsolicited; the firm could not wait until he found time to sell to them.[25]

Changes in accounting enhanced Hollerith's opportunities. Internal bureaucratic controls were increasing as organizations grew in size and with these the number of accountants.[26] Initially his and other types of equipment simply replaced existing manual applications. By World War I, accountants were employing his technology for applications that could not be done readily manually, for example, the immediate and continuous sales and cost analyses that, by the 1920s, were normal practice. One student of computing noted that just in factories alone "because the internal statistical data needed to control these flows had already been well defined, their application to cost accounting—given the necessary data-processing capability—proved to be relatively straightforward."[27] He reminded readers that at Pennsylvania Steel the data needed to use Hollerith's equipment was already understood and was being captured on a primitive basis.[28] The machines were employed in the overall reconstitution of basic processes such as mass production and more fact-based decision making.

Contemporary literature on accounting and business confirms these ideas. Inventions clearly supported accounting. From the thoughts of a business writer in 1909: "The trend of invention in the pay-roll and cost keeping field seems to be along the line of computing machines automatically controlled by the electric contact principle."[29] Hollerith's gear was used to tabulate sales statistics (1900–1905), sort and tabulate voucher distribution (1911), sort consumer trend analyses (1912), check bill extensions, allocate costs, and number job orders (by 1917).[30]

Our 1909 commentator reminds us that not everyone embraced the new technology quickly. "Some accountants fear the system because the record it produces is not displayed in the form of nice statements or reports."[31] That problem was solved quickly and by 1914, Hollerith's equipment was being applied so extensively "that engineering development was aimed at developing an overall automatic machine."[32] J. William Schultze, a widely respected commentator on office practices, in 1914 called his equipment "uncanny in its action," citing its use by AT&T for its complex accounting system.[33] In just one decade, the technology made it possible to use less skilled people in accounting, a development predicted as early as 1902 when a British writer argued that "when data are punched cards, the job can be put in the hands of a girl" instead of in the hands of "someone of marked ability."[34] The sorry fact then was that women were paid less for their deskilled services. Thus whenever women could be used to do such a job, that function became less expensive to perform.

As with typewriters and adding machines, tabulating equipment received considerable attention. The focus was on applications. What is important is how quickly such machinery received attention despite Hollerith's nearly decade-long struggle to sell his services in quantity. Billings wasted no time in describing punched card gear in 1887,[35] whereas cost accounting received its fair share of debate as early as 1902.[36] The use of tabulating equipment in factory-related applications, such as payroll, was discussed in widely read journals as well.[37] As railways accepted the equipment, articles on this fact appeared.[38] Each U.S. census either used Hollerith's equipment or someone else's through the first half of the twentieth century. In the early decades, its use was always the subject of considerable press coverage.[39]

Formation and Performance of the Tabulating Machine Company, 1896–World War I

Hollerith began his business as a one-man act, tinkering with equipment as he developed its design. He aimed initial marketing at the U.S. Census, but it scarcely was a leap in logic for him to realize that any government agency that gathered statistics would be a potential customer or, for that matter, any commercial operation. But in the beginning, like others in computing technologies, he did all the selling. Later, as Hollerith actually gained business, he set up a machine shop, hired workers, and began to piece equipment together. This casual approach gave way to a more formal corporate structure as business grew. In the 1880s, he had the nucleus of the Tabulating Machine Company, but he formalized the arrangement in May 1889 with a subsidiary called the Auditing Machine Company so he could continue to work on the New York Central Railroad project. Formal capitalization of the Tabulating Machine Company, before the merger with C-T-R in 1911, came on December 3, 1896, at $100,000 and with 1,000 shares of common stock at par value of $100 each.[40]

Why did he incorporate? Aside from the usual reasons given by lawyers (to limit personal liability), the motivation for Hollerith—as for other inventors—was easier access to both capital and advice on business matters from investors committed to gaining returns on their investments. It also meant that he could no longer operate on a shoestring with casual attention to business procedures or with "one-of-a-kind" devices to satisfy a census bureau here, a railroad there, and so forth. He would have to standardize his products and their manufacture with cost accounting and fix an eye firmly on profitability.

From 1895 to 1896, his business volumes were miserable while he focused on closing the Russian order. Soon after, the New York Central project became operational. The problem with government contracts was that they were of short duration and for one project, while what he needed and sought was a smoother, ongoing cash flow that could come only from continuous use of his equipment in critical administrative applications. Circumstances required a more formal, businesslike operation that would ensure a reasonable supply of machines and cards, which customers could rely upon, and a service organization available to all customers.[41] His firm did not take off until after the turn of the century, but when it did, he was ready. First there was the Russian Census in 1897. The New York Central signed its contract in 1902 for fifteen machines renting for between $3,000 to $4,000 total per year, with a budget of $3,000 just for cards. He built new devices for the census of 1900 that were more attractive to commercial customers.

The census of 1900 was very important for his financial health, but it was also a turning point that made possible broader expansion of the tabulating gear market. That year the Bureau of the Census contracted for 50 machines at an annual rent of $1,000 each—the same terms as in the 1890 contract but with an option to rent an additional 100 machines if needed. Hollerith brought out a new integrating tabulator that could add; that of 1890 could only count. The 1900 census was also going to trap more information than the 1890 census and the potential existed to sell 100 million cards. His machines also had to become faster simply to get the work done. Hollerith already had developed a new keypunch for the agricultural census (1893) that operated much like a semiautomatic tabulator by 1901–1902. These punches were also put under contract at $1,500 per year. Their added rental charge was justified bcause they could do six times as much work in a given time as older models. They were perfected over time and reached full function in time for the Philippine Census of 1904. During the U.S. Census of 1900, his tabulators worked at a speed of 415 cards per minute or 80,000 to 90,000 cards per day.[42] This census used 311 tabulating machines, 20 automatic sorters, and 1,021 punches for which Hollerith was paid $428,239 (including services rendered and cards).[43] His biographer noted that the equipment was technologically so superior at the time that "Hollerith made the sensing of the punched card itself control its passage through the machines—without human intervention."[44] This innovation led to a more integrated approach to information handling.

Thus Hollerith now began to recover his long-term investment. Based on data for 1905, one can see that tabulators broke even (cost of production and sales compared to rent) in twenty months, sorters in thirty. Sorters rented for $10 per month, tabulators for $40. To put breakevens in 1905 in perspective, computers in the 1980s had rent compared to purchase breakevens of about 30–33 months, whereas rent compared to manufacturing and marketing expenses required closer to 20–25 months. Hollerith's equipment increasingly became very reliable; declining maintenance expenses contributed to his bottom line. His agent in San Francisco, for example, made only two repair calls in 1915, both for minor adjustments. Controlling the sale of cards also helped Hollerith recapture his investment. Cards ranged in price from 85 cents to $1.00 per thousand with production costs of about $.30 per thousand, yielding a handsome profit on large volumes sold. Marshall Field used about 10,000 per day and both the Russian and American governments consumed millions. In 1907, the Southern Railway Company used over 200,000 per month for several months; demand from that firm reached 550,000 per month, which Hollerith could not satisfy fully. To drive the point home, at the same time (1907), Southern Railway was considering using another application that would require an additional half-million cards![45] He was clearly wise to insist on exclusive rights to supply cards, often using the argument that quality control was critical to ensure that his machines did not jam or malfunction.

Hollerith's business practices were crucial to the history of data processing because they were mimicked by many, not the least of which was IBM. IBM also rented equipment—almost exclusively until the late 1970s despite a consent decree of 1956 that forced the firm to offer hardware for sale—and sold supplies, particularly cards, during most of the same period. Hollerith controlled service and maintenance to manage performance levels of machines and, hence, preserve the reputation of his equipment. He discovered very early that high-quality cards did not jam and that responsive maintenance service and ownership of equipment made for good business.[46] These strategies were adopted by many firms in the industry over the next eight decades.

In the ten-year period just before the start of World War I, his company broadened its business base. The process was precipitated by the U.S. Bureau of the Census, which, after 1905, sought alternative sources of equipment so as not to be so dependent on Hollerith and to improve upon his designs. This circumstance forced Hollerith to find other customers faster, and that proved to be a successful effort. He had already begun to negotiate with other firms, which led to a series of contracts: in August 1903, with the Long Island Railway; in March 1904, with the West Jersey and Seashore Divsion, in June 1904, with the North Central Railway Company; then in August with the Philadelphia, Baltimore and Washington. The following month, the Philadelphia and Erie line adopted his equipment and, in January 1905, the Buffalo and Allegheny, with others later that year following suit. In that prewar decade, Hollerith introduced new products that looked better, were more ergonomic (e.g., making both horizontal and vertical sorters), used telephone plugboards for faster "programming," and operated faster.[47] Other customers included Eastman Kodak, National Tube, American Sheet and Tin Plate, Pennsylvania Steel, Western Electric, and Yale and Towne. Over one dozen new contracts were under negotiation in 1907 alone.

By 1908, growth had created problems; some customers complained that he was not delivering products fast enough. Hollerith responded by farming out manufacturing to Taft-Pierce Company, Woonsocket Company, and Western Electric to increase manufactured volumes. These problems of prosperity existed despite the fact that the U.S. economy was suffering in 1907. By 1909, railroads were his most enthusiastic customers in the United States. Other leading firms experimented with his new devices which, in turn, became solid references for yet more customers. Commenting on the demand for his products in 1909 Hollerith said, "Now it comes with a rush and I am simply taken off my feet."[48] Although. perhaps, not the greatest business manager capable of maximizing all opportunities, he nonetheless sported a collection of some one hundred customers in 1911 and more than three hundred in 1915. Sales in Europe also increased, leading him, in 1907, to formalize operations there by creating a syndicate called the British Tabulating Machine Company (BTM) which, until 1949, remained attached to his and successor firms, including IBM.[49]

By 1910, his company had reached a level of prosperity and complexity that gave it the necessary synergism and momentum with which to survive. In that year, sales reached $350,000, and in 1911, it joined others to become the Computing-Tabulating-Recording Company (C-T-R) because he needed an infusion of capital to continue expanding and supplying the needs of existing customers. The new firm, chartered in the State of New York on July 5, 1911, was the brainchild of Charles R. Flint (1850–1934), a colorful master of firm mergers. The new conglomerate consisted of the Computing Scale Company of Dayton, Ohio; the International Time Recording Company of Endicott, New York, and, of course, Hollerith's Tabulating Machine Company—all "high-tech" firms of their day.[50] Hollerith remained on the board of directors and continued to improve machines. A former NCR executive, Thomas J. Watson (1874–1956), was hired as general manager on May 1, 1914. It took him little time to realize that it was Hollerith's piece of the new enterprise that held the greatest potential and, hence, to focus attention and resources on it. His priorities were justified because for each six-month period from December 1909 to May 1911, rentals and sales of the Tabulating Machine Company had increased on average by 20 percent over those of the previous period.[51]

Part of the reason Watson's company was successful and a key element in appreciating the future of C-T-R (and, hence, of IBM) was Hollerith's constant introduction of new products. The pattern was also unfolding in the adding and calculating machine markets and still somewhat in that for typewriters. Product introductions in the tabulating machine world continued unabated for decades (see table 3.1). The most important introduction in the years immediately before the firm became IBM was the printing tabulator of 1917. World War I interrupted introduction of this machine, but reintroduced it in 1921 in a second version, which carried the firm through the 1920s. Printing capability satisfied the original request of accountants to see on paper all numbers manipulated by the Hollerith System.[52] Watson also made a firm commitment to research and development despite limited funds, which remained a problem before 1920 and reappeared in the early 1930s. From 1914 until his death in 1956, Watson viewed R&D as a critical success factor for his firm. In this he was following a pattern already very evident in many other technology-based companies of the day.[53]

The reasons for innovation came largely from customer demand and competitors. Even back in 1890 for the U.S. census, Hollerith had to compete to win the business. At that time, Charles F. Pidgin, of Boston, who had in-

TABLE 3.1
Innovations in Punched Card Machinery, 1917–1939

1917	Electric keypunch[a]
1919	Single-deck sorter
1919	Alphabetic printing tabulator
1921	Automatic control for tabulators
1924	Electric duplicating keypunch
1928	Typewriter attached to keypunch for simultaneous punching and typing
1928	80-column "computer," "IBM" card
1928	General-purpose accounting machine
1928	Devices for remote-control accounting for retail uses
1930	Offset-hole method of verification for numerical interpreters
1930	Universal printing-counting sorter
1931	90-column card
1931	Multiplying punch
1931	Summary punch
1932	Alphabetic printing tabulator
1933	Test-scoring machine
1933	Alphabetic printing punch
1934	Automatic carriage for printing tabulators
1934	Small cards (2″ × 2.75″) with 21 columns
1936	Collator to merge and separate cards
1938	Transfer posting machine
1938	Reproducing gang summary punch
1938	130-column cards (2 banks of 65 columns)
1939	Mark sensing for cards

Source: Gregory and Van Horn, *Automatic Data-Processing Systems*, 628–29.
[a] Majority of the developments listed in this table came from Remington Rand and IBM.

vented a device to handle Massachusetts census data for 1885, competed but lost the big order in 1890 because his equipment did not work as well as Hollerith's. But he came back in 1900 for the next matchup with his Automatic Mechanical Tabulation System, and the Electrical Typewriter Tabulator. In that test, Hollerith's equipment did the work in 185 hours, 53 minutes, whereas Pidgin's took 452 hours and so lost the bid.[54]

The Powers Accounting Machine Company

Of greatest seriousness to Hollerith after 1907 was the rivalry that emerged first from within the U.S. Bureau of the Census itself and, after 1911, from the Powers Accounting Machine Company. Very rapidly, it became the second largest vendor of tabulating equipment in the United States and, after World War I, a force to be reckoned with in Europe. By the end of the 1920s,

Powers had been acquired by Remington Rand, pitting that firm against IBM in the office equipment marketplace.

In 1907, the director of the Bureau of the Census, Simeon N. D. North, had begun planning for the 1910 census and sought improved technology that used faster, more reliable equipment than before, particularly for manual punching and verification of data on cards. Toward that end, he hired James Powers, an engineer. Powers built the Census Punching Machine (three hundred ultimately were manufactured) and a two-deck horizontal sorter. The big difference between what Powers ultimately made and Hollerith's equipment was electricity; Hollerith used it in his products before Powers did. Electrical components were more precise than manual equivalents and operations were faster even if they were subject to breakdown and required more complex maintenance.[55]

The U.S. government gave Powers the right to patent his inventions while he developed them on behalf of the bureau; he left the agency in 1911 to start his own firm to manufacture and rent tabulating equipment. The Powers Accounting Machine Company began with the punching machine and two-deck horizontal sorter. In 1912, he set up operations in Newark, New Jersey, and joined forces with another inventor, W. W. Lasker who, in 1914, completed the Powers Tabulator Printer. The machine could tabulate and print processed information, had the adding capability of a Comptrograph-type adder, contained components from the Dalton Adding Machine, and was mechanical.[56] Lasker modified other pieces of equipment, providing Powers with a set of competitive offerings with which to challenge Hollerith. In 1914, the firm moved to Brooklyn, New York, reincorporated, and the following year established its European operations through Powers-Samas Accounting Machine Limited.[57]

Powers's equipment gave Hollerith problems. Initial products from Powers were functionally superior. For example, Powers's punch had a feature protecting against punching errors by operators, and the punch itself came closest to looking like a typewriter keyboard. This came after Hollerith had sued the bureau over patent infringements involving Powers's work at the bureau; the courts rejected Hollerith's arguments. The basic patents for Hollerith's equipment had been awarded over twenty years earlier and were running out. The court allowed the agency to modify Hollerith's equipment and, of course, Powers built on that.[58] Hollerith was, therefore, obviously upset when the bureau decided to use three hundred punches developed by Powers at a cost of $250 each built by the Sloan and Chase Manufacturing Company. These did not work well and often jammed, forcing the bureau to do one-third of the work of the 1910 census on old Hollerith equipment first used in 1890, and some of these machines were used again in 1920. The bureau had simply found Powers's equipment less reliable, but that did not stop Powers from marketing his products.[59]

Hollerith-Powers Rivalry

The two firms were clearly at loggerheads, yet Hollerith's had the advantage of size and experience. His firm had sales in 1914 of $4.2 million, which, by the end of 1917, reached $8.3 million. The circumstances of World War I supported the emerging data-processing industry in America, and it was to become more supportive after the United States entered the conflict. In a nutshell, the war increased the demand for Hollerith's equipment to track army recruits, maintain and monitor business transactions as per government regulations, and even to manage increased tax collections. Earnings went from $490,000 to $1.6 million between 1914 and 1918. By the end of World War I, the firm had 1,400 rental tabulators and 1,100 sorters in more than 650 locations. Almost every large insurance company and railway used these machines, with only minor sales going to Powers. By the end of World War I, C-T-R's card-manufacturing facility in Washington, D.C., was producing 80 million cards per month, and in 1918, a second plant in Dayton began generating another 30 million, bringing worldwide production up to some 110 million per month. Best, but limited, evidence suggests that these volumes represented roughly 95 percent of the market for cards worldwide in 1918. And even then demand exceeded supply.[60] Powers could not supply demand fully either and experienced considerable manufacturing problems. Watson claimed that success was the result of superior salesmanship; in truth, it also involved efficient manufacturing. He was able to build more better-functioning quality products in a shorter time, even if the supply was never enough.[61]

Watson proved to be the better all-around manager, which accounted for much of the reason that his firm ultimately outpaced Powers's. One historian called him "one of the dozen or so great businessmen of his time."[62] Watson took advantage of Powers's control problems, which arose despite the fact that Powers had functionally better equipment when Watson came to C-T-R and had given the old Hollerith firm a hard time in 1912–1913. Powers was selling what appeared to be a better product for a while to Hollerith's old customers. The Hollerith firm had chosen to spend less on R&D in 1911–1914 than it might have, electing to rent existing products in Europe where Powers did not operate. Watson came in and emphasized salesmanship in the strong market of 1914 and 1915 while he increased R&D to combat Powers in the United States. In 1915, nearly 75 percent of C-T-R's revenues came from card sales, the rest from machine rentals, which provided Watson with the fiscal muscle to fight.[63]

Both firms saw a solid future ahead for tabulating equipment despite recession in the United States during 1913 and part of 1914. Sobel, in his history of IBM, pointed out that office appliances were in great demand because they "enabled employees to cut labor costs and conduct their business in a more efficient fashion. The business machine industry came as close as any in the nation to being divorced from the vicissitudes of the economic cycle."[64] Watson cultivated installed customers more than Powers did, avoiding cancellations of rental equipment unless the company replaced them with newer models (a marketing emphasis still alive in present-day IBM). The skill of IBM's sales force began to grow in those early years as led by Watson, an experienced and talented marketing executive. The effort proved costly to Powers who was a better engineer than marketeer and not a real challenge to Watson.

As would be done repeatedly in decades to come, C-T-R (IBM) increased the number of salespeople. A December 1917 organization chart showed a company with thirty-three sales offices in the United States reporting to eight district managers, who, in turn, answered to a vice-president of sales—a relatively new function in American industry—G. W. Spahr. During World War I, Watson also anticipated that pent-up demand caused by war shortages would make postwar sales enormous. So he committed resources and efforts to get ready. He consolidated all the salespeople from each piece of C, T, and R into one organization to market the entire product line from scales and recording equipment to tabulators. He also built up inventories threefold by the end of 1918 over what they had been in 1916. After the war, he announced a new printer-lister functionally superior to Powers's and less expensive. That was the first of many new machines introduced in the 1920s that gave C-T-R, and after early 1924, IBM, technological superiority over products from Powers. Initial returns on the strategy looked good: in 1919, total revenues at C-T-R were $13 million with earnings at $2.1 million.[65]

Other Punched Card Projects and Vendors

While C-T-R and Powers dominated the commercial market, others tinkered in various ways. The best-documented project was at the Prudential Insurance Company in Newark, New Jersey. In 1892, John K. Gore quit his teaching job at Woodbridge School in New York and joined Prudential as an actuary. In his early years (long before becoming vice-president in 1912), he saw the need for machinery to tabulate data and, with the help of his brother-in-law, installed them at Prudential in 1895; variations of his machines were still used there into the 1930s.[66] Before Gore's work, the insurance company had been an early user of Hollerith's equipment on an experimental basis but found Gore's machines, which had been designed with that company's needs in mind, more useful. Because of that specialized design, it was of little use to other firms and, hence, posed no competitive threat to Hollerith, only lost potential sales to Prudential. The experience with both systems gave the insurance company a healthy respect for data-processing technology, which it proved again when it became one of the first commercial enterprises to order the UNIVAC computer in the early 1950s.[67]

The other major effort, and one slightly competitive to Powers and Hollerith, was that of the Peirce Patents Company. Formed before 1915, it was a tabulating system firm that sold to American utility companies. Its product consisted of a card punch machine, a distributing device, and an automatic ledger machine, collectively called the Royden System of Perforated Cards. It was used to generate a bill, post debits and credits to ledgers, and generate monthly statements. Little else is known about the products or its organization. It never became a factor, and in 1921, C-T-R purchased the patents and assets of what was then known as the Peirce Accounting Machine Company. Watson subsequently dissolved the firm.[68]

Changing Patterns of the Office Workplace, Technology, and People

Each group of products discussed so far—typewriters, calculators, and punched card equipment—did well in the period from the 1880s to the end of World War I. There were the usual start-up problems, educating customers about their benefits, and then the effort to get the devices installed and used advantageously. It was done, and each of the companies surveyed performed well, grew, and was profitable. Their markets thrived and, in each instance, their devices continued to be used in one form or another down to the fourth quarter of the twentieth century. Clearly the potential and the optimism sensed by the early inventors was justified. The demand for aids to office work, in other words, not only was there but actually grew beyond initial expectations.

Expansion in the number of office workers boosted acceptance of data-processing technologies by providing the necessary environment needed to grow a new industry. The number of workers and managers kept growing up to World War II—during the great eras of the typewriter and punched card (see tables 3.2 and 3.3). Calculators continued to be adopted at even faster rates into the early 1970s despite the adoption of the digital computer in the 1950s. This phenomenon was not surprising because computers and calculators met different needs, at least through the 1950s.

Figure 3.1 (p. 62) illustrates what happened with the capital investments that supported these new office workers: furniture, buildings, and office appliances. In 1879–1899, expenditures quadrupled and tripled again by the end of World War I. Although getting ahead of the story, it is clear why the 1920s represented yet another good period, marked by an equal rate of

TABLE 3.2
Growth in U.S. Office Work Force, 1900–1940 (in percentages)

	1900–1910	1910–1920	1920–1930	1930–1940
Labor force	26[a]	23	15	6
Managers	45[b]	14	29	4[c]
Clerks	127[b]	70	28	15[c]

Source: U.S. Bureau of the Census, Historical Statistics 1:140–41. Beniger calculated most of the percentages, Beniger, Control Revolution, 393.
[a] Estimated.
[b] In 1900, managers and clerks were 8.9 percent of the civilian work force.
[c] In 1940, managers and clerks were 16.9 percent of the civilian workforce.

TABLE 3.3
Growth in Type of U.S. Office Jobs, 1900–1940 (in percentages)

	1900–1910	1910–1920	1920–1930	1930–1940[a]
Typists/Secretaries	189	103	40	11
Bookkeepers/Cashiers	93	38	20	−2
Office Machine Operators	178	102	30	31
Accountants/Auditors	70	203	63	24

Source: U.S. Bureau of the Census, Historical Statistics 1:140–41. Beniger calculated the percentages, Beniger, Control Revolution, 393.
[a] In 1900–1940, these four categories increased from 2.1 to 8.6 percent of the total civilian work force.

growth. Although the depression of the 1930s slowed investments, expenditures remained extensive. In figure 3.2, I compare the same investments in the office to those in manufacturing—a good indicator of whether funds were being diverted away from production and to the office or not. The evidence suggests that in the period 1879–1919 the investments tracked along similar lines. The decade of the 1920s was the exception, providing evidence of enormous growth in consumer demand for manufactured goods in an age when factory automation (which included the use of data-processing equipment) experienced significant growth.

A detailed look at what was introduced into the office after 1880 confirms strongly the circumstantial evidence presented by others, particularly Beniger, concerning a crisis of control that had to be fixed. His point is so relevant that it is worth quoting at length:

A crisis of control in office technology and bureaucracy in the 1880s, as the growing scope, complexity, and speed of information processing . . . began to strain the manual handling systems of large business enterprises. This crisis had

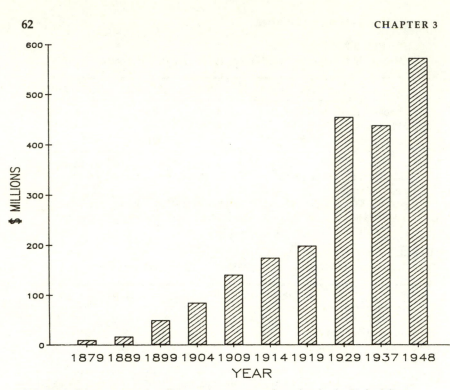

3.1 Capital investments in office equipment manufacturing in the United States, selected years, 1879–1948 (book value in 1929 dollars).

begun to ease by the 1890s, owing to innovations not only in the processor itself (formal bureaucratic structure) but also in its information creation or gathering (inputs), in its recording or storage (memory), in its formal rules and procedures (programming), and in its processing and communication (both internal and as outputs to its environment).[69]

Several refinements to his thoughts are called for, however, by the evidence. Clearly, there was a crisis of control. One might argue that it existed before the 1880s because it was in the 1860s and 1870s that inventors began to identify problems and to formulate initial thoughts on solutions. These problems were not fixed by the end of the 1890s, although all the fundamental directions for technologies had been set and were available. As sales volumes proved, they had not yet been widely distributed; that would come in the period from 1905 to World War I. Chandler's argument—that organizations formed to control economic activity in response to the same crisis mentioned by Beniger—described the period 1840–1870. The solution—large organizations with managers—was well underway to being implemented by the 1880s. Chandler argued that the process was essentially completed by the

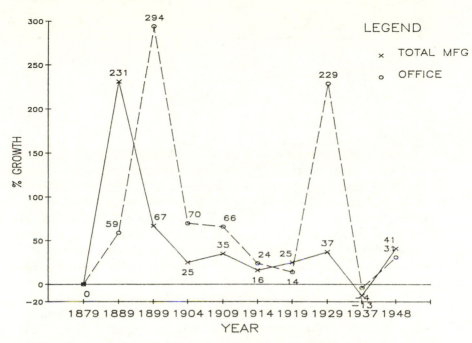

3.2 Growth rates: U.S. capital investments in office equipment compared to total major branches of manufacturing, selected years, 1879–1948 (book value in 1929 dollars).

1920s. Office equipment clearly was part of the process; its timing was no accident of fate.

Although the critical innovations were pretty much in place by the end of the 1800s, as the various lists of innovations and discussions indicated, more improvements came after 1900, almost always in response to new uses that either had not been anticipated or needed earlier, or that were not necessary until more basic applications had been implemented. Thus, for instance, a faster sorter was irrelevant unless a customer had one already that was too slow. Technologies were introduced and refined and their capabilities continuously stretched to their limits before they were replaced. Was that response any different than that to the computer chip, which went from 8K in the 1960s to over 1 million in the 1980s and continues to be enhanced?[70]

4

Cash Registers and the National Cash Register Company

CASH REGISTERS represented a unique element of the office appliance industry. Just because of the sheer volume of machines built, it was a major line of equipment. It was, perhaps, the most visible of all such hardware because one did not have to work in an office or for an insurance or railroad company to see one in use; increasingly, a person simply had to walk into a store. No symbol of engineering marvels at work at so humble a level appeared more obvious than the cash register supplanting the cash drawer. Its penetration across the economies of the United States and Europe was extensive by 1920. Even in places far from manufacturing facilities for registers, there they were in China, Russia, Central America and Latin America, and across Africa. The National Cash Register Company was the prime supplier, which made it a highly visible, well-recognized name in American commerce by the 1920s. Even more than a half-century later, with so many suppliers of registers, one would be hard pressed to think of any supplier other than NCR. The same was true many decades ago.

A second feature of the cash register business was precisely the founding of a major corporation (NCR) within the industry brought about by the cash register which gave the firm the market strength, manufacturing capability, fiscal reserves, and technical knowledge to foray into the office appliance industry for more than one hundred years. Technology developed at NCR surfaced in other products (e.g., in accounting machines) while its executives emerged elsewhere in the industry. The most notable example of the latter was Watson, founder of IBM. He admitted repeatedly to running his firm the way NCR had been run while he was there. Although NCR did not play as strong a role in developing the computer market as it might have, it always was a major player in the precomputer office appliance industry. If for no other reason than its size, NCR and the products it manufactured would have to be included in any history of the office equipment world. In short, the cash register and NCR were too public to ignore.

Development of the Cash Register

So far, this survey has focused on uses of information-processing equipment in offices and, to a lesser extent, in factories. Yet another major application lay in stores. The infancy of large retail chains, mail order enterprises, and many new stores (frequently with multiple departments) came in the period following the Civil War. Although the phrase "in-store processing" did not emerge until the 1960s, stores and, particularly, department stores, had information needs too and required control over operations and people that could be achieved through better and faster management of employees, goods, logistics, money, and information.

No product more symbolized the move to retail technology than the cash register. It was also important because the makers of those machines expanded their product lines into the general office appliance market in the 1920s. Later they built computers. No organization typified this process more than NCR. It rendered an enormous service to historians by dominating about 95 percent of the cash register market in the decade before World War I. Following that war, the role of the cash register must be traced through the histories of a number of rival firms as well.

Why was the cash register really needed by store owners? The question must be answered because the new technology came into existence during the same era as the large department store although ultimately the majority of users were small shops and other retail establishments. The worldwide spread of cash registers traveled at the same speed as that of adding machines, calculators, and typewriters. It penetrated its potential market more intensively so that, at least in the industrialized world, one could not imagine shops without cash registers by the start of World War II. Even by the time the United States entered World War I, NCR alone had built and shipped nearly 1.7 million machines, many of them shiny brass devices with ornate patterns with "NATIONAL" emblazoned across the front.[1]

Before the cash register of the 1880s, storekeepers managed cash either by using a drawer mounted under the counter with oval depressions for various sized coins or by using a box (perhaps even an old cigar box?). In time, drawers were built with compartments to sort paper money and coins. Because no informational feedback methods for control existed, clerks could steal cash without the store owner knowing it. Without some accounting process, it was also not easy to determine what the day's sales receipts were, a problem which grew extremely serious for enterprises that had multiple clerks and departments within the same store.[2] Fixing this lack of control was the fundamental motivation for using cash registers. Although writers frequently leaned on the issue of dishonest clerks, the evidence suggests that historians would be better served by thinking more of accounting controls as the critical factor. Clerk honesty was a secondary factor, to be sure, and an important issue. William H. Leffingwell, a well-respected business commentator in the 1920s, while commenting about business practices of the late 1800s put it this way:

> The old-time shopkeeper had a very rudimentary system of control over cash receipts—the old-fashioned money drawer. He kept no sales records whatsoever.

Eventually, however, merchants adopted the system of recording in a day-book the transactions handled in the store, but even for the one-man shop this proved to be insufficient. And as the shops grew into stores, with bigger stocks of goods and several clerks, it became impossible for the merchant personally to handle and record every transaction in his business.[3]

Leffingwell argued that merchants needed data on how and where cash was taken in and paid out to provide information to settle disputes that arose with customers or clerks. Storekeepers could reduce clerk errors in counting money and any pilfering. They heralded the cash register as a means of restoring trust between clerks and merchants.[4] An early NCR executive called the machine "an inanimate policeman," which evolved into "the keeper of the business conscience," controlling information as much as cash.[5]

Rise of the National Cash Register Company

NCR or, as it was known for some fifty years before World War II, "the Cash," was one of the preeminent companies in American business. It was the leading manufacturer of cash registers in the world for one century. Many American executives considered NCR one of the best-run companies in the United States; its alumni dotted executive offices on an impressive list of U.S. firms from its earliest days.[6] Its business practices and marketing methods became standard at IBM and in other office appliance firms by the 1920s. For these reasons, therefore, it would be difficult to overestimate the importance of NCR to the early history of data processing.[7]

The invention that led to the creation of NCR followed the familiar pattern noted with other contributors to information technology. James Ritty, who owned a restaurant in Dayton, Ohio, in the late 1870s, is generally credited with inventing the cash register. During the summer of 1878, while traveling to Europe, he saw a device that counted the number of revolutions made by his ship's propeller shaft. He thought that some type of similar device could measure money transactions just as well for his restaurant. Ritty suspected that employees were stealing cash from him and that such a gadget might stop them. Upon his return to the United States, he and his brother John (a mechanic) built the first cash register in 1879. It consisted of two rows of keys in front of a clocklike disk (or dial) that displayed dollars and cents, depending on which keys were pressed. It could accumulate totals of sales but had no cash drawer. They subsequently constructed a second, improved model for which they obtained a patent on November 4, 1879. A third variation, however, came closest to the appearance of a cash register. Called "Ritty's Incorruptible Cashier," it had a pop-up tablet that registered the amount of the sale rung up—a function evident in cash registers to the 1980s. Later, they added a roll of paper to record transactions, which, when removed at the end of the day, had holes that represented data, or a log, of each sale and sales total.[8]

The Ritty brothers decided to sell their machines, but, clearly, they were terrible salesmen. The evidence suggests that they sold only one machine, but what a sale it was. John H. Patterson (1844–1922) purchased for his retail coal business in Coalton, Ohio. Patterson was to become one of the most creative, brilliant executives operating in the American economy at the end of the century. His marketing and sales strategies remain legendary even after one hundred years. It was Patterson who would establish NCR and train so many executives, including Watson. Loss of fiscal control over the coal business that he and his brothers ran led to his purchase of Ritty's cash register. Patterson's cash losses subsequently diminished and the company finally turned a profit. After experimenting with another coal business, Patterson opted to try his hand at marketing cash registers.

Between 1881 and 1884, while Patterson tinkered with his coal business, James Ritty sold his cash register enterprise and patent rights to Jacob H. Eckert, of Cincinnati, Ohio, for $1,000. Eckert was obviously a better salesman because he sold enough machines to justify the creation of the National Manufacturing Company, capitalized at $10,000. Eckert modified the product by adding a cash drawer and the "bell heard around the world" to "ring up" sales. In 1884, Patterson bought controlling interest in the firm for $6,500. To jump ahead momentarily, in December 1894, he changed the name of the firm to the National Cash Register Company. Back in 1884, the firm had thirteen employees who could produce four cash registers per week. Patterson had acquired a company that made a product nobody knew about, wanted, or appreciated, and one that clerks would object to using because it cut down on their pilfering of receipts. He expanded the business and, in 1888, moved into a factory designed specifically to build these machines. He had a payroll of 80 souls located in Dayton, Ohio, corporate headquarters for NCR from that time to the present.[9]

Patterson saw the need throughout the 1880s to enhance the basic product to provide written records of transactions and receipts. Such features made the product more marketable. In the early 1890s, for example, he added the capability to print a receipt at the register for the customer. One NCR executive commented on the significance of the feature, arguing that it provided "protection for customer, merchant and clerk. For one thing it makes the customer the auditor of the transaction and thus promotes customer confidence."[10] Customers could ensure correct change and have proof of purchase should they have to return merchandise. Next came multiple drawer machines, which allowed several clerks to use a single register, each with his or her own distinctive bell; that sound prevented any other clerk from using the wrong drawer. Multiple counters, charge, and cash functions emerged during the 1890s as well. As with other technologies of the day, all the basic inno-

TABLE 4.1
Innovations in Cash Registers, 1879–1913

1879	First cash register patented
1881	Paper-roll register introduced
1884	Cash drawer added to NCR cash register
1885	Detail adder introduced
1890[a]	Receipt printout made a standard feature
1902	Total adder and printer
1906	Electric cash register introduced
1913	Register with ticket dispenser

[a] ca. 1890.

vations needed to create the modern cash register were in place by World War I (see table 4.1).

Charles F. Kettering (1876–1958), an inventor on NCR's payroll, built the first electrically run cash register in 1894, employing this form of energy in the same era as others did for the typewriter, adding machine, and calculator, not to mention Hollerith's tabulator.[11] By World War I, Patterson's machines had evolved into accountinglike devices that trapped information and went beyond simply keeping clerks honest. They looked like close relatives of the calculator and typewriter. In short, his machines were evolving into "high-technology" machines, even doubling the number of components in each by World War II.

One cannot understand NCR and its significance to the data-processing industry without appreciating Patterson's marketing and salesmanship. He made salesmanship into a science, a skill learned not inherited. He considered salespeople a precious commodity and, unlike most business leaders of the time, treated sales as an honorable profession. Patterson recognized that because nobody knew anything about his product, salespeople must educate merchants—a classic problem in the information-processing industry to the present. His sales strategy was not to pressure customers into acquiring machines but to argue logically about their benefits. This challenge was difficult because merchants strongly resisted change and clerks obviously did not want their activities to be controlled. NCR had to sell merchants on the positive impact such machines could have on profitability. Arguments in favor of the cash register were refined over time much as one would a product.

An outstanding salesman, Joseph H. Crane, wrote *The Primer*, a text that articulated exactly how to pitch the product to a customer. All salespeople were required to memorize the pamphlet. Patterson ran the first sales school in American industry on April 4, 1894. Salespeople were taught the functions of the machines and how to demonstrate them. They learned applications and how to relate these to the needs of customers. They even practiced selling in a mock-up store and in a butcher shop built at NCR's headquarters. One century later, IBM still ran a similar school, also called the Marketing School, and in a similar fashion. Patterson also made his sales staff dress neatly, admonishing them to "always conduct yourself in a manner that will reflect credit on your company."[12] And in many NCR offices, there was a little sign on the wall: "Think."

Patterson introduced three concepts that later were applied across the industry, particularly at IBM. First, all salespeople were guaranteed a territory; no NCR representatives could sell outside their own "patches." All commissions earned in a territory went to its designated representative regardless of who sold the product there. This practice was instituted to increase a salesperson's commitment to customer satisfaction and sense of ownership of marketing efforts, and it eliminated quarrels over who earned commissions as it reduced duplicate efforts. Similar practices had already begun to appear in other firms too, such as the Singer Sewing Machine Company, which encouraged NCR. It was a stupendous success; today, most sales organizations in almost every industry manage territories in that fashion.

Second, each salesperson had a quota that had to be met. Quota, argued Patterson, "establishes a definite measure of sales efficiency and accomplishment." Quotas were based on the size of the buying population, bank clearings, and previous sales records for the territory. This practice, in turn, led to sales forecasting, which made it possible to formulate manufacturing product construction plans tied to demand and to allocate fairly market support budgets and efforts in advertising and manpower. The effort as a whole also built up a "friendly rivalry which speeds up sales." Those who made quotas joined the Hundred Point Club, an important event in the life of an NCR salesperson and critical for career advancement. Both NCR and IBM have maintained the program to the present.[13]

Third, Patterson backed his salespeople with extensive advertising that was, by the standards of the day, new, innovative, and successful. He established a print shop in 1887 to manufacture circulars; advertising had started in 1885. In 1888, NCR shipped 135,000 copies of *Output* (a broadside on cash registers), using 25 percent of all the 2-cent stamps sold in Dayton that year. By the turn of the century, the U.S. Post Office in Dayton was building up a staff dedicated to NCR. *Output* was followed by a variable publication targeted at specific industries, called the *Hustler* which appeared, for example, as the *Store Hustler* or the *Saloon Hustler*. First introduced in 1890, it went to almost every storekeeper in the United States. By 1894, advertising circulars from NCR approached one-half million pieces. In 1913, that figure had risen to 9 million along with 35,000 color slides.[14] Publications were profusely illustrated and had catchy phrases: "You insure your life. Why not insure your money too! A National cash register will do it."[15]

Salespeople made many "cold calls" on merchants in their territories, emphasizing the accuracy of NCR's machines. They argued that having just a cash drawer was not good enough because they could offer no balances, no sales records, or any way to trace mistakes. Carelessness resulted, irritating customers, lowering profits, and inviting failures. Salespeople postulated that the "NCR Yard Stick—Information, Protection, Service, Convenience, and Economy" was applicable to the particular merchant in question. They offered to study a merchant's operation and then recommend a "system." It was application selling in its purest sense with emphasis on the benefits of the machine. They harped on quality, function, and service from NCR.[16] Salespeople were organized by branches, which, in turn, reported to a national sales office.[17] In this way, the number of calls made and volumes booked could be tracked while staying close to the customer. Patterson built a large, national sales network to drive sales as opposed to using agents and someone else's retail operations to move his products. With his own, highly skilled sales force, he could run volumes high enough to justify manufacturing in quantity and, hence, keep his products cost effective.

Firms that built and sold office appliances in volume survived the rough and tumble marketing environment of the late 1800s and early 1900s, remaining major vendors in the future data processing industry. NCR was perhaps the best example of this pattern. Patterson later commented that the success of NCR and the growth in the size of the cash register business owed largely the sales network he had established nationwide and, later, worldwide.[18]

One final prong of Patterson's strategy was product development. I have already noted some of the innovations that appeared. He felt that research and development was a critical element in his firm's ability to compete; salesmanship alone was not enough. One executive reflected back to those days, noting that "early developments came about largely through rectifying complaints from users." Customer needs determined product development, just as they usually do today. In its first sixty years of operation (1884–1944), NCR applied for 2,400 patents.[19]

NCR's Successes

This company represented yet another example of a successful firm in the "high-tech" world of office appliances although it identified itself with retail customers rather than with the emerging office appliance industry in the years before the Roaring Twenties. A quick first way to measure how well the firm did is to see how many cash registers it sold. Volumes for selected years to the 1920s are summarized in table 4.2. The volume is telling because the company (even by its own admission) dominated about 95 percent of the U.S. market and probably more than 75 percent of the overseas one too before the

TABLE 4.2

Number of NCR Cash Registers Sold, 1884–1922
(selected years)

1884	359	1900	200,000+
1886	1,000+	1906	500,000+
1890	9,000+	1911	1 million+
1892	15,000+	1922	2 million+
1896	100,000+		

Source: NCR, *1884–1922: The Cash Register Era* (Dayton, Ohio: NCR, 1984), 15.

1920s. By the period 1910–1914, one-half of its sales were overseas. Clearly, after 1905, NCR dominated the U.S. market, which places the extent of the entire American cash register market somewhere between 60,000 to 70,000 units annually. One gets a sense of what it must have been like in Dayton even as early as 1888 by reading in the company newspaper that the factory was "getting in so many orders and [is] so far behind that orders will be delayed somewhat."[20] Statistics on headcount provide yet another observation on volumes. In 1888—year of the above quote—123 people were on the payroll and in 1890, 444. The number kept growing, reaching 7,600 by 1914.[21]

Early data from this period also offers an answer to the question of how much investment was needed by a first entrant into a "high tech" market to sustain competitive advantage? Given that NCR dominated its market for one hundred years, whatever investment it made in these early decades offers a valuable response. Manufacturing floor space, for example, increased from 2 acres in 1890 to 17.19 acres in 1900 to 28.55 acres by late 1902. The total Dayton factory population increased from 283 in 1890 to 2,819 in 1902, supporting 6,829 orders in late 1902. In short, the investment required was substantial. The results were 50 registers sold in 1882, 9,091 in 1890, and, just in the first ten months of 1902, 42,403. The number of salespeople involved were 128 in 1890, 479 in 1900, and 976 in 1902. A factory worker in 1890 built 32 machines per year on average but by 1902, 15. In 1890, a salesperson on average sold 71 machines, 68 in 1900, and 43 in 1902. Equipment became more complicated to build (in 1890, the ratio of factory workers to salespeople was 2.2 to 1 and in 1902, 2.9 to 1), and the functions sold were more time consuming. Yet with substantial profit margins built into an increasingly complicated and more expensive product in its most complicated forms, the additional labor required to manufacture and sell these machines was not out of control.[22]

The relationship between volumes built and headcount indicate that management became astute on how to build, market, and price products profitably early in the company's life. Even in the earlier period, when a slow start-up

TABLE 4.3

Annual Volumes of Cash Registers
Manufactured, National Cash Register
and Their Sales Values, 1910–1913

Year	Number Manufactured[a]	Sales Volumes in U.S. (Dollars)
1910	144,000	15 million
1911	156,000	18 million
1912	156,000	21 million
1913	156,000	24 million

Source: *Standard and Poors* (1910–1918).

[a] In 1917, production was 6,000 per month or roughly 72,000 units that sold for $13 million; the decline was the result of World War I disruption of trade in Europe. NCR also was manufacturing war-related items for the government. In 1917, some 1.68 million NCR registers were in use worldwide.

might have been expected, NCR did better than other vendors in the office appliance business as a whole, increasing the number of registers built forty-nine times, headcount ninety-two times. Productivity went up as the company gained experience. Between 1895 and 1905, people increased threefold, but production rose nineteenfold. On a longer term, headcount increased almost twofold between 1905 and 1920; production went up fourfold, a positive story.

The number of machines installed from 1909 through 1913, using volumes of sales (see table 4.3), drives home the success. The data confirms the efficacy of Patterson's strategy, one that allowed him to create a firm that in 1913 was manufacturing 13,000 machines per month for a total sales value that year of $21 million.[23]

In the strategy, the crucial elements of success were having many good salespeople and a well-run factory and appealing to the self-interests of customers. Patterson hired outstanding managers and executives, groomed them, and when they posed a threat to his authority, fired them. That is how so many former NCR managers made it into other companies. His became an admired firm (as evidenced by press coverage), one noted for its "enlightened" personnel practices at the plant level. In fact, by 1905, between thirty thousand and forty thousand visitors came to tour the factory in Dayton annually. Yet his paternalism increasingly became a common pattern evident in many large manufacturing companies.[24] Salesmanship, executive talent, efficient manufacturing, a positive corporate image, and an emphasis on quality products are elements that traditionally have been stressed in explaining

TABLE 4.4
Names of Some National Cash Register Company
Subsidiaries, late 1890s

Germany	National Registrier Kassen Ges.m.b.h.
France	La Nationale Caisse Enregistreuse S.A.
Spain	Cajas Registradoras "National"
Italy	Societa Anonima Registratori di Cassa "National"
Japan	Nippon Kinsen Torokuki Kabushiki Kaisha

NCR's success. Clearly, after my research for this book, I cannot deny their importance. Overlooked, however, as yet another important success factor is the attention Patterson paid to foreign sales, an issue given insufficient attention by historians.

NCR, like typewriter and calculating machine companies, especially Hollerith's, sought to broaden the market quickly with overseas sales. The case of NCR represents the most successful model because nearly 50 percent of its sales came from overseas by World War I. Obviously then, foreign sales had been extensive in the prior decade because it takes time to build those kinds of volumes regardless of which decade is chosen. NCR's presence overseas hinted at activity taking place in other countries that would be worth examining. In 1886, NCR hired J. W. Allison as its first non–U.S. agent to work in Britain, France, Belgium, and Holland. NCR products were used at the International Exposition held in Liverpool that year and at the Australia Exposition in Melbourne the following year. NCR's first sale in China came in 1887.[25] By 1890, NCR had hired agents in Argentina, Uruguay, Brazil, Germany, Australia, Sweden, Italy, Spain, France, and elsewhere. In 1896, Patterson toured NCR territories in fifteen countries. He also followed the practice of hiring local nationals as heads of subsidiaries and blended the firms into local economic traditions. The names given these operations reflected that strategy and are sampled in table 4.4. Each country's agents were measured as were those in the United States—with quotas. Sales were logged and celebrated. Thus one knows, for instance, that the first register was sold in Spain in November 1896 for use in Bilbao. In 1901, 43 were sold and in 1903, 118 machines. E. C. Morse, agent in Japan, reported back to Dayton in 1906 his first sale and noted with excitement that the ratio of stores to people was far lower than in the United States, representing significant opportunity; that year he recruited 10 Japanese salesmen.[26]

By 1911, the company had 965 salesmen operating out of 271 branches outside the United States and factories in Dayton, Toronto, and Berlin. World War I interrupted normal marketing patterns—especially in Germany and throughout Central Europe—but by 1922, NCR had 28,000 people worldwide, all outside of the United States, operating in 50 countries. At that time, sales overseas had not exceeded 50 percent of the company's total.[27] Clearly, the significance of non-U.S. business on the office appliance business was important, specifically at the cash register end. Market demand was still growing rapidly, perhaps more so by the 1920s than before World War I. The broad question of overseas sales by such firms as Burroughs, NCR, and the Tabulating Machine Company remains an important avenue for historical research into early data processing outside the United States.

In the United States, at least, NCR's success came during an era of tough competition coupled with economic vagaries. To meet demand and competitors, NCR introduced many new products. In the period 1888–1922, NCR introduced twelve types of registers and already by 1897 had some ninety models of its products available. Interchangeable parts across models kept costs competitive by the mid-1890s when the average machine had some fifteen hundred parts.[28] The depression of the 1890s hurt although not much. The exception was in 1894 when the company was breaking even on costs and, although the depression lingered, sales grew to eighteen thousand units in 1897 alone.

Despite NCR's lead position in the market, obviously room for more suppliers existed because many other vendors were selling registers during and after the 1880s in the American market. In those days, patents were stolen and copied frequently. Competitors copied products, made them for less, and charged lower prices just like plug-compatible vendors of the 1960s and 1970s did with IBM's disk, tape, and computer products. Register competition was so fierce that salespeople had fistfights, lied to customers, and broke state contract laws. In the 1890s at one point, eighty-four companies battled it out in the cash register market, but by 1897, NCR's better marketing and corporate legal and manufacturing practices had reduced this number to three: the St. Louis, the Ideal, and the Michigan Cash Register companies. NCR established the "Knockout Department" to develop strategies to meet the challenge, particularly that presented by vendors who supposedly were impinging on patents. It passed on the results of its competitive analysis to NCR salespeople, who were always on the lookout for "silver bullet" arguments to discourage customers from buying non-NCR products.[29]

NCR's Legal Problems

As would occur within the information-processing industry during the 1960s and 1970s, as NCR's success grew so too did its litigation, following a pattern evident especially in the 1970s for IBM. Litigation occurred between NCR and competitors, on the one hand, and on the other between it and the U.S. Department of Justice. The latter went after NCR under the terms of the

Sherman Antitrust Act. Because of the analogy with future events, these cases are worth examining.

What little data historians have reviewed owes more to Watson's involvement than to any examination of the industry as a whole. Yet what happened in these pre–World War I years came again in the 1930s (Remington Rand and IBM versus the Justice Department), in the 1950s (with AT&T and IBM versus the Justice Department), in the 1960s and 1970s (IBM versus the Justice Department and other vendors) and in the 1980s (AT&T versus the Justice Department and being broken up). Seen in that broader perspective, the cases suggest the marketing or strategic value (or lack) of using litigation to go after a successful vendor. It offers perspective on the role of the U.S. Department of Justice within the data-processing industry, which is uncomplimentary to the government and evidence of how ineffectual it was in altering what appeared to be technological imperatives at work.

The earliest cases involved other competitors. It was a mark of NCR's influence that litigation began earnestly in the 1890s when the company was barely one decade old and the technology scarcely fifteen. Isaac F. Marcosson, an early observer of NCR, could scarcely recall a period when this company was not involved in litigation concerning infringement of patent rights. The problem was that NCR had the fundamental patents on the cash register, almost all of which originated out of Ritty's work. By January 1, 1890, the company had eighty-six patents covering hundreds of components or devices. John H. Patterson and his brother Frank were involved personally in other development work that led to twenty-two patents made out in their names between 1885 and 1895. Thus top management was very sensitive to the issue of patent protection when NCR's legal problems began in 1888. By 1895, when eighty-four companies were selling machines, there were, in effect, eighty-four sets of potential litigants, many of whom were challenged. Reflecting NCR's point of view, Marcosson noted that the majority of these firms had been formed "to force NCR into buying them out because of their nuisance value." They wanted "to capitalize on the good will, integrity of product, and the increasing market established by NCR through years of effort and expense." He accused them of maligning NCR when they could not compete fairly.[30]

The counterargument pictured NCR as monopolistic, often ruthless. Others claimed that their products (i.e., non-NCR machines) were innovative and not overpriced. The truth in most cases probably rested more with NCR than otherwise because the majority of the civil suits were settled with injunctions. Most suits were filed by NCR on the basis of patent infringement. During the cases, competitors continued to sell their own products and, in some instances, offered to sell out to NCR to end litigation. NCR's concern to protect its patent rights made good business sense. Competitive pressures enhanced the urgency to protect patent rights when possible. In the 1890s especially, the situation was urgent because it was in that decade that "premium" registers appeared. These machines were given away or sold way below NCR's prices (even at 50 percent or more discount), usually by wholesale distributors of cigars, tobacco products, liquor, spices, and chewing gum to retail operators in exchange for orders. These machines were often poorly made and unreliable but were so inexpensive that they threatened NCR's ability to compete. Nine such manufacturers of "premium" registers operated in the 1890s.[31]

The first phase of the cash register wars ended in about 1903. That struggle is best reflected in the case of *NCR v. Ideal Cash Register*. The Ideal Cash Register Company had been incorporated on September 30, 1897, in Bound Brook, New Jersey, capitalized at $1 million; that size immediately made it a serious contendor. Ideal's management wanted to manufacture a product line made up of lever-set, crank-operated registers to be sold along with medicines to druggists. The first machines were not marketed until nearly three years after incorporation. For several months before the first shipment, it published and distributed a house organ called *Every Now and Then* in which it attacked NCR's equipment, stating that "the detail strip, check printer, and other special attachments on the National Registers were ornamental jim-cracks which cumber the machine and add little to its value but serve as an excuse for exorbitant prices." In the next year, it published a circular called "Fourteen Ways of Beating the National Cash Register-79." NCR responded by filing suit on July 3, 1902, for patent infringement and a second suit on another patent two weeks later. While litigation proceeded, Ideal sold machines at a 50 percent discount to druggists provided they, in turn, bought $50 or more in medicines. Business slumped, however; Ideal closed its plant in 1903 and went into receivership in April 1904, which ended the need to pursue litigation.[32] If there is a lesson in the Ideal case, it is that a large vendor in the industry could, as did other firms in different industries, put sufficient pressure on a rival to neutralize it.

A second phase—involving the U.S. government when it was critical of NCR—was far more serious and would not result in the clear-cut victories enjoyed earlier. The battle grew out of litigation between NCR and the Hallwood Cash Register Company. In the early 1890s, Henry S. Hallwood, a street paver from Columbus, Ohio, bought the Stern P. Watt patents on a drawer-operated register and established a firm to build and sell the machine. Later in an affidavit, Hallwood admitted that the purpose of the exercise was to force NCR to buy him out. In March 1897, NCR sued for patent infringement. Hallwood countersued for unfair competition, conspiracy, and restraint of trade. The resulting legal battles lasted eighteen years with a variety of suits and countersuits dotting the story. In the process, Hallwood became insolvent and finally went out of business. He kept title to his patents and started another company called the International Register Company, followed by several others. To make a long story short, what emerged was the American Cash Register Company with his patents, which in turn was sued by NCR.

In 1910 the American Cash Register Company went to the U.S. government and filed a complaint against NCR. The government's investigation led to a federal civil suit against NCR based on its survey of the company's activities over the previous thirty years, using in some instances thirty-year-old data to build a case against NCR's activities of the 1910 era. The government would act similarly against IBM in the 1970s. The government concluded that NCR's practices had not changed in thirty years—a difficult conclusion for this historian to concur with. In December 1911, the Justice Department filed suit against NCR. In February 1912, a grand jury handed down indictments against John H. Patterson and twenty-one other executives (including Thomas J. Watson), charging them with criminal conspiracy "to restrain trade" under the terms of the Sherman Antitrust Law. They were also accused of trying to create a monopoly and then of maintaining it.[33] NCR pleaded not guilty while the government's attorneys pointed out that the company had about 95 percent of the cash register business, dominated it and, hence, was guilty. NCR was scarcely allowed to counter with arguments concerning strong marketing and patent rights. Marcosson noted in his account—the most complete available other than that embodied in the actual trial records— that of the thirty-two cases presented in the trial against the company, only three instances of interference were shown. "Records showed that in the three years immediately preceding the indictment the 1,000 agents and salesmen of the NCR made 3 million calls on merchants. This meant that approximately one call in each million was proved to be an interference with a competitor's business."[34]

The court found NCR guilty on all three charges on February 13, 1913. A $5,000 fine was levied and various prison sentences meted out to the defendants. The verdicts were protested by writ of error. In March 1913 (and before the case went to appeal court in October 1914), Dayton suffered a terrible flood. NCR responded by making its facilities available to the town; employees helped rescue and rebuild the community; and NCR financed relief work to the point where the city as a whole backed the company, placing pressure on the government to back off its case. The appeals court found defective the charges of creating a monopoly and of maintaining it, leaving only the question of where and when NCR had conspired against American Cash, giving NCR the opportunity to plead its case that it had not. The appeals court criticized the original trial court for not giving NCR the opportunity to plead its case. It remanded the suit back to trial court for retrial. The U.S. government attempted to reverse the decision of the appeals court but the U.S. Supreme Court declined to hear the case in June 1915. NCR and the Justice Department then negotiated a consent decree with NCR entering a plea of nolle prosequi in the criminal case.[35]

It was a major antitrust case, coming during a period of public criticism of big business practices. NCR was big business, and emotions ran high against the company. But as with subsequent antitrust cases, this early one was the first of a similar pattern. Civil suits preceded government involvement. But was there due cause? If the nation did not want a company to dominate market share for whatever reason, then NCR was unquestionably guilty. If the concern was about how dominance was attained, then NCR's hands seemed relatively clean in the United States but not absolutely so. In the world of salesmanship and marketing, it is impossible to be completely clean, regardless of industry, age, or circumstance because too much is subject to interpretation and someone's own perspective. Perceptions often meant more than facts. The NCR case certainly drew public attention, which complicated it. Students of antitrust law have also spent considerable time looking at it but with the narrow view of the law and not of the marketplace.[36]

It appears that this case may have represented the first instance in which the government based its argument on a poor understanding of the nature of the newly emerging data-processing industry for which it had no previous precedent or experience. The government had the same problem seventy years later with IBM, leading to mismangement of the case.[37] One economist's analysis of the case against IBM in the 1970s might just as easily have been written about NCR's, "First, the government and its economists approached market definition without concern for its purpose." Second, the government supposition "that a dynamically changing competitive market whose basic feature is technological change can be analyzed in terms of theoretical long-run equilibrium" was not possible. Clearly, the subject of the U.S. government's reaction to the office/computer market is one that will require historians' attention but not simply on a case by case basis, studied in isolation. Just as the IBM case in the 1970s "failed badly on every" count so did the NCR case.[38] NCR continued as the world's most important supplier of cash registers and, in fact, expanded its services during the 1920s and 1930s to include accounting machines. In the 1950s and 1960s, it entered the computer market, if in a faltering manner. The emerging data-processing marketplace dictated who survived and on a worldwide basis. To that call to arms, NCR responded and thrived while the U.S. government did not properly understand what was happening.

5

Rudiments of an Industry Identified

DEFINING the elements of an industry is at best fraught with controversy because no two students of an economic sector may agree. Differences are especially evident when an industry is in embryonic stages, in which it obviously lacks clear definition, or if it has not been defined before. The office appliance world reflects both conditions. Between the 1870s and the early 1920s, it was a conglomerate of office equipment vendors who initially operated in different market segments—cash registers, typewriters, adding machines, and so forth—with little identification with each other. That some shared related technologies did not mean that they had common customer sets, although they did by the early 1900s. Mutual customer sets, more than common technologies, caused vendors to operate with some identification of who they competed against or sold to and, later, what sets of products they should worry about.

As time passed, common sets of customers led to definition of sectors and, in turn, to identification with an industry. First came a self-awareness among vendors caused by an appreciation of each others' existence; indeed, that came quickly by sector (e.g., typewriter vendors recognized other typewriter manufacturers). Catalogs and advertisements helped as did, by the early 1900s, a secondhand equipment market. These elements encouraged a sense of identity. By World War I, catalogs followed by trade associations gave further identity to the industry as well. However, one event more than any other before the 1920s pulled various elements together into a clear definition—World War I. It was a war that called forth more organization and rationalization in the U.S. economy than any previous such struggle in North America. It was the war that led the U.S. government to monitor and direct many aspects of the economy and, most importantly for our purposes, to call forth coordinated activity by economic sectors. Rapid growth in sales volumes also helped vendors identify with a particular industry if they had not done so before.

It is difficult to define this industry in its very early stages with data collated decades later; identifying trends that occurred simultaneously may lead one to impose too great a structure on it, and using models and language common to the industry later (e.g., data processing or information processing) may lead to misrepresentations. For that part of the office equipment world most concerned with mechanical means of handling data, definition and self-identity did not begin to appear until after the turn of the century and most realistically not until roughly 1910–1912. By then, many vendors had stabilized and trade associations had begun to appear. The term "office appliance industry" also began to appear in print along with catalogs that showed the offerings of multiple vendors aimed at a common set of customers. The new industry also included important firms not studied in this book, such as those selling file cabinets, binders, and forms, initially to libraries and later to businesses and governments. By the start of World War I, the trappings of an industry clearly existed in the United States. This chronology implies that it took more than thirty years to acquire identity as an industry—a long process that suggests its original diversity and slow start. But once in motion it gained momentum rapidly. Its definition became clear-cut, recognizable, and public. By the time World War I had ended, it was an industry with a track record of growth and confident about its future.

World War I

As industrializing nations sought to enhance control over events with information-processing equipment, it was inevitable that such efforts would be turned to the war process. Each major war of the twentieth century directly influenced and encouraged enhancements in this kind of technology, a fact variously noted by most students of the history of data processing.[1] To varying degrees, wars, including World War II and the Korean War, contributed to developments in data processing.[2] War sped up current processes that had first emerged embryonically in peacetime or were outgrowths of the last major conflict. Wars caused existing technologies to be stretched scientifically to new limits rapidly to provide additional functions, often with the financial support of U.S. military organizations. For example, in World War I, the study of cryptoanalysis increased, which, in turn, created the need for faster or different computing devices that were developed during the period and through World War II. In the later and much larger conflict, "number crunching" had to be sped up to produce firing tables or to track millions of recruits and all the supplies they needed. Simulation of such activities as artillery firing conditions, flight training, and modeling of transportation problems (later called operations research) significantly forced data-processing technology forward and into new applications.[3]

Historians are fond of discussing how technology moved forward, particularly as a result of and during World War II.[4] Yet in each war, on a less glamorous but realistically more influential level, existing data-processing technologies were used to control data faster in larger amounts either to manage huge armies and navies or to control economic resources focused on war requirements on scales never before achieved by civilizations. World War I fit that pattern precisely. In the United States, after it entered the war in 1917, all office appliance manufacturers turned their skills, resources, and inventories over to the fighting effort. The growth in demand for equipment was to satisfy a need to increase the speed and accuracy of data processing and always in volumes massively larger than in civilian circumstances. Applications that had evolved before the war were used, for example, in production control and inventory management of munitions. Governments became more involved in economic activity and, through conscription, directly in the lives of a large percentage of the population. Both actions called for record keeping at new levels. Tabulating equipment was particularly in demand in all industrialized nations. Calculators also went to war, but the dramatic examples of data processing at work were punched card gear.

Watson was the major supplier of punched card equipment for the Allies because Powers was still a start-up operation. While C-T-R continued on its course toward product improvement, almost its entire newly built inventory and production went toward satisfying the continuously growing demand from government agencies and companies that supported war efforts. This circumstance went far toward explaining the sharp growth in revenues the firm experienced. Yet government applications were conservative; they replaced manual operations with mechanical means and, in many cases, used them to tabulate statistical data.

One by-product of this effort was the huge surplus of rental equipment at the end of the war that became available to commercial organizations. Rising inventories became a problem in 1919 and 1920 as governments relinquished equipment before commercial enterprises could shift production back to civilian levels. When they did, they supported the boom of the 1920s. Powers did not have as much inventory as he could have used (being new to the business) but had more modern equipment and was, thus, for several years, financially less at risk. He was, therefore, a serious competitor with his products such as the Tabulator Printer. Yet he obtained a market share because of the quality and functionality of his products. Watson emerged from his competitive, technological inadequacies by rapidly introducing more advanced products throughout the 1920s that were financed at first with earnings from World War I and later through retained earnings.[5]

During World War I, some very specific applications supported the nation's efforts. The War Industries Board, which totally dominated the U.S. economy, employed tabulating equipment to manage, for instance, transportation and communications. Production and distribution nationwide called for handling large volumes of data across the entire economy. Such tasks required so many of C-T-R's machines that total production had to be diverted to the government away from commercial customers.[6] Hollerith's biographer noted that the war made "the punched card a daily fact of life for thousands of clerks marshalling the nation's food supply and other resources."[7] The Germans plotted U-boat paths with some of his equipment. The U.S. Army used his machines for psychological testing and manpower utilization analysis; it conducted the largest studies of men done so far. It could sort cards also to find six hundred chauffeurs who spoke French.[8] The Department of the Army took measurements of soldiers' bodies in order to standardize uniform sizes, a project not completed until after the war.[9]

Technology was applied to sea warfare also. Besides plotting German U-boat paths, computational devices built before the war predicted tides. These machines also helped Allied captains determine when they could hug shorelines to avoid German submarines. By 1916, the Germans had their own analog brass brain to help direct submarines closer to Allied shipping.[10]

When one thinks of war, it is difficult to avoid images of the draft. Tabulating equipment went off to war along with telephones, telegraphs, calculators, and typewriters. Over twenty million pieces of data on recruits became holes in Hollerith's cards. The American Telephone and Telegraph Company manned 100 percent whole communication companies (military units) with its own operators and technicians; the same was true for telegraph services. Army war reports were typed for the first time while military staffs used Burroughs's products. Historians of both world wars commonly accept that a primary reason for the Allied victory was better management. As any good manager will argue, however, that comes less from genius or bravery and more from understanding what is going on, in short, from facts. The kind they needed came from office appliances. So much was this the case that in C-T-R, Watson never could satisfy fully demand and backorders built up before the war ended. Managers made military buyers insatiable customers.[11]

It was obvious and important that any asset of a nation would be employed in the kind of visceral struggle of life and death being played out on the broad scale of civilization as a whole. Data processing was certainly part of that war and one that has yet to be put into proper perspective. The role it played, less obvious at the time, has become increasingly more clear as it awaits thorough historical examination. Governments in Europe and in the United States became the single largest users of such equipment, thereby continuing a growing tradition that dated back to the 1880s of being some of the most avid and early customers of the new technology. The U.S. Army had, by the end of World War I, thirty years of experience with Hollerith's equipment and, therefore, complex data processing. The army would use data-processing technology extensively all through the twentieth century. Such equipment was always useful and met the need of the armed services to control huge quantities of information. The same held true for civilian agencies that controlled segments of the economy in World War I and later when gathering the data necessary to implement economic and social programs of the New Deal.

Millions of Americans and Europeans were exposed to statistics and data gathering. Thousands operated such devices, and in civilian life these veterans used such equipment in business and in civilian agencies during the 1920s and the 1930s in the United States. AT&T's communications veterans went back to civilian status to landscape the country with telephones. NCR's veterans went back to Dayton or to branch offices around the country while IBM's came back to plants in Germany and in the United States all to renew peacetime activities that were similar to what they did before the war. Accountants and analysts in companies increasingly relied more on calculators and tabulators. As I will show in chapter 8, technology appeared in almost every company and government department of any consequence by the start of World War II. Scarcely any photograph of offices in large enterprises in the postwar period was without telephones, typewriters, or calculating/tabulating equipment in the scene. Many stores used cash registers.

Size of the Industry

Numerical data helps establish the size of that portion of this new industry devoted to the use of mechanical aids to data handling just before its impressive growth in the 1920s. The exercise supports the contention that data processing was far more extensive earlier than otherwise supposed. Furthermore, it adds evidence that the "scientific" or "system" approach to office management had become a reality. Thus it was no surprise that the National Association of Office Managers was formed in 1919 to encourage the use of scientific management (along with appropriate technologies for information handling). Between 1914/1915 and 1921 these managers could select from more than one hundred new office machines appearing for the first time each year. These included everything from the kind of equipment discussed in this book to new office furniture and pneumatic tubes for delivering messages within a building.[12]

Critical factors were the growth and size of the office population and investments in the office. In the 1890s alone, capital investments in the office rose 194 percent and during the first decade of the new century, by 182 percent (as compared to 81 percent for all capital investments in the U.S. economy). One student of the period concluded that investments in office equipment during the early start-up decades frequently ran at four times the investments in manufacturing as measured by rates of growth.[13] Typewriter sales were instructive because they made up such a large portion of the embryonic data-processing industry and suggested patterns of demand. Nearly one-half million typewriters were manufactured per year between 1900 and 1921, triple the number assembled annually during the last decade of the nineteenth century. By 1922, more than 13 percent of all secondary school

TABLE 5.1
Sales Volumes for Office Furniture and Fixtures
in the United States, Selected Years, 1901–1937
(dollars in millions)

1901	30.2	1923	201.3	1932	74.9
1904	38.2	1929	288.7	1933	70.3
1916	51.6	1930	203.5	1935	111.1
1920	135.0	1931	151.7	1937	176.8

Source: U.S. Bureau of the Census, *Historical Statistics*, 421.

children in the United States had enrolled in typing classes; that figure rose to 17 percent by 1934—evidence of the rate of penetration within the economy.[14]

Sales of office furniture suggest that rapid growth in the ideal environment for data processing was taking place, even though information on data-handling equipment is difficult to separate from the available statistics. Between 1869 and 1889, sales nearly doubled from $13.6 million to $25.6 million, then remained constant through the difficult 1890s. Then came more growth. Sales for the first four decades of the twentieth century are shown in table 5.1. The long-term expansion of the office was a critical economic prerequisite for data-processing success during the twentieth century.

The office appliance industry began to draw attention from government economists before World War I, an indication of the growing importance of this sector and the magnitude of the new market. In 1909, these analysts determined that the factory value of typewriters was $20 million and of adding machines and cash registers, $24 million.[15] Tabulating products generated more than another half-million dollars. According to these data, industry size in 1909 was between $44 million and $45 million. If one factors in data on exports, between 30 and 40 percent of those volumes, or about $13 million, came from foreign sales. The U.S. domestic market, then, was roughly $32 million. In 1909, the U.S. gross national product hovered at $50 billion; thus the newly emerging data-processing industry comprised about .1 of 1 percent of the GNP. Exports to the United States, valued at between $2 and $5 million per year in the five-year period before World War I, added to the expanding market. In 1913, the United States exported $11 million in typewriters and $1.4 million in calculators. That year, cash registers shipped out of the United States were worth $4.5 million. In total, therefore, one can identify a $17 million export business. If one estimates exports at about 35 percent of the total U.S. sales, then in 1913, the industry's domestic and foreign U.S. market had grown to over $48 million, up nearly 50 percent in just four years.

Worker productivity indirectly confirms such growth. Labor productivity grew in the U.S. office and store machines market, which made it possible to

TABLE 5.2
Net Earnings for Two Typewriter
Firms, Selected Years, 1911–1917
(dollars in millions)

Year	Underwood	Remington
1911	1.5	—
1912	2.0	—
1913	1.9	1.7
1914	—	0.6
1915	—	1.1
1916	—	2.0
1917	—	2.3

Source: *Standard and Poors* (1911–
1917). The data are incomplete because
published data are lacking.

flatten unit prices. Reduced price increases encouraged customers to acquire
more equipment (despite inflationary pressures and always with additional
features on newer models), while ensuring manufacturers their profits. Productivity of this industry's workers tripled between 1899 and 1909 as vendors
learned how to manufacture more efficiently and in sufficient quantity to maximize plant capacity. Productivity improved yet another 40 percent between
1909 and 1919. Those efficiency rates continued through most of the twentieth century.[16] Although better manufacturing was important, along with improved marketing and distribution, demand and acceptance were also critical
elements in making productivity gains so positive.

Focusing specifically on individual companies within the industry helps
determine size and volumes for this period at a more micro level. I suggest in
table 5.2 what two typewriter companies accomplished in net earnings just
before World War I. They were very profitable. Underwood, for instance,
had net profits in 1906–1909 exceeding $700,000 annually on sales of twice
those amounts. Union Typewriter had similar ratios.[17] Remington, one of the
larger vendors (149th in size out of the top 200 U.S. corporations), had assets
in 1917 valued at $31.6 million.[18] When the Royal Typewriter Company was
incorporated four years later, it was capitalized at $8 million. These figures,
as disparate and incomplete as they are, still give a sense of the dollar volumes involved for the typewriter, an important piece of the office appliance
world.

Burroughs, representative of the calculator business, when compared to the
typewriter sector puts the industry's size in better perspective. It was capitalized in 1905 at $5.4 million.[19] A quick look at one of its competitors, the
Adder Machine Company (Wales) again suggests sales volumes. Its total assets between 1910 and 1913 and the surpluses it enjoyed are shown in table

TABLE 5.3

Adder Machine Company Assets and Surpluses,
1910–1913 (dollars in millions)

	1910	1911	1912	1913
Assets	1.47	1.79	2.06	2.18
Surplus	0.32	0.53	0.74	0.76

Source: Standard and Poors (1914), 1407.

5.3. As with typewriters, the calculator market expanded profitably with similar speed and sales volume sizes. Apparently Adder's business was also very liquid. In 1910 and 1911, for example, Adder's combined cash and accounts receivables were, respectively, $210,691 and $305,515. To be sure, receivables could also be viewed as a risk if uncollected.[20] Adder's debt was low, as was usual with companies in this new industry. When Adder was incorporated in 1906, capital stock was issued at a value of $750 million while debts totaled $61,500.[21] When created in 1911, C-T-R's capital stock outstanding amounted to $10.4 million, of which $7 million was funded. That year, revenues reached $950,000.[22]

Several features of this industry are of historical concern. First, most available statistics on sales, profits, and so forth were fragmentary and inconsistent from year to year. Second, they were only available for publicly held firms, yet the industry included many privately owned companies as well, Felt & Tarrant or Powers, for example. Third, many little enterprises came and went—perhaps as many as one hundred before World War I—about whose business volumes almost no data exists. Therefore, any discussion remains fragmented and rough at best and calls for more investigation. It is possible that further study would revise upward the estimates of volumes sold and reconfirm that if a company were successful it was very profitable and if a failure, it died quickly. The process could largely be attributed to the competitive edge that technologies provided temporarily, whether or not a national marketing and distribution process was established in time, and whether or not management paid proper attention to cost-effective manufacturing. Looking at more companies would underscore further that the market was truly international and came early. What can be said for certain as of this writing is that historians have underestimated the size and sophistication of this new industry for the earlier period.[23]

When one notes the patterns of economic activity within the new industry on the one hand and, on the other, the growth of the office, it becomes clearer that this part of the U.S. economy had become more purposeful before 1914, a finding that supports Chandler's thesis. The evidence for the U.S. economy is abundant. Marcosson, for instance, defined the motivation:

During all this evolution in equipment the merchant and the manufacturer looked for three things. The first was reduction of man labor; second, was the lowering of operating costs to be reflected in a reduced price of product and an increased market; third was accurate, systematized information which would enable management to formulate policies and make adequate decisions. The mechanization of accounting achieved these three objectives. It has made the office a source of profit and it produced the all-essential information.[24]

Mills, in his classic sociological study of American corporations, which he researched and wrote at the dawn of the computer age, underestimated the extent of the industry Marcosson described.[25] One office manual of the early 1920s, reviewing past achievements of the industry, listed dozens of uses for such technology. Its tabulation of industries that relied on information equipment covered the entire spectrum of the U.S. economy.[26] In short, by 1920 America was moving rapidly and extensively into an age of mechanized data processing.

Summary

Between 1865 and 1920, American inventors developed a variety of mechanical aids for calculation, data manipulation, and information handling. These emerged simultaneously but, initially, apart from each other. Main lines of development included the typewriter, adding and calculating machines, cash registers, and punched card equipment. Ancillary developments of greater importance to data processing in the 1920s and 1930s, but already evident before 1900, included the telegraph and telephone. By the early 1900s, but before World War I, technologies began merging (e.g., keyboards were used in each segment). Successful firms merged too, offering a growing variety of products through larger, fully integrated enterprises. Early on these companies operated worldwide and faced extensive competition. They frequently began by using agents while contracting out manufacturing. Then they (1) brought manufacturing in-house and (2) developed their own nationwide sales forces. The industry leaders were overwhelmingly early entrants in their markets. For their part, customers implemented new technologies to reduce labor costs and, subsequently, to enhance control over operations.

Technology was clearly a basic driver of business actions. It dictated, for example, the rate of innovation, influenced success of a firm's products, and, hence, had the ripple effect of causing companies to develop marketing, management, and manufacturing processes and structures that most effectively took advantage of product developments. The transfer of technological innovations from one product line to another in this industry was striking.

The pattern of development and use of technology offers evidence that evolution of office tools mimicked patterns identified by George Basalla. He argued that technology was changed by evolutionary strategies that favored increased utility over other criteria for selection. His basic contention was that "any new thing that appears in the made world is based on some object already in existence."[27] Equally relevant is his argument that devices changed to meet national requirements or new needs, citing telephones, televisions, automobiles; he could have just as easily called out bookkeeping, punched card and adding machines.[28] Basalla also noted that not all things were invented with a clear purpose in mind. Although that is very true for many items, such as phonographs and tape recorders, both of which are used for purposes not originally perceived, it appears that early office equipment was developed with specific uses in mind.[29] Over time, its application was considerably broadened and in the long run conformed to Basalla's contention.

Early customers were, as later, government agencies and large corporations that had growing armies of specialized office workers and multiple layers of management increasingly dependent on timely data with which to function effectively. Inventors started firms, often ran them poorly, then gave way to professional managers as they sought funding support, incorporated into publicly sold stock companies, or their businesses grew too large for one person to manage.

Although one cannot state that a data-processing industry existed before World War I that was obvious to its members (that identity became more clear in the early 1920s), it nonetheless had its rudiments and a population of probably more than fifteen thousand employees by 1910. Companies borrowed from each others' practices, which helped participants in the protoindustry become aware of each other. A. B. Dick, for example, copied NCR's use of a national sales force for his mimeograph, while it seemed that all typewriter firms watched what Remington did.[30] For instance, customers had to be taught what new devices did, and, because of the newness and complexity of the technology, strong marketing and service organizations had to be established. This was as true for Hollerith as for Burroughs. Salespeople required training and were more professional than those in many other industries. Therefore, these firms served as an obvious source for many innovations in marketing and salesmanship.[31] Patterns in marketing, manufacturing, and service appeared very consistent across each of the four segments by 1920, reflecting experiences of nearly a half-century. One can conclude confidently that by World War I a new industry existed in practice although it was not recognizable by name. That changed in the 1920s as this industry became identifiable, obvious, and significant. It would be a golden age for mechanical aids to information handling.

1. Christopher Latham Sholes (1819–1890). Sholes patented the first practical modern typewriter in 1868 (State Historical Society of Wisconsin).

2

2. William S. Burroughs (1855–1898). Burroughs developed an early adding machine and founded what became the Burroughs Adding Machine Company (Burroughs Papers, Charles Babbage Institute).

3. John H. Patterson (1844–1922). Patterson founded the National Cash Register Company (NCR Archives).

4. Herman Hollerith (1860–1929). Hollerith invented the modern punched card tabulating system, circa 1900 (IBM Archives).

3

4

5. An early cash register (NCR Archives).

FIRST ROUGH MODEL

6. The first adding machine built by Dorr E. Felt, early 1880s.

7. Hollerith Tabulator and Sorter Box, 1890 (IBM Archives).

8. Burroughs Adding Machine advertisement, 1922 (Burroughs Papers, Charles Babbage Institute).

9. A section of the Tabulating Machine Room, U.S. Bureau of the Census, circa 1910. (Left) tabulating machines built by the Census Bureau. (Right) carriage type-writers (U.S. National Archives).

10. Tabulator and vertical sorter, 1915 (IBM Archives).

11. Dorr E. Felt (1862–1930). Felt invented the Comptometer and was president of Felt & Tarrant Manufacturing Co., circa 1910.

12. NCR branch office, Philadelphia, 1902 (NCR Archives).

Factory and General Offices FELT & TARRANT MANUFACTURING CO.
1717-1735 North Paulina Street, Chicago, U. S. A.

13. First Tabulating Machine School for Salesmen, C-T-R, 1916 (IBM Archives).

14. The North Paulina Street factory, Chicago, 1913. As did many office machine companies, Felt & Tarrant had its headquarters and manufacturing in one building.

15. Burroughs factory, Detroit, 1904–1911 (Burroughs Papers, Charles Babbage Institute).

16

16. NCR factory, Dayton, Ohio, in the interwar period (NCR Archives).

17. C-T-R management. From left to right: George W. Fairchild, first chairman of the board of C-T-R; Thomas J. Watson, Sr., General Manager; and Sam Hastings, Flint's protégé, 1919 (IBM Archives).

18. Felt & Tarrant equipment used at the Pennsylvania Railroad, 1910.

17

18

Part Two

AN AGE OF OFFICE MACHINES, 1920–1941

6

Economic Conditions
and the Role of Standardization

USE OF mechanized data processing expanded enormously between the two world wars, particularly in the United States, along the lines established before 1917. The role of punched card equipment eventually became more significant than that of other data-handling technologies. By the end of the 1920s, that portion of the office appliance market most concerned with information-handling hardware was dominated by that technology. In short, an important aspect of the story of complex information processing in the 1920s and 1930s revolved around cards and closely related equipment known as accounting machines and "systems." Acceptance of and reliance upon mechanical aids came because of the country's growing wealth, not the newness of any particular technology. The most obvious example of prosperity at work was the acquisition of devices that had been available since the early years of the century, such as automobiles, radios, and telephones. In the 1930s, electrification of rural America extended dependence on technologically new and sophisticated products across all levels of American life.

Data processing acquired increased definition as a major subset of the office appliance industry. Its companies followed trends evident in other industries, such as consolidation (as among typewriter firms) and a combination of consolidation and expansion (as in accounting machine firms), while breaking away from identification with vendors that sold three-ring binders, file cabinets, and other office furniture or supplies. As in many other industries, verticalization of companies and product lines became a strong trend. Companies broadened product lines. For instance, typewriter companies folded into larger firms (four by the mid-1930s) or into office machine corporations, making possible more extensive product lines for the office equipment market. Others added manufacturing capability and nationwide marketing organizations. A great deal of the history of this period involves the story of how a number of giants emerged out of the prosperity of the 1920s, survived and thrived in the 1930s, and were thus well positioned in the 1940s and during the 1950s to enter the age of the computer. One can see IBM coming to dominate the punched card business along with Remington Rand (which tightened its grip on the typewriter market). NCR not only expanded its sales of cash registers but also, like Burroughs, became an important force in the accounting machine market. Finally, the industry grew in size, despite dips caused by the depression in the 1930s.

In the interwar period, the number of organizations using data-processing equipment increased and were in every state, as reflected by the increasing size and number of sales offices set up. Applications clearly identified as beneficial before World War I were implemented repeatedly again across the economic landscape of America and Western Europe and, to a lesser extent, in Eastern Europe, South America, and Japan. In short, data processing played a central role in accounting and inventory management. It appeared in factories and became a tool to support management decisions. Benefits of control identified before World War I were sought, particularly in the 1920s, by businesses positioned to make capital investments and, in the 1930s, by government agencies. In the 1930s, the need for efficiency or ability to respond to New Deal laws motivated new users.

Although economic historians traditionally have treated the 1920s as a period separate from the 1930s, the two decades lend themselves to consolidation when the history of data processing is discussed. Applications were the same in both decades, lines of research and development unfolded that were based more on science than on economic conditions, while product introductions, although timed and influenced by economics, built on previous offerings. To consider the two decades together accents lines of evolution evident before World War I.

The expanding economy of the 1920s made it possible for data processing to prosper. The economic climate of the 1930s, especially in the early years of the decade, was quite different and called for shifts in marketing and manufacturing strategies. The depression did not kill the industry, just slowed it momentarily. Business slowed too, but new applications for such technology were identified and implemented. Government policies, particularly at the national level through extensive New Deal legislation, boosted the use of data processing. World War II is a convenient historical break because that war, more than World War I, called forth such a concentrated economic focus that all industries changed their business focuses and used resources in new ways. For example, IBM's plant in Poughkeepsie, New York, manufactured rifles while NCR's huge facility in Dayton, Ohio, built other weapons. Large numbers of employees went into the armed services and new product development waned while the engineering of digital computing quietly came to fruition. Applications of existing 1930s–type technology, however, were evident, particularly those needed by the military. As the war progressed, the new technologies of the computer were applied to war-related activities, such as intelligence and the development of atomic weapons, while more mundane machines did inventory management and payroll. The excitement of the computer has caught the attention of most historians too much because during

World War II the bulk of computing was done as during the 1930s and with equipment manufactured before the war for traditional accounting and business purposes.

Economic Adjustments and Prosperity in the 1920s

Economic conditions in both the United States and in Europe following World War I directly influenced and shaped the course of events in the new industry, making prosperity possible. Simply put, a difficult period of adjustment to peacetime economic patterns immediately followed the end of the war as governments rapidly demobilized military units and war-related economic programs and businesses shifted to consumer and industrial demands. That process led to a short recession but one that by 1922 was passing, giving way to a period of enormous prosperity (particularly in the United States) that lasted until 1929. Then the Great Depression, with its severe shrinkage of economic activity of all types, which lasted until World War II, radically altered basic patterns of economic demand and supply. In each phase, the data-processing world thrived in different ways as it drew closer to becoming the core of basic economic activities of many organizations that needed to process information regardless of the overall conditions of the economy.

A few key features of the American economy facilitated expansion of the office products industry during the 1920s. The size of the population and trading market were obvious factors. The United States had a population of about 104 million in 1920; in 1930, that had grown by 16 percent to 123 million and to 132 million by 1940. Between 1920 and 1940, nearly 10 million Americans migrated from rural to urban centers. At the same time, the standard of living for factory workers rose. Between 1919 and 1929, the rise in annual real earnings approached 26 percent while the number of workers rose about 0.5 percent, strong evidence of substantial increases in labor productivity. Consolidations of manufacturing companies continued, as 274,598 enterprises in 1919 became 210,959 in 1929. Meanwhile, manufacturing output rose by 64 percent. Much of that can be attributed to a 40 percent increase in worker productivity, which largely came from more efficient and mechanized manufacturing and distribution.[1]

The role of technology in increasing productivity and the technological mindset it created cannot be ignored, especially because data processing was part of the process. During the 1920s, production procedures were enormously revamped in American factories. The same kind of reliance on technology took place in the office while-data gathering processes on the shop floor grew. Without recounting all too familiar ground concerning continuous production lines, mass production of automobiles, and so forth, it is sufficient to point out that investments in technology played a profound role along with the effects of "scientific" management touted in the two decades before World War I.[2] One obvious manifestation of increased faith in and use of technology is what happened in research and development.

AT&T consolidated all its major research into Bell Laboratories, which it formed in 1925 with a staff of three thousand. Its mission was to develop all the technologies needed to manufacture telephone equipment. In less than five years, it was developing devices to transmit voice and data over telecommunication lines.[3] IBM built and staffed a research facility at Endicott, New York, at about the same time. NCR, General Electric, Burroughs, and others simultaneously either consolidated their R&D activities with a greater focus on developing new technology-based products or increased their budgets for existing research facilities. By 1927, some one thousand U.S. companies had discrete research facilities or engaged in joint-venture projects to improve products or services. Many of the joint-venture arrangements included universities, which began a long association with businesses. For instance, during this period, MIT began contract research, or development work subsidized by industry, in the general area of telecommunications and computing (e.g., Vannevar Bush's differential analyzer used for complex mathematical calculations).[4]

Data-processing vendors, like counterparts in other industries, saw that research could lead to new products. Chandler noted that American companies continued to integrate production and distribution, which required a greater reliance on technology. Nowhere was this dependence and its concomitant requirement for capital more apparent than in high-technology firms like the Radio Corporation of America and General Electric. By 1929, more than two-thirds of the Americans employed in industrial research were clustered in five groups, two of which partly dealt with data processing—electrical machinery (31.6 percent) and nonelectrical machinery (6.6 percent).[5]

World War I stimulated research and development, and the military relied on technology more than during any previous war. The same held true for Europe. But more important in the European case was the fundamental decline in capital, which contrasted to the growth situation in the United States. Europe emerged from World War I with diminished buying power, the result of spending so much to fund the war. It had spent most of its savings, destroyed many factories, lost millions of people, established new relationships among currencies, and was living beyond its means. It responded to these problems by borrowing heavily from the United States, which had emerged from the war financially stronger than before. The result was a larger flow of scarce capital in Europe to American banks, which, in turn, invested these sums either in expensive loans to Europe or moved the capital directly into American industry. Total bank resources jumped from $47.6 billion to $72 billion between 1919 and 1929. Therefore, although loans to Europe were made, more funds were still available for U.S. firms to expand, consolidate, or retool. Consolidations led to larger office staffs dependent on office equipment, and modernized factories required more sophisticated control and communications equipment.[6] Despite Europe's depressing economic conditions, demand for productivity tools expanded as new factories were built, old businesses were reestablished, and urban populations grew. Europeans invested in new technology for the same reasons as Americans did.[7]

Mounting evidence suggests, however, that in large part the science-based technologies sold and installed in the 1920s in Europe and in the United States reflected a continuum from the turn of the century. The same seems to hold true for the 1930s and into the early years of World War II. Seminal innovations came at the turn of the century, setting the stage for the great spurt in the use of technology that one finds early in its life cycle.[8] Such developments in the years before 1917 initiated a trend in the use of technology that was only partially disrupted by war and resumed in the 1920s and 1930s.[9]

Increasing use of information technology reflected economic health, which, in hindsight, was evident in the U.S. economy. The U.S. GNP, during the period 1917–1921, on average stayed at $67 billion, while for the period 1922–1926, it grew to over $84 billion, leaving no doubt that it was the Roaring Twenties. In the next period, 1927–1931, despite the beginning of the depression, the GNP climbed to $83 billion.[10] The value of office and store machinery and equipment reflected macro national trends in this period, which suggests that it was central to economic activity. In 1920, this segment of the economy approximated volumes of $160.6 million and, as I suggest in table 6.1, in 1929 reached $217.8 million. Office equipment values in general had grown by 74 percent.

TABLE 6.1
Value of Office and Store
Machinery/Equipment, 1920–1929
(dollars in millions)[a]

1920	160.6	1925	196.4
1921	114.0	1926	200.1
1922	132.4	1927	201.2
1923	182.0	1928	213.6
1924	179.2	1929	217.8

Source: U.S. Bureau of the Census, *Historical Statistics*, 421.

[a] These figures represent value of output of finished goods destined for domestic consumption at current producers' prices. They do not reflect necessarily what was actually sold.

Control and Standardization

Between 1922 and 1929 many changes occurred in the way organizations functioned. Trends of considerable benefit continued throughout the decade of the Great Depression and beyond, so that by the end of World War II it would have been difficult for individuals in business or government to remember an era without them. An obviously important example was the attempt to standardize activities to enhance control. Rules and procedures mushroomed in most organizations along with processes to handle information.[11]

Control through the use of standardized forms caused people to organize information in a precise order and format. Precise organization, in turn, made it possible for equipment systems (e.g., tabulating machines) to process information more conveniently while reducing time and effort. Forms represented preprocessing at its clearest because they captured predetermined data, ignoring information not collected that otherwise might have hindered the processing of information deemed more relevant.[12]

By the 1920s, the U.S. government had become a major force in the U.S. economy, encouraging increasing use of standardized forms, and was followed closely by commercial firms creating their own. Government agencies used standardized forms to save expenses, which, increasingly throughout the 1920s, facilitated the use of business machines. In 1927, after various committees worked many years to develop a common purchase order, 400,000 U.S. businesses accepted a standard format. Throughout the 1930s, tabulating equipment was used to process and analyze purchase order data.[13]

On the heels of this spectacular standardization, which had been pressed by the U.S. government, came another. After strong lobbying by the U.S. Post Office, manufacturers of envelopes accepted standards for window envelopes to go into effect in 1929. As early as 1921, Herbert Hoover, Secretary of Commerce, had established within his department the Division of Simplified Practice. Throughout the 1920s, other agencies focused on similar problems, becoming major customers for all kinds of office equipment. In private business, the banking community spent a great deal of effort in the 1920s standardizing the format and size of checks.[14] That dramatic and important success for the banking world encouraged it later in the 1950s to set standards for the use of computers and related equipment to handle check sorting and electronic identification. Similar cooperative and independent actions were evident particularly in large enterprises, including those in retail, manufacturing, and transportation. The wisdom of using standardized forms and how they related to the use of office equipment was noted in numerous management books of the period.[15]

One author at the start of the 1930s argued that the use of forms made the application of information-handling equipment significantly easier. He linked forms to increased sales and the use of tabulating equipment in particular, arguing that as a result of using such hardware, one could increase clerical productivity by between 50 and 200 percent. These kinds of gains, obviously subject to much speculation, were not out of line with what was possible with various kinds of machines in the period 1880–1920. The key to such increases in productivity was simplification of work. The author cited many examples, such as the use of continuous billing forms, which could increase issue speed by 60 percent. The concept of continuous forms suggested a new systematic use of equipment by which data could be fed in, processed, and the result printed *continuously*. By the late 1950s, data-processing personnel would call the simultaneous input, processing, and output "concurrent processing." One estimate held that by 1930 over 600 million sets of preprinted multiple forms were in use in the United States. These were multiple forms, that is, several copies of a particular document sandwiched between carbon paper that could be filled in simultaneously. When printed, one had yet another example of various technologies merging to create a new application.[16] The use of forms in business machines was so extensive by the end of the 1920s that the author concluded, "American and world business today [1932] could not carry on without the assistance rendered by the business machines."[17]

The subject of control and standardization has a growing bibliography;[18] this literature also reflects evidence that in the 1920s and 1930s information processing through mechanical means was viewed as an important component of the broader movement toward extended efficiencies. Perley Morse, one voice from that period, observed, "Thousands of jobs requiring higher efficiency have resulted, and because of the labor-helping machine the wage index figure and standards of living have been lifted to heights never attained in any other period of the world's history or by any other nation than the United States."[19] Although the case was overstated, the enthusiastic writer made the obvious point that such equipment increased efficiency, control, and benefits. Morse showed in his study that while worker productivity was increasing sharply as more equipment was used, information-processing machines were having a similar impact within the office.[20] A little hyperbole drove home the point: "Today the click of the typewriter and the hum of the business machine can be heard wherever the commerce of man penetrates."[21]

The enhanced use of data-processing equipment in the 1920s reflected the overall acceptance of machines across the entire economy. Electronic consumer goods came into their own during the 1920s much as data-processing equipment had on a smaller scale some thirty years earlier. Automation on the shop floor and the construction of huge manufacturing facilities (particularly by automobile vendors) were dramatic examples of technology at work. Han-

dling information in more automated ways, however, was evident throughout
the economy. In the 1920s, many events were notable: regular transcontinen-
tal air mail between the east and west coasts (1924), commercialization of
radio facsimile transmission of photographs across the continent (1925) and
across the Atlantic Ocean (1926), transmission of checks in the same manner
(1926), transatlantic telephone service on a regular commercial basis (1927),
and air mail service between South America and Miami, Florida, ship-to-
shore radio telephone service, and introduction of a high-speed telegraph
ticker capable of five hundred characters per minute (all in 1929). Similar
developments came in the 1930s despite world depression, the threat of war,
and political uncertainty.

Yet historians have not fully put developments in office equipment into the
kind of mainstream historical perspective that they have the radio, automobile, telephone, and manufacturing processes and investments made during
the 1920s although that situation is beginning to change. Part of the problem
is that office equipment was not as visible as automobiles or radios. Information-handling equipment was buried in offices, playing an almost silent and
invisible role. Regardless of cause, by the 1970s and 1980s recognition increased that data processing influenced the economy.[22]

Market Segments and Suppliers in the 1920s

By 1924/1925, when various national manufacturers' associations were in
full bloom, collecting information on particular industries and categorizing
and cataloging market segments, one could take a metaphorical snapshot of
the proto-office industry at the precise time when the U.S. economy was
beginning to "roar" through the twenties. The major segments of that industry—if one leaves out suppliers of notebooks, accounting paper, stamp machines, and other office products of minor or unique applications—were
made up of those who supplied adding and calculating equipment, billing and
bookkeeping gear, and analysis machines. Buried among those groups of
vendors were tabulating machine suppliers, which suggests strongly that by
the 1920s, the market already was perceived as much broader and more complex than that defined simply by Hollerith's or Powers's customers. In table
6.2, I list major vendors of adding machines in the United States (many of
them in Europe as well) as of 1924/1925. These twenty-six firms represented
the largest constituency within the office equipment industry. Among them
were some that would become suppliers of computers and related products:
Burroughs, Marchant, and Monroe. Most were headquartered in the eastern
half of the United States; eight were in New York. The second largest concentration of headquarters and manufacturing facilities was in Chicago (the second largest U.S. city at the time), followed by Philadelphia (third largest)

TABLE 6.2
Adding Machine Vendors in the United States, 1924–1925

Company	Headquarters	Product[a]
Add Index	New York	
Automatic Adding Machine	New York	Golden Gem
Burroughs Adding Machine	Detroit	
Coxhead, Ralph C.	New York	Mercedes
Dalton Adding Machine Sales	Cincinatti	
Denominator Adding Machine	Brooklyn	
Doty Business Machines	Chicago	Record
Ellis Adding Typewriter	Newark, N.J.	
Ensign	Boston	
Federal Adding Machine	New York	
Felt & Tarrant	Chicago	
Lanston Monotype	Philadelphia	Barrett
Marchant Calculating Machine	Oakland	
Mechanical Accounting	Providence, R.I.	
Monroe Calculating Machine	Orange, N.J.	
Morschauser, W. A.	New York	Millionaire
Peters-Morse Manufacturing	Ithaca, N.Y.	The Peters
Portable Adding Machine	Chicago	
Reliable Typewriter and Adding Machine[b]	Chicago	
Reuter, Inc., Carl H.	Philadelphia	Archimedes
Sundstrand Adding Machine	Rockford	
Tim Calculating Machine	Chicago	
Todd Protectograph	Rochester, N.Y.	Star
Victor Adding Machine	Chicago	
Wales Adding Machine	Wilkes-Barre, Pa.	
Wren Adding Machine	Washington, D.C.	

Source: Office Equipment Catalogue, Inc., *Office Equipment Catalogue* (Chicago: Office Equipment Catalogue, 1925), xxxix.

[a] Listed if not named after the company (the normal practice).

[b] Known also as Pocket Adding Machines.

with two. Silicon Valley, then agricultural land, had an ancestor nearby in Marchant.

Other vendors considered themselves manufacturers of calculating machines. Many who sold adding machines included both types of devices by the mid-1920s. The list in table 6.3 includes the top fourteen vendors in the United States. Next in frequency were manufacturers of bookkeeping machines, of which eight were recognized as leaders (see table 6.4), whereas only six vendors sold billing machines (see table 6.5). Only three companies offered what they termed "analysis machines," which, in effect, were

TABLE 6.3

Calculating Machine Vendors in the United States, 1924–1925

Company	Headquarters	Product[a]
Burroughs Adding Machine	Detroit	
Coxhead, Ralph C.	New York	Mercedes
Dalton Adding Machine Sales	Cincinnati	Norwood
Denominator Adding Machine	Brooklyn	
Doty Business Machine	Chicago	Record
Ensign	Boston	
Felt & Tarrant	Chicago	Comptometer
Marchant Calculating Machine	Oakland	
Mechanical Accountant[b]	Providence, R.I.	
Monroe Calculating Machine	Orange, N.J.	
Morschauser, W. A.	New York	Madas, Millionaire
Reuter, Inc., Carl H.	Philadelphia	Archimedes[c]
Sundstrand Adding Machine	Rockford	
Tim Calculating Machine	Chicago	

Source: Office Equipment Catalogue, *Office Equipment Catalogue*, xxxix, xl.

[a] Listed if not named after the company (the normal practice).

[b] Known also as the Mechanical Accounting Company.

[c] A Brunsviga product sold through an agent in the United States.

TABLE 6.4

Bookkeeping Machine Vendors in the United States, 1924–1925

Company	Headquarters
Burroughs Adding Machine	Detroit
Dalton Adding Machine Sales	Cincinatti
Elliott-Fisher	New York
Ellis Adding Typewriter	Newark, N.J.
National Cash Register	Dayton
Remington Typewriter	New York
Sundstrand Adding Machine	Rockford
Underwood Typewriter	New York

Source: Office Equipment Catalogue, *Office Equipment Catalogue*, xxxix.

TABLE 6.5
Billing Machine Vendors in the United States,
1924–1925

Company	Headquarters
Autographic Register	Hoboken, N.J.
Burroughs Adding Machine[a]	Detroit
Elliott-Fisher	New York
Remington Typewriter	New York
Underwood Typewriter	New York
Wales Adding Machine	Wilkes-Barre, Pa.

Source: Office Equipment Cataloguc, *Office Equipment Catalogue*, xxxix.

[a] Vendor of the old Moon-Hopkins machine.

punched card tabulating and accounting systems: NCR, Powers Accounting Machine, and the Tabulating Machine Company Division of IBM.

Typewriter manufacturers played in increasingly broader markets (e.g., Ellis Adding Typewriter and Adding Machine Corporation). They dominated the billing machine market. Thirteen of the adding machine manufacturers in operation in 1924 (of twenty-four) were also active in the calculating machine market. Of the eight bookkeeping machine firms, three were adding machine suppliers while another four started out as typewriter manufacturers. The majority of the companies had existed before World War I, some (such as Burroughs and NCR) more than thirty-five years. Office equipment suppliers were increasingly seeing themselves as one larger industry offering a broad range of office machines as opposed to a more segmented view of multiple mini-industries defined by machine type. Many mergers took place during the 1920s as firms expanded into new geographical markets or enhanced their own product lines. One could detect a merger of function and technology—a process that started in the two decades before World War I and was only temporarily interrupted by the fighting in Europe.

A number of factors encouraged further integration of product lines in the 1920s, which consequently led to a period of significant enhancements and new products. One was improvements in fundamental technologies developed at the turn of the twentieth century. Another, already discussed, was the similarity of technologies that could be applied across a number of products, such as the typewriter keyboard or the mechanism of an adding machine. Economies of scale made possible by mergers to form larger companies also encouraged the process. Case studies illustrate the process at work. The other significant influence was customer demand.

As accounting, in particular, became more sophisticated and complex, customers voiced opinions about what the technology should look like. What one writer of the period noted became increasingly obvious to them, namely, that "any office or accounting detail can now be performed by machines with amazing results of which accuracy, control, speed and legibility are foremost."[23] That capability enhanced the position of accountants first in large organizations and later in smaller ones and placed them increasingly within the mainstream of such bureaucracies because they could provide current and useful data with which to do business or operate an agency.[24] Accounting had become an important profession integral to organizations partly because of data-processing technology.[25]

Accountants, by relying increasingly on the new technology, came in contact with vendors to whom they addressed their needs. In fact, financial and accounting communities were frequently the prime customers of vendor hardware by the 1920s, and this situation went far to explain why, during the 1950s through the 1970s, data processing was controlled by accounting executives more frequently than not. In the 1920s, as in the decades of the computer, financial and accounting personnel significantly influenced product development. For example, the Hollerith card of the early twentieth century did not hold enough data for accountants, which led IBM to introduce the 80-column card familiar to many people over the next sixty years.[26] Accountants caused vendors to link equipment during the 1920s to make possible continuous processing applications. Although the evidence is not conclusive, the influence of accountants on the evolution of various pieces of equipment linked together into systems was at least as pronounced as the actual activities of inventors and product managers (see fig.6.1).[27]

The process must be kept in mind because products that lent themselves most to systemization before the 1950s were punched card equipment, not stand-alone calculators, adding, or typing devices. One could conclude, with the absence of conclusive evidence to the contrary, that the need for computers was driven more by the type of work demanded of tabulating gear than by calculators. Some students of the history of computers would not share this view, particularly "pioneers" who have written on its past. Early computer engineers have argued that inventors of computers developed them largely out of frustration with the limitations of calculators that were incapable of complex, tedious processes or took too much time.[28] No evidence suggests that scientists and engineers who worked on computers were not frustrated by the limits of calculators and adding machines. Their documented testimony clearly confirms that they were.[29]

However, funding for research projects and, subsequently, significant financial and marketing endorsement of computer technologies, did not come first from typewriter or adding machine firms. These ventures came from either new ventures responding to new needs or from companies that had long experience with tabulating equipment (such as Remington Rand and IBM). Both had customers who could logically and relatively easily move from tab-

6.1 An IBM tabulator and summary punch (1935). Notice that IBM's products no longer look either like a wooden contraption (old Hollerith gear) or like engineering prototypes with no covers. The company had learned how to "package" machines (courtesy IBM Archives).

ulating applications to computer-based ones. Vendors of punched card tabulators and other systemlike devices saw the logic of moving to a new, evolving technology that enhanced existing uses and satisfied the needs primarily of business accountants and, early on, the computational desires of military agencies.

Summary

An expanding work force that was increasingly in offices, a healthy economy during the 1920s, and more complex, larger organizations all created an environment conducive to the greater use of information-processing equipment. The growth in complexity of organizations was tied to economic and demographic factors that consequently required greater control over information. One aspect of the response to changing institutional requirements for control was data standardization, accomplished, in part, through the use of more forms and preprocessing.[30] When a company or an agency structured information in a specific format and just as rigorously defined how to collect that information, the necessary discipline and tasks were in place to take advantage of mechanical data gathering and analysis. Much of the history of applications of computing equipment from the 1920s onward was a story of disciplined information gathering, channeling, and analyzing by increasing numbers of organizations. As the demand for more data increased, information-processing vendors simply built their successes on economic and organizational trends larger than any particular supplier or technology. Changes in product capacity, price, and function, therefore, were simply responses to environmental circumstances that made computing attractive in the first place. The effects of demographics, an expanding economy, increasing complexity of organizations, and the availability of various cost-effective technologies also drove accountants and office equipment vendors increasingly into each others' arms.

7

Products, Practices, and Prices

THE KINDS of products made, the way they were sold, and the terms and prices shed considerable light on how and why users received them. The cycle of events that culminated in the use of technology always began with interaction between customers and vendors. A look at the business from that perspective suggests the daily rhythm of activities that turned the potentials of specific technologies into tangible realities. Legal problems frequently complicated matters for vendors; therefore, the role of litigation must be understood, particularly that which involved the U.S. government. Ultimately, the accumulation of millions of individual manufacturing, marketing, and buying actions made possible an industry whose historically most significant sector was the card and tabulator business.

Punched Card Products and Development

From the end of World War I to the end of the Great Depression firms introduced products within the punched card business that were extensive both in number and functions. They significantly enhanced organizational dependence on such technology and created the very large user base that ultimately gave birth to the computer industry of the 1950s. The speed of product introductions leaves little doubt about how competitive the industry was at the time. Each major vendor felt the need to introduce new products every year: enhancements of existing lines, systems with compatible cards, or products that created customer dependence or the need to meet some niche requirement. In both decades, IBM and Powers/Remington Rand totally refurbished their product lines, a very expensive thing to do, particularly during the depression, but an absolute essential for success. Although IBM came to dominate this segment of the office appliance market by World War II, management's contention that it had to continue product introductions did not change. New products expanded the potential pool of customers by creating new functions and enhanced the abiltiy to compete on familiar turf. That position prevailed throughout the era of the computer.

The punched card market was characterized by reorganizations. IBM, for instance, restructured marketing to integrate salespeople from the original firms that made up C-T-R, dropped whole product lines, and shifted resources to focus and integrate product development and manufacture. Vendor shake-outs resembled those of computer hardware and software suppliers in the 1960s and 1970s. For example, Powers became part of Remington Rand. Consolidations continued, especially in the 1920s, as in all other industries. By the end of the 1920s, two firms dominated the tabulating equipment market in the U.S., IBM and Remington Rand.

Continued enhancements to basic technologies originally worked out before World War I broadened the applicability of punched card equipment in the 1920s. Encouragement from customers simply enticed vendors to develop product lines further, usually by adding functions. These advancements in turn heated up competition for existing markets while successfully forcing vendors to seek a broader customer base with new product offerings. The cycle never ended for successful firms; those that did not play the game were bypassed by newer, better products.

This cycle goes far to explain why there were so many technological and product enhancements throughout the 1920s and why they came so fast in comparison to earlier periods. C-T-R introduced its first 5-bank tabulator in 1920. Powers added a counter to its sorter in 1921, and in the same year, C-T-R introduced an automatic control function with its sorter. Powers brought out an alphabetic printing tabulator and then an alphabetic keyboard in 1924, pleasing accountants. In 1924, C-T-R (IBM as of February) introduced its electronic duplicating keypunch. In 1925, Powers countered with an electronic keyboard punch and the first synchromatic installation that allowed simultaneous typing of data on a typewriter and punching on cards. IBM introduced a motor-driven gang punch in 1926, and then its first general-purpose accounting machine. In 1928, customers could buy IBM's new 80-column card, rent equipment to use the new card, and use a fully automatic bill-feeding device on the tabulator. The many new products introduced that year evidenced considerable product development in the previous years. Remington Rand announced the Model 2 Tabulator in 1929 as IBM introduced a better keypunch with automatic feed and eject capability. Although the 1920s saw a richer set of product introductions than the 1930s, the press of new devices placed greater emphasis on product-processing capabilities than on data entry and output. Electrification and printing functions were milestones in the 1920s, but as those functions became widely available, attention shifted to enhancing the abilities of punched card equipment to process, calculate, and analyze data in greater quantities, at faster speeds, and to do more complex tasks.[1] The industry's success with the latter objectives by the late 1930s clarified the need for computers.

As the 1920s progressed, customers could choose from two very full product lines of punched card equipment: IBM or Remington Rand. Both sets of products were designed to do the same work and to compete head-on against each other. The IBM system (and the company did use the word "system" to describe its offerings by the late 1920s) consisted of an electronic keypunch. Cards at the end of the decade were of various sizes, but the main and new offerings were the 80-column type so familiar in future decades and subsequently called either the "IBM card" or the "computer card." IBM offered a Type 80 horizontal sorter, and a general purpose numeric printing tabulator. All used the new 80-column card, which could hold more data than earlier versions. Older machines depended on cards with 34, 38, or 45 columns. IBM machines could be configured to operate with specific card sizes. Auxiliary gear included a manual electric duplicating keypunch, a mechanical verifier and the addition of an automatic control function to the tabulator. IBM's systems had a reputation for being very flexible because all electric connections were on plug boards, which made changing processes (years later called "programming") easier than on older technologies.[2]

In table 7.1, I list punched card products of the Tabulating Machine Company (renamed IBM) available at the start of the decade. In table 7.2, I list punched card products available in 1933.[3] From the two lists one infers the enormous expansion and sophistication in the product line. No vendor in the office products industry had, up to that time, introduced as many new and complex products as did IBM between the two world wars. But their's was not an isolated case; executives at Burroughs, NCR, Remington Rand, and elsewhere also focused on new products during the same period.[4]

These successes were not simply the results of commonplace tasks of vendors or executive visions and policies. They were the outcome of individuals working on new problems. A little-known hero behind the many new products was James Wares Bryce (1880–1949), IBM's chief engineer for more than thirty years. He was one of the most important contributors to the evolution of IBM's product line and technical management in the early decades of the twentieth century. Bryce came to C-T-R in 1917 after a varied career as a draftsman and consulting engineer known to Watson. He went to work at Endicott, home of IBM's development and manufacturing for punched card equipment. There he linked up with another inventor at IBM, Clair D. Lake (1888–1958), to develop the popular Type 80 Sorter and then the famous 80-column card. Bryce directed all the efforts necessary to introduce a complete new product line to support the card. By the early 1930s, card sales of all sizes accounted for between 5 and 10 percent of IBM's revenues. All of the products of the 1930s, which relied on the new card, were the result of Bryce's work. In 1931, he perfected a multiplying punch (Type 600) and enhanced it with the Type 601 in 1933. He designed the Type 285 tabulator and the IBM Type 405 Alphabetical Accounting Machine. The 405 was perhaps the most popular IBM product in the 1930s; it remained in the product line until after World War II. Bryce personally accumulated 400 patents by 1936 and within IBM was known as the "patron saint of engineering." In 1936, the U.S. Patent Office honored him as one of the ten "greatest living

TABLE 7.1
Products of Tabulating Machine Company, circa 1920

Product	Model Number	Rental/Month or Purchase Price (Dollars)
Automatic Sorting Machine	10	20
Keypunch	15	75 (purchase)
Keypunch	20	75 (purchase)
Quick Set Gang Punch		75 (purchase)
Hand Set Gang Punch		50 (purchase)
Tabulator		varied

Source: Tabulating Machine Company, *Salesmen's Catalogue* (New York: Tabulating Machine Company, n.d. [ca. 1920]): 1–15.

inventors." He also encouraged his staff to invent; they generated an additional 299 patents.[5]

In Europe many developments occurred in punched card technology. Gustav Tauschek, an engineer from Vienna under contract to IBM, accumulated more than two hundred patents. Before working for IBM, he had developed a punched card electromechanical accounting machine for the Rheinische Metall- und Maschinenfabrik. During the 1930s, he consulted for IBM and built a reading-writing calculator. He constructed various storage devices that relied on magnetized steel plates and a banking accounting machine capable of storing the records of ten thousand accounts. His devices could also multiply and divide.[6]

Not to be ignored, however, was Powers. By the end of the 1920s, Remington Rand had absorbed the firm. The Powers system of the 1920s consisted of an electronic alphabetical and numeric key punch, a horizontal sorter, and an alphabetical and numerical printing tabulator, all using 45-column cards, the standard card across the industry at the start of the decade. Auxiliary equipment included an electric punch synchronized with a typewriter and a tabulator with automatic control. Powers and, later, IBM products expanded with the advent of the printing tabulator, which satisfied accountants' need for a printed audit trail output. Similarly, increases in demand for such technology surfaced after the introduction of alphabetic and numerical tabulating systems, which could manipulate both words and numbers.[7]

Despite improvements there were drawbacks. First, equipment was still perceived as expensive. One writer estimated that unless an organization was prepared to do about fifteen hundred operations daily, such equipment might not be cost justified.[8] Indirect evidence supports this contention because the bulk of IBM's customers through the 1930s were not small organizations. These products, however, were price sensitive. As prices for equipment

TABLE 7.2

Products of International Business Machines Corporation, 1933

Product[a]	Model
Punches	
Mechanical keypunch	No. 20, No. 23
Mechanical keypunch verifier	Standard, 80-column
Electric keypunch	H
Electric duplicating keypunch	D
Quick set gang punch	
Motor drive gang punch	
Automatic interpreter	
Automatic electric keypunch	Standard, 80-column
Automatic electric duplicating keypunch	Standard, 80-column
Motor drive verifier	Standard, 80-column
International automatic reproducing duplicators	45, 80 columns
International automatic summary card punch	Standard, 80-column
Automatic multiplying punch	45, 80 columns
Alphabetic duplicating punch	80 columns
Automatic check writing interpreter	34, 45, 80 columns
Alphabetic printing punch	80 columns
International reproducing punch	
Sorters	
Electric vertical sorting machine	
Electric horizontal sorting machine	Standard, 80-column
Sorting machine	No. 43 (Type 83)
Electric printing and counting sorter	
Electric counting sorter	45, 80 column
Tabulators	
Electric tabulating machine	42, 45, 80 columns
Electric automatic control tabulating machine	42, 45, 80 columns
Electric accounting machine	10 models
Tabulating machine	No. 63 (Type 83)
Chain grocery billing machine	
International 3 counter printing tabulator	45, 80 columns
Direct subtraction accounting machine	34, 45, 80 columns
Alphabetic accounting machine	
Automatic checking machine	45, 80 columns

Source: International Business Machines, *Manual of Business Instruction: Equipment and Supplies Furnished by International Business Machines Corporation Tabulating Machine Division in the United States* (New York: IBM, 1933). This publication was a sales rep's bible, known as the "sales manual" for decades at IBM.

[a] Prices are not listed because they varied by model and would have made this table too lengthy.

dropped, demand rose, and a broader base of customers built up. Second, users also had to pay staffs to operate the equipment. Considerable effort was expended to correct errors generated by operators and machines, both of which caused processing reruns that were both frustrating and expensive. Third, there was a growing need in the 1920s for the ability to multiply, subtract, and divide by way of card control. The inability to punch a summary card automatically began to sound much like the concerns and benefits offered by computers later. Product developers in the 1930s attempted to address each of these concerns, stretching punched card technology to its limits and, in turn, creating the need for the advanced function provided first by huge electronic calculators and finally by the digital computer at the end of the 1940s.

Changes in economic conditions and the evolution of technology gave the 1930s their own cast. The decade was a period of depressed business volumes but also one in which the variety and richness of product introductions showed. The latter, however, was not true of punched card equipment. In table 7.3 I list introductions made during the decade. Although IBM dominated the market, its competitors continued to respond aggressively with new offerings. Many of the developments were in the form of increased speed, capacity, and more continuous processing, often accompanied by decreasing human intervention as multiple devices worked as systems.

The evolution of punched card technology in the 1920s and 1930s illustrated two trends. First, vendors proved very sensitive to customers' requirements and demands. Second, product development did not call for major breakthroughs in physics, electronics, metallurgy, or other fields; it applied known scientific, engineering, and manufacturing principles. Technology's historians, such as Basalla, recognized this well-known scenario: technological innovation evolutionarily responding to newly defined problems or needs, often with responses based on existing knowledge of a solution's components. Punched card developments at IBM illustrated the process.

The horizontal sorter (Type 80 Sorter), developed in the 1920s, was a modification of a vertical sorter, with some functional improvements in movement and card sorting that responded to needs. It was an important product because sorting was crucial to users who needed to obtain subtotals. Good sorting required tabulating cards in proper order. The new sorter satisfied the need of accountants to obtain subtotals by predefined categories. The requirement for subtotals also caused IBM to design tabulators with multiple accumulators in which to "accumulate" subtotals as cards passed through the system. IBM went further by introducing in 1927 a tabulator that could provide automatic group control so that users could have subtotals within subtotals up to three levels.[9]

Various output devices were developed to print subtotal results: a summary punch, a duplicating keypunch, and others. These capabilities, in turn, in-

TABLE 7.3
Punch Card Product Introductions in the 1930s

Year	Innovation	Vendor
1930	Numeric interpreter to print on cards	IBM
	Model 2 interpreter and standard reproducer	Remington Rand
	26-column card and full product line to support it	Powers-Samas
	Automatic card verification	Powers-Samas
1931	90-column card introduced and full product line to support it	Remington Rand
	Automatic multiplying punch and duplicating summary punch	IBM
1932	Alphabetic printing tabulating device	IBM
	Verifier with automatic feed and eject mechanism[a]	IBM
	Automatic compensation feeding device for tabulators	Remington Rand
1933	Alphabetic key punch (Type 3) introduced with reproducing punch, test-scoring machine, alphabetic printing punch	IBM
	90-column synchromatic typewriter punch, summary punch, electric hand punch	Remington Rand
1934	Automatic carriage for printing tabulating machine, alphabetic direct subtraction accounting machine	IBM
	21-column card system	Powers-Samas
1935	Printing multiplying punch	Remington Rand
	New summary card punch	Powers-Samas
1936	Alphabetic verifier, alphabetic interpreter, collator (could merge separate cards)	IBM
	36-column card and full product line to support it	Powers-Samas
1937	60-column card and full product line	Powers-Samas
1938	Transfer posting machine, Type 513 reproducing gang summary punch	IBM
	Multicontrol reproducing punch	Remington Rand
	130-column capacity card	Powers-Samas
1939	Mark sensing equipment	IBM
	Model 3 Tabulator	Remington Rand
	Alphanumerical interpreter, combination automatic and visible key punch for 130-column cards	Powers-Samas Powers-Samas

Source: George Jordan, "A Survey of Punched Card Development" (M.S. thesis, Massachusetts Institute of Technology, 1956), 25–44.

[a] With this introduction, the entire punched card industry had both alphabetic and numeric systems products.

creased pressure on IBM and other vendors to develop cards with larger data storage capacity, which led IBM to the 80-column card. Each major product development of the 1920s and 1930s in effect built on the successes or failures of earlier devices. Thus, if a machine proved useful—punches for example—users invariably wanted it to work faster or to handle more cards, which led to newer and faster models. When users wanted a device to do more than just add, a variety of new equipment was developed, such as the multiplying punches of the early 1930s (e.g., IBM Type 600 and IBM Type 601).[10]

The way IBM responded organizationally to product development offers insight into the process. Hollerith originally developed machines to meet requirements he personally was aware of but did not undertake significant substantive market analysis. When C-T-R came under Watson's control in 1914, the new general manager and his salespeople began to focus on the concerns of all customers, listening to and reporting on their needs, understanding their operations, and appreciating their business objectives. Listening was encouraged throughout the company. Watson subsequently invested more in R&D, particularly in the punched card end of his business. He hired Bryce, Lake, and others to develop the company's future products. First Hollerith, first and then Bryce and others explored the idea of using electrical plug boards to program machines and, encouraged by customers, made such products increasingly easier to use.[11]

The institutional framework to support R&D was put up slowly. Before the 1930s, R&D was scattered in various locations, but in 1933, all efforts for punched card development were finally centralized in Endicott, New York, at the North Street Laboratory, a new four-story building that took up a city block. Seven engineers constituted the original R&D staff. Over the years, Watson began frequently to assign the same problem to two groups of engineers, creating a contention system whereby those who developed the best, most effective solution would see it adopted. Contention R&D, although expensive, continued in one form or another at IBM down through the 1980s and governed the nature of product introductions. Watson also concluded by the 1930s that no individual could keep up with the surge in customer demand; hence, he formalized a process to define product requirements. Throughout the 1930s, management kept product planning away from R&D and increasingly shifted the responsibility to corporate headquarters in New York City. By the end of the decade, a Future Demands Department existed, staffed by former sales representatives with engineering backgrounds, who not only defined requirements but began publishing articles on how to use tabulating gear in various "leading edge" applications, usually in scientific fields.[12]

Customers helped shape the environment for all vendors as the latter defined features and uses for products. None proved more influential on vendors than the U.S. government either as a user or through legislation. Laws again caused a surge in the need for more information both in and out of government, especially when legislation implemented the New Deal. For example, at the 32d annual National Business Show in New York (October 1935) Burroughs introduced a payroll and paycheck writing machine that generated the entire earnings record of an employee, personal deductions and all necessary totals while it produced a record consistent with the tenets of the newly passed Social Security Act. The Federal Home Loan Act motivated NCR to announce a machine at the same show to perform all the bookkeeping required by that law, which ranged from printing current entries into a borrower's passbook to consolidating these entries into office records, in one operation. Insurance companies increasingly depended on data–processing equipment, causing IBM to adapt a newly announced utility bill–issuing device to release premium notices.[13]

The 32d National Business Show was given considerable publicity in the national press because of the large variety of new products announced, which signaled a return to better economic times. All the key vendors in the office products industry showed off new products. Colonel Edward A. Deeds, chairman of the board of NCR, told a reporter there that "I've never seen a better one [National Business Show]."[14]

Consolidations, Courts, and Punched Card Vendors, 1920–1940

Between World War I and the end of the 1920s the same kinds of consolidations of firms and offerings witnessed in the typewriter segment of the office products industry occurred in other segments and for the same reasons. Typewriter suppliers merged into fewer organizations—a dramatic example of the process at work as dozens of organizations shrank to a few. Fewer vendors existed in the highly capital-intensive punched card market end of the industry so fewer absorptions occurred. However, the end results were just as impressive. As in the typewriter business, a very few firms dominated the market. Victors gained such a broad base of customers that they were able to survive the Great Depression, thrive during World War II, and prepare for the enormous potential growth that presented itself in the late 1940s and early 1950s. The largest punched card vendors were Powers (then Remington Rand) and, always, IBM. I will review the histories of Remington Rand and IBM in more detail later, but some structural elements of the industry need separate treatment because they define a pattern evident later across the industry, particularly in the 1960s and 1970s.

In broad terms, the 1920s were characterized by the actual formulation of new or different organizations whereas in the 1930s those that had not fully consolidated internally (such as Remington Rand) worked to do so. Those that had consolidated (such as IBM) took advantage of their integrated operations. In 1920, C-T-R bought the Peirce patents, eliminating a potential competitor. In 1922, the British subsidiary of Powers incorporated the Samas Company in France. C-T-R changed its name to International Business Machines Corporation, heralding corporate confidence in becoming a broad-based, worldwide supplier of office equipment. However, the big event of the 1920s was the merger of Powers and seven other firms to form Remington Rand, making it one of the largest general suppliers of office equipment in the industry. From 1927 to the 1950s, these two firms dominated sales of punched card equipment and cards.

In Europe, consolidations similar to those in the United States before World War I and during the 1920s were underway as new firms appeared and fundamental market patterns were established. In 1922, Bull came into existence to sell punched card equipment and, in time, became a major vendor. In 1923, C-T-R acquired 90 percent of the stock of DEHOMAG, the old Hollerith agent in Germany (Deutsche Hollerith Maschinen Gessellschaft mbH). At the same time, many new agencies were established on behalf of U.S. firms. For example, in 1926, the agency of Messrs. Bloch-Brun, of Warsaw, was created to represent IBM in Poland while another was established in Bulgaria. In 1927, Powers established representation in Spain and Finland. In 1928, IBM created the Internationale Geschaftmachinen Vertriebsgesellschaft mbH as a subsidiary to replace Furth and Company, thereby increasing direct control over local operations. Remington Rand followed a similar strategy when, in 1928, it created Powers GmbH in Germany. Powers and Samas merged in Europe during 1929. In the 1930s, names of organizations were changed, new agencies were established, and branch offices and plants opened throughout Europe. As in the United States, the demand for information-processing technology led to the emergence of larger, but fewer, major organizations.[15]

Both major American vendors emerged from the 1920s as suppliers of more than punched cards. The consolidated Remington Rand sold punched card equipment (Powers Accounting Machine Company in the U.S.), adding machines (Dalton Adding Machine Company), typewriters (Remington Typewriter Company), and miscellaneous filing, record-handling, and protecting devices and products (Rand Kardex Bureau, Inc., Baker-Vauter Company, Safe-Cabinet Company, etc.). The result on paper was a broad-based office equipment vendor that manufactured and sold products throughout the world.[16] IBM sold scales, microphones, clocks, office furniture, typewriters, and punched card cabinets. Using 1925 data, Powers' net profit was about $2 million whereas IBM's reached $4.5 million, which suggests that despite the consolidation of Remington Rand, IBM had surpassed many others in the industry by middecade.

IBM's success can be attributed to several factors. It continued to produce new products throughout the 1920s, which were priced competitively, with the intent to block Powers rather than simply to replace old lines. IBM created more efficient manufacturing processes to hold down product cost and raise profit margins. Finally, IBM's marketing and salesmanship was a crucial element.[17] Historians typically overemphasize its importance; it takes a variety of well-managed factors to make a company successful. Management within IBM in the 1920s already believed that no matter what was built (good or bad) the sales force could sell it. That folk wisdom survived for many decades, but in reality it took efficient teamwork among product developers, manufacturing engineers, and marketing specialists to sell high-technology products profitably. IBM, like NCR before it, succeeded better than its competitors.[18]

IBM benefited by not having many organizations to absorb in the 1920s. IBM kept a narrower product line, dropping items not directly compatible with its role in the office products industry. Remington Rand, however, wanted to play a major role in card filing systems, safes, and typewriters. IBM had fewer plants to worry about, and those it had more often than not produced similar products. Thus when capacity requirements dictated, plants were either expanded (e.g., Endicott) or built to order (Poughkeepsie) with knowledge and experience. The U.S. plants were kept modern and, in the early decades, were all located in New York State or around Washington D.C. During the 1920s, Watson completed his consolidation of marketing into one force whereas Remington Rand only began to work on that problem in 1927 and continued the effort into the 1940s. Thus when the depression became visible by 1930, Remington Rand was caught in the middle of its effort to digest various acquisitions and mergers. IBM already had in place all the key changes required to compete on an international basis. The one exception to generalizations about the two firms was the Powers Division within Remington Rand in the United States and Western Europe. It had not yet been tampered with organizationally and, thus, continued to introduce and market new products with its own agents during the early 1930s. But Powers's impact waned as its momentum slowed in the face of hard economic times on both sides of the Atlantic.[19]

Powers simply could not market as well as IBM and was hampered by the institutional turmoil at Remington Rand. By contrast, IBM's sales force was better trained and motivated to develop and maintain long-standing relationships with large customers, some of whom dated back to the 1890s. IBM's product development was also better tuned to customer needs through a formal management process not equaled by Remington Rand. Finally, all of IBM's resources—people, capital, and management—were focused on a narrower market than Remington Rand's. The net result was that IBM was better positioned to withstand the depression than its arch rival.

IBM's market share continued to grow during the 1920s. It came from two sources: new customers and Powers's customer base. One student of IBM argued that it had expanded primarily at the expense of Remington Rand, a statement more true of the 1930s than of the 1920s.[20] Although 1920 customer lists or how much each bought apparently were not preserved for either company, indirect evidence indicates that Powers increased its customers as did IBM and many other vendors. In the late 1920s, growth came from an absolute base of customers, with possibly some growth in numbers, but usually from encouraging existing customers to spend more either with rental price increases or by moving larger product volumes. At IBM, expansion of the world's economy and efficient management of product development, manufacturing, and salesmanship generated more customers, increased the amount sold to each, and, hence, brought dominance in the market. It would be difficult to rationalize in any other way an estimated 80 percent dominance of the punched card business by IBM during the late 1920s and early 1930s.

Rivalry between the two firms portended future relations between IBM and other vendors during the 1960s; the U.S. Department of Justice took issue with the growing dominance achieved by these two. For the same reasons that they went after NCR before World War I, government lawyers looked at Remington Rand and IBM practices. When IBM, for example, made tabulating machines available, it rented them and required that all cards be purchased from IBM, which, in effect, shut out supply competitors. Prosecutors viewed this practice as a monopolistic trade constraint. IBM and Remington Rand appeared to have "combined to restrain commerce" by renting machines and refusing to sell them "on condition that the lessee purchase at fixed prices and use the tabulating cards made by lessor, or pay an additional rental for the machines."[21] The U.S. government filed suit against both companies under the terms of the Sherman and the Clayton Acts within the first two weeks of the Roosevelt administration.

The government accused IBM of controlling 88 percent of the tabulating market and Remington Rand of controlling the remaining 12 percent. Newspapers reported that officials at both firms learned of the suit while reading their Sunday papers. They were presented with the formal suits the following Wednesday. Watson publicly exclaimed that he was not worried and welcomed an investigation of IBM's practices because they were aboveboard and legal. Much earlier, IBM had waived the requirement for the U.S. government that cards be purchased from the company; the government made its own cards. However, the suit alleged that even though the government saved money by not paying for cards, had it been required to acquire them from IBM, the cost of such cards would have been much higher, an expense private sector customers obviously had to bear.[22]

In December 1935, a federal district court in New York granted the U.S. government an injunction that canceled an agreement between the two companies and allowed each to make cards for the others' machines. It further ruled that neither could require customers to buy cards solely from them. Both companies had agreed to concur on whatever consent decree IBM finally settled for. Watson, however, let the case go to trial. After challenges and counter charges, IBM ultimately was told to stop forcing customers to buy all cards from the company. On April 27, 1936, the U.S. Supreme Court upheld the decision in the U.S. government's favor.[23] Before and after litigation, officials at both firms viewed their practices as progressive whereas government officials called them constraints of trade. Ironically, at least for Watson, while the case dragged through the courts, his personal relations with both President Roosevelt and key officials within the administration remained good.[24]

The problem for the industry presented by the cases of the government versus NCR before World War I, Remington Rand and IBM in the 1930s, IBM and AT&T in the 1940s and 1950s, IBM again in the 1970s, and AT&T in the 1980s was the relationship of antitrust legislation to an industry marketing high-technology products. The problem was exacerbated as the economy increasingly became more organized and, to use Chandler's phrase, "purposeful." Antitrust legislation had been designed in an era when lawmakers saw the economy as driven purely by market forces (demand) although, in fact, it was moving toward a more organized, controlled form. High-technology products not only reflected new patterns of management but visibly reflected the structural dichotomies presented by government policy at odds with changing economic realities in an industrializing society. Generally across the U.S. economy, the Sherman Act discouraged what Chandler termed "loose horizontal federations of small manufacturing enterprises formed to control price and production."[25] The growth of Remington Rand suggested the process at work. It went from a loosely tied to a more fully integrated organization by the late 1940s but never centralized as much as IBM. Yet that kind of centralization made larger organizations more viable in their efforts to control further the flow of products, terms and conditions, predictable business, and economic results. Antitrust legislation was as much as anathema in the 1930s (Remington Rand) as it had been in the 1910s (NCR).

The Sherman Act penalized those who attempted to monopolize industries characterized by integration and concentration. Although the government instituted public policy that allowed some of that activity for the common good (e.g., telephone service), it had not concluded that it should apply to information handling. The U.S. government was not willing to treat specific lines of office equipment differently from any other set of manufactured products. Thus with the clear example of a rapid and obvious industry concentration in the cash register business before World War I and among punched card equipment vendors in the 1920s one can see an inevitable clash brewing between IBM and Remington Rand on the one side and the U.S. Justice Department on the other.

Ironically, while each round of vigorous enforcement of the antitrust laws was taking place, vendors continued to count U.S. government agencies as their largest customers and supporters. Yet, the U.S. government perpetrated the largest, most publicized, and complex attack on industry practices over an extended period on information-processing businesses.[26] The case also highlights the fallacy of referring to the U.S. government as a monolithic enterprise with a common policy toward a particular industry; in reality, public agencies vary their practices, making it possible, for example, for the Antitrust Division of the Justice Department to prosecute a tabulating machine vendor while the Bureau of the Census cultivates such suppliers as welcome allies.

Lawsuits notwithstanding, leadership in technological innovations and marketing shifted from Powers to IBM by the end of the 1920s. During the 1930s, IBM brought out its full line of alphabetic and numeric equipment, a collator, and mark sensing equipment for scoring tests. Antitrust litigation by the U.S. government scarcely slowed the momentum. In 1930, Remington Rand's net profits reached $9.7 million while IBM's were $10.9 million. By 1940, IBM had expanded its lead, turning in net profits of $21.7 million against Remington Rand's $4.9 million.[27] So it appears that antitrust activities were only a severe irritant in the 1930s, not a permanent influence on the industry. One cannot argue that IBM simply took sales from Powers. Their combined net profits in 1930 totaled $20.6 million and in 1940 reached $26.6 million, an increase of 23 percent. The industry grew in absolute numbers of machines installed and dollars generated.

Government lawyers in the 1930s, as later in the 1970s, examined business practices by product type rather than by the industry's own definition of itself or by the totality of a company's presence in a particular industry. Thus lawyers looked at the dominance of card sales or tabulator presence and ignored the rest of IBM's or Remington Rand's product line. The government's very narrow definition of monopolistic activity was challenged in each decade by companies that viewed industry activities in much broader terms through multiple integrated product lines and whole customer sets. The narrowness of the government's view of economic activity prevented it from fundamentally hobbling the emerging data-processing industry. It undoubtedly influenced the practices of companies like IBM and NCR, but it did not slow either their technical imperative or the acceptance of new machines.

Practices and Prices in the Tabulating Machine Business

Given that IBM enjoyed the dominant position in the punched card business, its marketing practices, prices, and sales policies in general made it possible not only to maintain high volumes of sales but also to acquire a large customer base. Business practices were honed at IBM and elsewhere in response to the realities of the marketplace. Watson often reacted to the market before competitors by timing product delivery or responded to and built on the experience of a competitor. These tactics increased the firm's chances to hold and expand its lead in the interwar period.

During the 1920s in the United States, key vendors developed or expanded their direct sales forces. This was as true of IBM as of NCR, Burroughs, and, to a lesser extent, Powers (Remington Rand). In Europe, national firms used a combination of direct sales forces and agents in the 1920s, and direct sales forces increasingly in the 1930s. Direct salespeople were on the payroll of the manufacturer. Agencies were independent organizations under contract to market a particular vendor's products. Before World War I, it was customary for agents to sell goods from multiple vendors, particularly if that agent had an exclusive contract for an entire country. By the end of the 1920s, agents were specializing increasingly in one vendor's equipment (with the exception of typewriters). Agents ran stores and made sales calls. In the United States, the punched card portion of the office appliance industry was dominated overwhelmingly by direct sales representatives.[28]

In major cities such as New York, Philadelphia, Boston, and Chicago, IBM and Powers established sales offices that displayed products, provided facilities for demonstrating them, and served as offices for salespeople who made direct calls on customers. Figure 7.1 illustrates an early IBM office (when the firm still sold scales). One can conclude that the gentlemen in the picture represented the entire branch staff. Branch offices (as they have always been known) were staffed typically with less than one dozen salesmen and staff reporting to a branch manager, who had also grown up in sales. By the 1940s, branch offices in large cities also had repair personnel (later called field engineers [FEs] or customer engineers [CEs]) and administrative staff.[29] The IBM systems engineer, so widely evident in the late twentieth century, was created in the late 1950s and formally existed in sales branches beginning in the early 1960s. Their functions in the 1920s and 1930s were carried out by salespeople.

Territories were predominantly geographic before World War II except for large customers who might have one or more dedicated salespeople. In New York, for example, in the late 1930s, Thomas Watson, Jr., sold typewriters to customers in a single building.[30] When business expanded, IBM reduced geographical territories and opened branches. Business practices in Nashville, Tennessee, illustrate the growth process. Since the early years of the century, Hollerith and Time Recording salesmen came to town to call on state government officials, local insurance companies and banks, and other prospects. That pattern continued until 1934 when IBM opened a store with one salesman, who was joined by more than seven by 1946. During the 1950s, a large branch office developed with dozens of employees, and, by the late 1960s, it boasted a staff of more than forty. They added major customers in the 1940s and 1950s, including the Genesco Shoe Company and most major

7.1 The IBM branch office in Washington, D.C., 1924 (courtesy IBM Archives).

state agencies. During the 1970s, two marketing branches and another dedicated to field engineering opened.[31] The same pattern was evident in all states, across all Europe, and in most Latin American cities.

Whether in New York or in Nashville, marketing essentially prospected for new accounts or repeatedly called existing ones such as that typified by figure 7.2. The staff kept logs of whom a salesperson called and the results of the calls; at Friday afternoon branch meetings, they discussed marketing problems. They then tracked these issues until they resolved them.[32] At such meetings that salesmen sang songs, many championing the president.

Ever Onward

There's a thrill in store for all,
For we're about to toast

7.2 A punch card "data center," circa 1920. Notice single card punching on right, volume work on left, and the vertical sorter in upper left-hand corner (courtesy IBM Archives).

The corporation in every land.
We're here to cheer each pioneer
And also proudly boast
Of that "man or men," our friend and guiding hand.
The name of T. J. Watson means a courage none can stem:
And we feel honored to be here to toast the "IBM."

   Chorus

EVER ONWARD—EVER ONWARD!
That's the spirit that has brought us fame!
We're big, but bigger we will be,
We can't fail for all can see
That to serve humanity has been our aim!
Our products now are known in every zone.
Our reputation sparkles like a gem!
We've fought our way through—and new
Fields we're sure to conquer too
For the EVER ONWARD IBM.[33]

IBM's anthem, written in the 1930s, was more than panegyric music. Although it strongly suggests the cult of personality, in its time the music contributed to a sense of loyalty and identification with a militantly aggressive, "never say die" attitude typical of sales representatives in many companies.

Other vendors sang such songs, too, and had branches, often called "district offices," in the 1920s and 1930s.

Salespeople at IBM were carefully cultivated, often with Watson's personal attention. They were his favorite group within the company and, like executives at NCR in the late 1800s, he raised their level of prestige within the firm. He ran at least one sales school each year for new personnel, convened regional and annual sales meetings, and asked that each of his representatives sell applications for IBM's products, not just machines. He insisted on quality service, almost to a passion, and demanded that salespeople know their customers' businesses very well. During the 1920s, IBM began to instill what ultimately would be known as its "Basic Beliefs" (a term that originated in the 1960s) in each employee: respect for the individual, best customer service, and excellence in all that was done.[34]

Watson's style was impressed more on salesmen than on any other group for they were the individuals most closely identified with the man who set the tone for the company and whose pronouncements came nearest to providing peddlers with a philosophical basis for operating. "It is better to aim at perfection and miss than it is to aim at imperfection and hit it."[35] Others:

"All men should be judged upon their records."
"The best supervision is self supervision."
"Don't guess—know."
"Think in big figures."
"Organize the brains of your organization."
"Progress is improvement, not the performance of miracles."
"Time is money."
"Think."
"Learn the things to do."[36]

Watson recognized, however, that the way to ensure high customer satisfaction and, hence, more business, particularly in a world in which equipment was rented, not sold, required more than platitudes. It called for substantive ways to keep sales personnel involved and committed to customers. Watson accomplished this by the simple expedient of paying sales representatives commissions as machines were rented and cards sold, then deducting from their commissions when equipment came out of a customer's enterprise and off rent. That practice forced salespeople to make sure customers used equipment properly. When older devices were replaced, sales representatives worked hard to ensure that the new machines generated more revenue than the old ones had. A point system was used with each point equal to $1 of monthly rent. Thus, if in 1933 a salesperson convinced a customer to install a mechanical keypunch verifier at the rental rate of $5 per month for a year, it was worth 5 points of commission. If replaced with another device that rented for $6 (or six points), the salesperson was paid commission on one point (at x dollars per point, which varied each year according to the terms of the current sales compensation plan). On the other hand, if it was replaced with a $4 per month machine, he owed IBM one point of commission. Quotas were expressed in terms of points rather than by types of gear sold or in dollars. To "make quota" a salesman had to install at least as many points of equipment as his point quota. When he achieved this goal, he joined the 100 Percent Club—a significant distinction and a form of recognition all salespeople coveted. Between 65 and 80 percent of the sales force made quotas yearly with percentages of accomplishment higher in the 1920s than in the 1930s. As club members, sales personnel could attend a convention in which salesmanship was discussed, listen to speeches by company officials and special guests, and have a good time.[37] NCR followed the same practice and, in fact, pioneered the point process.[38] Individual recognition events were held around the world in North America, Europe, and Asia, even in the interwar period. The 100 Percent Club remained a viable and active institution into the late twentieth century.

Spending time with the customer was an important aspect of a sales representative's marketing effort, particularly in an industry in which salespeople frequently had to teach customers what a new device was, why they needed it, and how to use it and then convince them to do so. Getting the order was a major event. Each call was discussed, cataloged, and reported weekly back to New York to ascertain who placed what types of orders, which customers were receiving proposals, if surveys were being done and demonstrations performed, and the nature of a customer's interests.[39] Sales representatives installed machines during the 1920s and 1930s and, therefore, were asked to report to New York the exact day such equipment was rented so that correct billing might begin and commissions be paid. Sales personnel were admonished: "Great care should be exercised in seeing that machines are installed on a revenue producing basis with as little delay as possible after delivery. Sales offices may avoid delays in installations by following up customers to see that proofs of new card forms are approved, thus insuring delivery of cards in advance of date and delivery of machines."[40] In short, "nothing should be left undone which will assist in getting the installation started."[41] Obviously, discontinuances of rental equipment had to be reported as well. By the 1930s, branch managers prepared a number of reports each month:

prospect status	discontinued machine report
installation status	uninstalled machine report
bills	monthly consignment report
expense accounts	returned equipment report
idle machine report	commission statements.
goods returned report	

The centralized approach for ensuring a pattern of sales-oriented activities, Planned Sales Calls (taught to each new representative), and even the weekly branch meetings were structured. Salespeople had sales manuals that described many of their responsibilities and all the products and included copies of contracts, reports, and price lists. The central office mailed updates to the branches; the sales staff clipped them into the three-ring binders that made up the sales manuals. Management used weekly meetings to reinforce good habits and to inspect activities. They reviewed all installations within a territory and all marketing activities in "an open forum held for the purpose of securing ideas and recommendations from those present for rectifying the unsatisfactory condition," if one existed. Branch managers reviewed all forecasted orders scheduled for the previous week but not accomplished and then asked other sales representatives to suggest how to improve installation prospects. They looked at the next week's business plans, "securing a forecast from each man in the organization, with a view to securing this business as soon as possible."[42]

This pattern of activity for sales personnel almost matches those evident in the middle decades of the twentieth century.[43] In the 1920s and 1930s, customers came to know their "reps" well and sales reps studied their customers' businesses. Sales reps always focused on "growing" the installed base of machines while they added more customers. Contracts and practices from the 1920s and 1930s remained in force decades later (albeit in modified form). It was a pattern of selling that, at the street level, helped IBM grow. It was a relatively controlled process. The weekly sales reports, along with other communications with customers and branch personnel, gave Watson and other executives the specific details required to decide what new products were needed, how they should be priced, and in what ways competitors were attacking the firm. Justifications for new products and services thus were explicit and detailed and represented relatively current information.

This coordination between product development and marketing is one aspect of tabulating machine history that has been totally overlooked by historians who were more interested in product development or in Watson.[44] Not until they studied the 1940s, for which documentation is more complete, did historians see with some clarity the relationship between sales and practices, product development, and product demand. Yet the process had been locked in place much earlier and accounted for some of the efficiencies credited to IBM.

A critical concern to customers, sales reps, and company officials was prices of equipment and cards. Pricing actions, when coupled with new product announcements and appreciation of competitive activity, could influence profoundly a company's balance sheet. Industry leaders, such as IBM, NCR, Burroughs, Underwood, and Remington Rand, carefully priced new products so that they would be more attractive than older ones but not so much more that revenues for equal function dropped. Usually, the strategy was to offer new products with enhanced functions over older models at equal or greater prices. Inflation influenced prices for old and new models too. A comparison of IBM's price lists for the early 1920s to those of the early 1930s illustrates the dynamics at work.

A vertical sorter in the early 1920s rented for $20 per month on a yearlong lease and in 1934 at between $25 and $30 per month (depending on the model). These machines varied a little in function but not enough to swing the price, which was based on new features. Therefore, one can conclude that function for function users swung the price up between 19.5 percent and 33 percent. A gang punch sold for $75 earlier and for $125 later, reflecting a similar increase in price for the same function (and almost the same machine). Small keypunches sold for $75 and in the later period, for $100—a similar rise in cost.[45] Price increases either resulted from rising production and marketing costs or in response to declining competition or supplies. An examination of the sales manual from which these prices came reveals lead times for such equipment in the 1930s closer to thirty days, which suggests the punches probably were in inventory and, therefore, in ready supply.

A different situation applied when the firm introduced a new function. As a result of a much broader product line in the 1930s than in the early 1920s, function did influence price structures more dramatically and directly and across a larger number of machine types. Small keypunches in the 1930s rented for between $10 and $18 per month. If one uses a purchase-to-rent ratio of 1 to 25 (based on a 1930s' rental of $5 or purchase price of $125 for a gang punch), then a small keypunch (if it had been offered for purchase) would have sold in the 1930s for between $250 to $450 each, about three to six times the price of punches in the earlier period. Of course, in the 1930s, punches had more function to justify the expense. Sorters suggest a similar story. In 1934, one could rent a sorter for between $45 and $150 per month (the more expensive machine was an electrical printing and counting sorter). Tabulator rent ranged from $30 to $110, which again showed increased cost but also more function. An electrical accounting machine cost $150–$200 in rent, and the most expensive machine was the direct subtraction accounting machine, which went for $475 per month.[46]

Several factors were at work. More functions were added to newer models, such as electricity, printing, capacity, speed, and so forth, which partially drove up prices. Charges also rose on some devices that did not change fundamentally over time. A price increase of 20 percent or more contrasted with the U.S. national inflation rate of about 5 percent during the interwar period. What is not completely clear is the influence of competitors on pricing; however, competitive pressures made the introduction of newer models imperative. The last, and always influential, factor in pricing is what a customer is willing to pay. If a device is too expensive customers will find it cheaper to do the work by hand or with the aid of other, less costly technologies.

Card prices were a complicated issue for customers, vendors, and current historians because cards could be printed and prepunched, came in different

TABLE 7.4
Prices for IBM Cards, Early 1920s, Early 1930s

Quantity[a]	Price (1920s) (Dollars)	Price (1930s) (Dollars)	Change (%)
2,000	3.60	4.20	85
4,000	5.20	6.40	81
6,000	6.80	8.60	79
8,000	8.40	10.80	78
10,000+		1.25	

Source: International Business Machines, *Card Price List* (New York: IBM, Tabulating Machine Division, April 1, 1934), 8; Tabulating Machine Company, *Salesmen's Catalogue* (New York: Tabulating Machine, n.d., [ca. early 1920s]), 17ff.
[a] Data were based on standard manila or color-A stock cards (roughly 7 3/8″ × 3 1/4″).

sizes and numerous colors, thicknesses, and quantities, and sold under a variety of terms and conditions. By assuming that costs for varitions in cards were proportional to each other from decade to decade and type to type, one can look at the prices of standard stock cards (e.g., the larger ones that were roughly 7 3/8″ × 3 1/4″) to discern trends. Standard stock prices decreased according to how much one bought. Thus in the early 1920s, prices went from $3.60 per two thousand down to $8.40 per eight thousand. Prices rose from 78 percent to 85 percent, with the burden for the greatest increase as percentage of price borne by smaller users (see table 7.4). Part of that increase makes sense because costs are typically greater proportionately at the low-volume end, particularly for custom-printed or prepunched cards, regardless of the cost of pulp. What clearly stands out is that price increases for cards rose much faster than for machines.

Card sales were crucial to IBM and highly profitable, as they were for Remington Rand as well. In 1929, sales amounted to $3.6 million or just over one-third of IBM's total revenues. With the depression severely hurting customers, rentals of machines decreased, but those who used them had to buy cards. They did use the devices and so the proportion of card revenues to machine revenues actually rose. Cards contributed roughly 39 percent of IBM revenues between 1930 and 1935.[47] If a customer was prepared to purchase ten thousand or more stock cards in 1934, the cost was $1.25 per ten thousand as long as that customer acquired one million cards within one year. That offering suggests that many customers bought in bulk. Specialized cards could be twice as expensive as any price cited above. In either case, however, given the benefit to IBM of selling cards, the firm managed pricing and terms carefully throughout the interwar period.

Summary

What becomes obvious about the tabulating machine business during the interwar period is its clear organization of activities and the number of new products, their diversity, volume of sales, and the number of people involved in their use. IBM's punched card business carried the company to a position of dominance by 1940. Remington Rand, despite its highly diversified product line, also was a major player in the industry because of punched card sales. The marketing and product development practices worked out in this period enabled IBM management to enter the computer business with proven methods of marketing and support and a customer base that could migrate to the new technology. Any customer or vendor of the 1950s and 1960s would have found much that is familiar in Remington Rand and IBM methods for going to market with information-processing equipment in a profitable manner.

The activities of IBM sales representatives shed considerable light on the daily tasks of vendors in this industry. They offer a high-technology, business-oriented view of life at the micro level. In the next chapter I review application of this technology through the eyes of the customer. It was consumer receptivity to new technology that ultimately made IBM and Remington Rand successful despite the threats posed by the depression and government lawsuits.

8

Commercial and Scientific Applications of Punched Card Machines

DESPITE a massive body of contemporary literature on the subject, no aspect of the history of twentieth-century computing is less understood than the uses to which computers, tabulating equipment, and calculators were put. This corpus of published material (mostly articles) was usually written by users of such technologies, explaining what they did with the equipment and why. However, most were published in industry-specific journals or in other publications that were not widely distributed. After only a quick glance at the material, one begins to sense that the office appliance industry was not just populated with vendors but also with users, some of whom identified with the proto–information-processing segment of the economy. Tabulator applications, like calculator and adding machine applications, still await thorough historical examination. However, some observations on trends in the interwar period are possible. These observations are essential to understand because they portend patterns evident in the age of the computer.

Commercial and Administrative Uses

Powers and IBM can claim only half the credit for the success of tabulators; the remainder goes to users who elected to run their organizations with these machines and provided considerable guidance to manufacturers on what to build and why. Customers grew in numbers and became more creative in their use of equipment between the two world wars. The growth in IBM's revenues in the 1920s is evidence of the expansion in user numbers and their growing dependence on such technology. But why did this user base grow?

The answer remains largely the same as it was before World War I. One grocery store owner in Brooklyn in the 1920s specified cost savings: "Tabulating our labor costs by hand would, of course, be impractical as it would require at least six more people. . . . The machine is paying for itself every week."[1] For others it was efficiency in, for instance, municipal and commercial environments—to keep "a running check on exactly where they stand and to maintain a more nearly continuous contact with customers and prospects by frequent dunning and soliciting."[2] Increased accuracy of data provided yet a third incentive: "The elimination of errors . . . is a vital advantage of tabulating equipment, since it saves confusion and time wasted in checking besides promoting better organization and efficient management."[3]

A fourth reason was to take mechanization forward when new functions became available. Payroll procedures illustrate the process; accountants seized upon adding machines early in the century to calculate payrolls more efficiently and quickly than by hand. Adding machines did not solve the problem of errors caused by actual handling of cash (e.g., did the correct amount of money go into a payroll envelope?). Payroll and tabulating equipment could stuff envelopes with cash, keep track of what actually went into them and then update records, thereby reducing labor costs and conflicts with employees while getting a payroll out on time.[4] In large plants, such as those of the Ford Motor Company, that was a major application.

Decisions were forced by a variety of circumstances. Sales reps from IBM and Powers called on customers, encouraging decisions that favored increased use of tabulators. Increased publicity was given to applications that were successfully implemented. Many basic applications were defined by customers, vendor sales personnel, and product engineers by working through the problems encountered by early users as they applied tabulating equipment to their business processes. A survey of commercial journals of the 1920s and 1930s clearly shows that almost all coverage was positive and detailed. In the United States, these application briefs appeared at twice the rate they had in the decade before World War I. Key industry journals repeatedly published testimonials on the uses and benefits of punched card equipment. *Railway Age* and *Railway Review*, for example, reiterated repeatedly the interests of the transportation community in data processing.[5] The *American Gas Journal* and others did the same for utilities[6] while a variety of engineering and management publications echoed benefits for other communities of interests, especially in the 1920s.[7]

Some shifts in this literature in the 1930s reflected changes in the economy. As railroads declined in importance relative to other industries, particularly automotive, so too did their literature. However, other industries came forward, most notably banking. Banks experienced an enormous boom in the 1920s and, despite the Great Depression of the 1930s, bank holidays, and a bad press, they remained critical players in the American economy throughout the interwar period. Check management became a huge problem that called for specialized mechanical aids. By the mid-1920s alone, over six billion checks were being used annually in the United States—a figure that continued to grow.[8] It was no surprise that banking needs would gain attention.[9] The same was true for insurance requirements.[10] As before the war, discussion was considerable about the use of tabulating equipment in accounting.[11]

Such literature generally defined uses of machines and more often than not, their benefits. It was a body of "how to" publications that would become commonplace within the future computer/data-processing industry: "Punched

Cards Methods in Accounting," "Mechanization in Gas Offices," "How a Wholesaler Became Efficient," and "Distribution Methods by Hand and Machine."[12] Equally impressive was the growing number of books on the same subject in the 1920s and 1930s.[13]

Further evidence of increased equipment use appears in scattered statistics on education. Use of this hardware required some training. This was as true for users of calculators and tabulators as it was for typewriters. Each vendor operated training schools. For tabulating equipment, users were trained either in schools run by IBM and Remington Rand at sales offices that had equipment or on site at a customer's office. Felt & Tarrant operated 151 schools worldwide (100 in the U.S. and Canada) to teach people how to use its Comptometer, and they were only a small player in the office appliance industry by the end of the 1920s! Yet that company claimed to have trained 8,478 operators in 1930 while state government training programs handled another 27,500.[14] IBM trained individuals in major cities including New York, Washington, D.C., Chicago, and San Francisco while others visited the factory at Endicott, New York. There appears to be no extant data from IBM on the number of users it trained in the 1920s and 1930s; however, contemporaneous sales manuals detail how salespeople had, as a normal part of their responsibilities, to train customers.

One survey estimated that in 1931 in the United States, 51 public high schools had at least one course on the use of office machines. These schools taught 3,226 students. In that same year, some 1.2 million students took business classes in the United States.[15] Although the number of students in classes on business machines was small, the fact that 51 schools saw the need and acted upon it suggests awareness of the role played by office appliances. Other schools probably taught classes on business machines but were not surveyed. The same survey noted that of the 348 colleges and universities teaching accounting in the United States in 1931, none taught courses on business machine accountancy despite the fact that almost all major publications on the subject routinely discussed the use of such equipment.[16]

Despite the implication that many organizations were using tabulating equipment, not everyone rushed forward to convert their accounting and other data-management systems to mechanized forms. A notable example was the city of New York's Board of Taxes and Assessments, which was criticized in 1935 by *American City,* the municipal governments' industry journal, for being "almost unbelievably behind the times."[17] In fairness to this agency at the time (spring 1936), it had already done the necessary feasibility study on how to automate examination and data gathering for 812,000 sets of records and calculation of the more than 7 million transactions currently done by more than 110 assessors and clerks. The department's $1 million budget contained no allocation for office machinery. But the article points to three obvious facts: first, the tone of the trade press was hostile toward those who did not embrace the technology that already was more than forty years old; second, major conversions came later rather than earlier because of the volume of effort involved as the potential risk of failure increased; third, major projects of this type called for special budget appropriations.

A sampling of applications suggests uses for tabulating equipment in the 1920–1940 period. The Polish National Alliance of the United States—an insurance company—cut clerical expenses,[18] while a utility installed Powers equipment to manage 550,000 accounts.[19] Old Colony Trust Company and the First National Bank of Boston claimed to have cut by nearly half all duplicated data regarding trust accounting.[20] Management of perpetual inventory, stock control, and production accounting were major applications of the period.[21] Large organizations used tabulating equipment to compare expenses to budgets.[22] Liquor sales after the repeal of prohibition required efficient inventory control and order processing.[23] In another creative application, researchers ran data from electric meter readings through an IBM tabulating service bureau in the 1930s to do a market analysis.[24] At the other extreme, administrators addressed the age-old problem of inventory control and warehousing by using this equipment to coordinate management of multiple warehousing facilities within one company.[25]

What these uses point out is the development of a broad base of users across all segments of the economy who were comfortable with and dependent upon punched card equipment. Manufacturing, distribution, retailing, utility, government, transportation, banking, and finance sectors all had either labor- or capital-intensive functions. By the depression, not only the U.S. Bureau of the Census but many organizations used such hardware and depended on punched cards.[26] Many managers accepted as obvious that "the tabulating machine is the last word in accounting. It is the data analyzer par excellence."[27]

Thus when computers became available, their efficiencies were compared to those offered by tabulating equipment. Customers who had massive processing requirements that could no longer be met with punched card equipment were the first to jump to computers, which largely explains why civilian and military agencies of the U.S. government were the first major users of computers.

Displacing workers with office appliances was an issue that cropped up during the depression. Researchers concluded from one survey in the mid-1930s, which, perhaps, reflected extra sensitivity to the high unemployment during the Great Depression, that municipal governments had not laid off people when office appliances were installed. It cited the governments of Rochester, New York, and Newark, New Jersey, as examples. New York State's purchasing department not only installed new equipment but also requested permission to hire an additional ninety workers. Increased staffing was evident in other organizations as well.[28]

The automation debate hovered around many decisions to install tabulating equipment. Yet as these products acquired additional functions and increased speed or became operationally more reliable, additional users were found. For example, until printing tabulators appeared, accountants were reluctant to put their bookkeeping into this technology; they stuck with adding and accounting machines and books. However, by the late 1920s, printing tabulators were available, and the number of articles and books in the 1930s by accountants describing how they used punched card equipment increased substantially.

The same pattern was discernible as data entry began to merge with data processing. As more data was stored on cards, customers asked for and got new products that could transfer electrically, and with decreasing amounts of human intervention, information from one device to another while performing calculations, updating files, and generating reports. Various families of punched card equipment introduced, especially in the 1930s, reflected that pattern. Unknowingly, users were inching closer to the functions of a stored-program digital computer by systematizing applications of punched card equipment and, in the process, stretching to the limits the technical capabilities of such gear.[29]

The literature on the history of computers has largely been written by engineers and scientists who were more familiar with applications in their fields than in business, which creates the impression that the evolution of calculating and then computing devices was driven by the scientific community. In reality, the driving force came from a combination of the scientific/engineering worlds and business and government communities. However, although technological improvements could only come with contributions from scientists and engineers, they either worked on technologies in the 1920s and 1930s that were not widely applied until the 1940s and 1950s (relays, vacuum tubes) or were so limited in demand that the economic effect they had on the office appliance industry was miniscule (telephony, weather tracking, calculating differential equations). By the late 1940s and then beyond, as technologies became more complex, many improvements were driven by the scientific community, for example, parallel processing, paging, and fast chips, while customers asked for mass storage and higher level programming languages.

Minimizing the impact of scientists and engineers on the business side of the industry, that is to say, on the daily selling, installing, and use of equipment that supported industry, should not be confused with lack of interest in what scientists did because science and engineering were major sources of technical innovation. Executives of important office appliance firms saw scientists and engineers as useful contributors to the evolution of technology and applications. But they were viewed as delivering technologies and products that could later be useful to customers in business and government where real sales volumes and profits were to be made.

For instance, Watson developed a lifelong relationship with Columbia University that made it possible for Wallace John Eckert (1902–1971) to establish and run his Watson lab. There he used tabulating equipment in complex scientific applications and ran experiments to find new uses for such machinery. The experience at Columbia was repeated in other industries that invested in university-based research less out of any expectation of great sales than to accumulate technical knowledge for the future.[30] Interest in scientific markets came later with mini- and supercomputing. Vendors looked to commercial clients to define the nature of the market and treated government agencies as huge customers but scientists as small, usually underfunded allies. World War II, which brought a sharp increase in U.S. government involvement in defining needs and funding research on a massive scale, dramatically changed circumstances.[31]

Scientific and Engineering Uses

Scientists, mathematicians, and engineers were—and continue to be—users of computational equipment for many of the same reasons as those in commercial and government enterprises. They looked to such technology to ease the burden of an application's tedious or labor-intensive qualities, aspired to have information manipulated faster or in greater quantities than otherwise possible, and sought new insight into knowledge gained by comparing various pieces or quantities of data. But the differences between commercial and scientific users dictate why and how equipment was and continues to be used. Generally, commercial and administrative applications of punched card or computer equipment involved large amounts of data but relatively little computation. Scientific users required great computational capability and fewer volume data-handling functions, whereas the exceptions typically called for larger data-handling and computational capability than existing technologies could provide. With growing volumes of data or calculations came pressure to increase the capacity to store and manipulate information and the speed with which a job could be accomplished. These generalizations were as true for the 1920s and 1930s as for today. In large part, these characteristics provided much of the justification for development of the computer as another step in the ongoing process of expanding capacity, capability, and speed.[32]

Differences between scientific and commercial applications are important because scientists and engineers developed computers, not those working with commercial uses. One might argue that the computer grew out of their frustrating attempts to accomplish tasks that exceeded the capabilities of calculating machines and tabulators in the 1940s.

As early scientists, mathematicians, and engineers had to solve more complicated problems that required many calculations using the four basic arithmetic functions, the need to compute faster led most in this community to embrace adding machines and calculators from the 1890s onward. By the 1920s and 1930s, tabulating equipment became increasingly available to them through universities, government agencies, and corporate engineering and research departments. They found that tabulating equipment could do many jobs faster than desk top calculators. The only large impediment was cost; tabulating machines often required cash outlays in excess of what a laboratory could afford.

Technology, although an acceptance issue, was not as critical as the lack of adequate budgets. For instance, the IBM 601 could multiply and punch in 6 seconds. The same transactions on a desk calculator took closer to a minute, ten times as long, just for a simple transaction in which the user entered a multiplier, waited 15 seconds for the product, and then copied the result by hand on paper. By the end of the 1920s, those who understood both types of equipment could argue that productivity increased tenfold when users moved to the more expensive, complicated punched card equipment. As years passed, IBM also made available prepunched cards with mathematical data ready to use (e.g., logarithms, sines, and cosines). Users often went to an IBM punched card data center to rent time on machines or would, as they do today in university data centers, go to some central facility on campus to "run" their numbers after the day's normal commercial applications were completed.[33] For IBM and Remington Rand in the United States and Powers-Samas, Bull, and IBM in Europe, computational requirements and the slowly expanding size of the scientific community spelled some opportunity, if not as much as in the commercial world offered.

In the 1920s, astronomers needed to compute projections of flight patterns for stars and planets by iterative or analogous calculations of paths.[34] Ballistics experts needed more computing capability to calculate the trajectories of shells more accurately and rapidly.[35] Weather forecasters recognized the need for massive increases in computing power to do necessary mathematics with a given period but had to wait for the power of the computer. Thus the whole idea of "progressive digiting," an interactive method, called for the functions of a tabulator rather than a calculator. It was not enough to move to a tabulator; it had to be a fast one. Thus, an astronomical calculation involving 1.2 million implicit multiplications could be done on an IBM Type 405 accounting machine but ground on for 42 hours. On the IBM 601 the same job would have taken eight hundred hours.[36] A scientist could reasonably ask for more speed.

One of the first widely read proponents of the use of accounting machines in scientific applications was Leslie J. Comrie (1893–1950), the mathematician in charge of the British Nautical Almanac Office. He reported on the use of punched card equipment in Britain during the 1920s and 1930s and used many of the same arguments employed by commercial users: ease of use, speed, accuracy, and lower costs.[37] Others, for example, astronomers, also attempted complicated mathematical calculations and variable input volumes.[38] As superintendent of the Alamanac Office, Comrie was in a position to encourage use of such machines. In 1936, he left that job and established the Scientific Computing Service, expanding the use of such technology in both scientific and commercial applications. He is best known, however, for calculating the future positions of the moon with IBM equipment. In the project he used 500,000 cards, and the results caused other scientists to explore use of the technology.[39]

Scientists in the United States took an important step toward use of punched card machines when the Statistical Bureau at Columbia University, established in 1928–1929, mimicked Comrie's approach. Results and publicity again called attention to the benefits of such applications. Both Comrie's and Columbia's organizations did more to encourage scientists and engineers to use punched cards than any other force in the period 1928–1936. Afterward, enough had appeared in the academic press and sufficient numbers of individuals had worked with such equipment to lead historians to a few other locations that used scientific computing: the Massachusetts Institute of Technology (MIT), the Moore School of Electrical Engineering (University of Pennsylvania), and various government laboratories.[40]

At Columbia University the leading proponent of the use of punched card equipment was an astronomer, Wallace John Eckert (1902–1971). Eckert obtained grants of equipment and financial support for his university throughout the 1930s. Earlier, Watson and Dr. Benjamin D. Wood of Columbia worked jointly to establish the Statistical Bureau to which IBM gave equipment, including the one-of-a-kind IBM Difference Tabulator in 1929. It was used in educational and engineering applications. Eckert learned of the equipment and found ways to apply it and other devices in his study of astronomy. He went to work for the bureau and built up the laboratory, published on scientific computing, used punched card equipment in the 1930s, and encouraged scientists to use what was, by 1937, known as the Thomas J. Watson Astronomical Computing Bureau—a project involving IBM, Columbia, and the American Astronomical Society.[41]

IBM's interest grew out of a belief that if a university could develop and foster scientific applications for tabulating equipment, products would move into a scientific/engineering market. Another benefit would be suggestions from researchers for modification of products to better suit the needs of scientific customers. As one study noted, Watson's enthusiasm was an exception because "few universities or industrial laboratories obtained punched-card machines for their scientists."[42] Funding for research was never enough to justify creating other punched card laboratories, and so, whenever possible, scientists used existing administrative computing facilities or treked to Columbia and worked in Eckert's laboratory. In projects, researchers manipulated statistical data[43] and studied ballistics (also at government locations) and astronomy.[44] Most scientific calculations, still remained the preserve of less expensive, if slower, calculating machines.[45]

Engineers often still focused on formulas with exponential and trigonometric terms, which many tackled with handbook tables and slide rules. Yet their profession was rapidly changing in the early decades of the twentieth century to a mathematical discipline that relied on machines to compute. Sophisticated tools slowly became available in the 1920s and 1930s. The differential analyzer (an analog computerlike device), for example, was used at MIT to obtain numerical solutions to differential equations. However awkward it appeared, it allowed a few engineers to be trained in mechanical computation, some of whom went on to develop analog computing devices and digital computers.[46] But to put things in correct historical perspective, those engineers who had the opportunity to work either with MIT's equipment or traditional punched card gear were a minority in the 1930s; their opportunities came in the next decade. From the point of view of executives at IBM and Remington Rand, therefore, the scientific and engineering communities were incidental to commercial users.

Summary

Punched card equipment reached a broad user base in the 1920s for a far wider set of applications than evident in earlier decades. Once the machines were broadly accepted, demand fostered greater product innovation than before. Quality, function, and reliability improved while cost-effectiveness made these devices more attractive too.

Scientific and engineering communities, with their more unique requirements and often limited budgets, came to punched card equipment more slowly than commercial customers. Their experience mimed that of commercial customers in the first two decades of the twentieth century. Yet these communities contributed to the evolution of punched card equipment during the entire period of the interwar years and carried the burden of implementing technical innovations. Vendors gained sufficient strength to survive the effects of economic depression in the 1930s and to respond to their customers' enormous demand for products during World War II.

9

International Trade in Punched Card Machines

THE ROLE of international trade in the 1920s and 1930s was crucial to the successful expansion of information-processing vendors. Such trade gave manufacturers broader views of product requirements and a larger set of customers upon which to base their fortunes.

Because the American economy nurtured the tabulating equipment market, it is easy to forget that demand for punched card products existed internationally since the early 1900s. That world market may have been uneven in size, but once exposed to such products, customers in many countries bought them. Nowhere was this so obvious as in Europe, where preconditions for marketing such equipment were similar to those in the United States. Differences were more of degree than form. Because vendors operated primarily in the United States and earlier than in Europe, it is reasonable to expect higher sales volumes in the more fully exploited North American market than in Europe, Latin America, or Asia. The world market was not ignored however. Some of Hollerith's most important early contracts were signed by Europeans, and James Powers was scarcely in business in the United States before he sold in Europe well. World War I interrupted trade with Europe, but during the 1920s and 1930s, it was back to business as usual and expansion throughout the 1920s. Trade slowed, but did not cease, during the 1930s.

In 1910, a distributor of office and typing machines in Berlin, Willy Heidinger, established the Deutsche Hollerith Maschinen Gesellschaft mbH (DEHOMAG) as an agency to market Hollerith's products. BTM did the same in Britain. The Germans sold all over Europe, the British only in Britain and within the British Empire. Then in 1913, Powers set up subsidiaries in Europe: Società Machina Classificatrice Additionatrice (SIMCA) in France, another in Bulgaria, and licensed agents elsewhere, mostly in Britain.[1] By 1914, DEHOMAG had forty-four customers in Europe, Powers at least four; BTM's base remains unknown, but it was probably greater than the first two combined because the firm had been in business longer (it had fifty customers by 1918).

Following the war, all three vendors were still operating in Europe and some had agencies in Africa, Latin America, and the Orient. They had also started their own research and development. BTM and DEHOMAG began R & D before the war and subsequently expanded it in the 1920s and 1930s. Dialogue between developers in Europe and, in the case of IBM, American engineers made product lines international by the start of World War II.[2]

In the post–World War I period, C-T-R took the initiative by establishing a European headquarters in Paris managed by Andrew Jennings, a longtime employee who started out in the Bundy Manufacturing Company in the 1890s. Watson subsequently showed sufficient respect for the importance of the European market by visiting it each year and by naming some of the subsidiaries after himself.[3] Probably because of the lack of significant presence in Europe of any of these vendors and the confusion caused by the war to many segments of the local economy, expansion came quickly in the 1920s, especially to the aggressive Jennings. C-T-R established a subsidiary called SIMCO in France (1919) and licensed agents in Denmark, Sweden, Netherlands, Hungary, and Austria (1920). These agents operated in territories in addition to those managed by BTM and DEHOMAG. Powers's company in Germany (established in 1914) was a casualty of the war, along with operations in Bulgaria. Powers began its postwar thrust into Europe through the British Accounting and Tabulating Machine Company it had established in 1913 and with Società Machina Classificatrice Additionatrice (SIMCA) in Italy. Following C-T-R's tactic of licensing agents, it created Société Anonyme des Machines a Statistiques (SAMAS) and an agency in Belgium in 1919. Powers was back in the German market in 1923 with an agency. Thus, as in the United States, C-T-R and Powers competed for market share and volume. Their strategies were to expand coverage by increasing the number of agencies selling. DEHOMAG hired more salespeople and began producing its own products on behalf of C-T-R beginning with a horizontal sorter in 1920. That same year, DEHOMAG also ran the first training school for punched card equipment in Europe in Berlin.[4]

Customers for both firms were of the same kind as those in the United States: banks, utilities, railroads, large manufacturers, and governments. Applications were also similar: cost accounting and sales management, payroll, general ledger, and so forth. By the end of 1924, BTM had 100 customers whereas DEHOMAG managed an installed base of 116 tabulators and 100 sorters.[5] Powers had customers in most major European countries by the late 1920s. The prosperity generally enjoyed in Europe during the 1920s mirrored that in the United States in that it made possible increased demand for punched card products and for the same reasons: cost savings, convenience, and control.

But unlike in the United States, in Europe, a third, if very small, entrant emerged and in time became a serious rival. The predecessor of French Machines Bull began limited marketing after the war and became a fully established firm during the 1920s. As of 1926, all seventeen tabulating machines sold between 1922 and 1926 had been built by the firm's founder Frederick Rosing Bull (1881–1925). They were installed in Norway, Denmark, Finland, and Switzerland. After Bull's death, patents for the equipment eventually became the property of the H. W. Egli Company in Switzerland. This manufacturing firm grew into Machines Bull Company of France.

In 1927, with the formation of Remington Rand in the United States, Powers's European interests were taken over by the new firm, ensuring continued competition among the three companies.[6] In effect, Remington Rand left European operations as they were for the time being. By the end of the 1920s, IBM and Remington Rand had agents or direct sales offices in every country in Europe and in many Latin American cities as well. Equipment from one of the three major firms was installed in every European country except Turkey, Bulgaria, and Yugoslavia. Rivalry was not limited to the market either. Long, complex legal battles were fought over patent right infringements among the firms.[7]

European agencies were similar to those in the United States. Some were dedicated fully to selling one vendor's products; others also sold calculating and typing devices and, at least one in the Iberian Peninsula, also marketed Three-in-One Oil, Peerless automobiles, Eversharp lead pencils, Johnson wax, vacuum cleaners, and other items![8] Remington Rand responded overseas as in the United States to competitive initiatives taken by IBM more frequently than to any other vendor. Thus while IBM introduced the 80-column card, Remington Rand brought out its double-deck hole system worldwide. Bull conformed to the 80-column format rather than commit itself to the Remington Rand world or to the expense of developing its own system.

Despite what appears to be substantial expansion in the number of new agencies opened, overall market size remained small in the 1920s, starting at a lower base than in postwar America. European volumes grew, however, and business was profitable. In the case of IBM, European profits grew to 70–80 percent in 1927 over 1926 levels and experienced similar growth in 1928, the last year before the Great Depression began taking its toll. Yet in 1930 Jennings said, "I have long been of the opinion that the time will come when the European business will exceed that done in the United States of America."[9] Although optimistic and perhaps looking beyond immediate problems, his statement did reflect a positive mindset typical in this industry. Despite the existence of agencies all over the world, and small factories in Germany, France, and Britain, volumes remained low. In the peak year of 1935, net income for IBM from all overseas sales only amounted to $1.6 million. The bulk of resales came from tabulating cards.[10]

The depression created difficulties for this industry in both Europe and the United States. American vendors responded in part to the problem in Europe by servicing customers differently. They converted many existing agencies into company-owned operations, much as had been done in the United States during the 1920s. IBM, in addition to operations in Germany, Britain, and France,[11] opened subsidiaries in Finland, Norway, Belgium, Portugal, Yugoslavia, Poland, Hungary, Turkey, Bulgaria, and Japan to enhance control over market share while expanding sales coverage to match opportunities. It employed similar strategy in Latin America.

TABLE 9.1
IBM Products Marketed in Europe, 1930s

Device	Type
Numbering gang punch	501
Electric interpreter	550
Electric accounting machine	400
Summary punch	516
Alphabetical duplicating printing punch	030
Motor-driven duplicating punch	016
Automatic multiplying punch	600
Direct subtraction	285
Alphabetical printing punch	032
Test-scoring machine	805
Collator	077
Gang summary punch	507
Facsimile posting machine	954

Source: James Connolly, *History of Computing in Europe* (New York: IBM World Trade, 1967), 33.

Vendors' second response was to market the same product line on both sides of the Atlantic to simplify manufacturing, development, and cost controls. In short, they ran business at IBM and elsewhere on a global basis. For products available in the European market in the 1930s see table 9.1. Some products were assembled in Europe at company plants to avoid export taxes and transportation costs. In the same period, Powers marketed control punches, sight punches, alpha punches, adding punches, writing and duplicating punches, combinations of alpha punches and calculating typewriters, an adding punch–adding machine, and sorters—all on both sides of the Atlantic Ocean.[12]

Cie des Machines Bull appeared in 1932 as the reorganized third major competitor in Europe, a firm that would grow and survive to become, like its competitors, a major vendor of computer equipment later in the twentieth century. During the 1930s, it introduced a number of products including a horizontal sorter, printing tabulator (T50), electric alphametric tabulators types 36 to 120, and a calculator known as the C3. Despite the depression, the demand for new products did not wane sufficiently to halt product introductions.[13] Machines Bull claimed in mid-1933 that it had seventy-two customers in France, another three in Belgium, and one each in Italy, Switzerland, Denmark, and Argentina. All vendors expanded manufacturing in the 1930s. Even the Soviets began building equipment. The important German firm of Siemens (later a computer vendor) began assembling sorters for Powers. DEHOMAG went from less than five hundred installations at the start of the 1930s to more than one thousand by the end of the decade.[14]

How can one explain expansion in Europe, in the face of severe economic conditions? The office appliance industry was small, demand exceeded supply, and shrinkage of national economies was not sufficient to dry out the need for such equipment. In the United States, however, the market was more mature and, as will be seen later, the depression caused a decline in demand for tabulating equipment. This industry was so small in Europe when compared to segments like chemicals, agriculture, and general machine manufacturing, that it could, in effect, hide from economic shrinkage, much as adding and calculating machines and typewriters did during the depression years of the early 1890s in the United States. The ability to control expenses and tasks, increase usable information, and displace labor-intensive activities with faster, less expensive equipment would have advantages that were even more attractive in hard times. That equipment was rented and not sold eliminated the need for significant capital outlays or debt by customers and made possible contract cancellations should the machines not prove productive.

What gives credence to these thoughts is the assumption that customers in Europe were similar to those in the United States. They were similar in general and worldwide. Knowledge of the American customer can be ported to the European situation in general terms because the prewar markets were strikingly similar. Customers in Europe were also large organizations. Vendors marketed more to installed customers but did not ignore prospects; the latter simply did not contribute as much to a particular year's business. Major sets of customers were in business, industry, utilities, banking, insurance, and national governments. Many depended heavily on data manipulation to conduct their affairs. A list of specific customers suggests the breadth of the market that developed in Europe (see table 9.2). Customers depended on such technology despite the difficulties the depression created once applications had been converted from manual to machine processing. Tabulator sales volumes during the depression years offer the best proof of this dependence. As in the United States, where rental incomes for punches and tabulating equipment were either flat or declined, card sales remained strong or increased, which suggests that obtaining new customers was difficult but working with existing ones was easier.

When they compared their industry to others that experienced severe shrinkage, it is no wonder that executives in the office appliance market could be relatively optimistic in the 1930s both in Europe and in the United States. It was in that decade that Watson—always highly optimistic and always the consumate salesman—introduced his slogan "World Peace through World Trade," that was to grace company literature and even the sides of buildings for decades.[15]

European-based companies were not as effective in marketing products as their American counterparts throughout the interwar period, despite demand. BTM's historian convincingly has shown that both Powers and BTM were

TABLE 9.2
Major Users of Punched Card Equipment in Europe, Late 1930s

Customer[a]	Country	Vendor
Twentsche Bank	Netherlands	IBM
Milk Marketing Board	Britain	BTM
Stalina automobile plant	U.S.S.R.	IBM
Dispensarios Blancos	Spain	Powers
CAMPSA	Spain	IBM
Sickness Insurance for Vienna	Austria	Remington Rand
Gaz Electricity	Portugal	IBM
INA	Italy	Remington Rand
Savings Bank of Verona	Italy	IBM
Ministere du Travail	France	Bull
Staatsmijnen	Netherlands	Bull
Ministry of Finance	Greece	IBM
Gasworks of Budapest	Hungary	Remington Rand
Nestle	Switzerland	IBM
Alcohol Monopoly	Finland	Powers
Exchange Control Board	Denmark	IBM
Rumanian Government	Rumania	IBM

Source: Connolly, *History of Computing*, 35.
[a] Customers came from banking, insurance, automobile, iron, steel, manufacturing, utilities, petroleum, mining, food processing, governments, radio broadcasting, and service bureaus.

afflicted with weaker selling skills. Selling and marketing practices had the same structures as in the United States. But selling, particularly in Britain, "was generally conducted on amateurish lines" in very sharp contrast to the deadliness of purpose seen, for example, in the American IBM company.[16] The British could not be made into aggressive sales reps as easily as Americans, and he discounted the effectiveness of local management.[17] However, during the depression (1929–1932), BTM sales did not decline, the company simply failed to expand. Afterward, expansion reflected improving economic conditions and more advanced products. Indeed, BTM's historian characterized the period 1936–1939 as "the heyday of the punched-card-machine industry."[18] His evidence confirmed that for the United States, namely, that demand, both latent and explicit, was sufficient to support the punched card end of the office appliance industry.

Our understanding of the punched card business worldwide in this period is limited by lack of more than impressionistic evidence concerning Latin America, European colonies in Africa, and Asia as a whole. Although it would be reasonable to assume that large organizations in important urban centers had important tabulating machine installations and for the same applications as documented in the United States and in Europe, nonetheless, judgments will have to wait for further research on the office appliance business in these areas. However, the bulk of the picture concerning punched card sales in the 1920s and 1930s can rest comfortably on what is known of European and American patterns.

10

The Great Depression in the United States

IT IS ALMOST obligatory for historians of the interwar period to treat the Great Depression as a topic worthy at minimum of its own chapter, but in reality it represented a link between prosperous times and war days. The depression in the United States, which began at the end of the 1920s, remained intense until the mid-1930s and lingered until World War II presented a whole series of complications for the national economy that rippled with varying effects across each of its segments. The depression posed serious questions for economic historians, which have yet to be answered fully. On a parochial plane, what were the effects on the office appliance business? For data processing in general, what role did technology (or high technology-based products) play? Historians will entertain these and many other questions for a long time because it is becoming increasingly obvious that too little is known about the role of technology on the economy during this period. What little is known indicates that technology was more significant than previously understood.

Over the past two centuries in the Western world, societies adopted technological innovations, and dependence on them extended right through major periods of societal disruptions. In fact, some disruptions, like world and civil wars, sped up the adoption of new technologies whereas others, such as recessions and depressions, were only momentary irritants. Whenever a major national economic crisis occurred, senior executives in the office appliance industry, often with more than thirty years of experience, could be called upon to remember what had happened during the last crisis and to plan accordingly their responses. But they did not fully document their reactions; historians have only the evidence drawn from the marketing efforts of the firms. However, the economy's dependence on technology increased, which represents a possible unifying theme across both centuries.

Technology's role in hard economic times has not yet been adequately defined by historians. Although positions remain tentative on many points, consensus is growing that technological innovations came regardless of momentary economic difficulties because they increased centralized and controllable activities, even if they were inegalitarian in establishing a new economic order.[1] But at the same time there are conflicting opinions over whether technology always increases productivity or contributes to economic swings.[2] In the subsequent chapter, I will explore the specific responses of high-technology–based firms to the crisis, in part by presenting what annual reports offered and by suggesting some answers to the questions raised.

One ultimate reality of the Great Depression was that despite disruption and shrinkage in economic activities and the actions of governments and businesses, some buying and selling took place. Economic activity did not shut down 100 percent. Those elements considered most vital or most advantageously poised to survive in that portion of the economy still active were preserved. Where did data processing fit into this situation? To answer one must acknowledge that the study of the mechanized use of data, which focuses on applications, benefits, costs, and effects of such technology—which appears now to be a necessary core element for the operation of any twentieth-century economy—is critical to the overall discussion of the role of technology in the American economy, especially in times of great stress. Although it represents a narrow slice of the American economy, the information-processing segment of the office appliance industry nonetheless provides a view of the economy as a whole. More important than the actual number of dollars funneled through this industry is the fact that it had altered the fundamental capability of institutions to grow and control their own activities and organizations by the time of the Great Depression; thus a look at this industry offers a glimpse at the emerging infrastructure of organizations that dominated American economic activity in the decades following the Great Depression.

What happened to suppliers in the Great Depression speaks directly to the value the economy placed on control and feedback mechanisms derived from the better management of information. By studying the results of the economic crisis, the historian can examine the effects of depression on specific companies and establish some sense of their durability in difficult times. Some facts may have been known to executives at the time but subsequently lost to historians. As I indicated in chapter 9 and will reinforce in the next five chapters, institutions valued information-handling tools even in the most difficult times, both in depression and in war.

If measured by the short-term impact of economic behavior in the early 1930s alone, data processing was not as significant as, for example, the very large agricultural sector of the economy. What appears most obvious is that although the depression hit hardest much larger, better established sectors, causing significant shifts in governmental policies along with actual redistribution of wealth and people, data processing's role was to facilitate some of these changes. Put another way, the social policies of the New Deal would not have been implemented in as cost-effective a manner without punched card equipment to manage payroll deductions, unemployment insurance, and massive welfare programs.

There is no evidence to suggest that adoption of office equipment did more than slow down in this period. Data from earlier periods indicate that during the recession of the 1870s the industry was not established well enough to be affected, but by the recession in the 1890s, information-handling technology had begun to offer control and the promise of cost efficiencies with minimal capital outlay. Therefore, business continued to adopt it. During the Great Depression, the long-term trend of adopting such technology continued. The numbers of punched card equipment flattened and momentarily dipped, but with the actual implementation of New Deal programs by the mid-1930s, social policy rescued the balance sheets of all major vendors in the industry. As evidence will show, this response was true also of calculators and, to a lesser extent, typewriters.

A few statistics suggest the severe impact of the world depression on technology's rate of acceptance and the challenge posed to office equipment suppliers. Despite swings down and then up in overall economic activity during the 1920s, industrial production throughout the world reached a level in 1929, 48 percent above that of 1913 (as measured in constant dollars). American growth in productivity was spurred outside traditional economic sectors by including new ones: automobiles, electricity, and rubber. But for three years between that peak year and 1932, those productivity gains were all but lost in the United States and Germany, leaving the output of goods worldwide in 1932 actually below that of 1913. Despite much hype to the contrary, the New Deal programs never brought the nation back to 1929 levels; World War II did that. In fact, between 1939 and 1944, the U.S. GNP increased by 125 percent while the volume of manufacturing almost tripled.[3]

IBM's situation suggests the pattern for the period. Revenues rose continually during the 1920s, peaking at some $20.3 million in 1931. So it managed to continue growing during the early stages of the depression. But then it felt the results, causing revenues to decline to $17.6 million in 1933.[4] In short, IBM's commercial customers resisted acquiring more as prospects waited. However, after 1933, New Deal programs began to be implemented, creating significant additional demand for information management upon which IBM was able to capitalize. Although well-established government agencies accounted for some of this new demand, a great deal of it came from new agencies, such as the Social Security Administration (SSA), which led to enormous increases in sales.[5] In IBM's case, demand pushed 1937's revenues to $31.7 million. The company closed the books in 1940 with $45.3 million in revenues. Profits went from $1.4 million in 1922 to $9.1 million in 1939, while retained earnings jumped from $5.9 million to $28.7 million.[6] IBM, in short, was now a major vendor within the industry and was rapidly headed toward a similar status within the economy at large. Although the Great Depression slowed economic activity momentarily, on balance the company— hence the tabulating machine business generally—grew. Customer dependence on such technology was so great that they could not fall back on older methods.[7] While machine rentals dropped for IBM and Remington Rand, card sales remained strong. At the worst moments of the depression, IBM sold 100 million cards per year at $1.40 per thousand. That performance grew until, for example, in 1938, out of its total revenues of $34.7 millions, card sales brought in $5 million and were the most profitable items in the product line.[8]

By 1934, the worst of the depression seemed over, and industry leaders were becoming increasingly optimistic. All the major vendors anticipated that older equipment, not replaced over the previous several years, would begin to wear out, particularly typewriters. They introduced a raft of new alternatives in anticipation of new demand and increased competition. This was as true for IBM as for Addressograph-Multigraph, Underwood-Elliott-Fisher, Burroughs, NCR, and others. Significant increases in sales revenues in 1934 over those in 1933 that ranged from 20 to 80 percent seemed proof positive that better times were ahead.[9]

All accounts of the period also pointed to the increased role of the U.S. government as a factor to be reckoned with. One contemporaneous writer noted that "the New Deal in business competition requires the keeping of records in more detail and in greater variety than ever before." Specifically, the National Recovery Administration (NRA) was "making us a nation of cost accountants."[10] The NRA, SSA, all the armed forces, the Agricultural Adjustment Administration (AAA), the Civilian Conservation Corps (CCC), and others were solid IBM customers; indeed, the government had become IBM's largest customer by the end of the decade, replacing railroads and insurance companies. IBM depended heavily on it for significant sources of revenues for decades to come. By the mid-1930s some four hundred IBM tabulators and sorters were on rent to government agencies.[11] IBM gained market share during the 1930s at the expense of others, particularly Remington Rand but also from vendors of large accounting machines (e.g., Underwood, NCR, and Burroughs). Remington Rand did not win the SSA contract or any other major government bid because their products were more costly and less technologically advanced than IBM's at bid time and were not marketed as effectively.

Competition remained stiff, but investors liked the results. In 1934, stocks of all major office equipment suppliers (NCR, IBM, Underwood-Elliott-Fisher, Burroughs, Remington Rand, Addressograph-Multigraph, and Dictaphone) collectively outperformed the market and, in at least the case of IBM, the corporation paid dividends throughout the depression.[12] The last thing Watson wanted was to be shut out of sources of capital as he constantly refurbished IBM's product line and preserved intact manufacturing and marketing organizations. Thus the combined strategy of keeping the manufacturing force together (e.g., at IBM) or of introducing new, effective products (Burroughs and IBM) made it difficult for less competitive companies (e.g., Remington Rand) to keep pace. Survivors and thrivers were those who were able to expand their customer bases in the only direction that spending took place—U.S. government agencies—and the first to get there happened to be IBM.

During the U.S. depression, Britain experienced disastrous economic conditions, with unemployment jumping from 1.5 million to 2.5 million in 1930–1931. Equipment sales of all types declined by 60 percent, but by 1933, rapid recovery became evident, and by 1936, sales were back to predepression levels. As in the United States, tabulating revenues, declined momentarily but did not dip as much as income from other types of office equipment primarily because the practice of leasing rather than selling, in the words of BTM's historian, "smoothed out the troughs and peaks experienced by the rest of the office-appliance industry."[13] Sales to government agencies were important but did not have the same apparent effect as in the United States. In the rest of Europe, sales of tabulating equipment services dipped but, again, less than in other segments of the industry.

In summary, the evidence suggests that momentary worldwide declines in revenues were caused by customers who attempted to get by with the minimum amount of data-processing equipment. Because large organizations relied on equipment that absolutely needed cards to manage, control, and operate administrative processes, companies could not afford to drop below a minimum level of dependence without jeopardizing their existence or competitive posture. The response of the New Deal administration of President Franklin D. Roosevelt to the economic crisis was more control and vast spending programs to reenergize the economy. These initiatives created significant demand for information-control products that existing companies, such as IBM and Remington Rand, could supply, especially IBM. Finally, enhancements to product lines continued across the industry in rapid response to new market conditions in the mid-1930s. The industry had made it through yet another economic crisis in the same way as before: by offering control over costs and administrative efficiencies and cost-effective leased products and expanding into new market segments.

11

IBM and Powers/Remington Rand

IN THE INTERWAR period, the history of tabulating equipment sales was dominated by IBM and Powers/Remington Rand. Where they simply well-run companies? Or, were they firms that happened to be at the right place at the right time? The same charge would be levied again in the 1980s against those selling microcomputers and software. What influence did demand, economic conditions, and the availability of technology have on these companies? How did they come to dominate the distribution of what, in hindsight, was a crucial technology? These questions strike at the very nature of the information-handling business of the 1930s and 1940s. These two company cases also suggest a model of behavior that others in the industry emulated later.

The Case of IBM

Students of IBM's history always have been fascinated by how the company did so well, became a major player first in the office appliance industry and then in the data-processing industry, and made the *Fortune* 500 list as one of the largest corporations in the world. Many have almost implicitly argued the inevitability of IBM's success.

Many explanations have been offered for this success. One argument holds that IBM was in the right place at the right time.[1] A favorite approach employs the "great man theory" of history: Watson was a man of vision with a plan that worked.[2] To IBM's enemies and critics, the company ruthlessly crushed its competitors while restraining trade in its favor.[3] Many think that IBM was a well-managed company.[4] It was recognized as having good sales personnel.[5] Some suggest that the company was influenced by a series of factors that worked in its favor.[6]

True, IBM had a competent chief executive officer in Thomas Watson. He did craft an organization that developed good management, sound marketing, and effective salespeople, and his executives watched the balance sheet. Fortunately for the firm, its important organizational childhood (1920s) coincided witht the period when receptivity to information-processing equipment expanded sharply for all vendors. In 1929, Watson was able to note that his equipment had been placed in only one out of every five organizations that realistically could use them. Although such observations coupled to substantial increases in sales from year to year suggest opportunity, his was still a very small company.

All available evidence points to the effectiveness of having a corporate strategy that works as opposed to simply allowing market conditions to control business rhythms opportunistically. In reality, a combination of the two increases a company's ability to thrive and compete; IBM was simply an early example.[7] Otto E. Braitmeyer, vice-president of sales during the early years of IBM, imposed a philosophy on the company often quoted by IBM executives as "make your plans and then work your plans."[8] It was a mindset of control and purposefulness that attempted to minimize the effects of others' attempts to dictate market conditions or cause the company to operate reactively. Abhorrence of reacting as opposed to responding proactively remained one of the fundamental characteristics of IBM's culture deep into the twentieth century. If there was a difference between IBM and other companies in the industry during the 1920s and 1930s, it was that Watson's organization implemented restructuring earlier and, perhaps, more effectively than most.

Usually, companies develop strategies out of their experiences with previous ones; in effect, they correct ineffectiveness and experiment with new approaches while they improve existing ones. In this respect, IBM was no different. Watson, Braitmeyer, and others in the small, young company had worked in larger organizations (some, for instance, at NCR) and thus had been exposed to a more disciplined approach to market analysis and product development than one might expect in a firm as small as C-T-R. Therefore, it was no surprise that from the earliest days of the firm, practices commonly seen at such companies as NCR or Burroughs would be employed.[9] One crucial feature included formal statements of which markets to serve. Watson and his small staff elected to focus resources increasingly on the information-handling market (tabulating equipment and cards) during the first fifteen years of his management (1914–1929).[10] IBM shed unprofitable products and, more importantly, nonstrategic items, a process that took an additional fifteen years to accomplish. It dropped meat scales, time-recording clocks, microphones, radio equipment, podiums, and sundry "office" supplies. Increasingly, in their stead, a sales rep's product manual was filled with punched card equipment, related parts, and a variety of card products.[11]

With increased focus on a narrower market, IBM came to understand better customer needs and, hence, responded more effectively with the kinds of practices noted earlier.[12] Concurrently, management emphasized selling to the company's traditional punched card customers: large organizations. It sold products less often to very small companies and agencies. Powers sought large customers, too, but also attempted to go after market segments ignored by Watson. The customer set IBM sought was overlaid by a growing network of direct salespeople who, by the mid-1920s, sold the company's entire product line. Specialized product sales reps were phased out and replaced by representatives who ran a general territory. Territory salespeople came to know the features of the entire product line and operated with good sales skills. Those developments made it possible for IBM to react quickly to changing circumstances throughout the 1920s and profit from a boom that was not completely appreciated or understood until it was well under way.

"Plan your work and work your plan" was both a top down and a bottom up approach that increased focus where it had to be. It facilitated management's coordination of activities across the entire company from sales to manufacturing and from sales rep to chairman. It worked well at IBM, allowing the company to emerge from the 1920s as an organization better prepared to survive the 1930s than its rivals, some of whom were newly organized (e.g., Remington Rand).

It is difficult to imagine a time when IBM was small; but indeed it was, despite successes during World War I. It began the 1920s still fragmented into four little firms that made up C-T-R, each with its own sales force or collection of agents and manufacturing and accounting organizations. Much manufacturing was farmed out to vendors or manufacturing companies (e.g., Western Electric). There were few sales offices and the product line did not always respond to the needs of the office appliance industry. Monthly sales were erratic, which must have encouraged more purposeful planning because too much variability in performance would have been an anathema in such a company culture. In 1922, for example, Otto Braitmeyer was told that production of keypunches varied from a low of forty-one units per month to a high of ninety-nine with monthly swings in volumes. That year the company added more than nine hundred units to its inventory of rentable machines. Verifiers in the same period were built at the rate of anywhere from four to twenty-eight per month with the average closer to nineteen to twenty-four; more than two hundred were made that year.[13]

According to the U.S. Department of Justice, by the end of 1935, IBM had installed in the United States 4,303 calculating machines, 4,106 sorters, and 8,412 punched card devices and had sold some 4 billion cards. Translated into percentage of market share, IBM had under lease or rent 85.7 percent of all installed tabulating machines. The government maintained that IBM also controlled 86.1 percent of all sorters and 81.6 percent of all punches; these figures were never vigorously challenged by IBM.[14] During the same period, the centerpiece of IBM's cash and profits—cards—continued to be lucrative, with sales growing from $2.6 million in 1926 to approximately $4 million during the mid-1930s. This data suggests that the focused approach to the market had been effective and that it was still small.

IBM's net income and profits and, for perspective, selective sales, during the interwar period are given in table 11.1. It was an enviable record of ex-

TABLE 11.1
IBM Net Income, Net Profit, and Select Sales Revenues, 1919–1941 (dollars in millions)

Year	Net Income[a]	Net Profits[b]	Sales Revenue[c]	Year	Net Income[a]	Net Profits[b]	Sales Revenue[c]
1919	2.5	2.5	—	1931	7.4	11.4	20.3
1920	2.4	2.4	16.0	1932	6.4	10.6	18.4
1921	1.6	1.6	10.6	1933	5.7	10.1	17.6
1922	1.8	3.1	10.7	1934	6.6	11.0	21.0
1923	2.2	3.6	—	1935	7.0	12.2	21.9
1924	2.5	4.0	—	1936	7.5	9.1	26.2
1925	3.5	5.0	—	1937	8.0	10.4	31.8
1926	4.5	6.0	—	1938	8.7	10.8	34.7
1927	5.3	6.9	—	1939	9.1	11.4	39.5
1928	5.3	8.3	19.7	1940	9.4	13.1	46.3
1929	6.7	10.0	19.4	1941	9.8	19.5	62.9
1930	7.4	11.0	20.3				

Source: *Moody's Manual of Investments*, 1919–1941; IBM Annual Reports, 1923–1941. Annual reports of IBM reflected these patterns and often slightly different data than reported by Moody's but not sufficiently different to alter performance assessments. Variations in accounting reporting suggests why historians of the company have never reported IBM's performance in such complete tabular form.

[a] Net income (earnings) was defined in this period as net profit less maintenance, depreciation, and so forth.

[b] All data were publicly available; blanks for net profits in 1920s was the result of lack of reporting by CTR/IBM.

[c] The same was true for sales in late 1930s.

pansion and growth, with revenues doubling between 1922 and 1929, dipping momentarily during the hardest period of the Depression, then doubling again by the end of the 1930s, riding the wave of New Deal customers. By the end of the 1930s, IBM was the largest firm operating in the business machine market in the United States. As illustrated in tables 11.2 and 11.3, the only firm outstripping it in revenues was Remington Rand, which generated sales from many other products besides office machines (e.g., safes, paper items, and typewriters).[15] IBM's growth in revenues and, especially, profits was consistent, particularly in the 1920s.

Leasing contributed significantly to IBM's success. IBM encouraged customers to try equipment and, during the depression, made it possible for them to use such hardware without capital expenditures. Powers also had a rental strategy, whereas many other office appliance vendors simply sold outright or offered both purchase and rent options. Rentals illustrate how IBM coordinated accounting practices, manufacturing flexibility, and marketing strategies. The process worked so well that renting/leasing remained the central focus to IBM's offerings for hardware until the end of the 1970s, when ac-

TABLE 11.2
Comparative Statistics for Selected Business Machine Firms, 1928, 1939
(dollars in millions)

	1928			1939		
Company	Revenue	Profit	Rank[a]	Revenue	Profit	Rank[a]
Burroughs	32.1	8.3	1	32.5	2.9	3
IBM	19.7	5.3	4	39.5	9.1	1
NCR	49.0	7.8	2	37.1	3.1	2
Remington Rand	59.6	6.0	3	43.4	1.6	5
Underwood-Elliott-Fisher	19.0	4.9	5	24.2	1.9	4

Source: Annual issues of *Moody's Industrial Manual*.
  [a] Ranking by largest profits earned. Note the sharp declines of major firms over the ten years and the significant position of IBM's profits compared to others in 1939.

TABLE 11.3
Comparative Rankings within the Top Two Hundred
U.S. Corporations by Size and by Value of Assets, 1930
(dollars in millions)

Rank within Top Two Hundred	Firm	Assets
118	Remington Rand[a]	68.4
155	National Cash Register	52.1
171	International Business Machines	43.6
175	Burroughs Adding Machines[a]	42.9
191	Underwood-Elliott-Fisher	38.3

Source: Chandler, *Scale and Scope*, 649.
  [a] In 1917, only two of the top two hundred firms in the U.S. were in the office appliance business: Remington Typewriters and Burroughs.

counting and tax practices merged with new economies of scale and realities in the market to dictate other approaches. Thus renting and leasing were some of the oldest and most important business practices in the industry. IBM excepted its small items, like clocks, electric typewriters, cabinets, and so forth, which were only sold but represented a decreasing portion of the total revenue of the firm. IBM's definitions of rent and leasing varied over time, but essentially rent was a lease that ran from thirty to ninety days whereas a lease represented a commitment for one or more years.

By leasing at fixed annual rentals, profits did not have to be calculated on the number of devices built in a given year but on the number of machines in use on rent/lease. Machines were carried on the books as capital assets while new ones were built with profits derived from rented and leased equipment. In 1922–1933, on average IBM paid out only 50 percent of its net profits in common dividends. It eliminated a debt of $5.9 million while funding expansion. Working capital dropped from $4.2 million in 1922 to $3.6 million in 1933, which at either amount remained adequate for company needs given that IBM also had recurring income from rentals and leases.[16]

The business appliance world of the 1920s and 1930s shared many characteristics evident in other industries that influenced IBM. The most visible was the dominance of key executives over their firms. They were often well known to the reading public both within corporate America and in their own industries partly because they stayed in power so long. Watson ran his company from 1914 to the mid-1950s. Joseph Boyer managed Burroughs from 1905 to 1930, while at Remington Rand, James H. Rand, Jr., presided from 1926 to 1968. They were princes of their industries. Many presidents and vice-presidents were also in positions of authority for decades, reinforcing the culture of continuous management. Ahead of all executives in this industry in name recognition and identification of a company with an individual was Watson. The *New York Times* called him "an industrial giant," while *Time* magazine said he was one of the most astute businessmen in the world. *Forbes* saw him as a "master salesman," and *Fortune* acknowledged that he was a visionary.[17]

The leading historian of the company, Robert Sobel, gave Watson high marks for creative management, noting, "he was considered an unusually enlightened and intelligent industrial tycoon, one of a new breed who not only understood the nature and potential of modern technology and the importance of planning, organization, and efficiency but realized that cooperation with government was necessary and could prove beneficial."[18] In short, the story of tabulating machines and its industry of the 1920s and 1930s rapidly became very intertwined with IBM and Watson.

The Case of Powers/Remington Rand

From the days of the U.S. Census of 1910 Powers and Hollerith competed, chasing the same customers around the world. The institutional history of Powers—later part of Remington Rand—when coupled to IBM's, provides almost the entire story of tabulating machine vendors. Little historical research has been done, however, on the Powers Accounting Machine Corporation, except as an aside to Hollerith,[19] even then only for the period before the mid-1920s. Yet Powers accounted for about 10 to 15 percent of the tabulating machine business by the end of the 1920s. That market share equated in revenues to an estimated $2.2 million in 1934. In the face of inadequate data to the contrary, one suspects that Powers's revenues were higher when taking into account European operations. Yet one fact is incontestable: IBM perceived Powers as a major competitive threat long before the rival became part of Remington Rand. IBM also considered Burroughs and various typewriter firms as threats because they sold products in IBM's market as well. Clearly, Powers concerned Watson because it had good products and an adequate size to compete. When Remington Rand was formed with Powers as part of it in 1927, the threat became potentially far greater because two titans were battling in the industry with broad product lines that went beyond mere punched card equipment.

James Powers, it will be recalled, worked for the Bureau of the Census and developed for that agency tabulating equipment for the census of 1910. He then formed his own company in 1911, with excellent sorters and tabulators. Throughout the 1920s, both Powers and IBM competed, which kept prices and functions comparable. Powers thrived on both sides of the Atlantic, making it an attractive takeover candidate. When the creators of Remington Rand began to put together their organization in the second half of the 1920s, they looked for companies that would enhance the new firm's position across the entire office equipment market. Powers was a logical choice.

Remington Rand was largely the work of James Henry Rand (1886–1968) who, helped by friends on Wall Street and within academic circles, put together a company that could market a broad product line covering all large sectors of the office appliance industry: his Kardex systems, typewriters, adding machines, and Powers' tabulating equipment. The conglomerate also included other devices and products when it opened its doors in 1927 as Remington Rand. As first formed, it comprised thirteen old companies consolidated to five and then merged into the new firm. By 1932, it employed eleven thousand people backed by 3.8 million square feet of manufacturing facilities. On paper at least, a major new corporation had been born on January 25, 1927.[20]

However, all during 1927 additional pieces were put into place, including Powers, which officially became part of the new empire on November 3, 1927. The initial process of acquiring one company or another continued through 1933.[21] Consolidations within the firm faced it with the same kinds of problems it experienced more than a half-century later with the merger of Sperry (successor to Remington Rand) and Burroughs in the 1980s into Unisys: multiple product lines with redundant goods, services, and expenses; internal competition for resources, for example, R&D; and split focus from senior management. In the late 1920s, management elected initially to leave Powers alone to function as before; in time, its activities were more integrated into the new company. The legal battles in Europe over punched card patents were resolved in the fall of 1934 when Siemens and Halske A.G. allowed Remington Rand to market products in Europe called Powers-Siemens & Halske equipment, sold in Germany by Powers GMBH.[22]

Low profit margins in an increasingly competitive industry made consolidations of the type initiated by Remington Rand attractive. It first became a recognizable pattern with typewriter manufacturers and then with adding and tabulating machine vendors. The economies of scale made possible by consolidation were also real provided that true integration of marketing and manufacturing could take place—a process that eluded Remington Rand during the 1930s. Nonetheless, it had become a large company with sales by the end of 1928 reaching $60 million. As suggested in table 11.2 (p. 153), Remington Rand's potential economic power was enormous, provided that the firm rationed resources, which were so diversely spread from Kardex systems to paper, three-ring binders to adding machines and tabulating gear. In sharp contrast to IBM, a firm that had already integrated most of its operations, Remington Rand's sales were two-thirds greater but profits were closer together ($5.3 million for IBM versus Remington Rand's $6 million), hinting of possible profits proportionately larger if properly organized, managed, and committed to a focused market.[23]

The feeling at the time, particularly in the business press, was that Remington Rand could fully displace giants in the office machine market, NCR and Burroughs, chase IBM, and do it all within a few years. Its anticipated dominance failed to materialize when the depression and management's inability to organize effectively led the firm to lose market strength, especially to IBM. By 1939, IBM was in second place after Remington Rand. NCR held third position with $37.1 million in sales and, like Burroughs in fourth position with $32.5 million, was better placed than the new giant with its sales force organized and coordinated with manufacturing. To jump ahead a little, by the end of World War II, IBM had annual sales of $141.7 million, Remington Rand $132.6 million. IBM's assets (net worth) and earnings had now far exceeded Remington Rand's. Both companies, however, were giants facing a decade of battle over many products not the least of which was the computer when it became commercially viable.[24]

Summary

The experiences of these two firms in the interwar period were partially duplicated by typewriter firms, of which four companies were the major providers. Typewriters were more of a commodity item that sold on price and availability and, only marginally, on functional differences. On the other hand, the kinds of goods sold by Powers and IBM were complicated and required far more skill to operate. Therefore, both vendors and customers needed to make considerable investments in staffing to sell, maintain, and use such devices effectively. The cost in capital required to fund rental inventory of machines as expensive as tabulators and assorted peripherals precluded entry into the punched card market for many; in sharp contrast, many vendors existed in the typewriter market. Manufacturing remained more complex; product lines were carried on a vendor's books as assets, not as inventory as with typewriter firms. It also took years to develop manufacturing and marketing staffs to sell and install these products. Thus a series of circumstances led the punched card business to be essentially the story of IBM versus Remington Rand and distinct from the world of typewriters.

The abilities of both firms were a function of economic prosperity and the desire of large organizations to control events through better management of large bodies of data. Both grew because of their ability to respond reasonably well to specific customer requirements. IBM had the edge in superior marketing, but both had responsive manufacturing and product development. Each nurtured their loyal bases of customers and made them dependent on their brand of technology, ensuring a revenue stream from year to year. The exception was IBM's ability to take opportunity for future customers away from Powers. Revenue streams made it possible for both to develop new products and to enhance their offerings with additional lines of goods and services (as at Remington Rand) or to expand market coverage (as at IBM). Remington Rand's senior executives reacted to the market very much as did those at IBM in the 1920s and 1930s. Both were successful, grew, and were well positioned to take advantage of the unique opportunities presented by World War II.

12

Other Accounting Machines and Their Uses

THE NEAT classification implied by IBM leasing tabulating machines, NCR offering cash registers, and other parties distributing typewriters breaks down when one looks at the market for adding machines, calculators, and other accounting equipment. Companies sold such machines with an enormous diversity of products to a wide variety of customers, both single users and in quantity to large firms. Companies in the office appliance industry were multidimensional in that some were fully integrated and vertical, building, selling, and maintaining a combination of products that ranged across many segments of the industry. Remington Rand was an example but so too was Burroughs, which sold adding machines, calculators, and various other equipment. Burroughs was chased by an NCR eager to broaden its base. Vendors of diversified product lines numbered in the dozens; tabulator suppliers numbered only two in the United States.

Industry Structure

While IBM and Remington Rand said grace over the future market for computers by selling tabulating equipment, punched cards were only a small part of the industry in the 1920s and 1930s. To put things into a quick perspective, IBM's sales in 1930 for all products and services totaled $20.3 million while Powers added an additional $1.7 million to $2 million. The U.S. government estimated that the office appliance industry as a whole that year shipped products valued at $165.3 million. In 1937, IBM's total revenues for all products and services reached $31.9 million while for the entire office appliance industry it had climbed to $204.9 million.[1] Because of the enormous variety of products in other segments of the office appliance industry, almost all office workers were potential customers, and that community was growing fast. The office appliance segment of the market employed an expanding number of workers who made, sold, and serviced an ever-growing variety of products. By 1927, seventy-eight thousand employees worked in the industry, and in 1930, that figure had grown by another 14.9 percent.[2]

Understanding market segments within this industry is important because of the variety of offerings. The year 1925 offers the first vantage point from which to view customers and segments (see table 12.1). The market was

TABLE 12.1
Important Types of Information-handling Hardware, circa 1925

Accounting and Tabulating	Check certifiers, endorsers
Adding	Check protectors and writers
Adding machine–cash and credit registers	Credit registers
Adding machine–cash registers	Dictating
Autographic cash registers	Duplicating
Billing	Intercommunicating systems
Bookkeeping	Photocopying
Calculating	Time-recording
Cash registers	Typewriters

Source: William H. Leffingwell, *The Office Appliance Manual* (Chicago: National Association of Office Appliance Manufacturers, 1926).

complex, with many classes and models of different sizes, options, and functions, adding up to hundreds of available products. Definitions of all the permutations filled hundreds of pages in catalogs of the period.[3] However, the important products were the adding and calculating machines and associated billing and accounting (bookkeeping) devices. Closely tied to these were typewriters and cash registers; but as the 1920s and 1930s passed, their importance for the history of data processing declined. However, IBM competed against Remington Rand over typewriters very strenuously, and by World War II, IBM had the emerging electrical typewriter market pretty much to itself. Their competition over typewriters publicized and enhanced their rivalry in more data-processing oriented markets as well. Leading typewriter and cash register companies increasingly expanded their product lines into the broader area of information handling, and for this reason, I will examine NCR later.

Large Accounting Machines: Uses and Types

Accounting machines (also called bookkeeping machines during the 1920s and 1930s) were used to enter data on forms and then to perform normal accounting calculations. They could be used to prepare balances and print results. The reasons for using such equipment were, as before World War I, to take advantage of the "savings resulting from the elimination of unnecessary operations, the assurance of greater accuracy through perfect accounting control, and making the work easier for the personnel engaged in performing."[4] These machines reached a high point of development during the 1920s and 1930s and modifications continued down to the end of the 1950s. Advertisements used the term "accounting machines" deep into the 1960s, although by then vendors were marketing either computers or accounting de-

12.1 A Burroughs Automatic Bookkeeping Machine in use in 1933 (Burroughs Papers, courtesy Charles Babbage Institute).

vices with computerlike technologies and functions. The device from before World War II illustrated in figure 12.1 suggests kinship to the typewriter and adding machine.[5]

Scores of different uses—all related to accounting and finance and the posting and recordkeeping associated with them—drove demand for such variations. Competitive pressure and a growing demand for niche applications (e.g., for just insurance, utility billing, and banking) provided incentives for vendors to enter the market to offer additional products. The demand for niche products also was true of adding and calculating machines. Large accounting machines were used in many sectors of the economy: banks, in particular; insurance companies almost as much; then railroads; payroll departments of large organizations; governments; and retail firms.[6]

Bookkeeping machines competed head-on with another accounting process—punched cards. This market comprised IBM's way (punched cards) or everyone else's (accounting machines). By World War II, IBM's way was chosen most often. The punched card option should not be confused with sales for accounting applications that used accounting and calculating machines because that was an entirely different market. For large accounting requirements, a customer could elect to use punched cards from the two vendors in the United States or the three in Europe or to use bookkeeping machines from various companies that came and went on both sides of the Atlantic.

Bookkeeping machines were so varied in size and function that they could be used more selectively and for smaller applications as well as large. Thus besides competing in areas usually inhabited by Powers or IBM, they played well with smaller customers. To complicate matters more, customers who used equipment from Powers and IBM also employed bookkeeping machines and adding and calculating devices. Banks, for example, used IBM equipment for companywide applications and specialized accounting machines for backroom processing or for managing something as simple as a savings account passbook. A variety of specialized equipment sold to niche markets and, hence, to a larger mass of customers than IBM could reach with tabulating equipment (see table 12.1). With so many firms and customers by the end of the 1930s, the phrase "accounting machine" could be used to describe devices for either approach; however, in the 1920s, it was more associated with punched card equipment.[7] Major categories of other devices included billing machines used to generate invoices, check protectors and writers for banks and accounts payable departments, cash registers, duplicating machines, and addressing machines (e.g., those sold by Addressograph-Multigraph, known in the 1920s as Addressograph Company). Time-recording devices were also sold by many vendors and provided data-gathering capabilities that influenced the design and marketing of other products.[8]

Larger vendors of bookkeeping machines included Burroughs, Dalton Adding Machine Company (later part of Remington Rand), Federal Adding Machines, Sundstrand Adding Machines, Elliott-Fisher, Remington Rand after 1927, Underwood Typewriter, and NCR. Remington Typewriter Company marketed such devices before it merged into the larger Remington Rand. Customers asked each firm to build machines to perform specialized work. Suppliers had to educate customers about specific features of their machines, suggest how best to use them, and provide a systematized approach to accounting problems. The key was to adapt a machine to a particular customer's problems. A normal sale, therefore, involved taking into account the individuality of each customer and the complexity of that prospect's accounting problems. As with tabulating machine sales, a direct marketing force, who could sell well and were trained in the functions and uses of specific machines, had to propose, install, and train customers, then maintain and repair the equipment. Thus "sell cycles"—a sales term—could be as short as two months or as long as several years.[9]

Customers in the 1920s and 1930s acquired products that obviously delivered considerable productivity and which could be important to the timeliness and efficiency of an organization. From a vendor's perspective, it was also a complex, expensive process to produce precision-built devices. Expenses were compounded because machines were leased or rented, which placed the risk of obsolescence on the vendor as newer devices appeared from competitors. With purchase to rent ratios of 56–60 months:1, which suggests that machines had to be rented for five years to recapture cost and assigned profit, vendors had to design products that could not be displaced sooner. Both customers and vendors looked to these devices as long-term commitments to the way an organization managed specific applications. Thus it was not so onerous to think in terms of five years, even if leases were for less. But to reach a profit target that might stretch to five years (with breakevens of less than four years)[10] vendors had to make sure that products matched critical customer needs. While vendors staffed branch offices with salespeople knowledgeable about applications, customers populated accounting departments with people that were comfortable using specific machines. Vendors always helped with formal training programs.[11] Burroughs also tried using agents and dealers to sell such products and, to help them, operated a "systems department" from 1907 to 1937. This department had the sole mission to help sell applications and was an early example within the industry of a market support function. Over time, Burroughs' management concluded that customers and the company were better off with a direct sales force in branches (like IBM) to manage increasingly complex and long-term relationships involving application selling.[12]

Adding Machines: Uses and Types

In sharp contrast to either punched card tabulating equipment or bookkeeping machines was the adding machine. It performed far fewer functions and, thus, could be used by more people with less training. It was a mass-produced device that shrank in size over time. Its smallness meant that it could be used in many places, most commonly on an accountant's desk, and less expensively than a large machine. This class of device caused some engineers and scientists to complain about the limitations of adding and calculating machines and motivated a few to develop very large calculating engines.

To buy or sell adding machines required less effort than marketing bookkeeping devices. No systems had to be designed or sold; one ordinarily determined the capability of a particular machine to speed up calculations, established whether or not the purchase price was reasonable, and then walked out of the store with it or had it delivered. Despite this simplified view of what happened, one could also argue that in the 1920s the machine's technology had evolved substantially since William S. Burroughs constructed his first in 1885. They now could be bought with, for instance, wide carriages for listing amounts directly onto various forms (in which case one could not carry it out of the store). They were either manual (handcranked) or electric; some

TABLE 12.2

Age of Base Technologies of Adding Machines by Vendor and Type, 1885–1940

Company[a]	Approximate Date of Machine Origin[b]	Machine Type	
		Full	Ten-Key
Burroughs	1885	X	—
National (Ellis, Wales)	1900	X	—
Remington Rand (Dalton, Monarch)	1903	—	X
Underwood (Sundstrand)	1910	—	X
Lanston Monotype (Barrett)	1910	X[c]	X[d]
R. C. Allen	1912	X	—
Victor	1916	X[e]	X[f]
L. C. Smith & Corona	1923	X	—
Monroe	1924	X	—
Swift	1937	—	X
Clary	1939	X	—

Source: "Adding Machines," Typescript (ca. 1949), 2, Burroughs Papers.

[a] Note the number of typewriter firms selling adding machines. In addition to the above machines, several foreign vendors also sold in the United States: Addo, Precisa, Olivetti.

[b] Date of origin refers to the date of incorporation or patent, not necessarily the date of the first machine sale.

[c] 1910–1940.   [e] 1916.

[d] 1935.   [f] 1940.

had a direct subtraction feature whereas others could carry a credit balance for recording negative results. By the late 1940s, they could also subtract, multiply, and divide and still be called adding machines because each operation was based on addition. Adding machines were still divided into two types: full keyboard and ten-key keyboard. The ten-key device by the end of the 1920s had a keyboard similar to that of a modern simple electronic hand calculator. The two fundamental designs had not changed that much since before World War I. In table 12.2, I list the years in which base patterns of machines were first introduced.[13] The technology of adding machines was less volatile than punched card or bookkeeping technologies.

Adding machines were mass produced and sold in larger quantities. Exactly how many were sold in the 1920s and 1930s is not fully known. In 1929, however, 157,740 adding machines, 57,201 calculating devices, and nearly one million typewriters were built in the United States.[14] Burroughs conducted a market survey in 1949 that described the market as of 1947–1948, which they also believed had patterns similar to those of the 1920s and especially, the 1930s. It turned up the fact that for every adding machine built in the late 1940s 2.5 typewriters were made. The same ratio applied to automobiles as well. In the United States, 132,000 adding machines were built in

1939, a period when the industry was back in a growth spurt. That statistic and its circumstance tempts one to conclude that annual volumes in the early to mid-1920s were much lower, perhaps by as much as 25 percent each year, placing manufacturing volumes around 100,000 units, of which about one-fourth or more would have been exported, leaving a U.S. market of some 75,000 units annually.[15] These numbers are also supported by the facts that such machines did not wear out and, hence, were used for years. As of the late 1940s, closer to 1.5 million units were installed in the United States alone. Extrapolating backward, one could conclude that there were at least 750,000 adding machines by the start of World War II. Without more detailed information constructed out of sales data for most of the key vendors, a more precise number is difficult to establish.

Businesses of every size typically acquired their machines directly from sales offices. Small businesses, and those run out of homes, generally acquired their equipment from dealers, vendors who often sold multiple products and not necessarily only those from one manufacturer. Although specific data on buying patterns do not exist for the 1920s and 1930s, data on the 1940s do and, in the case of Burroughs, reflected buying habits of the previous twenty years. That meant 58 percent of sales to small businesses came from office machine stores or dealers, another 38 percent from local agencies, 2 percent from department stores, and the remaining 2 percent from other miscellaneous sources. Businesses buying machines included light manufacturing, wholesalers, retailers, restauranteurs, and other organizations with very small clerical staffs. Home businesses (e.g., insurance agents, accountants, dentists, lawyers, doctors, and so forth) acquired 54 percent of their machines from dealers, another 40 percent through local agents, 3 percent through department stores, and the remaining 3 percent from miscellaneous sources. The combined total of small and home businesses accounted for 57 percent of all new adding machine sales within the United States as of 1947, again suggesting where business came from in the 1920s and 1930s.[16]

What were the advantages that so drove sales? I list advantages and disadvantages of full- and ten-key keyboard devices as perceived by users in table 12.3. Their opinions were important because much of how a buyer acquired a machine depended on function, not simply on price or who was selling it. Customers bought more ten-key machines, a trend that became increasingly obvious over time. Many vendors responded by introducing more such devices. New ten-key machines were introduced for the first time by Barrett (1935), Swift (1937), and Victor (1940). Barrett withdrew its full keyboard product (1940); the only firm to come out with such a device for the first time in that era was Clary (1939). Large vendors, like Burroughs, NCR, and Underwood, carried both types. Customers ultimately preferred the ten-key machine because of its greater speed (operators could use the touch method) and the belief that it caused less operator fatigue. On the other hand,

TABLE 12.3

Functional Advantages and Disadvantages of Full- and Ten-key Adding Machines

Full Keyboard Advantages[a]	Ten-key Disadvantages
Faster because all ciphers print automatically.	30 percent more key depressions needed; ciphers estimated to be 30 percent of all figures.
Faster because a number of keys and the motor bar can be depressed simultaneously.	Individual key and motor bar depressions necessary.
Faster, more convenient to enter digits in any order in any direction.	Digits must be entered in exact sequence, left to right.
More accurate because fewer keys are depressed.	30 percent more chance of error in key depressions; operator must track number of ciphers entered in machine.
More accurate because operator can correct keyboard entry before figures are printed or added in machine.	Entry must be printed and added before operator knows if it is correct.
Faster because single digit corrections are made without disturbing the rest of the entry.	Entire entry must be erased and reentered correctly to eliminate one incorrect key depression.
Faster because operators need correct errors only when they see a figure is in error.	Operator must correct items thought to be in error; no way to tell what figures have been entered in machine.
Easier to learn to operate because operator can visualize entry on keyboard and see after entering it that it is correct.	Requires practice to operate by touch; each key has constantly changing value.
Less tiring to operate because fewer keys are depressed.	Extra strain and effort to enter ciphers and keep track of all digits.

Full Keyboard Disadvantages	Ten-key Advantages
Operator must refer to keyboard continually.	Faster because small, compact keyboard permits touch operation.
Hand and arm must travel back and forth, up and down larger keyboard.	Faster because only fingers move within small area of ten keys.
If operators enter figures as they read them, increases hand and arm travel.	Faster and easier for operators to enter figures in the order in which they read them.
Short-cut operator must mentally group figures, select columns, and arrange fingers to depress more than one key at a time.	Faster because ten-key operator can depress several keys individually while full keyboard operator thinks out shortcut methods.
Operator must shift attention from data to machine; loses place.	Faster to work down long columns without shifting attention to machine.

TABLE 12.3 (*cont.*)

Full Keyboard Disadvantages	Ten-key Advantages
Operator must shift eyes from paper to machine; on latter must locate correct column and correct one of nine keys.	Reduces eye strain because operator does not need to shift eyes from paper to machine and back again.
Ciphers print automatically but entire amount must be reentered one column to the left for each digit of the multiplier.	Faster in multiplication (repeated addition) because single depression of cipher key automatically moves entire amount one column to the left.

Source: Edward Littlejohn and C. J. McClain, "The Accounting Machine Industry," (Burroughs Adding Machine Company, June 1950, Report) 146–48, Burroughs Papers.

[a] Such advantages and disadvantages appeared in advertisements for adding machines throughout the 1920s to 1940s, adding to the confusion.

they perceived full keyboard devices as easier to learn to use. Contradictions were so numerous (e.g., one customer said the ten-key machine was more difficult to learn to use and another said the reverse) that vendors had difficulty defining market demands exactly and developing good selling techniques. Lack of precision was in itself a feature of this market and most difficult in comparison to other portions of the proto–information-processing industry which had more clearly defined and consistent views about the functions and benefits of specific machines.[17]

Adding machines were used for the same reasons in the 1920s and 1930s as before World War I. By World War II they had been available in American and European markets for more than a half-century. The industry responded to "ease of use" concerns by enhancing models so that one could perform basic mathematical functions while printing results or not. I did not find substantial evidence to suggest that these machines were yet treated as commodity items, as they would be by the 1950s, or as personal computers would be in the late 1980s.

Enhanced tasks of accounting and record keeping made usage of all machines more diverse over time. Adding machines were used by banks and insurance agencies first then by most medium-sized firms by World War II. But the key to demand and applications was accounting. As additional accounting functions became the norm, new uses also emerged. These included calculation of payroll deductions (in part thanks to SSA regulations), weekly labor and work summaries, managing petty cash expenditures, and tracking and calculating weekly travel expenses. They were also used routinely in the more complex tasks of footing inventories, developing profit and loss statements, and preparing balance sheets and income reports.[18]

Some of the major vendors in this market included Burroughs, Victor Adding Machine Company, Dalton Adding Machine Sales Company, Sundstrand

Adding Machine Company, Wales Adding Machine Company and, on and off during the 1920s and 1930s, nearly one dozen others. Competition proved intense, and became even more so because customers bought by weighing many considerations (functions, preferences for local dealers in some instances and agents in others) and price. Suppliers entered what was a relatively low-capital, low-cost segment of the office machine market and experimented with numerous combinations of distribution ranging from direct sales offices to dealers and agents, with many variations in products.

Calculators: Uses and Types

Calculators were products sold to satisfy needs somewhere between adding machines (low function, low data volumes) and large accounting/bookkeeping devices (greater function, large data volumes). Calculators were commercially in greater demand than tabulating machines but sold in fewer numbers than either adding machines or cash registers. In this text, I deal only with machines that were commercially available to businesses, government agencies, engineers and scientists at universities, and the general public—the commercial market for such products. Specialty items, often one-of-a-kind machines in research, were constructed at universities or government laboratories. These devices have been cited by historians as precursors of the modern computer but were not part of the commercial market for office equipment in the 1920s and 1930s.[19]

As with adding machines, by the 1920s, various technologies had stabilized that were then simply refined and repackaged in response to competitive pressures or customer demands. These machines shrank in size during the 1920s and 1930s—a process that continued to the 1960s. As with other types of adding devices, parallel types of calculating machines evolved; they were key driven and rotary. Key-driven products offered full keyboards, usually with visible keys or dials (the latter to accumulate totals). Such machines performed the four basic arithmetical functions and were sold by such firms as Felt & Tarrant and by Burroughs. The Burroughs Duplex machine provided a second register at the rear that permitted direct subtraction and accumulation of grand totals of individual calculations without recapping subtotals. The second major design type, rotary machines, also had a full keyboard and, usually, a ten-key multiplier keyboard. Some models sported actuating keys and motor bars, added over the years to control calculations and carriage location. Such devices were marketed, for example, by Marchant and Monroe. Most were made of iron painted black and sat on desks or on specially designed stands.[20]

Unlike adding machines, which could perform only simple arithmetic functions, by the mid-1920s, calculators could carry out transactions to the eighth decimal and support more complex engineering and mathematical calculations. Sophisticated applications not conveniently possible on a mere adding machine but clearly in the domain of the calculator included "reducing quantities of grain, expressed in pounds, to bushels, and computing the value at a given price per bushel."[21] Figuring out different rates for various hours of work for payroll became possible. Many customers faced a real problem in deciding whether to acquire the less-expensive, limited-function adding machine or the more expensive, functionally enriched calculator. Adding machines would record every numerical entry and, hence, be slower than a calculator, which only printed end results. Buyers in the 1920s valued "speed . . . one of the most important important considerations in the selection of a figuring machine of any sort."[22] By then both key-driven and crank-operated machines were available. The scientific community in the 1920s frequently still used machines acquired by their laboratories before World War I.[23]

Major vendors included Burroughs, Marchant Calculating Machine Company, Felt & Tarrant Manufacturing Company, Monroe Calculating Machine Company and, by the 1930s, Remington Rand (which owned the old Dalton Company). Machines were placed in banks, insurance companies, railroads, large factories, public utilities, retail operations, oil companies, architectural firms, schools and colleges and sold to engineers and government agencies.[24] I list common applications performed on these machines in the interwar period in table 12.4. Organizations often also had other types of machines, such as bookkeeping and tabulating gear.[25]

No single vendor dominated this market and, as suggested in table 12.5, many offered products. By the late 1940s, Marchant, considered the dominant vendor in the U.S. market, only had about 30 percent of an estimated calculating machine market of between $25 and $30 million in the United States.[26] Clearly, it was a much smaller market in the 1920s and 1930s than for adding machines. Exactly what size it was proved difficult to establish because Monroe was privately held and did not publish financial statements, whereas publicly held companies did not differentiate between sales of calculators and other adding machines, let alone between foreign and domestic volumes. However, rotary calculators dominated sales, by the 1940s, nearly 70 percent of all dollar volumes sold.[27]

Most commercial applications called for key-driven devices sold, for example, by Burroughs and Felt & Tarrant. They were seldom employed to do division. Rotary devices were more popular with engineers, but only about 15 percent of these machines actually went to such professionals, a small percentage of the total customer set for these products. Engineers were important, however, to historians because it was from the community of electrical and radio engineers that some developers of the computer came.[28] Burroughs sought to satisfy a wide customer set with a broad product line. It entered the calculating machine market in 1911 and in 1933 gained some

TABLE 12.4
Sample Commercial Applications for Calculators,
1920–1940

Adding and balancing cash books
Adding daily sales, vouchers, charge sheets
Providing daily posting
Balancing ledger accounts
Adding trial balances
Averaging accounts
Figuring and providing freight bills
Discounts on purchase invoices
Figuring interest, commissions, foreign exchange
Providing postings by adding vouchers to cash slips
Balancing cash books
Determining piece costs, totaling job costs
Figuring pro rata or percentage of cost
Profits by salesperson, department, territory
Original figuring of invoice extensions
Totaling weights or quantities on bills
Establishing freight allowances
Figuring taxes
Adding fractional quantities

Source: Leffingwell, *Office Appliance Manual*, 98–100.

TABLE 12.5
Calculating Machine Vendors in the United States,
1920–1930

Burroughs Adding Machine Company
Dalton Adding Machine Sales Company
Denominator Adding Machine Company
Doty Business Machines Company
Felt & Tarrant Manufacturing Company
Ensign Company
Marchant Calculating Machine Company
Mechanical Accountant Company
Monroe Calculating Machine Company
Morschauser, W. A.
Reuter, Inc., Carl H.
Sundstrand Adding Machine Company
Tim Calculating Machine Company

Source: Office Equipment Catalogue, *Office Equipment Catalogue*, xxxix–xl.

competitive advantage by introducing a duplex (two-register) model that helped sales against a major rival, Felt & Tarrant. Yet both sold roughly the same number.[29]

Despite Burroughs's apparent technological superiority since at least 1933, Felt & Tarrant had just as effective an alternative strategy. Since 1905, it had run operator training schools and, by 1950, had 140 around the world that taught only on its own machines and then made these graduates available to customers. Once trained on the Comptometer, it became difficult for Burroughs to argue that they be retaught a different brand. Felt & Tarrant also helped its users obtain employment and, if a customer needed extra operators, found them. Burroughs, on the other hand, followed a strategy of "on the job training" and, consequently, operated only 20 percent as many schools.[30] Felt & Tarrant was also a well-established firm with at least fifteen years more experience in the calculator business than Burroughs; the latter was (in the 1920s) a relative newcomer to the field. It must have meant something because as late as 1950, company employees were still complaining about the competitive "edge" held by Felt & Tarrant for having been in the market longer.[31] Yet it was the loyal following of thousands of operators trained by Felt & Tarrant that helped sales go to Burroughs's rival, just as thousands of operators and programmers trained by IBM would do for Watson's company in the 1960s and 1970s.

Summary

The world of adding and calculating machines differed substantially from that of punched cards. Vendors were different; customers frequently were too, particularly in smaller organizations. Prices were lower than for tabulating and punched card peripherals, and dependence on these smaller devices was less. The market had fewer rigidly defined buying patterns. In both, function and value were crucial factors in a sale. It was easier to enter the adding and calculating machine markets but also more competitive, hence, riskier for a vendor. As I will show in the next chapter, such machines made up an important part of the proto-information–processing world.

13

Vendors, Practices, and Results

DAILY activities of that portion of the office appliance industry most concerned with adding and calculating machines illustrates how vendors varied their responses to market conditions from those selling and servicing activities associated with tabulating and punched card machines. To examine how effective vendors of adding and calculating machines were and in what ways they responded to their customers adds insight into this industry. Effectiveness can be determined by measuring sales volumes and studying marketing practices. The market for cash registers was related also to this segment of the industry, and, thus, a look at NCR will round out the analysis of key vendors and market segments before the start of World War II.

Players and Practices

The rhythms of buying and selling adding machines, calculators, and bookkeeping devices varied less than the forms of distribution. Why certain types of equipment were bought and to what uses they were put had been reasonably understood by World War I; in the period between the two world wars, previous trends of acquisition and distribution continued but at an accelerated pace.

Snapshots of some practices and comments of major vendors suggest patterns of marketing. The Elliott-Fisher Company, headquartered in New York with manufacturing in Harrisburg, Pennsylvania, operated branch offices in major U.S. cities. It sold a Writing Machine, a Simplex Accounting Machine, and a Universal Accounting Machine. It bragged that it was the "largest exclusive manufacturer of Accounting-Writing Machines in the world." The firm also maintained a staff of accountants to show customers how to use this equipment.[1] The Peters-Morse Manufacturing Company, which sold adding and listing machines called the Peters, was headquartered in Ithaca, New York, and claimed to have sales representatives around the United States (probably agents).[2] The Marchant Calculating Machine Company had its single plant and headquarters of the 1920s in Oakland, California, with sales offices around the United States (mostly dealers). Its calculating machines offered, according to the company, "simplicity of operations" while the firm saw itself as the "Master of Mathematics."[3] The Monroe Calculating Machine Company's general headquarters in the Woolworth Building in New York, a plant in nearby Orange, New Jersey, and sales and dealer offices in the United States, Canada, and Europe marketed descendants of the Baldwin calculator of the late 1800s.[4] The company stressed speed and ease of use: "The mechanism of the Monroe is simple, durable and made with such precision and care that it is not only a very smooth-running machine, but insures a great many years of service at exceptionally low cost."[5]

The Victor Adding Machine Company had its product, the "Victor" on the market as an adding and listing machine for $100 FOB. (1925). Prices for other brands of products ranged from $100 to nearly $900 (for some fully configured accounting machines). Victor's products were sold by retail dealers, not by a direct sales force. Victor stressed technology in its advertisements: one thousand fewer parts than comparable machines. It emphasized its permanence by announcing in the mid-1920s that it had sold over sixty thousand machines. Its references suggested the kind of customer it sought and gained: E. I. du Pont de Nemours and Co., Southern Pacific Lines, Willys-Overland, American Steel and Wire, Tidewater Oil, National Biscuit (Nabisco), railroads, Eastman Kodak (already a giant in its own industry), and Armour and Company. The firm sold its machines for cash or on "moderate terms." Its dealers were also authorized to install trial machines at a customer's site.[6]

Wales Adding Machine Company of Wilkes-Barre, Pennsylvania, marketed adding machines, commercial ledger posting and statement devices, cash registers, and other products. It stressed "feeds and speeds." The firm had existed since 1903 and claimed to have been successful on the basis of the accuracy, speed, and durability of its products. The WALES machine was available through dealers.[7] Dalton advertised various models (as opposed to Wales, which offered a limited product line) and distributed products through sales agents reporting into headquarters at Cincinnati, Ohio.[8]

It is interesting to see the commonality, say, between IBM's approach and those of vendors marketing accounting machines. In 1925, for example, IBM was arguing that it maintained "a staff of representatives who, without obligation, co-operate either directly with a company or its outside accountants in devising plans for securing accurate results in its accounting and statistical work."[9] Like other bookkeeping machine vendors, Powers followed a similar tack by providing "constructive recommendations for replacing existing clerical operations."[10] Both suggested what types of organizations bought from them. A sidelight was the International Time Recording Division of IBM, which made electric time systems, master clocks, secondary clocks, time stamps, and time recorders that were advertised as the product of many decades of experience. Size was obviously important because this division of IBM claimed in the 1920s to be the largest manufacturer of such systems in the world. It also stressed the same features as most office equipment manufacturers: quality, function, and support.

Instructions to Burroughs's marketing force of the 1920s and 1930s illustrate daily activity. They were addressed to representatives in more than two hundred cities around the world where customers could be trained by "figure experts." The company's motto in the mid-1920s was "Better Figures Make Bigger Profits." It advertised that over 750,000 of its machines had been placed worldwide. The company communicated with its dealers, a direct sales force, and a national network of repair facilities within agency offices.[11] Burroughs also competed against used equipment, yet sold its own second-hand hardware, about which it communicated to its sales force.[12]

Since before World War I, managers at Burroughs headquarters had sent instructions to its agents admonishing them to adhere to discipline and company policies. Thus in 1921, agents were told that "machines must be sold at established prices."[13] Marketing representatives reported directly to marketing managers whereas agents saluted district managers. In some cities, agency managers also reported to district managers, all of which suggests an organized distribution network meeting various market needs but also capable of receiving and sending information.[14] Regardless of title, sales and service functions were in the same field organization, a formula employed by other vendors. Service quality was always a concern to management. The national service manager reported that there were "indications, strongly supported by facts that many inspectors do not study their instruction books." Quality service was a competitive tool and the problem thus had to be addressed.[15] The company's eighteen hundred member sales force, in September 1920, ran a "Fall Drive" sales campaign to sell more equipment during an economic slump.[16] Such emphasis programs continued to the present and have been sponsored by all vendors in the industry. In 1921, one also saw another stock approach to hard times: more generous payment terms extended to customers.[17]

By 1931, management expressed concern over basic skills of sales reps; the result was, for example, a memorandum to all marketing personnel on how to demonstrate equipment.[18] Admonitions to do better were mixed in the mail with news flashes of successes to be emulated. In 1933, one broadcast to the field noted, "If the large volume of business obtained since breweries resumed is any criterion, we're in for plenty more sales when distilleries and wineries start again. We can use any information on this type of accounting."[19] The New Deal was obviously good for business. By 1936, continued worry about marketing effectivness led to a sermon on quality over quantity.[20] All of these communications expressed the typical concerns of any normal marketing organization regardless of industry and rather suggested health in the company.

Such instructions appeared when the industry was beginning to show signs of maturity. For example, the National Association of Office Appliance Manufacturers that came into being during the 1920s published materials and catalogs and sponsored meetings. It had thirty-three company members of which sixteen made information-handling equipment. It showcased products, commented on their use, and advertised on behalf of the industry. Its actions were typical of those in other industry groups, for example, automotive, consumer goods, and transportation. During the interwar period, name recognition grew for Burroughs, NCR, Victor, and others as did the public's association of these firms with office equipment.

Performance of the Burroughs Adding Machine Company

I have said much already about Burroughs because it was an important vendor within the industry. During the interwar period, sales made it one of the top half-dozen suppliers. As of 1928 (the last full year of prosperity before the depression), it ranked third with $32.1 million in revenues after Remington Rand ($59.6 million and NCR at $49 million). If one left out typewriters, cash registers, and other types of nonaccounting products, Burroughs was the single largest vendor in the 1920s. In 1928, it brought in the most profit ($8.3 million), followed by NCR ($7.8 million), Remington Rand ($6 million), and IBM ($5.3 million).[21] IBM was the most profitable with a yield of 26.90 percent on revenues, followed closely by Burroughs at 25.86 percent. NCR's efficiency was far behind with 15.92 percent. Remington Rand (at 10.06 percent) clearly had major problems with productivity and efficiencies, which were probably caused largely by its merger during 1927.[22] By 1939, rankings by revenues placed Burroughs ($32.5 million) fourth after Remington Rand ($43.4 million).[23] Clearly, relative positions and efficiencies within the industry were shifting.

Burroughs has been typically characterized as unimaginative in this period, content to sell adding machines, calculators, and bookkeeping equipment. There is no evidence to suggest that it went after market share and expansion with the same intensity as either NCR or IBM. Most management teams in this industry were conservative, but demand outpaced their conservatism enough to make it a low-risk decision to expand product lines and manufacturing capacities. That is why, for example, each time a major firm entered a new sector of the office appliance market, it rarely stumbled. The one exception was during the depression when demand fell off for everything. Burroughs's marketing effectiveness appeared reasonable and it applied traditional methods of distribution and service. Burroughs also introduced a stream of new products at a comparatively predictable pace, often in response, however, to competitive pressures. The Duplex exception represented technological leadership. The Burroughs Class 16 machine, another exception, allowed a user to accumulate numbers in several registers as opposed to adding numbers in simple columns. It came out in the 1920s and was dubbed by Leslie J. Comrie as a "modern Babbage machine." Conservative management at Burroughs should not be confused with incompetence because senior and middle management had been in the business machine market for a long time. They knew how to sell to banks, insurance companies, and railroads. Like others, they too knew how to make acquisitions (although very few) to root their business solidly in the office equipment industry. Their major acquisition during the 1920s and 1930s was the Moon-Hopkins Billing Machine Company. They also built factories in Europe and expanded marketing worldwide.[24]

The Great Depression severely hurt Burroughs because, as in many other sectors of the U.S. economy, purchased items were in far less demand as buyers put off even leased acquisitions. But the company survived. As of 1934, it had about 17 percent of the industry's market share, which dropped to 13.9 percent by the end of 1939.[25] Burroughs was the strongest vendor in the rapidly growing banking industry during the 1920s and 1930s, providing a solid base that served it well in the post–World War II period. Burroughs, however, had not been overall as competitive as it needed to be to sustain or expand market share. In an internal assessment, one Burroughs writer noted that "it is probably common knowledge that during the thirties and early forties the company had fallen behind in the competitive race to the extent that sales and profits rose less than that of certain other competitors and the rate of profitability declined."[26] Sales along with after-tax profits (earnings) during the interwar period are given in figure 13.1. It is very obvious that the firm

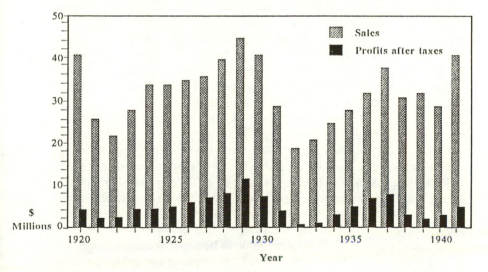

13.1 Historic Record of Burroughs Adding Machine Company Sales and Earnings, 1920–1941 (Burroughs Annual Reports).

TABLE 13.1
Sales and Profits, Burroughs Adding
Machine Company, 1942–1945
(dollars in millions)

Year	Sales	Pretax Profits	Posttax Profits
1942	44.04	11.50	4.51
1943	44.48	6.52	3.72
1944	37.44	3.46	2.53
1945	37.60	2.27	1.26

Source: Burroughs Annual Reports, 1942–1945.

could not generate profits evenly in the 1930s. Noticeable also is how hard the depression hit the firm; it was far more severely and quickly struck than, for example, IBM. The momentum of the 1920s, although eroding quickly in 1930, had become a disaster in 1931 and 1932. Burroughs also was not able to take advantage of wartime spending to restore volumes and profits in the early 1940s (see table 13.1). Consequently, other vendors were better positioned to lead during the late 1940s.

Not being competitive enough was a severe problem made even more complex by the fact that the industry was so diverse and, therefore, required specific, aggressive, and intense responses to different types of vendors in varying market niches. In the calculator market, for instance, Felt & Tarrant was the arch rival. In accounting machines it was IBM, NCR, and Remington Rand, while in adding machines (and in the 1930s, typewriters) it was nearly one dozen organizations. On the plus side, the firm had established a worldwide marketing organization that included, by the mid-1920s, some twenty-five or more marketing subsidiaries addressing specific market segments. In Europe, local competitors also battled against Burroughs's marketing organizations; some U.S. firms, like IBM and Remington Rand, were there too. Yet despite competition, between 1890 and the end of the 1920s, the firm had delivered virtually continuous profitable growth.[27]

In the 1920s, the chairman of the board, Joseph Boyer, ruled with his son-in-law, Standish Backus, as president. The board of directors in the mid-1930s included Backus as president and many of the original 1920 top management still ran the company—perhaps a hint of why the firm increasingly did not respond to change differently than it always had.[28] However, this team could brag in January 1926 that the company had just manufactured its millionth machine, a source of personal pride to Backus.[29] Yearly in the 1920s, management reported that Burroughs had "released for sale many new models, features and improvements and has many more in preparation for the future."[30]

Joseph Boyer died on October 24, 1930, bringing to an end his era but certainly not his style of management or view of business opportunities, which ensured that much would remain the same. As a result of the severe drop in sales and profits in 1931, management finally had to comment on the problem to stockholders. Backus wrote in March 1932 that "during 1931 the Company introduced substantial economies into practically every branch of its operations, and is continuing to do so. On the other hand, there has been no diminution in the Company's efforts to develop, expand and improve its products." He also announced that the company would begin to sell typewriters.[31] The following year, Backus reported on recently introduced machines, including additional cash registers.[32] Reduced budgets throughout the firm accompanied product announcements and became a way of life for the rest of the decade.

Backus shared with his stockholders a more detailed analysis of what happened during the 1930s in his annual letter of March 1940.

> The low point was reached in 1932 when earnings amounted to $655,329.43, but beginning with 1933, earnings increased each year to 1937 when they reached $8,163, 404.29. Another decline in business which started in 1937 continued well into 1939. Because of rising costs, prices were increased during this period. However, the price increase did not fully cover the increase in wages and taxes together with the additional depreciation on new buildings and equipment. Hourly wages paid to production workers have been increased in keeping with the general level of wages. Labor forms a much higher percentage of the cost of our products than of manufactured products generally.
>
> Anticipating that the decline in business which started in the last half of 1937 and continued until the second half of 1939 would be temporary, we maintained our factory and field organizations intact throughout this period although many departments were temporarily on shortened time.[33]

In short, he had followed tactics used by others in the industry. His business overseas turned in a mixed performance. Roughly two-thirds of foreign revenues came from Western Europe. From 1936 to the end of 1939, none came from Spain, Germany, or the Soviet Union.[34] Although the outbreak of war in Europe made the company nervous, managers recalled business had improved during World War I and might again.[35]

Performance of the National Cash Register Company

The "Cash" had been selling cash registers for some forty years by the mid-1920s, for fifty-five by the start of World War II. It would not be until October 1987 that any company (IBM) would sell more cash registers in a year (called "point-of-sale terminals" by the 1970s) than NCR. As companies increasingly became dependent on data-handling devices, the importance of NCR's products became less relevant to the main stream of data processing. The transfer of technology that occurred between register manufacturing and other device fabrications of the 1890s, for instance, had ceased to be a source of innovations by the 1920s. Cash registers did not manipulate data as well as other devices did until the 1960s, when they acquired processing capability. However, what made NCR important in the 1920s and 1930s was that it chose to market accounting machines, and its successes with cash registers gave it the economic strength, customer base, and managerial talent necessary to compete in new arenas.[36]

Before one can speak of NCR as a vendor of accounting machines, one must review its role as the leading supplier of registers. It had 95 percent of the market at the start of the 1920s.[37] Its volumes remained strong in subsequent years; in 1924, it built over 145,000 registers in Dayton, and by 1929, it had 8,500 employees there.[38] Yet it was not the only vendor of cash registers. Major competition in the United States came from the Federal Cash Register, the St. Louis Cash Register, and the Remington Cash Register (a subsidiary of the Remington Arms Company). Of the adding machine firms that also competed, Wales, Sundstrand, and Dalton were the most recognizable. Less known but still important players included Indiana Cash Drawer, Add-Index, and the McCaskey Register Company. The same vendors competed for credit registers as well. As in other segments of the office appliance industry, extensive market share did not discourage competitors from participating in this business because it required minimal technological expertise and capital.[39]

In 1923, NCR introduced its first accounting machine because customers were moving toward more complex transaction processing that exceeded the capabilities of normal cash registers and because of demand. Nowhere had this become more obvious to NCR's management than among its most important customers in retailing, railroads, hotels, and banking. Yet its initial steps into the world of accounting machines were tentative and limited. All during the 1920s, there were those within the company who wanted to expand its product line to meet new demands, while others wanted to remain predominantly with cash registers; the latter prevailed during the decade. Frederick B. Patterson, Stanley C. Allyn (comptroller and director), and the general manager, John H. Barringer, were key decision makers. The first accounting machine from NCR was the Class 2000, which Allyn later called "a sophisticated cash register that printed data on inserted forms and provided 30 totals rather than a half dozen."[40] Given its position of strength, NCR generated $29 million in sales during 1921, turning in profits of $2.8 million. By the time the books were closed on 1925, that year's sales had reached $45 million with profits of $7.8 million; executives claimed the Class 2000 had played an important, yet unspecified, role in that growth. It was no surprise, however, that the Class 2000 had been sold to existing register customers. The first machines were acquired by the Statler Hotel chain to manage all charges and credits for valet, porter, restaurant, and laundry services, posting a voucher and a detached record of all transactions in one operation.[41] A modified version, called the NCR Bank Posting Machine, was used by banks to record deposits in passbook savings.

The company expanded and, in 1926, made its first public stock offering (large by contemporaneous standards) for $55 million to fund growth. In January 1929, NCR bought the Ellis Adding-Typewriter Company because it had a machine that could produce a description of an entry, not just numbers. Announced as the NCR Class 3000 accounting machine, it was designed to handle such applications as preparation of payrolls, stock records, billings for utilities and insurance companies, and cost accounting.

Yet not all was well at NCR. The senior Patterson died in 1922, leaving the company in the hands of his son, whom one historian called "a feckless executive who practically reduced the firm to bankruptcy."[42] So the experience in innovation in product development and market expansion was not taken advantage of as well as it might have been during the boom of the 1920s. By 1931, NCR could not maintain the value of its stock, which led its bankers to try to take over the firm.[43] Although they failed, their effort proved once again that just because the demand for data-handling equipment was growing, that, in itself, was no guarantee of prosperity for a firm. Basic statistics on the company quantify the period of decay (see table 13.2). Revenues in 1928 had reached $49 million, making NCR the second largest vendor in the industry; but in 1939, its volumes only climbed to $37.1 million, putting it in third position.

The depression had a great deal to do with NCR's troubles, not just weak management. With customer spending declining, the demand for cash registers did too. To hold onto business, NCR offered customers installment payment options. However, that did not work well. In 1931 alone, repossessions of cash registers from failed businesses amounted to $5.2 million in the United States.[44] Yet in 1934, the firm was in the black again with net profits of $1.1 million on sales of $26.6 million. Colonel Edward Deeds (chief executive officer) complained in 1934 that part of the problem with sales stemmed from "commercial treaties, tariff barriers, trade restrictions and money complications" that took "productivity from the Dayton factory."[45] With foreign sales still accounting for 45 percent of the company's revenues, it is no wonder that he made such a statement. In the late 1930s, sales overseas became relatively strong again, which helped the company. As with Burroughs, sales in Spain diminished to zero but were up almost everywhere else, leaving the company with plants and sales offices scattered around the world that employed sixteen thousand people by end of 1937.[46]

NCR continued to experience fluctuations in sales. In 1938, for instance,

TABLE 13.2
National Cash Register Company Sales and Profits, 1922–1941
(dollars in millions)

Year	Revenues	Profits[a]	Year	Revenues	Profits[a]
1922	31.73	5.49	1932	16.50	(3.30)
1923	40.05	7.88	1933	22.80	(0.58)
1924	42.49	6.87	1934	26.61	1.12
1925	46.99	8.16	1935	29.75	1.67
1926	46.07	6.76	1936	35.11	2.92
1927	46.96	7.04	1937	42.28	3.98
1928	49.00	7.80	1938	36.23	2.41
1929	57.60	8.30	1939	37.10	1.81
1930	45.40	3.50	1940	38.78	2.05
1931	28.90	0.82	1941	52.40	3.26

Source: Moody's Manual of Investments, 1922–1941.
[a] Note the uneven performance from one decade to the other. The firm lost money in 1932 and 1933. It took a world war to turn volumes upward in 1941.

domestic volumes dropped nearly 20 percent, and the contribution to revenues from outside the United States decreased to 42.9 percent. During the 1920s and 1930s, the company sought to increase productivity in sales by converting its branch offices (called agencies) across the United States fully into company-owned marketing offices. It completed 100 percent of the transfers to direct ownership in the United States and in Canada by 1942, reflecting the same pattern of distribution seen with Burroughs and IBM.[47]

Despite its efforts, NCR was nearly a casualty of weak management and of the economy. The value of its stock told the story. In 1927, a share was worth $3; in the following two years it went to $4 but by 1931 sold for only 69 cents. The pattern of decline was more extreme with "A" stock, which went from $154 per share in early 1929 to $6.87 after the stock market crash in October. Employment reflected problems; the plant in Dayton went from eighty-six hundred employees in 1930 down to thirty-five hundred by March 1933. Employment then began to grow slowly for the rest of the decade.[48]

NCR survived the young Patterson partly because he was forced to turn control of the company over to Deeds in 1931. Deeds set about to rebuild the corporation, expand further into the accounting machine business, and improve efficiencies. But by then the accounting machine market was being serviced by better-run organizations already armed with products and marketing experience. They forced NCR to rely on cash register volumes for support through the 1930s. Thus, despite large sales figures (mainly for registers), NCR was not as significant a player in the office appliance industry—or in the embryonic stages of data processing—as one might otherwise have expected.

Non-U.S. Activities

Patterns within the industry and among customers were similar outside the United States and Canada to those here. American manufacturers continued to dominate trade in the interwar period in all information-handling equipment, especially in Latin America and in Asia. The second-largest market after North America remained Europe. Market segmentation was the same on both sides of the Atlantic. Methods of distribution reflected American practices. The number of vendors not of American origin in Europe remained higher than, for example, in Japan. No indigenous vendors seem to have emerged in South America. Americans held a virtual monopoly on tabulating equipment worldwide. That was not the case with easily mass-produced items such as cash registers, adding machines, and typewriters. Each of these items were manufactured in the millions in the first four decades of the twentieth century.

Major suppliers of smaller office equipment in Germany, an important trading area for such hardware, included the Brunsviga-Maschinenwerke, Grimme, Natalis (better known as Brunsviga). This firm was well known in Europe and had a distinguished history dating back to the late 1800s. It had a broad product line and a national distribution network.[49] Other local firms operated in Britain, Italy, France, and Scandinavian countries. They were smaller than Brunsviga and American firms, and most had come into existence in the late nineteenth or early twentieth centuries under circumstances similar to those of their peers in the United States. The greatest amount of research and development of new products, however, took place in Germany.[50] Development also occurred at the same time, however, elsewhere in Europe.[51]

The size of the European market remains unknown; however, because American manufacturers still dominated sales of calculators, adding machines, bookkeeping devices, tabulating machines, typewriters, and other miscellaneous items, by looking at American exports, one gets an inkling of volumes and patterns. In general, sales to Europe by the American industry were within 30 to 45 percent of all output. The market for secondhand equipment remains a complete mystery for both the United States and Europe. The market as a whole and worldwide clearly grew during the interwar period. Vendors expanded distribution networks and built manufacturing facilities outside the United States for the first time.

Expansion of distribution was a strong indicator of increased demand. NCR, for example, opened sales offices or agencies in Europe, throughout the British Empire, and in the Middle East while it expanded facilities in South America and in Asia. It also either expanded or established plants in Canada, Germany, and Japan.[52] NCR's case is important because it reflected patterns evident throughout the office appliance industry, including those portions relating directly to the origins of the data-processing industry. As did other vendors, NCR's management focused on worldwide marketing and competing head-on in each major national market.

Industry Volumes

Another way to measure growth and attributes of the industry is to use the same measurements employed by these companies. These measurements document extensive activity by firms that nearly failed (NCR), were created (Remington Rand), competed weakly (Burroughs), or were able to establish the solid base required to be a major fixture on the U.S. economic landscape (IBM). Information-processing vendors had mixed results but, overall, contributed to fundamental growth. Volumes came through the number of products sold but also from broadening product lines to include more variety of goods and services. Expanded product lines, in turn, made it possible to sell more goods to a wider set of customers. Statistics on volumes, values, and numbers of participants suggested how much and by whom. The only major difficulty involves the inability to separate neatly nondata-processing items from raw data, such as typewriters, microphones, and furniture. Yet even with that problem and an almost total lack of information on the size of the secondhand equipment market (which is ignored in table 13.3. statistics), existing data quantifies the extent of growth. It also hints at the growing dependence of American organizations on information-handling hardware.

In 1929, at the height of business volumes before the onset of depression, total value of all products in the office equipment market reached nearly $500 million as measured by factory prices. When profits and expenses for distribution were added, they had a retail value of $900 million.[53] Those numbers were pushed higher by typewriters sold in the 1920s. However, some extraction of data processing volumes from overall figures suggests more closely the portions coming from information-handling products (see table 13.3). Included in the $500 million were office furniture and fixtures. Nonetheless, volumes continued to rise in 1930 by 19.4 percent over 1929's volumes in at least typewriters and bookkeeping-billing machines for a value of $66 million. In 1927–1930, these devices had gone from $55.32 million to $66 million, representing growth of 19 percent with an estimated one-third plus going to overseas markets.[54] That placed sales within the United States at about $36.51 million and $43.56 million, respectively, for these kinds of products.

The numbers reflected an optimism that spilled over into the depression decade and caught the industry off-guard. Writing in 1931, one contemporaneous observer of the industry noted that "despite the great progress made in the business machine industry in the last quarter century, it is regarded by its leaders as yet in its infancy."[55] In hindsight, that turned out to be true. It was

TABLE 13.3
Shipments of Office Appliances in 1929
(dollars in millions)

Cash registers and punched cards	54.783
Adding machines	25.559
Calculating machines	11.732
Other devices	16.440
Total[a]	108.514

Source: Perley Morse, *Business Machines* (London: n.p., 1932), 34.
[a] Data are based on results of forty-six firms.

TABLE 13.4
Value of Office and Store Machinery, 1920–1937 (dollars in millions)

Year	Value[a]	Year	Value[a]	Year	Value[a]
1920	160.6	1926	200.1	1932	78.5
1921	114.0	1927	201.2	1933	78.8
1922	132.4	1928	213.6	1934	—
1923	182.0	1929	217.8	1935	140.6
1924	179.2	1930	165.3	1936	—
1925	196.4	1931	116.5	1937	204.9

Source: U.S. Bureau of the Census, *Historical Statistics*, 421.
[a] These were values of products destined for U.S. domestic consumption at current producers' prices. They do not necessarily reflect what actually was sold.

an industry that created new jobs within itself in the late 1920s. By the end of 1925, just in the United States, sixty-nine thousand employees worked in the industry. That work force expanded to seventy-eight thousand by late 1927 and climbed another 14.9 percent by 1930 to nearly ninety thousand.[56]

In the 1930s, values of output dipped and only began to climb late in the 1930s when increased spending at the federal level began to affect buying decisions by customers. In table 13.4, I summarize values of manufactured goods for the 1920s side-by-side with the 1930s to show the pattern. At the worst moments of the depression, vendors did not expand their inventories; they simply sold or rented what they had. That was a normal tactic in hard times. Pretax income as a percentage of sales declined all during the 1930s, not just in the earlier years, as illustrated in table 13.5. That also held true for typewriter manufacturers, organizations that built and marketed in a similar fashion to the same customers (see table 13.6). In short, declining volumes of inventories in themselves did not protect vendors from an overall shrinkage in economic activity early in the decade nor allow them to take rapid advantage of the moderate increase in demand that came in the later 1930s.

TABLE 13.5

Pretax Income as a Percentage of Sales for
Major Vendors, 1935–1939

Firm	1935	1937	1938	1939
Burroughs	21.5	26.2	11.3	9.4
IBM	37.2	32.3	30.7	28.4
NCR	7.0	12.6	8.6	6.6
Remington Rand	8.4	8.7	4.8	6.3
Felt & Tarrant		34.4	18.7	20.9
Marchant	22.4	22.9	15.7	21.3
Monroe	20.7	20.6	11.7	12.7

Source: Burroughs Papers.
[a] Data were drawn from published U.S. government
sources; data not collected for 1936.

TABLE 13.6

Pretax Income as a Percentage of Sales for
Major Typewriter Vendors, 1935–1939

Firm	1935	1937	1938	1939
Royal		19.3	12.2	11.2
Smith Corona	6.1	10.9	5.2	3.5
Underwood	14.8	24.2	12.4	9.0

Source: Burroughs Papers.
[a] Data were drawn from published U.S. government
sources; data not collected for 1936.

A breakdown by major vendors identifies the extent of competition and
their positions within the industry. Position influenced the policies and practices of suppliers worried about market share. Net sales for ten companies
during the late 1930s and early 1940s demonstrate that no single vendor dominated, although some had a lock on specific market segments (e.g., IBM and
Remington Rand on tabulating gear) (see table 13.7). This conclusion is reinforced by examining sales of one to another as a percentage of total sales by
major vendors in the industry. The results for the entire industry appear in
table 13.8. However, if one took out typewriter companies alone, the total
percentage of all volumes related to data-processing products ranged from
roughly 75 percent in 1934 to 70 percent in 1939 (the last year before war-
related purchases for or by the U.S. government began). Most importantly,
competition remained intense, for no single vendor came to dominate the
industry.

The overall market shares of major players remained roughly the same.

TABLE 13.7
Net Sales for Ten Major Office Equipment Suppliers, 1937–1941
(dollars in millions)

Company	1937	1938	1939	1940	1941
Burroughs	38.5	31.1	32.5	29.4	41.3
IBM	31.8	34.7	39.5	46.2	62.9
Marchant	—	—	3.9	4.3	7.5
NCR	51.4	45.4	40.4	39.9	52.7
Remington Rand	49.4	42.7	43.2	49.2	77.3
Royal	11.1	15.7	18.2	18.8	24.4
Smith, L. C.	13.1	11.9	12.1	11.2	14.9
Underwood	30.8	23.3	24.2	26.3	36.5
Addressograph	14.5	12.1	11.6	6.2	14.6
Pitney-Bowes	3.1	3.3	3.6	4.2	6.0

Source: *Standard and Poor's Basic Analysis (01-B) of Office Equipment Industry*, copy in Burroughs Papers.

TABLE 13.8
Sales as a Percentage of Total Industry Sales, 1934–1939

Firm	1934	1935[a]	1937	1938	1939
Burroughs	16.8	16.4	14.7	14.0	13.9
IBM	14.3	12.9	12.2	15.6	16.9
NCR	18.3	17.5	16.2	16.3	15.8
Remington Rand	23.8	24.0	23.4	19.6	18.8
Addressograph	5.8	5.6	5.5	5.5	4.9
Royal	—	—	4.2	7.1	7.8
Smith-Corona	2.5	4.9	5.0	5.4	5.1
Underwood	14.1	14.1	11.8	10.5	10.3
Felt & Tarrant	—	—	2.3	1.7	1.9
Marchant	0.9	1.2	1.6	1.5	1.7
Monroe	3.5	3.3	3.1	2.8	2.9
Total	100.0	100.0	100.0	100.0	100.0

Source: Calculations performed by Burroughs, Burroughs Papers.
[a] Data not available for 1936.

This result is reasonable because large vendors marketed essentially similar products at comparable prices in common ways to the same types of customers. Whatever expansion occurred and disappeared was shared by key vendors proportionately (roughly) during the decade. That performance also points out that while IBM, which was always praised as growing enormously during the period, in fact, only increased market share slightly, all others lost share. Overall increases in demand, which several vendors were able to seize upon slightly more effectively than others, accounted for growth in dollar volume sales in the late years.

Profits also added definition to the performance of these firms. Profits of the five largest vendors in 1928—Remington Rand, NCR, Burroughs, IBM, and Underwood-Elliott-Fisher—illustrate the point. That year they generated revenues of nearly $180 million and turned in profits of just over $32 million, providing a gross yield of roughly 18 percent. The same group in 1939 turned in revenues of $177 million with profits of $18.6 million or a yield of 10.50 percent on essentially flat growth in overall revenues—a clear squeezing caused by reduced sales and fiscal belt tightening. Yet it was usually a profitable business with attractive margins; the only major exception was NCR, which actually lost money during 1932–1933.

Impact of Office Equipment

The role of such products cannot be measured solely by how they were used, let alone by raw statistics on profits and revenues; it was still a business that influenced workers' roles primarily in white collar jobs. The proto–information-processing business came at a time when office workers began to constitute a significant portion of the total work force that was, as a percentage of the total, growing rapidly. One sociologist found that such technology increased specialization of jobs and led to the creation of new ones. Given that more people used accounting machines than punched card equipment, his observations ring more true for the former than for tabulator users: "Machines and social organization had begun to interact and . . . it is a true mark of the 'era of scientific management in the office'."[57] This environment also made it possible for increased numbers of women to continue to take socially acceptable jobs, much as they had in the three decades before World War I. One reliable source estimated that by 1930 one-third of all female office workers used "machines other than typewriters for some of their routine duties."[58]

Such equipment had, by the start of World War II, become an integral part of an office's rhythm of life. As with other technologies—electricity, automobiles, telephones, and so forth—office equipment took approximately fifty years to penetrate deeply and substantially into the economy and into the fabric of office work life. When one adds the growth the industry experienced as a whole during World War II, early data-processing equipment seems to have followed the same pattern. The same amount of time would be required by computers and many of the same patterns of behavior within the industry. But before that happened another world war came, which profoundly influenced the American office machine industry.

Our Deepest Gratitude, Little One — You Brought Us Here

19. Cartoon from *Burroughs Journal*, 1926 (Burroughs Papers, Charles Babbage Institute).

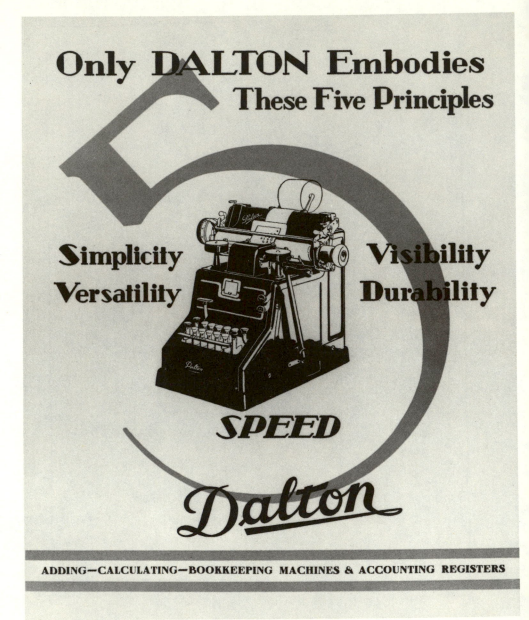

20. Dalton adding-calculator machine advertisement, 1929 (Hagley Museum and Library).

A NEW TIME-SAVING TRIUMPH IN MECHANICAL BOOKKEEPING

REMINGTON
FRONT FEED
BOOKKEEPING MACHINE

THE Remington Bookkeeping Machine has always been noted for its *surpassing speed*, its *ease* and *simplicity* of *operation*, and its *complete adaptability* to every individual need in every line of industry.

A new emphasis has been added to these points of outstanding leadership by the introduction of the *simplest*, *fastest* and *most accurate* method of collating, inserting, and registering any combination of forms that may be necessary to meet the most exacting requirements.

21. Remington Rand front-feed bookkeeping machine advertisement, 1930 (Hagley Museum and Library).

22

22. A keypunch installation, circa 1920. Only men supervised (IBM Archives).

23. Thomas J. Watson. Watson at age forty (1914), was the new general manager of C-T-R (IBM Archives).

24. IBM's first logo. It was used during the interwar period (IBM Archives).

23

24

25

25. An NCR cash register in China, circa late 1930s, early 1940s (NCR Archives).

26. Burroughs Desk Model Adding Machine, 1937 (Burroughs Papers, Charles Babbage Institute).

27. James Rand (1886–1968). Rand was the founder and chief executive officer of Remington Rand (Hagley Museum and Library).

26

27

28. Keypunch assembly, IBM Endicott Plant, 1936 (IBM Archives).

29. IBM Horizontal Sorter, 1938 (IBM Archives).

30

31

32

30. Dr. Ben Wood and IBM punched card equipment, Columbia University, 1935 (IBM Archives).

31. Thomas J. Watson, Sr. (1874–1956), CEO of IBM in 1935 (IBM Archives).

32. Edward A. Deeds and S. C. Allyn, NCR's senior executives, early 1940s (NCR Archives).

33. NCR C-2000 Accounting Machine, 1930s (NCR Archives).

34. John Coleman, CEO of post–World War II Burroughs Corporation (Burroughs Papers, Charles Babbage Institute).

35. Card layout department at IBM plant, Endicott, N.Y., 1935 (IBM Archives).

36. The first IBM graduating class of women systems service workers, 1935 (IBM Archives). IBM pioneered employing women in nonoffice jobs and outside manufacturing.

Part Three

WORLD WAR II AND THE POSTWAR OFFICE APPLIANCE INDUSTRY, 1941–1956

14

Economics, Government Controls, and Applications

NOTHING disturbs the routine of a nation's economic life more or more quickly than a major war, and World War II was no exception. It disrupted lines of communication, altered patterns of distribution, and, at the source of goods and services, caused mining and manufacturing companies to focus on the military needs of a wartime economy. Economies of the entire world were bent to the needs of war. In the United States, the process of focusing the energy and capability of the economy to support war was directed by government agencies. They dictated the course of manufacturing and distribution in all major industries by establishing priorities. To convert to a wartime economy and then ensure effective control and feedback on results required information in ever-increasing quantities. Data-processing equipment was used extensively to gather and manage this information. Given the growing dependence on such technology in the interwar period, it would have been difficult to imagine a world war fought without reliance on typewriters, adding and calculating machines, or the punched card tabulators. In a nutshell, data management played an important role in World War II.

It is customary to describe development of the computer as a new way to provide the extensive processing capabilities required to decipher codes, manage fire control systems, train pilots, perform extensive calculations in ballistics, and then support development of the atomic bomb. The role of the U.S. and British governments in the evolution of the modern computer is also standard material for any history of data processing during the war.[1] In fact, World War II brought to a head the need for and consequent construction of the digital computer. However, its development was also the culmination of a process that had begun earlier. Yet it was during World War II that the first functioning electronic digital computer (ENIAC) was built. It symbolized a new era and was the hallmark of data-processing's wartime history.[2] But, the role of data processing during this war had a far richer history that made the ENIAC a minor event even if, however, it rippled with potential for the future.

The industry that existed before World War II continued to function throughout the war years—a story that has not been told adequately but which is relatively more important than the construction of a few specialty computers. Weapon production, supplying food and materials to soldiers, and general harnessing of economic power in the early 1940s would have been impossible without the help of data-processing equipment. The volumes of machines used, their applications, and the concerns of the U.S. government regarding them are eminent proofs of the industry's significance. The roles played by vendors, customers, and government alike represent the central historical issue for the history of data processing during the war. The period was also bracketed by government controls (1941–1946) that dictated how and what would be built and sold. It was an extreme example of the purposeful economy at work. Such controls also reflected application of the foreign and economic policies of the Roosevelt administration. Lend-lease, begun in 1941, was a clear example. Put another way, for the first time in the history of the office appliance industry, actions of the government fundamentally influenced events within the industry. That had not happened during World War I. Growing government influence began in the 1930s within civilian agencies of the New Deal but during the war the government went the extra step of also managing production and distribution through quotas. From World War II to the present, the role of the government has remained significant for the industry.[3] This pattern of increased involvement was evident in many other industries as well. A result was that the government went from consuming roughly 19 percent of the GNP in 1939 to over 30 percent by the 1970s.

The period 1941–1946 saw the American economy expand and develop depth and strength, capacity and reliance on science-based products, making possible the dominant U.S. position in the world economy in the immediate postwar era. The office appliance industry benefited from that growth, and, as will be shown, business volumes expanded across the industry. It also emerged from the war with the financial and intellectual resources needed to tackle effectively a new field of technology—electronics. With that capability, products could evolve into the computer as commercially viable merchandise.

Economic Environment

First, with the outbreak of war in Europe in September 1939 and, second, with the formal entrance into the conflict by the United States in December 1941, the economies of the Western world underwent profound change. In the United States, the depression was already coming to an end. Industrial production increased enormously with war. In the period 1939–1944 GNP expanded by nearly 125 percent. Manufacturing production climbed in the same period to nearly three times prewar levels. Explosive growth came in almost every basic sector. The supply of raw materials required to manufacture additional goods climbed some 60 percent in actual output while demand outpaced that. Additionally, many older products were recycled into new ones, such as those made out of various metals (e.g., steel furniture, aluminum in office appliances). Economic historians today argue almost universally that one reason the Allies won the war was because the United States outproduced the Axis powers. In munitions, U.S. production outpaced that of the Axis by 50 percent. In fact, the United States manufactured approximately 45 percent of all armaments made by all parties at war![4]

A fundamental ingredient in all this production was increased manufacturing capacity. Many American companies either expanded existing facilities or built new ones. Within the office appliance industry, expansion of existing facilities occurred at IBM (Poughkeepsie, New York), NCR (Dayton, Ohio), and at Burroughs (Detroit, Michigan). These expanded in response to increased demand for office equipment in general and, more specifically, war-related items. Burroughs manufactured the Norden bombsight while IBM made rifles, gas masks, and components for submarines.[5] In the period 1939–1944, U.S. companies invested more than $13 billion in expansion and construction, positioning themselves well for a postwar civilian production boom. Wartime expansion was also fueled by an equally large investment in plant facilities by the American government. Some of this federal investment went directly to war-related materials such as synthetic rubber and chemicals or to manufactured goods (e.g., aircraft and computers).

U.S. Government Controls over the Industry

Normal free-market conditions, driven by the role of competitive rivalry in response to customer demands and technological evolution, both of which had become a way of life in this industry, were shelved during the war. The government picked up on a formula first developed during World War I by erecting an elaborate bureaucracy to control the flow of raw materials, to specify quotas for the amount and type of manufactured products, and to allocate distribution of finished goods. The umbrella organization most responsible for the activities of the American economy was the War Production Board (WPB) and, as with each industrial sector, it had a staff dedicated to the office supplies industry called the Service Equipment Division of the Consumers Durable Goods Bureau. The Office of Price Administration and Civilian Supply (OPACS), later called the Office of Price Administration (OPA), was created to influence events within the industry. Much of the next story illustrates how such agencies satisfied needs of military organizations by influencing production and sales within the proto–information-processing industry. The government designated the industry as two: office machines and typewriters. Thus a variety of agencies actively affected the industry.

Until the United States officially entered the war, government influence on the industry had been more ad hoc and less organized than afterward. The war in Europe caused the American government to increase acquisitions of office machines on behalf of the Allies to the point where events in the industry were affected, particularly by the increased sales now going to government agencies. Yet the earliest impact actually came from the British government and portended things to come later from Washington. The British declared a sea blockade against all trade between neutral countries in Europe and the rest of the world. Exporters had to obtain applications to export to Europe. The process of British licensing scarcely deterred exports of office machines to Western Europe in 1939 and 1940, something that would change later. After the United States entered the war, it took over this licensing function through the Economic Defense Board (EDB). On March 6, 1942, office machines were explicitly put on the list of items requiring formal export licenses. The fall of France to the Germans on June 22, 1940, posed a more practical restriction on Allied exports to Europe, and as countries fell under German control, overseas markets shrank. Simultaneously, however, the American government was demanding that output go increasingly to the war effort. The government treated exports, therefore, as a serious issue. Under the War Powers Act, the president could control exports. Additional legislation on June 30, 1942, and July 1, 1944, expanded his authority in such matters. The Economic Defense Board (created on July 30, 1941) and later called the Board of Economic Warfare (BEW) (as of December 17, 1941), were the agencies created to exercise this authority. On July 15, 1943, BEW became the Office of Economic Warfare (OEW).[6]

Very important to all exporters was the Lend-Lease Act of March 10, 1941, which allowed the U.S. government to increase the movement of goods of military value to the Allies. The Office of Lend-Lease Administration (OLLA) (created October 28, 1941) played an important role in the affairs of many office machine companies. Just to clear up any possible misunderstanding about agencies influencing the industry—and there were many saying grace over its activities during the war—OLLA and OEW merged into the Foreign Economic Administration (FEA) and then with the U.S. Commercial Company, Export-Import Bank, and other agencies on September 25, 1943, providing thereafter a single focal point for most foreign economic affairs. This new agency—FEA—had as its mission "to implement the general economic programs and policies of the Government by controlling the commercial exportation from the United States and its possessions of articles, materials, supplies and technical data."[7]

Obvious objectives included keeping useful materials and goods from the Axis powers, ensuring that war production and the civilian economy in the United States was supplied first, blocking the flow of useful technical data to the enemy, supporting the United Nations (Allies, as they were known), using goods to leverage favorable treatment by neutrals, and in general, making sure that the war effort was being supported effectively.[8] These objectives remained in effect until August 21, 1945, when the Lend-Lease Program was terminated and lifted further on September 10, 1945, when other office machinery restrictions were removed although not completely abolished until 1946.

Lend-lease represented an early and important government effort that influenced the industry. A foreign government (usually at the instigation of an office products vendor or distributor) petitioned the government for permission to acquire goods under lend-lease, at which point, if approval was granted, a company such as Burroughs or IBM quoted a price for specific goods. FEA or OLLA then looked at the specific proposal to see if it was consistent with the law, objectives of suporting the war, U.S. economic needs, and so forth. Once it was finally approved, the actual order for equipment came from the U.S. Treasury Department, which acted as the purchasing agent on behalf of the lend-lease nation. The series of transactions were also subject to repeated government audits. To facilitate the process, all major firms employed agents in Washington, D.C. They herded paperwork through the system, answered questions, and explained situations in a favorable light.[9]

Role of the War Production Board

The WPB covered all activities for most industries during the war whereas Lend-Lease, FEA, and others were concerned only with export aspects. One of the earliest concerns of the WPB was to convert civilian manufacturing to military purposes. Until Pearl Harbor was attacked, the office appliance industry had been, for all intents and purposes, left alone in recognition of the practical and productive effects such goods had on the economy. But after Pearl Harbor, pressure increased for fundamental changes in production.

This quickly became a sensitive issue because demand for office equipment ran at an all-time high in 1941, caused largely by "purchases of the Armed Services; the establishment of new war plants; the conversion and expansion of existing plants; the great increase in service activities such as transportation; the legal requirements that war producers keep complete records of payrolls, production costs, etc.; substantially increased overall employment; increased circulation of money and probably a considerable amount of buying in anticipation of restrictions," according to the WPB.[10] Such demands made it difficult for these firms to manufacture anything else (such as guns) without considerable disruption because they were already dedicating increased capacity to military needs. This circumstance came at a time when the requirements for manufacturing equipment with low tolerances were needed—for decades the industry's strong suit in manufacturing. The WPB initially restricted civilian sales to conserve the industry's resources so that they might be used to manufacture military goods. The board increasingly restricted sales across the industry to the Armed Services, lend-lease customers, war plants, and others who had convinced the WPB that such goods would be necessary to carry out war-related activities.

During 1942, the WPB gathered and analyzed the requirements of various government agencies and allocated purchases of office equipment. In turn that led the WPB to issue formal production schedules to vendors. But because agencies could never accurately define their needs, additional production schedules were issued periodically for specific types of equipment. Business was initially prorated on the basis of what share each had of the 1941 billings for specific classes of machines. Thus, in the case of typewriters, in March and April 1942, production of new machines was set at 326,215 nonportables and at 75,115 portables for the remainder of the year. These targets were, respectively, 59 percent and 17 percent of 1941 volumes.[11] At the same time, the government authorized acquisition of a million secondhand machines and by the end of the war had purchased some 300,000 of these. Members of the National Typewriter Dealers Association had an estimated inventory of some 3 million machines, which suggests the number of units of office equipment in the American economy.

During 1942 and 1943, the government attempted to stop production of various types of office equipment; by the end of 1943, those battles were over and it set larger production quotas for each year as early as 1942.[12] It was clearly a case of equipment being deemed essential to the war effort. Determination of production volumes resided with a committee composed of representatives from the army, navy, Board of Economic Warfare, Division of Civilian Supply, and OLLA. The first subject tackled by this group during April and May 1942 was the typewriter. Of all the industries discussed, office equipment came up at 75 of the first 130 meetings.[13] Second in importance to the group after typewriters was punched card machines. During 1942 and 1943, the government denied about 50 percent of all civilian requests for new office equipment, allocating the bulk of production to the military, followed by other agencies. Civilian pressure on the government mounted, and on March 1, 1943, the chairman of the WPB, Donald M. Nelson, called for a review of allocation of all types of office machines because "inadequate production" was "particularly burdensome on the business world, due to the vastly greater amount of paper work necessitated by additional payroll deduction for taxes, [and] for saving bond purchases," among other things.[14]

Volumes in 1941 (the base period used to allocate subsequent supplies) together with the 1943–1944 anticipated amounts that the chairman called inadequate are given in table 14.1. In fact, Nelson took a strong stand on the matter:

In short, during a period when the national product of this country is increasing from $97 billion in 1940 to $120 billion in 1941 to $175 billion in 1943 . . . the

TABLE 14.1

Office Machine Sales 1941 Compared to 1942–1944 Authorized Availability (dollars)

Class of Machines	Business Volumes[a] 1941	Supplies Authorized 5/31/42–6/30/44
Accounting, bookkeeping, billing, continuous forms handling	32,519,849	30,752,032
Adding	32,484,807	20,829,629
Addressing	5,711,469	5,722,596
Calculating, computing	34,430,086	32,711,313
Duplicating	11,708,477	14,183,099
Office composing	459,600	757,485
Shorthand writing	605,643	1,281,421
Time recording	5,896,964	7,687,917
Time stamping	576,139	811,086

Source: Donald M. Nelson to Nathaniel Burleigh, March 2, 1943, app. 5, War Production Board, "History of the Administration of Regulations of the Office Machine and Typewriter Industries, 1942–1945" (Report, August 1945), copy in Burroughs Papers.

[a] The data include export volumes and government-designated classes of machines (except typewriters, which are treated as a separate group).

production of business machines is being drastically reduced. Since such machines increase the productivity of our manpower in a substantial way and since manpower is fast becoming an important limiting factor in war production, I feel that careful consideration should be given to meeting essential needs for these machines.[15]

As a result of his pressure, revised production quotas were issued by the end of March 1943. Throughout the fall and winter of 1942–1943, numerous vendors had lobbied in Washington to get their production quotas set higher; their efforts, obviously, were effective.

One internal WPB report, however, noted that the new "allocations were never sufficient to meet even the most urgent demands of actual war industry let alone meeting the real needs of war industry and essential civilians."[16] The demand for equipment as formally submitted to the government by civilian organizations for the period June 1942–June 1944, as approved in August 1942 and March 1943, and then the twelve months between 1944 and the 1941 billings (sales) base period is indicated in table 14.2. Officials at the Office of Civilian Requirements acknowledged that demand for such equipment exceeded the numbers needed just for war plants and essential office functions.[17]

Based on the WPB records one could conclude that democracy could not be saved without the typewriter, and, indeed, many discussions were held con-

TABLE 14.2
Office Equipment Requirements, 1942–1944, 1941 Sales (dollars thousands)

Class of Machine	Requirements Determined[a]		Requirements for 1944[b]	Sales
	As of 8/42	As of 3/43		
Accounting	4,986	16,751	27,718	35,519
Adding	2,362	10,305	14,584	32,484
Addressing	1,225	4,349	4,724	5,962
Calculating	3,800	22,759	20,809	34,485
Duplicating	1,421	5,938	4,401	12,053
Dictating	687	1,094	2,127	9,948
Office composing	99	366	232	459
Time recording	3,154	7,030	4,662	6,219
Time stamp	60	241	201	807
Total	17,794	68,833	79,458	134,936
By units of machines Punch card tabulating	9,890	19,119	14,093	18,539

Source: War Production Board, "History of the Administration of Regulations of the Office Machine and Typewriter Industries, 1942–1945," (Report, August 1945), 13, Burroughs Papers.

[a] Requirements determined for June 1, 1942 to June 30, 1944.

[b] Requirements established February 2, 1944.

cerning the supply of this tool of modern bureaucracy! However, the role of the typewriter in World War II awaits its historian; more important here, it was significant because, as WPB's records suggest, it led to increased focus on other data-handling equipment of greater importance to the origins of the data-processing industry and to the successful execution of the war. Between June 1, 1942, and December 31, 1943, eleven classes of equipment were built and shipped, amounting to $109.52 million as compared to billings of $135.37 million in 1941. In addition, suppliers delivered 15,141 units of punched card equipment compared to production and delivery of 18,539 units in 1941. How these types of machines were distributed among claimant agencies is shown in table 14.3.

The WPB held meetings with industry representatives, known as the Office Machine Manufacturing Industry Advisory Committee, to discuss issues and volumes between April 2, 1942, and April 7, 1943. That the industry took these meetings seriously is evident from the members: Lawrence V. Britt (a senior sales executive at Burroughs), Harmon P. Elliott (CEO at Elliot Addressing Machine Company), Stanley C. Allyn (a senior executive at NCR), A. B. Dick, Jr. (soon after the war to become president and CEO of A. B. Dick Company), Watson (CEO of IBM), and Carl M. Friden (of the Friden

TABLE 14.3
Distribution of Machinery among Claimant Agencies, June 1, 1942,
to December 31, 1943

	11 Classes in Dollars		Punch Card Tabulating Units	
	Shipments	% of Total	Shipments	% of Total
Army	31,417,523	28.69	5,138	33.94
Navy	15,498,558	14.15	1,538	10.16
Lend-Lease	7,999,470	7.31	3	0.01
Canada	1,242,521	1.13	50	0.33
Export-OEW	3,363,446	3.07	486	3.21
Civilian	49,892,271	45.56	7,926	52.35
Total	109,516,194	100.00	15,141	100.00

Source: War Production Board, "History of the Administration of Regulations of the Office Machine and Typewriter Industries," 43, Burroughs Papers.

Calculating Machine Company). Other members came from the Standard Register Company, Addressograph-Multigraph Corporation, Dictaphone Corporation, Todd Company, Standard Duplicating Machine Corporation, and Simplex Time Recorder Company. This committee reflected the industry's concern that the U.S. government was influencing its fortunes and future, a situation entirely different from that of the 1920s or even the 1930s.[18]

Because during 1944 the same individuals who had established and administered the government's regulations were still in their positions, procedures ran relatively normally. The one major change was the increase in requests from potential customers to order equipment to a rate of 3,700 per week for a total of nearly 190,000 applications. Equipment valued at $440 million was manufactured by the office equipment industry for war production purposes that year. An additional $23 million in machines went to the U.S. armed services and other amounts to the Allies.[19] The single largest problem facing the government was allocation of manpower within the industry. As backlogs of unfilled orders increased in 1944 because of restrictions on manufacturing, so too did industry pressure rise to hire additional labor or, at least, to allocate manpower to normal production of goods. The government had a difficult time dealing with the issue because the allocation of manufacturing quotas did not always match actual production as a result of discrepancies in manpower and raw materials allocations. For instance, in 1943, the production of 24,818 nontypewriter units was authorized for the industry but only 10,073 were built; 278,788 typewriters were authorized and 206,279 made. Manufacturing to quotas remained a difficult process during the war.[20]

By early 1944, it was obvious to federal and industry officials that the economy demanded additional supplies and that, therefore, the 1941 base

TABLE 14.4
Summary of Production, Shipments, Inventories, Unfilled Orders for 1944 and 1943
(dollars in millions)

Type	Production		Shipments		Inventory[a]		Unfilled Orders[a]	
	1944	1943	1944	1943	1944	1943	1944	1943
Accounting	20.2	18.2	21.8	18.6	3.6	5.0	18.9	8.8
Adding	12.9	9.4	15.3	11.6	1.1	3.0	7.2	1.8
Calculating	23.5	19.1	25.0	20.9	2.1	3.5	3.2	3.1
Punch Card & Tabulating (units)	9,637	9,124	10,191	9,240	479	806	5,052	2,067

Source: Arthur Sanders, "Office Machine and Typewriter Industries in 1944," (Report of the Service Equipment Division, WPB, May 1945), sec. 2, add., copy in Burroughs Papers.
[a] As of December 31.

lines used to determine production runs were inadequate. An internal WPB report concluded that "production ceilings for specified periods based on historical sales volumes was not a wholly satisfactory plan for securing the production of the proper makes and models of machines needed during wartime. The makes and models of machines required by the normal peacetime economy during the base period of 1941 were entirely different from those required by the wartime economy of 1942 and later on."[21]

Production and distribution quotas were raised each quarter during the war and "as a practical matter, studies showed that there was little likelihood that any individual manufacturer would be able to produce up to the ceiling permitted because of the lack of facilities and manpower and because of the very low rate at which they had been producing since June, 1942."[22] The volumes for selected equipment manufactured and shipped in 1943 and 1944 across the entire industry are given in table 14.4. Manufacturing quotas compared to actual production in 1944 document the relationship between demand and production realities (see table 14.5). It suggests the effects of such constraints as insufficient manpower or inaccurate demand forecasts.

Between January and May 1945, some sixty thousand applications for equipment orders flowed into the government; forty thousand were approved. As a result of the Germans trying to break through the Allied lines in Belgium on December 16, 1944, both the U.S. Army and Navy requested more armaments, which, in turn, absorbed the additional supplies of carbon steel needed in the office appliance industry. The Office Machinery Branch of the Service Equipment Division (within WPB) managed the supply problem with a staff of twenty-four individuals. They also helped to redirect the industry's manufacturing capability toward the fabrication of war supplies valued at $310

TABLE 14.5

Maximum Permissible Production of Office Machines Compared to Actual Production, 1944

Class of Machines	Delivery Authorizations	Unfilled Orders 1943	Permitted Production for Inventory	Maximum Permissible Production	Actual Production
Accounting	33,274,293	8,802,014	1,666,659	43,742,966	20,241,475
Adding	16,652,764	1,861,529	3,505,975	22,020,268	12,905,990
Calculating	25,027,394	3,139,563	3,339,629	31,506,586	23,500,143
Total all Classes[a] (dollars)	103,376,659	16,479,174	15,499,809	135,355,642	81,454,273
Punch Card & Tabulating (units)	18,804	2,067	2,901	23,772	9,637

Source: Arthur Sanders, "Office Machine and Typewriter Industries in 1944," copy in Burroughs Papers.

[a] Total of all classes consisted of twenty-two types of equipment; shown above were only data-processing machines.

million annually. In the first three months of 1945, actual shipments reached $77 million, a rate continued until summer.[23] Then government contracts were canceled across all industries as the war ground down. Companies in all industries shifted production to civilian manufacturing, including office supplies. The only major exception was NCR which, when its contracts were canceled for gun sights and the Oerlikan gun magazine, sought other military contracts, obtaining one from the U.S. Navy to build rockets. That allowed the company to avoid layoffs, keeping its staff intact for the peacetime demand that would call for their services.[24]

Price Controls and Sales Deliveries

A feature of the American economy during the war was the extensive system of price controls imposed by the American and Canadian governments that limited the more natural forces of supply and demand, competitive pressures, and management prerogatives. The Office of Price Administration and Civilian Supply (OPACS), later converted to the Office of Price Administration (OPA) on August 28, 1941, was the principal vehicle used by the Roosevelt administration to control prices. Its objectives were to stabilize prices, to prevent speculation, profiteering, and hoarding, and to ensure that supply costs to the military were not excessive. OPA also wanted to minimize hardships on fixed incomes. The power to implement these objectives proved almost total and was usually effective. Controls stayed in force until July 1946, with some minor regulations remaining in place until the following summer. Once again, from an economic perspective, World War II did not end until nearly one year after Japan surrendered.

The base regulations affecting the office equipment industry came on July 29, 1942, when OPA issued the Maximum Price Regulation 188 (known in the industry as MPR 188). Simply put, it set maximum pricing at the manufacturer's level by prohibiting vendors from evading price limitations that altered normal discounts, allowances, or other pricing differences in effect in March 1942. Other restrictions on pricing actions were imposed to block changes on commissions, service, transportation, and other charges and discounts. In short, practices within the industry in force as of March 1942, were preserved relatively unchanged until late 1946. After enormous pressure to raise prices, the government allowed the industry to do so in September 1946, at which point they went up approximately 12 percent. Price controls regulated rentals, leases, sales, service charges, costs of new and used equipment of all kinds, and, thus, profitability of suppliers.[25]

These controls effectively froze prices for many years. How it was done can be gleaned from comments made by a Burroughs employee of the period:

> The office machinery program within OPA was administered by an industry representative at practically all times during its effective life. His industry viewpoint enabled him to protect the industry position insofar as it was consistent with the overall OPA program; he was receptive to suggestions and advice from the various members of the industry; when the OPA objectives had been achieved, it was his incentive to work toward a prompt termination of the controls in effect. The work of such individuals was always more practical and more direct, than the work of other sections which did not operate in this manner (through industry men).[26]

It appears that both the industry and the government were trying to make the best of an awkward situation.

The OPA and other agencies also regulated what priority system could be used to fill orders. They called for orders from the army and navy to be filled first, followed in descending order of priority by manufacturers of defense material; manufacturers of defense supplies; direct U.S. government agencies; other offices, such as those in state and county governments; utilities; and, finally, civilian organizations. To obtain delivery, thousands of customers tried to gain higher defense ratings than they might otherwise have been qualified for, which led one supplier to complain that "the cumulative effect was a build up of preferred demand beyond the capability of the supplier to meet."[27] The government monitored deliveries to ensure that priorities were observed. Auditing requirements imposed a considerable administrative burden on the industry, which had not existed before the war.[28] In addition to the concern about whose orders to process first, normal marketing and sales activities were also bothersome for management and government alike because sales could not be encouraged, especially among those potential customers who did not have a defense priority. Although that may have been less of an issue for IBM, which had many customers supplying the war effort, it hurt others, such as NCR and Burroughs, who had many customers in small, civilian markets.

In Canada, sales and prices were managed in the same way as in the United States. But instead of the WPB, Canada had the Wartime Prices and Trade Board. The U.S. government treated Canada as a claimant agency; both governments thus coordinated carefully their controls over the North American economy as a whole throughout the war.

Wartime Applications

Clearly, the largest set of applications for office equipment was the traditional set of accounting, inventory, and manufacturing functions that had become commonplace earlier and that continued to meet war production needs. Bureaucracy in government, followed by additional administrative pressures on industry (coming from more government controls) represented the majority of users.[29] American industry expanded the use of data processing at the same time that it modernized its manufacturing capability. For example, tabulating equipment was used to design aircraft,[30] implement automated inventory control,[31] manage transportation routing,[32] stabilize and control office salaries with cards as required by the Wage Labor Board,[33] install automated methods for handling payments at Consolidated Edison of New York,[34] and account for new government regulations and circumstances.[35] They found new uses as well in mining,[36] mathematics,[37] parts and material control,[38] and in maintaining and locating people on the National Roster of Scientific and Specialized Personnel.[39]

Expansion of the armed forces drove added demand for accounting equipment. almost all army and navy accounting relied on IBM technology. They used this equipment to track people and supplies, forecast demand for material, record expenditures, and plan battles. Millions of Americans drafted into the armed services were tracked with 80-column cards. These were present at induction, training, and mustering out. IBM's products were employed in bomb surveys, tracking missing-in-action personnel, prisoners, displaced persons, relief materials, and inventories of captured items. Equipment from IBM and NCR was also used for breaking codes, which built on relations with the military intelligence community dating back to the 1920s and 1930s.[40]

Product introductions, historically driven either by competitive pressures or the need to perform some new function, came to a virtual halt as manufacturing capacity went to supply either immediate demands for existing devices or to make war goods. However, in response to some demands for different products and services, a few new devices appeared along with changes in the industry. For example, in tabulating equipment, in 1941, IBM announced the Type 416 accounting machine, a tape-controlled punch, and the 404 alphabetic accounting machine with a multiple-line printing capability from a single card—all the culminations of prewar development activities. The following year, Remington Rand launched its first direct sales program for tabulating machines, followed in 1943 by Powers-Samas bringing out a cross-adding punch.[41] These represented the major tabulating events of the war and suggest the degree to which product introductions had been put on hold. Many items currently sold during the war, however, were relatively new, having been brought out during the second half of the 1930s. Consequently, most machines in manufacture were of reasonably current technology. Almost no technical advances were made in the late 1930s and early 1940s, however, with typewriters, and the production of cash registers came to a virtual halt to conserve metal.

One of the most publicized uses of data-processing equipment, and the one that provided specific incentives for the U.S. and British governments to finance development of the modern computer, was wartime intelligence or, more specifically, cryptoanalysis—the breaking of enemy codes in messages. A number of projects in this field had been underway since the turn of the century, with initial work in Germany; by World War I, various naval and army agencies in Europe and in the United States were involved. Such work drew elements within the military community increasingly closer to the office appliance industry during the first four decades of the twentieth century and built a solid basis for close ties with the data-processing industry, which has continued to the present day. The U.S. Navy led the way within the U.S. government in supporting work in cryptoanalysis and radio communications because it needed airborne links to ships and to translate encoded foreign telecommunications. Beginning in 1921, the navy operated a cryptological unit, which was better financed than the army's by a factor of three or five. By 1939, the U.S. Navy's operation was mature and sophisticated. During the 1930s, IBM punched card equipment was used to process codes and, by the end of World War II, the navy had also installed seven specially developed machines built at MIT.[42] The navy's work in the area of high-speed analytical machinery for cyrptoanalysis caused some in the military to appreciate the potential value of electronic and mechanical data handling in general, an appreciation made even more firm by concurrent support for MIT's studies of servomechanisms during the 1930s and 1940s. This later work contributed to electronic feedback devices to control movement.[43]

The U.S. Army devoted considerable attention to code breaking but also added a third line of development: the computation of ballistics tables for artillery and, later, rockets, building on research dating back to World War I. This research relied heavily on differential analyzers such as those developed by Vannevar Bush at MIT.[44] This interest led eventually to construction of ENIAC during the war, the first functioning electronic digital computer. Rivalry between the two services was not excluded even from the decision to support development of ENIAC at a time when the U.S. Navy had made significant progress with its own computerlike projects.

Yet the centerpiece of early World War II applications remained cryptoanalysis. The British and Polish governments had been more active and effective in employing hardware and electronics in this field than the Americans in the interwar period. British, French, and Polish intelligence communities had, by the early days of World War II, copies of a device known as Enigma developed by the Poles to translate encrypted German and Japanese codes. At Bletchley Park, in Britain, workers refined equipment, which led to construction of various computers.[45] The Germans were constantly changing their coding methods, which, in turn, caused the Allies to change theirs, find faster means to do so, and be more effective. Incentives were enormous. For example, when the Germans in 1942 complicated even further encryption on Enigmas, Allied intelligence stopped receiving German messages regarding activities of U-boats in the Atlantic. Consequently, many Allied ships were sunk with horrible losses of life. The British reacted by promptly investing more resources in applying electronics to breaking codes. Results of this work were shared with U.S. military intelligence, which too had seen the value of code breaking. It was, for example, the U.S. Navy that had developed enough information through code breaking to warn high government officials that the Japanese were planning to attack Pearl Harbor. By the end of 1942, the British had developed a high-speed computerlike device to break codes, which they nicknamed Heath Robinson.[46]

The U.S. Navy had several of its own projects in cryptoanalysis. The most notable involved the Naval Computing Machinery Laboratory (NCML) housed on the grounds of NCR's plant in Dayton. NCML began with a staff of 20 in 1942 and ended the war with 1,100. It used nearly 1,200 machines of some 140 varieties.[47] With increased losses of shipping in the Atlantic during 1942, pressure mounted to get results, and this led the U.S. Navy to take direct control of all developmental work with cryptoanalysis then under NCR's management. During the period when NCR primarily managed the work and subsequently when the Navy did, IBM participated by building special-purpose punched card equipment for breaking codes.[48]

The Harvard Mark I and work done at the Moore School of Electrical Engineering were funded by the military. The army turned to the University of Pennsylvania's Moore School to construct ENIAC for ballistics analysis while the navy, in conjunction with Howard Aiken at Harvard and IBM's

TABLE 14.6
Combat-related Applications Using Office Equipment and
Special Purpose Computers, 1939–1945

Applications	Devices[a]	Start Date
Cryptoanalysis	IBM Punch Hardware	1920s
	NCR Accounting Machines	1941
	Heath Robinson	1942
	Colossus	1943
Ballistics	IBM Punch Hardware	1930s
	Differential Analyzer	1930s
	ENIAC	1944
	Harvard Mark I	1944
Flight Training	MIT Equipment	1944
Atomic Bomb	ENIAC	1945

[a] This highly selective list does not include the use of traditional office products of the 1930s and 1940s for normal accounting for personnel, payroll, inventory, ship scheduling, and so forth.

engineers at Endicott, built Mark I, one of the last giant electromechanical calculators before the advent of electronic digital computers.[49] The ENIAC, primarily, but also the Mark I were used to calculate trajectories for ballistics and to develop firing tables more rapidly and accurately than before.[50]

Various war-related applications that involved use of equipment from IBM, Remington Rand, NCR, Burroughs, and others are summarized in table 14.6. The list indicates the speed with which vendors and government alike turned to computing and information-handling technologies to help conduct the war. It is proof of the perception that such equipment could make a difference. For the industry, such dependence on these classes of machines bonded a relationship with the U.S. government that encouraged the construction of early computers, creating the earliest demand for such machines before they were commercially attractive.[51] The same happened in Britain.[52]

Summary

Activities of the U.S. government illustrated the radical and rapid change in the economic environment in which information product vendors and users had to operate. Government agencies controlled both activities and economic incentives in sweeping fashion. Even during World War I, the U.S. government had not so totally attempted to control the economy, let alone succeeded. The information-processing world served as a useful example of the manner in which the government accomplished control as purposefully as it did. Despite such control, major vendors were kept busy supplying products deemed crucial to the war effort. How they met such demand while attempting to maintain profit margins and qualified staffs is the subject of the next chapter.

15

The Role of Major Vendors, 1939–1946

THE EVENTS of World War II presented a unique set of challenges and opportunities to all businesses in North America. Vendors in the proto-information–processing industry were not exempt from these new circumstances. The intensity of the economic focus on war-related activities far exceeded the experience of World War I. How they responded contributes to the economic history of the war. It also suggests further evidence of the growing dependence of the North American economy on information-handling technologies. Ultimately, delivery of equipment deemed useful for the war effort by major vendors was as important as the use to which they were put. Without effective distribution, the benefits of such equipment could not be enjoyed. Senior management in at least the major firms had some experience with controls from the days of World War I to help them as they guided their companies through the next world war. By examining specific actions taken by some of the major vendors, one can see how the office appliance industry fared during the early 1940s.

Burroughs Adding Machine Company

The role played by Burroughs during the war is a good case study of what other vendors did. Business patterns were disrupted, yet Burroughs' products were in demand for the war effort. Manufacturing military products proved important, particularly the Norden bombsight, while its employees served in the armed services. The war affected volumes of sales and profits, yet the distribution of products remained essentially the same. International sales stopped to the Axis powers from the United States while those to Allied and neutral countries were subjected to U.S. government controls. Burroughs management did not enjoy the same kind of successes as say, IBM, partially because so much of the productive capacity and effort of the firm went to highly regulated items (e.g., war goods), which resulted in its products not being able to contribute significantly to sales in the later years of the war. Executives were also older, perhaps more set in their ways, but clearly not as effective as those in some other firms within the industry.

Burroughs reacted to the uncertainties of war by setting up a reserve fund to cover the eventuality that all of its foreign investments might be destroyed except for those in Canada and Central and South America. That accounting step in 1941 alone meant that the firm carried on the books its foreign assets as investments valued at $901,713 (after deducting $1.2 million in reserves of which $500,000 were charged against 1941's income). This action reflected uncertainty but was, nevertheless, effective. By the time the war had ended, all overseas assets in Europe and Asia had been retired from the general ledger this way and were then folded back into the balance sheet in 1946. This cautionary move also balanced against growing demand anticipated for office products in general. Standish Backus, president of the company, reported that "the demand for our products has increased due to the War Production activity. The total production of bookkeeping and accounting machines of all concerns in this country is not very large, and we have now reached the point where it appears that all machines of this type may be required by the Government and other industries doing direct war work."[1] That meant an almost guaranteed demand for everything he was allowed to make for the duration of the war.

The company sold increasing proportions of its products to the U.S. military community and to government contractors and civilian agencies. The president of the firm in the spring of 1943 boasted that "qualified by long experience, the Company's combined servie and marketing organizations are aiding the Army, Navy, other governmental units and war contractors in setting up, simplying, and mechanizing accounting and auditing procedures for countless war activities both here and overseas."[2] Burroughs's customers also used its equipment to track new taxes, rationing, coupons, and other controls.

On February 15, 1943, the company changed its leadership, a shift that had little positive effect on it during the war. Standish Backus, president since the 1930s, retired because of ill health and was replaced by Alfred J. Doughty, executive vice-president and long a key executive at the firm, who served until the end of the war.

The volume of business done during the war and the lack of any positive influence by management changes is shown in table 15.1. What becomes obvious is growth in dollar volumes until 1944 followed by decline as the business shifted resources to war production and away from normal sales of office equipment. Profits also declined largely because of restrictions in the manufacturing of business machines and price controls. Clearly, opportunities to improve efficiencies throughout the firm were not seized upon, particularly in manufacturing. Furthermore, foreign sales declined because of the war.[3] The company's problem with profits stemmed from the fact that the rate of return on sales of office equipment was always higher than that on war goods.[4] However, its rate of return on office products was not as great, for example, as IBM's. Thus a combination of reasons—loss of economies of scale as office product sales slowed, needs of war production, price controls, rising labor costs—all played havoc with the bottom line.

TABLE 15.1
Revenues and Profits for Burroughs Corporation,
1939–1946 (dollars in millions)

Year	Revenues	After Tax Income	Assets[a]
1939	28.46	2.99	28.86
1940	30.17	3.02	29.38
1941	41.86	5.33	30.71
1942	43.48	4.82	32.13
1943	45.46	4.28	33.01
1944	39.51	2.68	33.13
1945	32.31	0.90	33.31
1946[b]	39.99	1.75	32.64

Source: Burroughs Corporation, *1946 Annual Report*, 22–23.

[a] Assets were added (less liabilities and reserves) to show how little the company had actually grown in worth.

[b] Data for 1946 were included because many U.S. government controls were in effect until late that year.

The centerpiece of war-related manufacturing at Burroughs was the Norden bombsight, a delicate device that gave engineers considerable experience with electronics that was useful after the war in developing new products, including computers. The bombsight, known as the Type M9 Bombsight Unit, was manufactured on behalf of the C. L. Norden Company. The initial contract negotiated in 1942 called for 6,900 units at an estimated cost of $50.5 million. On November 1, 1944, this contract was modified to call for manufacture of 5,511 units at a total cost of $53.6 million plus the company's fee. The 1944 order was completed at a cost of only $16.8 million, leaving a savings to the government of some $15 million. Burroughs was paid $1.9 million for building the 5,511 units. Other aircraft-related manufacturing included 2,500 Directional Stabilizers, 2,500 Glide Bombing Attachments, and the necessary links to match 965 stabilizers with the bombsight. The entire bombsight contract cost the U.S. government $20.4 million on a cost-plus basis for which the company was paid just over $2 million, making Burroughs's fee 10.15 percent of cost.[5] At the height of the war, revenues from this contract approached nearly one-third of the company's total.

The war did not prove as profitable for Burroughs as one might otherwise think. If measured on just the basis of earnings per share of stock, in 1941, that figure had climbed to 95 cents and, thereafter, declined annually to a low of 25 cents per share in 1945, then rose to 39 cents in 1946. Dividends paid out exceeded earnings per share in 1944 through 1946, which insured that the

TABLE 15.2

Sales for Burroughs and Major Competitors, 1939–1946
(dollars in millions)

Year	Burroughs	NCR	Marchant	Underwood
1939	32.49	37.08	3.89	24.15
1940	29.36[a]	38.78	4.27	26.30
1941	41.28[a]	52.40	7.46	36.49
1942	44.04[a]	79.88	8.62	33.26
1943	44.48[a]	99.17	5.69	47.60
1944	37.44[a]	93.78	8.02	37.52
1945[b]	37.59	68.44	9.05	28.98
1946	46.24	77.38	12.02	37.16

Source: Goldman, Sachs and Co., "Burroughs Adding Machine Company," Report of August 28, 1947, Burroughs Papers.

[a] Parent company only.

[b] Dips in revenues in 1945 were caused largely by government contracts canceled for war goods as the war came to a close.

value of the stock would not falter. The company emerged from the war with no debt to speak of and strong financially. During the war, the major shift in expenses came in salaries. In 1939, these accounted for 66.6 percent of all income from products and services and climbed to 80.8 percent during 1946. Factory hourly workers in 1946 made approximately 55 percent more than they had in 1941.[6]

The company had not grown in volumes or market share during the war as had some rivals, either because of lackluster management or, as it explained, because of too many government controls. The conventional "street wisdom" of the time may have proved correct: the company was not as effective as some rivals in marketing (see table 15.2). Largely, that weakness, along with poor management of manufacturing processes, accounted for the change in top management in 1946 and for fundamental alterations in company policies. The firm emerged from World War II, for example, with a manufacturing plan to build 582 special purpose models that it then slashed to 95 high-volume models to streamline and control costs.[7] A whole generation of management was replaced with younger senior executives in their forties and early fifties.

Burroughs, as an organization of people, was caught up in the events of war like its peers across the economy. Management invested corporate funds up to the maximum amount allowed in Series "F" Defense Savings Bonds while more than 90 percent of all employees bought Series "E" Savings Defense Bonds through payroll deduction (made convenient by accounting equipment). The savings bonds program for employees was initiated at Burroughs in January 1941 and remained in force throughout the war. By the spring of 1944, 1,476 employees were also serving in the armed forces of the United States.[8]

National Cash Register Company

NCR represented a very different model of an office equipment vendor during the war in that its main product—cash registers—were not allowed to be manufactured in the belief that the raw materials, manufacturing personnel, and capacity involved could best be used for other, more war-related items. Consequently, NCR had to approach the crisis of war differently than Burroughs, which had products more central to the war effort. NCR responded by becoming mostly dedicated to the production of war-related goods. It also invested increasingly in data-processing technology, such as accounting and adding equipment, while refurbishing thousands of old cash registers and related devices. This was a company whose foreign sales had historically been a significant portion of its revenues (35–45 percent), and these too came to a halt owing to the war and the government's prohibition on the manufacture of registers, which cut off marketable inventory. When all these factors were taken together, NCR's wartime experiences were unique.

The restriction against cash registers grew out of the government's survey of its agencies at the start of the war to determine what should be built and how many. These agencies and the armed services did not request registers and so the WPB had no recourse but to deny all cash register vendors permission to make such devices. Issued on May 5, 1942, general conservation order M-126 restricted manufacture because cash registers were made from steel. Vendors were told they could continue to use up to 75 percent of such metals in any product they wanted for up to 45 days, until June 20, 1942. An exception was made for cash registers, which they were allowed to continue making until August 5, 1942. Thus firms like Burroughs, McCaskey Register Company, NCR, and others virtually stopped construction of cash registers to conserve metal for other products or because of the absolute ban. The government did not lift its prohibition against cash registers until May 15, 1945, despite numerous protests and appeals by NCR and others. Some exceptions were granted, but they were few and far between. For example, NCR was given permission to manufacture a few machines for the U.S. Navy during 1944.[9] Additional supplies were allowed in 1945, but controls remained in place in one form or another until 1946 when, late in the year, all restrictions were lifted.

The government's prohibition was a shock to NCR's business. It came on the heels of a major decline in business worldwide caused by the war. In the fall of 1939, sales to Europe virtually stopped. In 1940, production ended in

Japan; NCR's plant there was ordered sold to Japanese interests. In countries at war, about the only sales were of secondhand and rebuilt machines. In 1940, foreign exports out of the Dayton plant were 50 percent below 1939's. Sales in Latin America continued to grow, up 20 percent in 1940. Remaining shipments in 1940 and 1941 additionally went to Australia, New Zealand, South Africa, Hawaii, and the Philippines. Overall sales that year from all sources (foreign and domestic) were up 16 percent over 1939.[10] But that changed with WPB's order of 1942.

The company responded to the prohibition on manufacture in a number of ways. First, it worked hard to maintain existing machines at their customers' locations and encouraged them to use these to meet increased demands. Thus, for example, store owners were shown how they might handle more customers with the cash registers they had.[11] Second, NCR scoured the world, acquiring every used, secondhand NCR register and Class 2000 accounting machine it could find, shipping thousands of units to Dayton for refurbishing and modernization. This allowed the company to have products for sale while keeping intact and enhancing the skills of its manufacturing force, with an eye to being able to make new machines when war ended. A side benefit of the hunt for old machines was that secondhand dealers could not compete against new products after the war was over. It was an effective program, one that an NCR executive said "stripped clean, worldwide, all obsolete NCR products."[12] Concurrently, the engineering community at NCR designed new models in anticipation of the postwar market. In all, these steps made up a series of creative responses to a serious problem.

NCR also joined other major office supply vendors to convince the WPB to allow increased production of accounting machines above 1941 levels. It cooperated in a study sponsored by the WPB that showed if a machine took three hundred hours to make, it could save three thousand man-hours of work. This study took place as business expanded by roughly 60 percent and accounting by 20 percent across the economy during the early days of the war in large part because of the fighting. As a consequence, NCR, like other office machine suppliers, was allowed to build additional accounting machines late in 1942 and in early 1943. One NCR executive recalled that a major issue weighing on the minds of the WPB was the "conservation of man power" which "was proved to be more important than conservation of raw materials."[13] WPB's records lead one to conclude, contrarily, that this agency was concerned about raw materials almost as much as manpower.

NCR had capacity and manpower that it needed to employ elsewhere as long as registers could not be built. The firm could not build accounting machines in sufficient numbers to make up the shortfall in capacity owing to production quota limits nor venture into new products because of similar controls. Its only option beyond refurbishing old machines, and the one it went after aggressively, was war-related manufacturing. That was one reason why,

TABLE 15.3
NCR's Sales, After-tax Profit, and Net Current
Assets, 1939–1946 (dollars in millions)

Year	Sales	After-tax Profits	Net Current Assets
1939	37.08	2.46	29.75
1940	38.78	3.15	30.34
1941	52.40	4.91	31.70
1942	79.88	10.84	33.00
1943	99.17	10.72	31.27
1944	93.78	8.52	32.03
1945	68.44	2.25	29.55
1946	77.38	3.37	37.07

Source: Moody's Manual of Investments, 1939–1946.

for example, NCR persuaded the U.S. Navy to work with it on cryptoanalysis at the Dayton plant. As early as 1940, NCR had begun making bomb fuses. From then to the end of the war the plant made the MK4 rocket motor used in 5-in. antiaircraft rockets. It built Chandler-Evans aircraft carburetors for various bombers. The K-3 and K-4 analog computerlike gunsights used in bomber defense systems also came from NCR. As at IBM and at Burroughs, skills in electronics grew during the war years. At Dayton, for instance, Joseph R. Desch had begun working with electronics in 1938 and all during the war gained further experience.[14] By early 1945, almost 100 percent of manufacturing at Dayton was directly related to the war, and that kind of effort continued to dominate manufacturing and engineering into midyear. By October, however, the U.S. government had begun canceling contracts across the economy, damaging NCR severely. The firm put on a brave front to its employees, announcing in its company magazine that "the door opened for the unrestricted manufacture of our regular products."[15]

NCR's revenues had grown steadily during the war but dropped sharply in 1945, mostly because of the decline in government business (see table 15.3). Yet overall, the company came out of 1946 twice as large (as measured by sales revenues) as in 1939. Net profits declined sharply and for essentially the same reasons as at Burroughs. At NCR, government contracts had covered the company's overhead while profits came from the sale of reconditioned machines.[16] The only major business event of the war for NCR related to data processing occurred in 1943 when it acquired the Allen-Wales Adding Machine Company in recognition that it would give the company a greater presence in the banking and insurance communities—both seen as significant users of information-handling equipment.[17] Pricing and expenses mirrored conditions at Burroughs. Prices were controlled by the government, which at

NCR meant that between 1939 and 1946 sales prices for its products rose only 25 percent whereas manufacturing costs by 65 percent, mainly for salaries. Price controls and cost increases had squeezed profits.

Human resources presented a significant problem for management. Like other manufacturers, NCR sought on the one hand to keep intact experienced staffs to renew business after the war and to survive government controls at the moment but, on the other, could not discourage or stop people from serving in the armed services. On occasion, a whole group of skilled people was absorbed into the military. For instance, of 1,914 NCR field maintenance personnel, 935 eventually served in the armed services, making it very difficult for NCR to repair the equipment in its customers' hands. Like most corporations in the United States, it backfilled many positions with women for the first time, beginning in 1942.[18] This move made it possible for thousands of men from NCR to serve in the armed services without restricting day-to-day operations within the company. That strategy allowed the firm to preserve the size headcount it wanted. On VJ Day in September 1945, it had eighty-two hundred employees at the plant in Dayton and more than ten thousand by January 1946.[19]

Throughout the war, NCR's management knew it was constrained by the ban on register production compared with the potential demand identified by marketing. In 1944, for instance, they knew that retail outlets generated $69 billion in sales in nearly 1.8 million stores across 125 lines of business with some 7 million employees. Experience dictated that such retail volumes had been made possible in the past partly by the use of cash registers and other products and that in 1944 the economy was continuing to expand. They were frustrated also by the fact that their best customers were department stores, which also were growing, representing 10 percent of all retail business transacted in the United States. Another major set of NCR's customers was supermarkets, which, in 1944 alone, numbered 7,980 and generated $2 billion in sales.[20] Yet the only manufacturing of new products for all these customers came in 1945 when some 27,000 registers and accounting machines were built at Dayton. By 1947, NCR had a backlog of unfilled orders worth $100 million![21] That volume was equal to the maximum capacity of the Dayton plant for one full year, working around the clock.

Employees responded to the war in personal ways, thereby contributing to a corporate image of fully supporting the war. They bought savings bonds and gave blood. Management strongly endorsed war-related programs. NCR's registers were used at the New York World Fair in 1939 and for many war loan drives. NCR installed a "mammoth model of a National register in Times Square" to record progress of war bond purchases.[22]

Management clearly, and against a tougher situation than faced by Burroughs or IBM, had proven relatively effective, creative, and able to preserve the firm through potentially disastrous times. In the process, it had become stronger, learned about electronics, and acquired experience in dealing with the U.S. government. When combined with even better management in 1946, NCR was well situated when the postwar period brought significant changes to the industry.

International Business Machines

IBM's executives managed the company effectively during the war, expanding and strengthening the firm more than any other company did in the industry. In sales volumes, in 1939, IBM ranked second with $39.5 million after Remington Rand, which had sales of $43.3 million. In 1945, IBM was the largest at $141.7 million with Remington Rand at $132.6 million. In earnings, in 1939, IBM ranked first with $9.1 million and ended the war in the same position with $10.9 million. In the value of net assets, IBM in 1939 was first at $79 million compared to NCR at $56.9 million. In 1945, IBM remained number one with $134.1 million, Remington Rand number two with $75.4 million, and NCR third with $57.4 million.[23]

Watson, apparently earlier and more enthusiastically than most of his peers in the industry, offered the U.S. government his support. That meant making available IBM's manufacturing and managerial resources while shrewdly expanding the number of contracts he had with various government agencies. IBM already had extensive relationships with military and civilian offices within the government developed during the early decades of the century that were expanded extensively during the depression. These were extended even further when IBM's products were declared critical to the war effort. IBM also held the advantage over many companies from the government wartime rulings on pricing because the firm entered the conflict making as high or more of a return on sales as any of its competitors. The company had skilled precision manufacturing capabilities that it used to produce military products. IBM—like its peers—publicly endorsed war-related programs for its employees and went further than many in providing special benefits as a result of the war. The sum of all these circumstances and programs meant that IBM prospered, continued to be a leading provider of office equipment, and emerged well positioned to maintain its prominent position.

It began with Watson, who cherished patriotic feelings that left no doubt in any employee's mind about where he stood on national issues. His views always prevailed at IBM and were highly publicized and open. At the start of the conflict, he offered the company's manufacturing capabilities to the War Department, which, in turn, immediately asked him to manufacture 20 millimeter machine guns and munitions. Other requests followed quickly for some three dozen products by the end of the war. They ranged from parts for airplane engines to bombsights, components for submarines to hand grenades,

TABLE 15.4

Revenues and Profits for IBM during World War II, 1939–1945 (dollars in millions)

Year	Revenues	After-tax Income	Assets[a]
1939	39.5	9.1	79.0
1940	46.3	9.4	83.1
1941	62.9	9.8	97.6
1942	90.7	8.7	120.6
1943	134.9	9.2	154.2
1944	143.3	9.7	136.5
1945	141.7	10.9	134.1

Source: *Moody's Manual of Investments*, 1943, 1948; Robert Sobel, *IBM: Colossus in Transition* (New York: Times Books, 1981): 104.

[a] Assets more than profits tell the story of IBM's financial success during the war.

rifles to ammunition. Some of the company's major wartime customers included the U.S. Navy Bureau of Ordnance, the U.S. Army Corps of Engineers, and the U.S.N. Bureau of Ships. IBM also served as a subcontractor to other firms building military products, most notably General Electric.[24] In addition to these products, IBM continued to sell its own tabulating supplies and to rent equipment.

Watson was prepared to compromise profits and normal business practices to support the war. In fact, through various wartime economic controls, the risk of weakened profits was real. Yet he was creative and supportive of responsible business practices while IBM produced war-related goods. For example, to focus on the manufacture of military products he created the Munitions Manufacturing Corporation in 1941. He limited profits on all military contracts to 1.5 percent. These profits were set aside for widows and orphans of IBM employees killed in action and, thus, did not flow to the parent corporation. Wives of IBM employees in uniform received one week of their husband's prewar salary for each month served in the military. Watson kept his own salary at the 1939 level throughout the war.

Roughly 10 percent of the company's volume directly concerned production of weapons and related products, another 10 percent with parts and supplies for war, and the remaining 80 percent with normal office equipment. The office machinery end of the business expanded largely because of the government's need. Results of IBM's overall financial performance are summarized in table 15.4. Wartime excess profit taxes kept IBM from otherwise probably tripling profits during the period and kept the rise to a modest 20 percent. Yet the net worth of the company expanded from $79 million to $134 million between 1939 and 1945; cash and other liquid assets went from $6.5 million in 1939 to $23.5 million in 1945.[25]

During the war, IBM's factory space tripled while the number of employees doubled.[26] The number of products on rent kept rising too. At the end of 1943, IBM had approximately 10,000 tabulators on rent of which 64 percent were the Type 405 alphabetic accounting machine, another 30 percent the numeric printing tabulator (primarily Type 285), and the final 6 percent nonprinting devices. It had installed 2,000 Type 601 multipliers, 24,500 keypunch machines, and 10,200 Type 80 sorters.[27]

Unlike most other American firms in the industry, IBM's foreign sales grew during the war with earnings doubling. Local IBM employees managed to keep open facilities in Germany, Italy, and France. Tabulating equipment was thus used by both sides in the war. Given the exigencies of warfare, keeping operations going in Europe was no minor accomplishment. Yet what helped was that other governments had the same need for office appliances as the U.S. government and, therefore, ensured that these kinds of operations remained productive. Because some of IBM's overseas operations remained in working order, it was able to reorganize foreign activities relatively quickly into the World Trade Corporation in 1949 with the necessary focus to make that portion of the business grow continuously.[28]

As at other firms, IBM employees bought war bonds, some $27 million at maturity, while public sales through war bond drives amounted to $53 million. The army and navy gave the plant at Endicott the coveted "E" award of excellence five times, that at Poughkeepsie four.[29]

Although IBM's early work in computer technology is beyond the scope of this book, one notes that as a result of research projects with universities (e.g., Harvard and the University of Pennsylvania), government agencies (e.g., army and navy ordnance communities), and other companies (General Electric, AT&T, Bell Labs), IBM acquired some expertise in electronics and contacts among scientists, engineers, and government contractors that was useful after the war.[30]

Remington Rand

If one looks at just calculating and computing products and markets, striking similarities appear between the experiences of IBM and Remington Rand during the war years. Like IBM, Remington Rand had its punched card line and was subject to the same governmental controls. But IBM had a considerable edge because it controlled the largest portion of the punched card market in 1941. IBM also enjoyed the benefits of a well-oiled selling organization whereas Remington Rand still struggled with establishing a fully integrated, effective marketing enterprise. Those efforts continued throughout the war despite the loss of labor to the military and the disruption of normal trading patterns. Unlike IBM, Remington Rand had to be concerned with other office products, such as furniture. Much of the furniture had been made out of steel in the 1930s, and government proscriptions against such manufacture slowed the company's financial performance.[31]

Retailing billings for accounting machines amounted to $2.68 million at Remington Rand during 1941, placing it fourth after Burroughs ($14.23 million), NCR ($9.69 million), and Underwood-Elliott-Fisher ($5 million). Other competitors such as R. C. Allen, Allen-Wales, IBM, and Monroe had less than a half-million dollars in billings each for accounting machines that year. The key vendors—Burroughs, NCR, Underwood, and Remington Rand—combined had sales that year of $33 million, giving Remington Rand just over 12 percent of the market.[32]

In adding machines, Remington Rand billed $5.58 million in 1941, placing it in third position after Burroughs ($8.64 million) and Underwood-Sundstrand ($6.31 million). Other rivals with at least $1 million in sales that year included R. C. Allen, Allen-Wales, Monroe, L. C. Smith, and Victor. When joined by the three large suppliers, all generated a total domestic U.S. sales volume of $32,587,887. Therefore, Remington Rand owned 17.2 percent of the market, a better position than it had in the accounting machine market.[33]

A third market segment, calculators, represented a field in which Remington Rand played a minor role at the start of the war. In 1941, sales amounted to $1.5 million in a market of $34.44 million. The top five vendors were Monroe ($9 million), Marchant ($7.63 million), Felt & Tarrant ($6.82 million), Burroughs ($5 million), and Friden ($4.18 million).[34]

Remington Rand was, however, a major supplier of typewriters. In 1941, it shipped 235,755 desktop machines out of a total sold by all vendors in the United States of 718,435. That gave Remington Rand roughly one-third of the market. Out of 558,768 portable typewriters shipped by the top four suppliers, Remington Rand sold 145,205, placing it second after Royal, which had 184,643 to its credit.[35] Typewriters represented, therefore, an important aspect of Remington Rand's business and, in all probability, a highly profitable revenue stream milking a stable, well-understood technology. Certainly, it was a line of business not overlooked by the company throughout the war; it represented a far more significant piece of the business than punched card equipment or calculators. Typewriters competed successfully for attention and resources against accounting, adding and other machines, office supplies, and furniture. Unlike many other vendors in the industry, Remington Rand had a very broad product line at the start of the war, which, by drawing attention and resources, did not lead to the singular focus evident at IBM, where the product line was narrower and management could concentrate more on specific market segments.

TABLE 15.5
Net Sales for Remington Rand Corporation,
1939–1945 (dollars in millions)

Year	Net Sales	Year	Net Sales
1939	43.2	1943	132.9
1940	49.2	1944	132.5
1941	77.3	1945	108.0
1942	91.4		

Source: *Standard and Poor's Basic Analysis (O1-b) of Office Equipment Industry* as reproduced in table 3, "The General Nature and Size of the United States Business Machines Industry: Notes for Technical Seminar of 14 November 1951," Burroughs Papers.

Net sales for Remington Rand during World War II are given in table 15.5. During the early 1940s Remington Rand did extremely well in revenues. Although it did not double revenues as did IBM, they rose by one-third, which bested the performance of its key competitors. In large part that success can be attributed to having products relevant to the war—tabulating and punched card equipment, typewriters, and military devices. Actions continued the reorganization of the firm started before the war. It announced additional products in punched card equipment and reorganized marketing to sell such equipment directly. The latter move made sales to the military, for example, more effective. Overall during the war, Remington Rand picked up considerable momentum, which gave management the confidence and the necessary fiscal power to survey the horizons of the postwar period and conclude that the firm should include electronics in office equipment and move into commercial computers earlier than many other well-established companies. Computers were simply another line of office machines to add to Remington's collection of products.

Momentum caused by sales, revenues, and profits is a psychologically motivating factor frequently ignored by economists and economic historians but which is recognized by executives as a positive and real factor. World War II had that kind of effect on the office appliance industry. Growth rates were constantly monitored by competing vendors as signals of a rival's potential future effectiveness. Between 1937 and 1948, for example, analysts at Burroughs documented increases in their company's gross revenues at 2.1 times and, correctly, those of major competitors—IBM, NCR, and Remington Rand—at 3 to 5.7 times. To Burroughs, the trend represented a long-term threat while offering impetus to others as they defined new market niches.[36] By such measure, Remington Rand appeared in good shape.

TABLE 15.6
Number of Patents Issued, 1940–1946

Company	1940	1941	1942	1943	1944	1945	1946	Total
Burroughs	10	14	6	8	7	4	0	49
IBM	87	72	68	59	55	52	25	418
NCR	19	25	15	12	10	12	20	113
Underwood	36	55	43	37	27	16	9	223
Remington Rand	9	22	21	16	11	5	2	86
Monroe Gardner	5	11	9	8	6	6	2	47
Annual Total[a]	76	199	162	140	126	95	58	

Source: Edward Littlejohn and C. J. McClain, "Accounting Machine Industry," 37, Burroughs Papers.

[a] The annual totals suggest the culmination of prewar research results and decline during the conflict. The number of inventors with patents peaked in performance with 103 from IBM, 65 from NCR, 42 at Remington Rand, 38 at Underwood, 10 out of Burroughs, and 9 from Monroe.

Yet not all was well at Remington Rand. IBM's punched card line during the war had been technically superior, hence, more attractive to customers. A larger portion of IBM's offerings were electric whereas many more in Remington Rand's line remained mechanical (hence, less effective). Throughout the 1940s, IBM's sales organization was recognized as superior to Remington Rand's, which meant the former was more persuasive in convincing customers to use IBM products.[37]

It is a commonly accepted axiom in business that the best leverage on market share and profits always is derived more from efficiencies in product development and manufacturing than from sales. This clearly was the case in the office appliance and later, computer business, whether in the 1870s or in the 1970s. One measure of innovation has traditionally been the number of patents issued, a cautious signal of newness and, hence, possibly improved efficiencies of things to come. During the war, the two companies most aggressive in filing for patents were IBM and NCR (see table 15.6). Remington Rand's performance was the worst on the eve of U.S. entry into World War II and remained relatively poor all during the conflict. Patents have always been portents of product futures, measurements of currect effectiveness in R&D, and witnesses to previous decisions and investments when the future arrives. Remington Rand's performance, along with Burroughs's, reflected little prowess in R&D, which may help explain why, after the war, when it sought entry into the computer market, it bought expertise in electronics such as that offered by Engineering Research Associates (ERA) and Eckert and Mauchly. Remington Rand's exposure, as measured strictly by expired patents, is illustrated in table 15.7; it joined NCR and Underwood in paying less attention to the future than did IBM and Burroughs.

TABLE 15.7
Expired and Unexpired Patents by Company, circa 1950

Company	Expired	Unexpired	Total	Increase[a]
Burroughs	440	190	630	15
NCR	1,590	450	2,040	41
Remington Rand	2,035	343	2,378	24
Underwood	2,634	1,021	3,655	64
IBM[b]	252	1,150	1,402	165

Source: Littlejohn and McClain, "Accounting Machine Industry," Burroughs Papers.

[a] Increase since October 8, 1944.

[b] IBM employees had been granted 2,356 patents since 1914 and had some 380 applications pending as of April 1950.

Summary

Two questions leap to mind as one looks back on the experience of the industry during the war. First, did all the various government controls achieve the desired results? The topic is of immediate concern for the war's economic history because of the massive attempt to place vast quantities of resources at the disposal of the military in a large economy. The second question deals more with the complex of events following the war. What long-term effect did the extensive influence of government in the war have on the industry as a whole? The answers offer evidence of government's influence on the industry for at least the next two decades through its research agendas and buying practices.

Government regulations and interferences can be measured by their success or failure in meeting the primary goal of funneling the nation's resources toward a victorious conclusion to a war. Did data processing help in that effort? Clearly it did, as demand for its goods and services illustrated, particularly during the ramp-up phase of 1941–1943 when the economy adjusted quickly to war needs. Testimony on the effectiveness of regulations came from Arthur Sanders, chief of the Office Machinery Branch at WPB. Writing in August 1945, he summarized the efforts of WPB as regards this industry:

> To summarize it may be said that in the main the principal objectives of the regulation of the office machine industry were achieved. Through limitations on productions, it was made possible for the industry to very substantially convert its facilities to the production of equipment of war. In this respect the industry has done an exceptional job.
>
> The restrictions on distribution of office machines have made it possible to channel the limited output to the uses where the machines would make the greatest

contribution. These limitations and restrictions have at times been burdensome to the industry and certain hardships have resulted therefrom, but by and large the industry seems to have been satisfied with the treatment it has received from Washington.[38]

Patriotism, realities of war, and various commentaries in internal memorandums from corporations of the time lead one to conclude that the industry concurred with Sanders's assessment.

Historians of the data-processing evolution in the postwar era are unanimous in acknowledging the importance of the government's role in funding R&D. They also recognize that government practices also affected many activities within the industry.[39] Government funding and encouragement of specific types of research led directly to the development of electronic digital computers while postwar efforts improved on the original work and led to miniaturized electronics. Specific types of software and programming languages evolved also because of the government's concern and its use of economic muscle. The acquisition of millions of dollars' worth of equipment first in significant quantities in the 1930s and more so during the 1940s, made all federal agencies collectively the largest customer in the world. Thus its wishes and practices were translated quickly into customer demand and vendor offerings.

This pattern of influence has a long history dating from the 1880s when Hollerith began working on equipment for the Bureau of the Census. Added reliance on such equipment, for example, at the Social Security Administration, encouraged other agencies to do the same with a snow balling effect during the 1930s and 1940s. World War II exacerbated the situation because there was already a history of mutual government/industry dependence. That dependence made it easier for the government to justify mandating how those relations had to continue during the war. The industry was effectively used largely because federal officials understood it, an appreciation borne out of previous use of office equipment. Sales figures of the period would also lead one to conclude that it was the American government more than any other institution that led the industry to acquire expertise in electronics and, subsequently, to adopt the computer as a product.

After World War II, the industry was never the same. It had grown quickly during 1936–1945, creating momentum its leaders wished to continue afterward. Larger volumes meant more resources that could be used to develop products and meet demand through new manufacturing techniques while using tried and tested methods for marketing and distribution.

16

Industry Structure, Vendors, and Practices, 1945–1956

RUMBLINGS of a new base of information processing technology, later to be seen in the form of computers, were only part of the forces of change evident in the old industry in the period 1945–1956. Other elements included the enormous economic strength of the United States following the war. That power directly influenced the industry by increasing demand for its products. It came in an era when automation appeared in ever-increasing and different forms in many sectors of the economy. White collar populations spelled growing demand for faster, more reliable products again. As in previous decades, a combination of the U.S. economy's health and growing number of workers significantly influenced the nature of the industry.

The period after the war also reflected much activity in all sectors of the old office appliance industry, where traditional product lines remained the mainstay of business while some changes came. For instance, IBM moved more aggressively into typewriter sales by introducing electric machines in the 1930s and improved models in the 1940s. All traditional lines of business did well at the same time that new electronics carried the efficiencies of these products to more impressive levels of reliability and cost effectiveness. Competition remained keen despite growing concerns of the U.S. Department of Justice about possible antitrust violations by AT&T, IBM, and Burroughs, a worry it also expressed about many other industries as well. But in many ways the office appliance industry in 1945–1955 reflected structure and substance evident in earlier decades. Leaders in the industry of the 1930s remained the same in the 1940s and 1950s. New executives took charge at NCR, Burroughs, and IBM, where even the venerable but aging Watson, Sr., began slowly to share power with his son by the early 1950s. Not until approximately 1955 did it become obvious to many both in and outside the industry that computers would create different circumstances and enormous growth comparable to that in the years 1895–1928.

Economic Environment

The population of the United States increased substantially during the 1940s from 132.1 million in 1940 to 151.3 million in 1950; many of those new citizens obviously were members of the "baby boom" generation who joined the work force in the 1960s. Better health services drove down deaths from

10.9 per thousand in 1940 to 9.5 in 1960, ensuring a more effective, longer-lived work force during the period 1945–1956. Higher standards of living, greater economic output, and a larger population helped drive growth in GNP from $200 billion in 1945 to $400 billion in the mid-1950s.

At the end of the war, the U.S. economy began a period of enormous growth caused by consumer desire to dispose of savings accumulated during the war, continued massive spending by the government, pent-up demand for goods and services by local and state governments, and needs of businesses to retool or replace worn-out equipment and to support growing demand for goods. The Marshall Plan, cold war politics, and the Korean War also contributed enormously to demand. The United States exported more than it imported. Expenditures by businesses alone in new plants and equipment went from about $8 billion in 1945 to $28 billion annually by 1955. During the second half of the 1950s annual expeditures remained consistently more than $30 billion.[1]

The American labor force grew from 56 million in 1940 to 74 million in 1960.[2] The biggest change—and the most important to the office appliance industry—was the increase in the number of workers in the service sector. Between 1920 and 1970 that portion of the work force rose from slightly under 30 percent to nearly 60 percent. Given the absolute growth in the number of workers in the same period, the overall shift actually is more impressive than percentages might suggest. After 1947, net increases in employment came only in the service sector.[3]

Potential users of office equipment, therefore, increased. In 1945, some 4 million workers and, in 1955, 5.9 million were in the service sector alone. In government, the work force in 1945 totaled 5.9 million and, in 1955, 6.9 million. The total work force in the U.S. economy went from 40 million in 1945 to 50 million in 1955.[4] The clerical population went from 4.9 million in 1940 to 7.2 million in 1950.[5] Vendors of office equipment were aware of these growth figures and translated them into market potential. Proof of commitment to growing markets came in the form of many investments, not the least of which were factory workers in the industry, expanding from 24,000 to 40,000 between 1940 and 1950.[6]

In any year between 1945 and the mid- to late-1950s, the U.S. economy proved fertile for the office equipment industry. The environment was an almost perfect set of economic conditions for the continued growth of this industry. It supplied necessary incentives to sell modernized products while affording change to a new technological base.

Postwar Industry Structure

The challenge facing the industry in the immediate postwar period was to return to normalcy in a peacetime market. By 1946, wartime price controls and restrictions on the use of raw materials were being shed quickly in the United States. In Europe these were less a factor, except in Germany where Allied occupation forces imposed restrictions, including some that prohibited "high-technology" items. Veterans who had worked within the industry were either back at work or soon would be. Demand was identified as other companies and agencies turned to peacetime activities. Vendors shifted production to meet these requirements while they updated products. By 1947–1948 they were back on a peacetime basis in the United States. In Europe, Latin America, and Asia, recovery proved much slower because of the destruction and the greater effort required to recover to peacetime economic levels; but even here, the effort was made to get back to prewar patterns of behavior. Business grew overseas despite the aftermath of war. American companies expanded marketing and manufacturing outside the United States and, as in the case of IBM, creation of an entire new management organization called IBM World Trade. In time, that arm of the company rivaled the domestic firm in revenues and profits.[7]

The major suppliers were the same top five as before the war.[8] The industry's self-identification in the late 1940s, however, began to shift, reflecting changes occurring over the previous decade that led to differentiation between vendors of data-processing equipment and those that also handled other types of products such as coin changers (e.g., Abbott Coin Counter). The U.S. Federal Trade Commission still thought of the office equipment industry as including typewriters and stenotype, bookkeeping, adding, addressing, calculating, duplicating, and dictating machines, autographing registers, and other office equipment. It also thought monolithically about the "top three," "top four," or "top five" vendors in the industry.[9]

Yet all firms within the industry itself saw that the only common denominator in that list was where products were used—in the office—but that otherwise commonality broke down because of differences in the marketing, distribution, and manufacturing of these items. For example, Remington Rand's office furniture did not compete against Underwood's typewriters.[10] Leading vendors primarily manufactured and sold information-handling equipment such as one would expect to see in the nascent data-processing industry (see table 16.1). The relative position of these firms remained the same through the first half of the 1950s with only business volumes changing. The sources of income for top suppliers still came from traditional sets of customers (see table 16.2).

The industry was as complicated as before the war. One cannot assume that the largest firms competed equally. They did not use their resources with the same effectiveness or for the same ends. Competitive product-by-product battles occurred in various sectors of all industries. Skirmishes were fought division by division. For example, Remington Rand sold computers that challenged NCR's small computer organization in the 1950s but did not compete

TABLE 16.1

Assets, Revenues, Employees of Ten Largest Office
Equipment Firms, 1948 (dollars in millions)

Company	Assets[a]	Revenues	Employees
IBM[b]	242	162	20,000
Remington Rand[c]	126	148	29,182
NCR[d]	121	168	16,400
Burroughs[e]	67	94	15,202
Underwood[f]	42	57	
L. C. Smith[g]	19	26	4,888
Monroe	14	21	2,226
Marchant	10	15	2,600
Felt & Tarrant	9	12	1,885
Friden	7		1,500[h]

[a] If one adds Lanston, Victor, Clary, R. C. Allen and Swift, total assets for all the above ten and five just listed totaled $674 million; revenues approached $738 million; employment was nearly 99,000.

[b] United States and Canada only.

[c] all sources, all subsidiaries.

[d] United States and subsidiaries.

[e] Parent firm only.

[f] U.S., domestic subsidiaries, foreign subsidiaries carried as investments.

[g] U.S., Canadian, and British subsidiaries.

[h] In addition had agents.

against cash registers to any degree. When one looks at product segmentation, competitors varied. In the adding machine market of the late 1940s and early 1950s, major suppliers were Burroughs, Remington Rand, Underwood, and Victor. In calculating machines, they were Burroughs, Felt & Tarrant, Marchant, and Friden. In accounting machines, one could turn to Burroughs, NCR, IBM, or Remington Rand as industry leaders. In cash registers, there was, of course, NCR but also Burroughs, R. C. Allen, and McCaskey. Seventeen typewriter firms competed in the market, however, it was dominated by less than a handfull.[11] The American economy had more than sixty vendors providing office equipment products despite the concentration of sales by market segment to three or four within each sector of the old office appliance industry.

Thus, for instance, in the late 1940s, some eleven vendors sold adding machines. Patent restrictions did not exist because the product line's technology was mature, so lower barriers to entry into that market existed; two companies entered the American industry during the 1940s.[12] The process was also easier because newcomers needed less capital than for other machine

TABLE 16.2
Sources of Revenues for Top Five Vendors, 1948
(percentage of dollars)

IBM	
Rental income & service	75
Sales of cards & supplies	15
Sales of other equipment	10
NCR	
Cash registers	55–60
Accounting & bookkeeping machines	30
Adding machines	5–8
Supplies & service	9
Remington Rand	
Cabinets, filing & index equipment	40
Typewriters & supplies	20
Tabulating, accounting machines, etc.	25
Electric shavers	5
Photographic equipment	1
Miscellaneous	9
Burroughs	
Adding machines	24
Calculators	10
Accounting machines	61
Cash machines	2
Other	3
Underwood	
Typewriters	50
Accounting machines, adding machines	35
Supplies	15

Source: Littlejohn and McClain, "Accounting Machine Industry," 8–9, Burroughs Papers.

types. The two that entered had assets worth less than $2 million.[13] With calculators, more capital was required, and marketing proved more difficult because it called for some application selling. By the end of the 1940s, the seven suppliers had all been in business since at least the 1930s. The concentration was greatest, however, in the accounting and tabulating machine market as it had been earlier and for the same reasons: complexity, patent protection, high volume of capital and R&D required, and sophistication of application marketing and services. In this segment, IBM continued to dominate. As one industry watcher put it, Watson's management had "made IBM the synonym of mechanized accounting."[14] Some 75 percent of its income came from tabulating equipment in this period.[15]

Profits remained strong in the postwar period for the largest vendors.

IBM's net profits after taxes ranged from a low of $10.9 million (1945) to a high of $33.3 (1949). In 1949, IBM's net profits after taxes represented 18.1 percent of sales. In the prewar period, these profits had been between 23 and 32 percent. In contrast, Burroughs served as a good model for the small end of the data-processing product line, turning in a 1949 profit margin of 9.1 percent. Average net profit margins of other competitors, such as NCR, Remington Rand, and Underwood, came closer to 7.2 percent.[16]

NCR continued to dominate cash register sales. Its serious competition came from other data-processing manufacturers who sold against NCR's calculators and accounting machinery and, later, computers. In the postwar period, between 50 and 60 percent of NCR's revenues came from cash registers. Remaining sources were wrangled primarily from IBM, Remington Rand, Burroughs, Underwood, and Monroe.[17]

The more specialized a product line, e.g., coin changers or cash registers, the greater was the concentration of a few suppliers. By the postwar period, concentration was a natural process because the narrower the product, the smaller the demand, and thus it made economic sense only for a few firms to participate. That process was clearly at work when commercial computers were introduced; demand was limited and so, too, were suppliers.

Distribution remained the same as before the war and for the same reasons (see table 16.3 for how many sales offices, dealers, and agencies major vendors had in the United States in 1949–1950). The more complicated the equipment sold, the more likely it was that it would only be acquired through direct sales offices.[18] Less complex equipment came through other well-understood channels, such as dealers or even department stores.

The volume and variety of machines shipped in the postwar period was impressive. The figures for adding machines in 1947 suggests the volumes: in the United States over 340,000; in 1949, 350,000, of which 50,000 came from Burroughs.[19] By 1950, customers had a choice of more than fifty models of calculators. IBM, in 1956, offered five major accounting machines, seven calculators (including the IBM 650), and hundreds of input/out devices, special items, or attachments. The IBM sales manual for 1956 ran into hundreds of pages, only a few of which were devoted to the well-received IBM 650 computer.[20] At the other end of the market—very small hand-operated adding machines, which sold at prices from $89.50 to $250—customers had a choice of over forty-five machines. In 1947, some 340,000 of these were sold in the United States alone.[21] At the very low end (less than $100 each), Victor dominated.

All these data suggest a healthy industry with as much diversity as in the prewar era. They also indicate that computers had rivals at the high end in the form of products to compete against and later displace in the 1950s and early 1960s.[22] As sales volumes show, the industry grew between 1945 and 1955 supported by traditional market conditions and lines of business.

TABLE 16.3
U.S. Distribution Outlets by Product Type, 1949–1950

Product Line/Vendor	Branches	Dealers	Agencies
Tabulating Equipment			
IBM	159		
Full Line			
NCR (& Allen-Wales)	209	300	
Remington Rand	200	8,500	
Burroughs	133		
Underwood[a]	225	—	
Monroe	180		
Calculators			
Marchant			86
Felt & Tarrant	83		
Friden	12		250
Adding Machines			
Victor	22	500	
R. C. Allen[a]		—	
Clary	50	170	
Swift		Limited[b]	
Typewriters			
L. C. Smith & Corona		7,200	
Lanston Monotype (Barrett)		Limited[b]	

Source: Littlejohn and McClain, "Accounting Machine Industry," 65, Burroughs Papers.

[a] Underwood and R. C. Allen had nationwide coverage.

[b] Limited sales.

International Business Machines

IBM emerged from the war large and influential. Its more than $140 million in annual revenues made IBM second in size in the industry; in value of assets, it led the industry in 1948. Historians are often fond of speaking of any organization's history as one of transition, and so they have written about IBM's in the decade following the war. More relevant, however, were three sets of events between 1945 and 1956 because they influenced the structure and direction of IBM and the industry over time.

First, the creation of IBM World Trade signaled an expanded commitment to sales outside the United States on a more effective basis. Second, in the natural evolution of management, older executives gave way to younger ones who increasingly differed with previous managers on how to run IBM. Third, an antitrust suit between IBM and the U.S. Department of Justice was settled with terms that influenced the company's marketing practices down to the present and contributed to the end of the tabulating machine era. Closely tied to these legal issues were those resolved in another legal skirmish between IBM and Remington Rand over antitrust issues.

The event that became visible most immediately was IBM's restructuring of foreign operations. In 1949, it divided into two pieces: a domestic U.S. company with corporate headquarters and a subsidiary called IBM World Trade Corporation. The latter was presided over by Tom Watson, Sr.'s son, Dick Watson, whereas the U.S. organization increasingly came under control of Tom Watson, Jr. The largest piece of the market was still the United States. Available evidence suggests that Watson, Sr., took this step to provide each brother with an opportunity to be his own person with minimal rivalry.[23]

The organization proved a workable business decision. Although foreign revenues (exclusive of Canadian) in 1949 only reached $6.3 million, the potential was enormous, particularly in Europe after it recovered economically; Watson, Sr., saw that capture of this market required focus. The components of World Trade, in some cases dating back to Hollerith's early work in Europe, were important. For example, the British Tabulating Machine Company (BTM), with which Hollerith entered business in 1908, had become an important part of IBM's European business. In 1949, IBM BTM signed a licensing agreement to market IBM's products while IBM established a British subsidiary. IBM also had the plants and sales offices it had established after World War I in Germany, France, Italy, Portugal, and Spain and others in Latin America and Asia. When establishing IBM United Kingdom, for the first time IBM made it possible for foreigners to purchase stock in a subsidiary. That formula would be repeated elsewhere, opening a new source of capital to the firm in later decades while allowing local companies to identify more easily with the nations they served.[24]

On the first day of World Trade's operations (January 1, 1950), the foreign company consisted of ten factories making machines, twenty producing cards, and sales offices in fifty-eight countries. The parent U.S. company provided the design of products, management as needed, and financial backing. During the early 1950s, World Trade expanded in response to growing opportunities outside the United States; ultimately, it established its own R&D to build on developments in the United States but tailored to the requirements of its own customers. IBM as a whole soon felt the impact on revenues of the new organization's effectiveness and expanding demand for its products. By the close of 1955, World Trade's revenues had reached $132.8 million compared to $564 million for the U.S. firm. In the following year, revenues were $157.7 million compared to $734 million.[25] During the 1950s, its rate of growth parallel that of the domestic company.

IBM World Trade's success was the result of several factors. Practices and products of the domestic company along with its past relationships with customers ensured an initial momentum of activity. At least as important was the ability of national subsidiaries to alter marketing practices to meet local requirements, ranging from pricing based on local tax laws or competition to the needs of a particular economy or customer, or to respond to the requirements to use products in non-European alphabets (e.g., Japanese).[26]

An important change at IBM was the attrition of aging executives and their replacement with younger ones who were often allies of Tom Watson, Jr. Nowhere was this process more at work than within the Watson family itself. Watson, Sr., was seventy-one years old at the end of the war, Watson, Jr., 31. Many of the firm's top executives had been at their posts since the late 1930s. Watson, Sr.'s two main lieutenants in 1945 were Charles Kirk and John Phillips, each a vice-president. Both were reputed never to implement a policy without Watson's approval, although of the two Kirk was more likely to suggest fresh ideas. Watson, Jr., slated to manage the firm after his father, was groomed by Kirk. However, in 1947 Kirk died while Watson, Jr., was a vice-president but regarded as not yet ready to take over his father's responsibilities. Kirk's death left the firm in what one historian called "a drift, as though it was awaiting Watson junior's coronation."[27] In 1949, Phillips became president of IBM, Watson, Sr., took the title of chairman, which he had never held before, and Watson, Jr., was promoted to executive vice-president.

Watson, Jr., began to place people of his own choosing in key positions in the early 1950s. They infused electronics into products and even dressed with soft collars instead of the stiff ones characteristic of Watson, Sr. Watson, Jr., focused greater attention on R&D than had been done in the earlier 1940s, while he managed a company growing rapidly both in number of employees and markets during the early 1950s. In 1952–1955, as president, the younger Watson presided over the doubling of IBM's revenues. Throughout the 1950s, he decentralized the firm as the volume of decisions became too many for one or two individuals to make. The final event symbolizing changes at IBM was Watson, Sr.'s death on June 19, 1956, following a heart attack. Watson, Jr., remained president and was elected chairman of the board in 1961.[28] In his last years, Watson, Sr., had increasingly yielded day-to-day operations to his namesake, which, in effect, caused a graceful transition to a new generation over some nine years. By 1956, the firm was stamped with the mark of Watson, Jr., by more modern buildings and products and practices that reflected a much larger company now dependent on new technologies.

IBM's antitrust problems illustrated the growing power of the younger Watson. Legal issues reflected the continuing concern of the U.S. Department of Justice with office equipment vendors. Settlement of the case with a consent decree represented a break with the past that was both symbolic and real for IBM. The issue was the same as in the 1930s: the government accused IBM in 1952 of monopolizing tabulating machines sales and supplies of cards. Federal authorities wanted IBM to lease and sell equipment, not just lease or rent, and to allow customers to obtain cards from other sources as well. Watson, Sr., protested passionately, even arguing that Harry Truman was punishing him for supporting Dwight D. Eisenhower for president. He also contended that the Justice Department was practicing bad economics—the charge that Burroughs leveled against the government and that IBM would in the 1970s—by improperly defining the industry and competition within it.

Watson, Jr., who had just been made president before the government filed charges, viewed the situation differently. Rather than get mad as had his father, he focused more on IBM's future and less on past practices. Watson, Jr., and IBM's legal staff believed the government's criticism only concerned cards and tabulators whereas the future promised other products such as tape medium and computers, although in 1951–1953 that was a distance away but closer in 1955–1956. If IBM moved toward use of magnetic tape and computers, the charges would become less relevant. When the case was filed in 1952, the declining importance of tabulating equipment was not as apparent as it would be by 1955–1956. The period of some four years and the events that took place in the industry, accounts largely for why Watson, Jr., and IBM's lawyers were more willing than his father to accommodate the Justice Department. Watson, Sr., eventually bowed to his son's arguments that a consent decree should be negotiated and that the company had to get on with its affairs without the burden of legal problems about aging technology.[29]

Evidence from Watson, Jr., on the matter is direct. On wanting to settle the case: "We knew that sooner or later the government would come after us. Our equipment was in the accounting departments of virtually every major American company, and the government knew all about us because we were in every federal agency too. We charged premium rents for a premium service, and our growth and profits were astounding—year after year we were making about twenty-seven cents, pre-tax, on every dollar of revenue." IBM had little competition in the tabulator business because his firm "held about 90 percent of the market for punch-card machines."[30] A congressional report available to him at the time estimated that 16 percent of all accounting work done in the United States was performed on IBM equipment, and the U.S. Department of Commerce also reported that 9 percent of all manhours of production workers in offices and in store machine functions relied on IBM's equipment. Watson's father estimated in the early 1950s that IBM had 2 percent of all the numerical calculations going on in U.S. industry.[31] Regardless of how IBM came to such a dominant position, the son knew he had a problem, and so "I determined to settle the suit before it went to trial" (1955–1956), which, when accomplished, "cleared the way for IBM to keep expanding at top speed."[32]

The consent decree was signed in 1956. In hindsight, it was a most significant one for the industry (at least until the breakup of AT&T in 1984) because it affected IBM's practices for decades, although that consequence was not fully anticipated at the time. It called for IBM to sell or lease its machines, a provision that had scarcely any effect on tabulating machine revenues. IBM had to divest itself of its capability to produce more than half the cards required by the American economy within seven years. Although of concern in 1956, card sales kept declining over the next ten years anyway. IBM had to establish the Service Bureau Corporation (SBC), a subsidiary, to compete against IBM and service bureau companies. SBC was a means of encouraging rivals in that market segment to enter the fray. In 1962, IBM sold SBC to Control Data and stayed out of that market in the United States over the next three decades. IBM agreed to grant licenses for a fee to any firm that could afford them to sell or rent current and future machines in tabulating, accounting, and computing. In practice, this license would be for existing innovations; a rival would thus signal its lack of innovation if it had to rely on such a method to acquire technology. IBM consented to severe restrictions on its ability to remarket secondhand equipment, a term of the agreement that was subsequently strictly honored by IBM for more than three decades. The consent decree applied only to IBM's practices in the United States and, by implication, to territories under the jurisdiction of U.S. law.

Meanwhile, Remington Rand, which had accused IBM of antitrust activities in the late 1940s, conducted ongoing negotiations with IBM over the matter during the early 1950s and agreed in August 1956 to cross-licensing of patents on computer technology or others applied for before October 1956. The net result of these two settlements—with the government and Remington Rand—was that IBM gained access to new technology with no legal exposure for previous R&D potentially at odds with Remington's. IBM also gave up minor concessions to the government and could now focus increasingly on computers and related services without legal impediments or risk.[33]

Given the changes in products, executives, competitors, legal problems, and organization, how did the company perform financially? Table 16.4 tells the story. From 1946 to 1957, gross revenues and net income rose faster than in the office appliance industry as a whole. Long-term debt climbed in the 1950s as a reflection of Watson, Jr.'s growing commitment to R&D and expansion. Given the size of increased revenues, however, growth in long-term debt can be considered prudent and proportional to the amounts assumed by Watson, Sr. (see table 16.4). By the early 1950s, the definition of the office equipment industry was changing, a process that accelerated during the mid- to late 1950s with the introduction of commercial computers on a large scale.

TABLE 16.4

Selected Statistics for IBM, 1946–1956
(dollars in millions)

Year	Gross Revenues	Net Income	Long-term Debt[a]
1946	119.4	18.8	30.0
1947	144.5	23.6	50.0
1948	162.0	28.1	85.0
1949	183.5	33.3	85.0
1950	214.9	33.3	85.0
1951	266.8	27.9	135.0
1952	333.7	29.9	175.0
1953	410.0	34.1	215.0
1954	461.4	46.5	250.0
1955	563.5	55.9	295.0
1956	734.3	68.8	330.0

Source: Table reproduced with permission from Robert Sobel, *IBM*, 125. Data originated in *Moody's Handbook*, 1957, 193.

[a] IBM avoided long-term debt before the mid-1940s and funded growth and R&D out of current earnings.

Although the definition of what constituted the industry thus became a problem for historians and economists[34] and lawyers involved in antitrust suits in the 1970s,[35] in tabulating gear, IBM still had its 85 to 90 percent market share. When compared to other vendors and to all types of products and services, it perhaps held up to 25 percent of the business equipment market. Clearly, its revenues were very large in comparison to those of its arch rivals. IBM's position remained intact, as strong as it had been in the early 1940s, and financially capable of expanding in the second half of the 1950s.[36]

Remington Rand

The major news at the second-largest tabulating and most-publicized computer vendor, Remington Rand, during the period 1945–1955 was continued growth through its merger in 1955 with Sperry Corporation to form Sperry Rand. General Douglas MacArthur became chairman of the board and James Rand, the old chairman of Remington Rand, vice-chairman. Chief executive officer of the new firm was Harry Vickers, a senior executive at Sperry Corporation. Both companies intended to merge two compatible firms. Sperry enjoyed a good reputation as a successful supplier of various types of technologies to the U.S. military establishment, most recently reinforced during

World War II. It also held considerable expertise in electronics, particularly in leading-edge technologies that included work on semiconductors. Sperry shared a similar heritage with ERA (also acquired in this period along with the Eckert-Mauchly computer enterprise by Remington Rand) in that some of Sperry's engineers had conducted research for the U.S. Navy that involved computerlike hardware. The combination, at least on paper, made the new firm potentially significant in the emerging computer field.

Sperry Corporation was incorporated on April 13, 1933, as a holding company made up of numerous older organizations. One of these was the Sperry Gyroscope Company, incorporated on January 21, 1929, and a descendant of earlier structures, famed as manufacturer of the gyrocompass used by merchant marines and navies worldwide. During World War II, it manufactured the gyroscope used in bombsights and torpedoes. Another subsidiary, Ford Instrument Company, employed electronics for artillery control, such as rangekeepers, directorscopes, and mechanical computing devices for anti-aircraft fire control and artillery batteries. Sperry had annual sales of some $2.8 million during the 1930s and, by the end of 1939, turned in a gross income of $10.7 million on revenues of $24.4 million. During the war, it had prospered enormously. In 1944, for instance, sales reached $460 million but in 1946 dropped to $85.8 million because of decreased demand for military products.[37] That experience led management to seek domestic nonmilitary customers, hence the attraction of a firm like Remington Rand that had civilian/government-related products and customers and a distribution system for goods and services. The lesson of not being too dependent on the military was probably forgotten momentarily, however, during the Korean War. Sales climbed to the same levels as those of World War II although as after the previous war, they subsequently dipped.[38]

Experiences of the past were recalled. Sperry emerged from World War II with money to invest and had even more coming out of the Korean War. It saw Remington Rand as a compatible acquisition. Remington Rand's civilian loyal customer base was particularly appealing. Vickers was prepared to invest heavily in R&D and to take on IBM. Remington Rand had already taken key steps to engage IBM in the computer market at the high end, often where customers were either government civilian agencies or the military. Sperry could sell to Remington Rand's customers, thereby broadening Vicker's outlets. In short, it appeared a logical merger. Industrial analysts saw the merger as a winning one that could challenge others in the office equipment market and everyone in the newly emerging computer world.[39] In that year (1955), sales of the UNIVAC I reached their all-time high; the future never looked better.[40]

Remington Rand was not a small acquisition as shown by the company's net sales during the late 1940s (see table 16.5). The data suggest, however, something less than consistent or expanding sales volume. The transaction

TABLE 16.5
Net Sales for Remington Rand, 1946–1949
(dollars in millions)

Year	Net Sales[a]	Year	Net Sales[a]
1946	147.1	1948	148.2
1947	162.4	1949	135.7

Source: Standard and Poors, 1946–1950.
[a] Net sales are sales charged to customers and do not include income from other sources.

showed why it was a good takeover candidate for Sperry or any company large enough to acquire a firm moving into technology-based products and smart enough to manage it effectively. Size restricted the number of companies able to consider a takeover because Remington Rand was not small; in 1950, it had 29,909 employees, a work force that continued to grow. The number of employees alone made it the second largest employer in the industry after NCR (with 30,000) with IBM in third (28,604).[41] Measured by pretax income as a percentage of sales, these figures went from a high of 18.2 percent in 1946 down to a low of 9.7 percent in 1949 then back up to 16 percent in 1951. Subsequent computer sales and other investments altered the financial picture again. To put the firm's performance in perspective, throughout the same period, IBM's pretax income as a percentage of sales remained consistently between a low of 26.2 percent (1946) and a high of 29 percent (1949, 1951), whereas at NCR they were a low of 4.3 percent in 1946 but, thereafter, 14.8 to 18.9 percent.[42] In short, Remington Rand's performance was uneven in comparison to better-managed firms.

The diversity of its products and organization, fractured attention by senior management, and consequent dispersal of available capital across too many projects made it a decreasingly serious rival to others entering the computer field while making it a good merger/takeover candidate. Computer sales did not grow there as rapidly as at IBM. In 1955, the Univac Division's revenues hovered at $711 million, in 1956 near $868 million.[43]

National Cash Register

The immediate challenge facing NCR at the end of World War II was to revitalize quickly its cash register business while it enhanced sales of accounting machines. As war-torn economies overseas recovered, the demand for registers became a function of the growth of retail operations much as it had in previous decades. In the United States, the same notion applied but was compounded by the need to replace older accounting machines that customers had to use during the war when they might otherwise have acquired more advanced models. In the second half of the 1940s, the company refurbished the entire product line, including some machines that went from three hundred parts to more than seven thousand. NCR also brought out more advanced accounting machines that often used electronics for the first time and new styling. The majority of the company's business during the period 1945–1956 concerned cash registers and accounting machines. Revenues from government-related projects and computers were minor.

The future looked good for NCR with 1.9 million merchants and some .5 million other businesses as prospects. NCR went after that market in the late 1940s with more than 500 possible combinations of machines. By 1948, it had 206 sales offices in North America. As of 1947, it had 333 marketing representatives and managers with 25 or more years of service with NCR. Each sales office on average had at least one highly experienced marketer providing guidance and serving as a floor leader to newer employees. Such a pool of skilled individuals helped to develop effective sales personnel rapidly, allowing the company to take proper advantage of pent-up demand and a modern product line.[44] By the early 1950s, the company had made the transition to a worldwide peacetime market.[45] NCR retained its name recognition from the interwar period and built on its traditional customer base with the same kinds of goods and practices as in the past.

Executives were concerned about the new electronics, asking the same questions about computers that were on every other vendor's mind in the office and electronics industries. Where was the demand for computers? Like others, NCR concluded initially that it existed with scientific and military applications. There was reluctance within NCR—as at IBM—to deflect any resources or attention from current lines that generated revenues and profits unless there was little risk in so doing. If the firm entered the computer business, as its president, Stanley C. Allyn, put it, "We knew it meant many millions of research and development dollars, plus the retraining of manufacturing, marketing and service personnel."[46] By the early 1950s, the company could see that it had to make a foray into this new facet of the office equipment business or, as Allyn believed, otherwise live "on with a declining opportunity."[47]

The company responded by buying the talent needed to enter the market. In 1952, it acquired Computer Research Corporation (CRC) and made it NCR Electronics Division in 1953. It was capable of building computers for commercial uses. NCR asked that computer development be linked with creation of efficient input mechanisms to trap data in machine-readable form, recognizing that commercial applications were characterized more by input and output of data than by extensive calculations. NCR had to catch up with IBM and Remington Rand, whose existing tabulating and accounting systems already sported good input/output punched card equipment. Both of NCR's

TABLE 16.6
Net Sales for NCR, 1946–1950 (dollars in millions)

Year	Net Sales	Year	Net Sales
1946	77.4	1949	167.3
1947	138.5	1950	170.5
1948	168.2		

Source: Standard and Poors, 1946–1950.

rivals understood such machines both on the manufacturing and sales sides of the house. Both also had manufacturing facilities geared to build such equipment. They could add computers to such a system of devices. NCR's products did not use punched cards but were "original-entry" devices. That is, one typed data directly into machines. For these reasons, it was understandable why NCR's initial foray into computers was hesitant and mild. CRC's first product was a digital differential analyzer used by North American Aviation for airborne operations and from that base CRC reached out with more commercial products only in the mid-to-late 1950s.[48]

But computers were in the future for NCR's expansion was fueled by traditional electromechanical products. By 1953, NCR had ten manufacturing plants producing such equipment and several others to make supplies and business forms for its traditional product line.[49] Sales expanded worldwide in the late 1940s and in the first half of the 1950s. In Japan, NCR became the first American firm to be "legally reconstituted" (July 1949).[50] During 1947, a new plant for cash registers opened in Dundee, Scotland. It was expanded in 1952 and, by 1957, built $40 million worth of registers annually. In 1947, some 478 employees built registers in Berlin, and by the early 1950s, the combined work force of plants in Berlin and Augsburg exceeded 2,000 and made more than 17,000 cash registers annually.[51] In 1950, it had a work force of some 30,000—the largest in the industry, which, without more evidence, suggests either how labor-intensive electromechanical products were to build and sell or inefficiencies. Sales dipped in 1945 as NCR shifted from a wartime environment to a peacetime one, and this conversion had been completed by 1947. Sales then began rising and took off in 1951 with a 24 percent spurt over those in 1950 (see table 16.6). By then some two-thirds of NCR's total revenues were coming from U.S. sales, the rest from overseas. In that important year of 1951, earnings reached $11.7 million, making it possible for NCR to acquire CRC.[52] In 1955–1956, NCR's sales jumped to over $300 million, with less than 5 percent coming from computer-related services or products.[53] To give perspective on the early growth of computer sales, by 1960, these had only climbed to 7.2 percent of total revenues.[54]

NCR's market share, measured by the volume of revenues against the ten largest vendors, was 15 percent in 1946, 22 percent in 1949, then settled down to 18–19 percent during the early 1950s.[55] Market share was consistent with what it had been during the 1930s. Measured by pretax income as a percentage of sales, in 1946, it was 4.3 percent (disastrous and the worst in the industry). But it grew in 1947 to 14.8 percent, hovered at 15–16 percent in the late 1940s, reached 18.9 percent in 1951, and then continued at that level into the 1950s.[56] NCR's overall performance was slightly below that of Burroughs (a good comparative example because of similar types of manufacturing and marketing) and, when contrasted to mechanically intensive products such as typewriters, was 4 to 6 percentage points better.

In short, NCR's history of 1945–1956 was similar to that of the 1930s. Although one knows little about personnel changes among policy-making executives after the war, some took place but not at the top. Chairman of the board Edward F. Deeds did not retire until 1957; at that time he had served as chairman for twenty-six years and was eighty-three years old. Robert S. Oelman was a relatively new figure, having served as executive vice-president only since 1950; he became president in 1957. Allyn, an executive since the 1920s, served until 1961. One could conclude that an important reason for returning after the war to practices and products reminiscent of the 1930s, might be the result of lack of changes in the management team and many of its employees or because of the commonality of market conditions prevailing after 1945. It is an unresolved issue about NCR worth examining elsewhere because it may answer the question of why NCR took so long to get into the computer business and why, when it did, it proved ineffective.

Burroughs

Of all the major vendors in the office equipment market in the first three years following World War II, the one that launched the greatest number of changes to improve marketing, manufacturing, and products was Burroughs. It changed many of its key executives in 1946, advancing younger, more energetic and creative individuals than the company had seen since the 1930s. These managers and executives, in turn, improved production efficiency through a combination of redesigned products and manufacturing processes.

Burroughs expanded marketing worldwide. It also invested substantially in electronics in the belief that this technology must be imbedded throughout the product line. Despite its failure to move as quickly into the computer market as IBM and Remington Rand, Burroughs, nonetheless, recognized the need to address this new field as early as any major vendor. In 1956, it enhanced its own internal skills by acquiring talent to go after the computer market, giving it the critical mass to keep computers as an important and visible piece of the business for decades to come. All through 1945–1956 Burroughs performed well financially, which positioned it to thrive in the late 1950s. That it did not grow to the degree its management wanted is a story chronologically outside the scope of this book, but for a brief moment in the late 1940s and early 1950s, Burroughs enjoyed an era of renewal and health.

Given that during the war profits had fallen below expectations and it seemed that Burroughs was saddled with a lackluster senior executive team, the board of directors took action by naming John S. Coleman president in 1946. He was a disciplined, professional, and energetic executive who, over the next several years, infused new life into the company. He hired engineers and college graduates with degrees in business administration and promoted rapidly younger managers with fresh ideas in all sectors of the company. He also made the crucial decision that led to very large investments in R&D in electronics. Between 1946 and 1956, revenues grew from $46 million to $273 million, yielding an average annual growth rate of 19 percent. Net earnings went from slightly less than $2 million to $14 million, a 22 percent annual growth. Ray W. Macdonald, chairman of the board in the 1970s, argued that this success was the result of a total refurbishing of the product line, expansion of markets by adding paper forms and supplies to service new machines, and expanded overseas sales.[57]

The truth was more complex. Overseas sales increased, but the proportion of revenues contributed from outside the United States remained at first below prewar levels and it was not until the 1950s that they were back to normal at between 20 and 30 percent. The product line was totally replaced; but manufacturing processes for making them was too, driving down unit costs while increasing efficiencies of personnel. Manufacturing changes probably had more to do with success of the product line than marketing. When manufacturing and engineering redesign are counted together, sales reps represented the least expensive piece of doing business and could take advantage of market demand to help close sales.

In 1948, product lines consisted of adding-subtracting machines, desk bookkeeping machines, calculators, typewriter accounting machines, bookkeeping machines, statistical machines, billing machines, cash registers, microfilm equipment, office chairs, and business machine supplies. Burroughs saw itself as a producer of "a complete line of attractively designed and carefully engineered figuring and accounting machines to save time, effort and cost in every business."[58] The firm could not capitalize on demand because it lacked adequate amounts of materials in 1946, plant capacity of the right mix, and enough sales and service personnel to call on customers. Burroughs retooled and expanded plants and increased engineering efforts, then complemented these moves either by improving or expanding the 558 sales and service centers in North America and the 215 sales and dealers offices in other countries. Coleman increased the number of employees in 1946 by 21 percent worldwide, 16 percent in North America. Production that year, an indicator of demand, rose by 71 percent over that of 1945. In the spring of 1947,

Coleman thought his firm's future was outstanding and, consequently, chose to invest a large portion of Burroughs's profits in that future.[59]

Coleman stayed the course in 1947, using his fourteen thousand employees to continue revitalization, making Burroughs, as its logo phrase put it, "a better place to work." By the spring of 1948, he was able to report that "Burroughs has an extraordinary backlog of orders and new orders are being taken in large volume."[60] Production was shifting by late 1947 from simply satisfying backlog and replacement orders to increases in the demand for productivity tools, especially in American offices. Inflation in the second half of the 1940s, especially in salaries, made such products attractive as a means of containing office costs while providing tools for increasing numbers of office workers. As the company observed, "Burroughs products in high demand include all types of adding and bookkeeping machines, calculators, and a wide variety of other specialized figuring and accounting equipment."[61] Exports went from 19 percent of total contribution in 1946 to 24 percent in 1947 on the way back to prewar levels of roughly 30 percent. In 1947, Coleman also started increasing the number of sales reps and service personnel by 50 percent to satisfy new demand. By early 1948, R&D had stepped up to such an extent that he could report that "particular emphasis is being placed on the further development of electronic circuits for high-speed calculations," in short, replicating what was happening at IBM and Remington Rand.[62]

By the end of 1948, the bulk of the first round of refurbishing had been completed. This carried the company deep into the 1950s. It had been financed largely through internal funds; 70 percent of 1948's profits, for example, were plowed back into the business to pay for plant expansion and increased costs of work in process, finished goods inventories, and carrying charges for accounts receivable.[63] Demand softened in 1949 as the initial blush of postwar business slowed. Coleman warned stockholders that inflation, shrinking of postwar demand, uncertainty in world affairs, and the value of the dollar would hurt despite continued expansion, increased efficiencies, and continued product introductions.[64] Yet he moved ahead, expanding engineering and R&D staffs by 10 percent in 1948 alone. He achieved his target of adding 500 new salesmen and 300 service representatives. However, in February 1949, Burroughs laid off roughly 450 employees in manufacturing because of softened demand for products.

During the early to mid-1950s, the momentum of the late 1940s slowed, although revenues continued to grow, masking problems concerning strategic directions for the future. The fundamental problem was, to use Macdonald's words, that "the company did not make satisfactory progress from the standpoint of developing a cohesive range of electronic data processing products for the commercial market. Our participation in advanced government projects had diverted our relatively limited research and engineering resources away from the commercial areas."[65]

By the mid-1950s, the product line would not carry the company but it seemed that perhaps computers could. The internal battles over direction were similar to those at IBM at the same time. However, in reaction to its inability to respond to the computer market now being developed rapidly by IBM, Burroughs bought ElectroData Corporation in 1956. That firm had a commercial computer that Burroughs could sell. Yet despite this acquisition, it was not until the 1960s that Burroughs could react seriously with a product line of computers, despite some installations in the 1950s.[66] Apparently, Burroughs, in the early to mid-1950s, as had other firms, relied too long on its existing product line, finding it difficult either to invest in new machines or to shift to a more advanced technology quickly enough. If IBM's experience is an indicator, pressure from the financial community within Burroughs, always with an eye cast to immediate profits and dividends to stockholders, might well have pressured senior management to move more slowly toward a product set that had questionable levels of profitability when a product line with known financial performance was in hand. In hindsight, shifts to new products or technologies seem obvious but, in reality, they have always represented some of the most difficult decisions for any CEO. Every major vendor of office equipment looking at the market for computers in the late 1940s and throughout the 1950s faced difficult decisions of this type. Burroughs was no exception.

Indeed, Burroughs faced the same problem of timing the shift to computer-based products as other companies. In 1953, for example, management did not yet see commercial demand as significant enough: "The automatic office cannot be expected in the near future."[67] This technology was also determined to be as yet impractical and not sufficiently cost-effective. The latter was IBM's view at the time as well. However, Burroughs did introduce a commercial computer in 1954 called the E-101, taken from ElectroData, which was sold as a small scientific processor. The E-101 failed. Its functions were too limited, the market for it never developed, and it was not sold effectively. There was a subsequent shift of R&D risks to military projects, which Macdonald's previously quoted comments confirmed.[68] The company had found, as had IBM and others, that it was safer and more cost-effective to fund computer-related R&D through military contracts.

The bulge in demand following the war is obvious along with the settled pattern of the 1950s (see table 16.7). Market share grew nicely as well. In 1946, as compared to ten other vendors in the industry,[69] Burroughs enjoyed an 8.9 percent share that grew to 11.8 percent in 1948, dipped in 1949, and rebounded to an 11.2 to 11.3 percent share.[70] That share did not change until IBM took off again with commercial computers in the second half of the 1950s. Pretax income as a percentage of sales in 1946 was a poor 8.2 percent. Management turned that situation around quickly, raising it to 16.8 percent in 1947 and to 21.1 percent in 1948. As could be expected once the bulge in

TABLE 16.7
Net Sales for Burroughs, 1946–1956
(dollars in millions)

Year	Net Sales	Year	Net Sales
1946	46.24	1951	127.37
1947	69.14	1952	150.82
1948	94.05	1953	162.04
1949	82.46	1954	168.65
1950	86.93	1955	217.81
		1956	271.76

Source: Moody's Manual of Investments, 1946–1956.

postwar demand had passed, pretax income percentages declined to 13.3 percent in 1949. It began climbing as overall volumes expanded and capital investments were recouped in 1950 (15.7 percent) and in 1951 (19.6 percent). By then, its yields were comparable to the industry at large.[71]

For many companies in the industry, 1955–1957 represented a watershed. Either they committed to computers and remained major suppliers in the office equipment industry or faced hardships. Burroughs confronted the same issues. It made the decision to enter the computer business and, by 1955, was large enough to carry it off. Its revenues that year were substantial—$220 million—and that critical mass grew to $273 million the following year and then to $283 million in 1957. Sales of general purpose computers in 1955 amounted to some $10 million, grew by $2 million in 1956, and again in 1957. By the end of 1960, general purpose computer revenues reached $20 million on a total revenue base of $389 million. Proportionately, therefore, computer revenues remained the same within the company.[72] All data-processing revenues added for 1955 (computers, peripherals, supplies, and services), totaled 10 percent of total revenues and reached 20 percent in 1960. In short, Burroughs's traditional lines of business remained very important just as tabulating equipment did at IBM in the same period.[73] For all vendors, profits still came from traditional products in the 1950s, not yet from computers.

U.S. Antitrust Activities

The office appliance industry and, later, the data-processing industry were riddled with the remains, memories, and practices caused by numerous battles with the U.S. Department of Justice. The government faced off with NCR, Burroughs, IBM, and Remington Rand in almost every decade. Part of the problem was simply the early and continued concentration of goods in a handful of companies. Occasional indiscretions and periodic legal victories for the government's lawyers encouraged the Antitrust Division at the Department of Justice to maintain vigilance. Consent decrees also justified its suspicions of business while they made vendors cautious. In short, the industry's relations with the Department of Justice has been a long-standing but inadequately studied historical issue. The legal events of the period 1945–1956 were very important because they occurred when the activities of the Antitrust Division were being reinforced by major decisions of the Supreme Court.

Confrontations began much earlier and have been documented throughout this book. However, in the 1940s, activity picked up again when the government came back to Burroughs, IBM, Remington Rand, and AT&T to explore the possibility of antitrust behavior.

Nationally, a number of factors affected the office appliance industry as other sectors of the economy. During the twentieth century, the U.S. government played an increasingly proactive role in ensuring the availability of competitive activity in each major industry by enforcing the Sherman Act and the Clayton Act either through legal action or through negotiated settlements (consent decrees). Periodically, however, the Antitrust Division had to go to trial; important cases ultimately were decided by the U.S. Supreme Court. In 1945, a U.S. court ruled against the Aluminum Corporation (Alcoa); it had been accused of controlling some 90 percent of the industry's output. More importantly, an American court relied on market structure rather than upon market behavior to test the legality of the antitrust charges leveled against Alcoa. Then in 1946, in a case seminal for office machine vendors, *American Tobacco v. United States*, the Supreme Court sustained the government. It concluded that the crime of monopoly could be committed just as much by possessing power to suppress competition and to raise prices as by actually committing illegal acts. It also ruled that the Justice Department did not have to prove collusion to set prices if this could be inferred reasonably from observing actual market conditions. Thus, if a firm like IBM or Remington Rand had a sufficiently high percentage of the tabulating market—70, 80, 90 percent—it could be perceived as fitting that definition. The same held for NCR with cash registers or for Burroughs with adding machines.

The Antitrust Division won a series of other victories across several industries from 1946 to 1948; Congress altered the Clayton Act in 1950 to prohibit a company from purchasing the assets of another when such an acquisition could tend to reduce competition or lead to a monopoly. Thus by the start of the 1950s, it had been clearly established that the government had authority to preserve competition; the issue became how to use that power. During the Truman and Eisenhower administrations (1945–1960), between forty-three and forty-six antitrust suits were filed annually. The Antitrust Division also continued to win cases throughout the 1950s, which strengthened its hand.

Cases prosecuted during the 1950s reinforced the Supreme Court's position that the possession of sufficient power to control a market could be declared as much illegal as overt acts. That doctrine was cemented through the important victory against E. I. DuPont de Nemours and Company in 1957 that caused the firm to divest itself of General Motors Stock.[74]

Already by the 1940s, companies in the office appliance industry with antitrust problems were arguing that the government's definition of their industry was faulty, that the government was practicing poor economics. As the industry underwent structural changes in the 1950s and 1960s with the sale of computers and software, one can imagine how corporate lawyers would advance this argument more aggressively. Their line of reasoning was taken up by IBM in the 1950s, but the most spectacular example came in the IBM antitrust case of the 1970s. When it came to an end as the government dropped it in the 1980s, it had become obvious that the Antitrust Divsion's definition of the industry, and, hence, the basis for defining a monopoly, had proven invalid.[75] The charge of poor economics has continued to the present. As recently as the late 1980s, a government economist involved in the suit against IBM, Richard Thomas DeLamarter, published a book that critics attacked as biased, in which he assumed that IBM's behavior in the late 1980s was exactly as in the 1960s and used twenty-five-year-old data to condemn the company's behavior across many decades.[76]

The case against Burroughs in the late 1940s showed the positions taken by both sides. The Federal Trade Commission (FTC) and the Department of Justice had defined the office machine industry as consisting of several major vendors, the "big three" or "big four." The government assumed that these firms operated monolithically, that is to say, the same in the tabulating gear or adding machine markets. Government lawyers did not distinguish between market segments and, hence, argued that Burroughs dominated monolithically. The Antitrust Division had, in effect, declared vertical integration of companies suspect without, in the opinion of vendors, taking into account specific requirements of office machine marketing. Manufacturers, specifically Burroughs in this instance, argued that one had to look at segments of the market and that upon investigation, one would see active competition. Practices in the adding machine world differed from those in calculator sales for example. A company might have to compete against one dozen firms over adding machines but for another product, such as cash registers, only with three or four rivals. Vendors contended that no reasonable test of competition could be performed simply by considering size or percentage of market penetration based on revenues. Rather, one had to view marketing behavior at the point where a sale was made to see if, in fact, a customer had a number of vendors to choose from. If so, antitrust legislation was not violated.[77]

Much could be said for the defense presented by the industry. Despite concentration in certain segments (e.g., cash registers, typewriters, and tabulating machines) customers could buy different types of technology to process information. Thus instead of using punched cards from IBM one could use an accounting machine from Burroughs, NCR, or someone else. Various sectors of the economy or slices of the office appliance world had features uniquely different from each other to cause vendors to react more in marketing terms than simply to the availability of some new technology. One study prepared for Burroughs in 1950 concluded that industry structure stemmed

> naturally from the nature of the products. Thus, the larger size of some firms is the *sine qua non* of their ability to develop and manufacture a costly piece of technical equipment; and branch distribution is the means by which they must guarantee the customer appropriate standards of sales counsel and maintenance service. On the other hand, smaller machines which are not so complex or so expensive may be manufactured by both small and large concerns and may be distributed with less dependence upon branches.[78]

Vendors defined their industry in product terms. They spoke not of customer types but of segments based on the size and complexity of machines. These fell into several categories: tabulating and accounting machines at the high end followed in descending order by calculators, adding machines, typewriters, cash registers, and other devices. Computers were at first considered specialized equipment but in time fit into the tabulating/accounting machine niche. By the end of the 1950s, small and large general-purpose computers were discretely segmented.

Excessive pricing was another concern of the Department of Justice during the 1930s and 1940s as a manifestation of monopolistic behavior. In one study on rents of tabulating equipment performed outside the circle of either the Justice Department or vendors, researchers concluded that the prices charged led to very favorable profit margins for Remington Rand. These were the result, however, less of profit-producing possibilities gained from leases and more of management driving down unit cost and distribution expenses. Capable executives used leases efficiently as marketing tools in conjunction with other actions.[79] In short, there was no attempt to exploit or inflate prices because there were only two suppliers of tabulating machines. Either customers had other technical options or, as in previous decades, could retain older methods until newer ones became more cost efficient.

Although the Antitrust Division's relations with the office machines world awaits its historian, some obvious questions can be asked. Why did the government define markets without paying attention to their purposes? Why did the government's lawyers continuously misunderstand the speed and nature of technology's role in a particular industry? Was faulty, incorrect, or outdated economics practiced in each decade by the government? This writer suspects that the answer is yes for all decades.[80] The concept that branded possession of potential power to monopolize as illegal was introduced in the mid-1940s and influenced behavior in the industry. It made the likes of IBM cautious after 1956.[81] There is, as of this writing, no evidence to suggest that the industry as a whole reacted that way for legal reasons in the decades before 1956, with the possible exception of NCR and then only insofar as concerned domestic sales of cash registers. Clearer is that the activities of the Antitrust Division had a greater impact on the industry *after* 1956 than before and brought about important changes in patterns of behavior, particularly in the marketing activities of large vendors.[82]

17

Business Volumes

WORLDWIDE trade, sales, expenses, assets, and profits and losses are the terms used by managers of key suppliers to define characteristics of the office appliance industry. The data suggests how well the industry moved from a wartime to a peacetime economy, from one completely based on pre–World War II technologies to one moving toward reliance on computers. I begin the discussion of business volumes by presenting foreign trade data because volumes from outside the United States were rolled up into American attainments.

Foreign Trade

American office equipment manufacturers responded to the end of war by restoring quickly prewar manufacturing and distribution processes worldwide. The need to reestablish business was particularly urgent in Europe, the largest non-U.S. market of the 1930s. To reestablish prewar levels of business Americans effectively recruited former employees from before the war. Many were glad to have employment in what otherwise was a relatively bleak economic situation in 1946–1948. IBM restored plants in Germany and added onto or built production facilities in the British isles as did Burroughs, among others. Sales offices reopened while others were added. During the late 1940s and throughout the 1950s, companies established national subsidiaries, first in Europe and in Japan, later in Latin America, Asia, and Africa.

One immediate problem to resolve was the location and reinstallation of equipment sent to Europe before the war. IBM tabulators in Germany were carried off to the Soviet Union while French machines were dispersed or lost. In Spain, the economy was in virtually the same condition as at the end of the civil war in 1939, so local inventories were low and machines were worn out. The strategy employed by all American vendors was to locate old machines and refurbish or cannibalize them for parts while bringing to Europe additional inventories, particularly of older models from the 1930s. By the end of the 1940s, volumes approached prewar levels as a percentage of total revenues. Sales in Europe, Asia, and Latin America exceeded prewar volumes by the early 1950s, another reflection of how quickly the world's economy recovered from the war.[1]

The same local vendors operated as before the war. In France, Machines Bull challenged IBM and Remington Rand. In Italy, Olivetti expanded its product line. In Germany, Siemens marketed products by the 1950s. Loyal customers from before and during the war were cultivated although supplies of equipment to them often remained scarce until the early 1950s. For enterprises like Siemens the challenge was to develop a customer base for the first time. In some cases, joint projects were initiated to increase leverage. For instance, in 1949, Machines Bull and Olivetti formed an alliance, a venture that served as a model for others, especially for electronics and office equipment vendors during the 1960s.[2]

A number of events signaled a return to traditional patterns. In 1946, German Powers was back in business. IBM enlarged its plant in Milan the same year to supply reopened sales offices all over Europe. In 1947, Arithema was set up as Czechoslovakia's only indigenous punched card manufacturer. Almost at the same moment, the Société des Machines à Cartes Perforées was established in Zurich. That same year, IBM set up European headquarters in Paris. In 1948, IBM opened a card plant in Lisbon, and in 1949, World Trade came into existence. Europeans went on the offensive against American firms as early as 1949, when Machines Bull established the Italian subsidiary called Olivetti-Bull. In that same year, Machines Bull opened a plant in Amsterdam. In Castlereagh, Northern Ireland, BTM did the same. In Belgium, IBM's card plant made more than one million cards per day. In 1950, an important agreement reached between Remington Rand and Machines Bull called for joint marketing and cross-licensing. Machines Bull allowed the American firm to sell its products outside France, but within France, Remington Rand could not sell its own machines or cards.[3] They followed up with a patent exchange agreement in 1952. The history of American firms in Europe was a litany of opening sales offices, expanding manufacturing, and sales of more equipment year-by-year in the late 1940s and early 1950s. A similar process was underway for European firms as they responded to the Americans and to expanding demand. By the mid-1950s, European vendors were able to offer stiff competition to the Americans worldwide. None, however, even seriously competed in the U.S. computer market.

Little is known about indigenous office equipment vendors in the years immediately following the war, yet Europe represented the largest non-U.S. market. The case of Machines Bull suggests rates of growth in the French market and, to a lesser extent, across the rest of Europe where the company did business. It responded to demand effectively against IBM and Remington Rand. Its success with punched card products hints that American vendors were not able to capture as much of the market, at least in Europe, as they had enjoyed in the 1920s and 1930s. Gross revenues for Machines Bull in 1946–1956 were achieved without the benefit of computer sales (see table 17.1). Although sales of national products were nurtured in France as public policy,

TABLE 17.1
Annual Income for Machines Bull, 1949–1956
(francs in billions)

Year	Income	Year	Income
1949	2.12	1953	4.57
1950	2.08	1954	6.08
1951	2.59	1955	6.70
1952	3.47	1956	8.77

Source: Connolly, *History of Computing*, E-18–E-23.

revenues also came from Italy, Switzerland, and elsewhere in Europe. Growth in revenues suggested a well-run company and a recovering Europe that had at least the same level of demand for information-handling equipment as that evident in the United States.

Machines Bull expanded quickly. In 1947, it set up a subsidiary in Switzerland and opened a sales office in Oslo. In 1948, it sold its first machines in Poland. In 1949, Joseph Callies became the general manager of Machines Bull and subsequently led it through a period of remarkable growth. He negotiated the agreements with Remington Rand (1950, 1952), opened a sales office in Sweden (1950), introduced the Calculator Gamma 3 (1952), opened a sales office in West Germany (1952), a subsidiary in Portugal (1954), and two plants in France (1955). The following year, Machines Bull expanded one plant and built two others in France. This activity went on simultaneously with an equally growing IBM World Trade.[4]

There was no indigenous European computer industry until the late 1950s. Only one firm started serial production of computers before 1955— Ferranti—whereas LEO II (an early British commercial product) was really part of the post-1955 history of British computing. As a result of minor economic activity with computers outside the United States, any measure of non-U.S. business machine activity can omit computers for the period 1945–1955.

The majority of activity concerned adding and calculating machines, cash registers, and, to a lesser extent during the late 1940s at least, punched card equipment. During the early 1950s, production and competition in adding and calculating machines and cash registers increased sharply. Between 1953 and 1958, the United States went from a position as the largest exporter in the world of such equipment to third. In 1959, it became a net importer for the first time. In part, the shift was caused by American manufacturers setting up or expanding production facilities overseas to reduce labor costs, shorten transportation routes, and leverage local tax or import/export laws. Part of the answer, perhaps, lay with the growing use of digital and analog computers by 1959 that displaced the need for more traditional accounting and tabulating equipment. Yet another part of the answer rested in more effective competition from an increasing number of vendors not of U.S. origin. The same occurred with typewriters.[5] From the late 1940s to the late 1950s, industrial resurgence in Europe coupled with general economic development in Asia, Africa, and Latin America created enormous demand for such relatively simple, less-sophisticated products. Worldwide demand made possible U.S. exports, almost doubling in the period 1953–1958 from $56 million to some $100 million. These figures did not include output of local American plants, especially in Europe. The latter volume was counted in the national outputs shown next.

Italy exported $7.2 million during 1953, $23 million in 1958. Sweden went from $9.7 million to $16 million in the same period. These figures only cover adding and calculating machines. While NCR was restoring its export trade in cash registers to one-third of its revenues, the rest of the industry was busy selling machines too. Primarily because of NCR, the United States was still the largest exporter of such devices in 1953, shipping one-third of the world's value, or roughly $3.4 million. By 1958, this figure had climbed to $4.3 million but represented only 20 percent of the total, one-third behind Sweden and Germany. Worldwide volumes had thus reached some $21.5 million annually. Sweden had gone from $2.5 million to $7.9 million, or to 37 percent of the world market; Germany had reached $5.1 million in 1958, or 25 percent of the market.[6]

Lower-cost models of all three types of machines did best in the least industrialized economies. The most industrialized—Europe—tended, by the mid-1950s, to buy the largest volume of the most sophisticated models along with punched card equipment and a few computers. One U.S. government analyst observed that with the service sector of both the U.S. and world economies expanding rapidly in the 1950s, demand for such devices would continue to grow, and, despite expanded use of punched card equipment and computers, "the market for these conventional machines is far from saturation."[7]

Exports of these three types of machines to the United States came in large volumes during the early 1950s, representing new levels of global sophistication in the manufacture, distribution, and use of such equipment. The volume just before computers became commercially important in European and American markets is illustrated in table 17.2. The percentage of consumption in the United States of imported machines is evidence of the improved effectiveness of foreign vendors in placing products in the United States (see table 17.3). Adding machines were shipped from plants in West Germany, Sweden, Italy, Switzerland, the United Kingdom, Norway, and Denmark. Europe more than doubled exports of calculators between 1953 and 1958, from $3.3 million to $5.8 million in 1958 with foreign trade dominated by Italy, Netherlands, and the United Kingdom. Demand for calculators in the United

TABLE 17.2
U.S. Imports of Adding and Calculating Machines, Cash Registers, and Parts, 1953–1959 (dollars in millions)

Year	Adding Machines	Calculating Machines	Cash Registers and Parts	Total
1953	2.00	3.36	1.59	6.95
1954	2.33	2.71	1.48	6.52
1955	3.52	3.14	2.32	8.98
1956	5.35	5.81	2.48	13.64
1957	5.75	5.81	3.28	14.84
1958	6.01	5.84	3.61	15.46
1959	10.60	9.10	6.20	25.90

Source: U.S. Department of Commerce, *World Trade in Adding Machines, Calculators, Cash Registers, 1953–1959* (Washington, D.C.: Government Printing Office, 1960), 13.

TABLE 17.3
U.S. Imports as a Percentage of Consumption, 1953–1958

Year	Adding Machines	Calculators	Cash Registers
1953	—	8.3	3.7
1954	5.2	7.7	3.2
1955	6.3	7.4	4.3
1956	8.9	10.8	4.0
1957	10.3	10.3	5.5
1958	14.0	12.5	6.5

Source: U.S. Department of Commerce, *World Trade in Adding Machines, Calculators, Cash Registers*, 13.

States that existed at the same time commercial computers were coming into their own remained strong. If one left aside the success companies like Burroughs enjoyed and just looked at the products that came into the United States (see table 17.4), one glimpses the growing demand for such devices, which could not be satisfied totally by domestic suppliers. It also testifies to a rapidly expanding European market. Europe was right behind the United States in the manufacture and use of such machines.

Italy tripled production in the mid-1950s while increasing its export trade from 16 percent in 1953 to 30 percent in 1958. Production volumes, evidence of Italian activity, are summarized in table 17.5. Italy had at least ten manufacturers of these three classes of machines, only two of which were U.S.

TABLE 17.4

U.S. Imports of Calculating Machines and Parts by Country of Origin, 1953–1959 (dollars in thousands)

Country	1953	1954	1955	1956	1957	1958	1959
Italy	1,927	1,725	1,814	2,695	3,081	3,170	5,908
Netherlands	335	75	227	842	1,374	954	1,498
United Kingdom	635	605	215	208	458	738	917
West Germany	111	20	15	180	80	527	248
Sweden	144	192	247	256	373	295	201
France	—	3	521	608	289	32	17
Switzerland	172	48	67	20	73	18	60
Canada	27	30	25	982	24	11	29
Other Countries	12	10	7	17	62	95	220
Total	3,363	2,708	3,138	5,808	5,814	5,840	9,098

Source: U.S. Department of Commerce, *World Trade in Adding Machines, Calculators, Cash Registers*, table 7, 15.

TABLE 17.5

Production of Adding Machines, Calculators, and Cash Registers in Italy, 1953–1958 (thousands of units)

Year	Adding Machines and Calculators[a]	Cash Registers	Locally Manufactured Exports[b]
1953	82,737	1,953	8,290
1954	101,800	3,783	10,989
1955	132,651	4,480	20,144
1956	141,902	3,675	24,397
1957	193,154	4,804	30,551
1958	230,689	5,627	42,493

Source: U.S. Department of Commerce, *World Trade in Adding Machines, Calculators, Cash Registers*, 17–18.

[a] Data for adding machines were not discrete.

[b] In each year imports of all three classes of machines into Italy were in volumes significantly below local production levels.

subsidiaries. Right behind Italy was Sweden, which also became the single largest exporter of cash registers in Europe by the late 1950s. Roughly 45 percent of her exports went to satisfy European demand, another 43 percent to the United States, the rest around the world (see table 17.6).

West Germany and the United Kingdom present slightly different experiences. By 1956, West Germany was the fourth largest exporter behind Italy, Sweden, and the United States. Germany sold 42 percent of its exports of

TABLE 17.6
Production and Foreign Trade, Adding and Calculating Machines and Cash Registers
in Sweden, 1953–1958 (dollars in millions)

Device Type	1953	1954	1955	1956	1957	1958
Production						
All office machines	20.96	25.27	29.95	35.60	41.50	—
Adding, Calculating, Type- writers, cash registers	17.12	20.26	23.94	27.97	31.60	—
Exports						
Adding, Calculating	9.70	11.53	12.53	15.14	16.02	15.16
Cash Registers	2.53	4.12	4.65	6.97	6.42	7.95
Imports:						
Adding, Calculating	0.25	0.28	0.43	0.37	0.59	0.61
Cash Registers	0.43	0.40	0.70	0.46	0.55	0.68

Source: U.S. Department of Commerce, *World Trade in Adding Machines, Calculators, Cash Registers*, 19.

TABLE 17.7
Production and Foreign Trade, Adding and Calculating Machines and Cash
Registers in West Germany, 1953–1958 (dollars in millions)

Device Type	1953	1954	1955	1956	1957	1958
Adding Machines						
Exports	—	—	—	6.38	7.82	6.55
Imports	7.62	8.25	3.85	4.81	4.95	3.13
Calculators						
Production	11.61	13.28	16.51	19.22	22.43	22.60
Exports	—	—	—	3.48	3.81	4.19
Imports	—	—	—	2.62	2.30	4.86
Cash Registers[a]						
Production	—	—	11.62	15.91	16.29	20.12

Source: U.S. Department of Commerce, *World Trade in Adding Machines, Calculators, Cash Registers*, 20.

[a] Cash register dollar volumes are high because they contain German punched card, book-keeping, and accounting machines.

adding machines in 1958 to the United States while European customers absorbed another 27 percent. West Germany sold more calculators to France (18 percent of total) than to any other trading partner. West Germany had become a major supplier with some twenty-five firms producing these three classes of machines, only four of which were U.S. subsidiaries (see table 17.7). Although Germany started later than Italy, Britain, France, or Sweden because of Allied occupation regulations and wartime destruction, once active it man-

TABLE 17.8
Production and Foreign Trade, Adding and Calculating Machines and Cash Registers
in the United Kingdom, 1953–1958 (dollars in millions)

Device Type	1953	1954	1955	1956	1957	1958
Production (all office machines)	82.43	98.36	109.47	126.23	136.35	145.05
Adding Machines						
Exports[a]	8.30	4.91	4.89	4.54	4.94	5.41
Imports	0.32	0.50	0.89	0.82	1.20	
Calculators[b]						
Imports	0.94	1.25	2.01	1.86	0.81	2.01
Cash Registers						
Exports	1.61	1.62	1.77	1.49	1.56	1.91
Imports	0.57	0.98	1.63	2.41	2.88	4.00

Source: U.S. Department of Commerce, *World Trade in Adding Machines, Calculators, Cash Registers*, 21.

[a] Includes calculators.
[b] Exports included with adding machines.

aged to increase volumes rapidly. The United Kingdom contrasted sharply to most European examples. During the 1950s, Britain's export volumes and percentage of market share actually shrank (see table 17.8). Commonwealth markets were taking roughly half of Britain's exports in the mid-1950s, other European states 20 percent, and another 15 percent went to the United States. Britain had ten companies building equipment in these classes, of which five were U.S. subsidiaries. That activity represented the highest American penetration in Europe.

Volumes were far less for other countries. Lists for all Europe of the number of firms building these machines and how many were subsidiaries of U.S. enterprises are in table 17.9. The smaller volumes from Switzerland, the Netherlands, Norway, France, Denmark, and elsewhere indicate that local manufacturing plants either were small or were also making other devices, such as duplicators and dictating equipment (as, e.g., occurred in Denmark). The Canadian market was dominated by U.S. firms as it continued its historic role as an extension of the U.S. office equipment market.

The volumes of adding and calculating machines and cash registers produced in Western Europe show that the office equipment industry outside the United States continued to be dominated by noncomputer equipment sales throughout the 1950s and deep into the 1960s. Local firms were active, outnumbering American enterprises to a far greater extent in the postwar period than ever before. Additional research on the European office equipment industry for the entire twentieth century would probably uncover a larger, healthier indigenous industry than data on U.S. exports/imports would lead one to believe.

TABLE 17.9
Number of Firms Manufacturing Adding and
Calculating Machines and Cash Registers in
Western Europe, 1958–1959

Country	U.S. Subsidiary	European	Total
Italy	2	8	10
Sweden	1	5	6
West Germany[a]	4	21	25
United Kingdom	5	5[b]	10
Switzerland	1	11	12
Netherlands	3	5	8
France	3	3	6
Denmark	0	2	2

Source: U.S. Department of Commerce, *World Trade in Adding Machines, Calculators, Cash Registers*, 17–27.

[a] Plants existed in Czechoslovakia and in East Germany but no data are available on how many. Production facilities also existed in South Africa, Spain, Argentina, Brazil, Colombia, Japan, and Mexico for local consumption; almost all were subsidiaries of U.S. or European vendors.

[b] One firm is an Italian subsidiary.

U.S. Industry Volumes

The American industry was not small, rather one that enjoyed expanding sales, a strong capital assets position, and a visible presence in American offices (see the raw sales statistics in table 17.10). It competed effectively against airplane manufacturers and traditional electronics firms for the latest information-handling device—the computer—winning control over its manufacture and development by the late 1950s. One important consequence of that victory was the change in the industry's self-identification from purely an office equipment community to the data-processing industry of the 1960s. That metamorphosis led to different types of products both, however, built in a period of considerable prosperity generated by the sale of traditional products. Another consequence was the industry's commitment to being technology-based to a degree it never had been before. The demand for capital for R&D and to change manufacturing processes constantly was huge.

From the end of World War II until the early stages of the Korean War, prewar marketing habits were reinstated and results achieved in familiar ways. The only changes were in additional use of electronics and fashion. A snapshot of total sales for eleven companies appears in table 17.10.[8] As one might expect and as was reflected in letters to stockholders in almost every

TABLE 17.10
Office Machine Company Sales, 1947, 1949, 1951 (dollars in millions)

Year	Sales Volumes[a]	Year	Sales Volumes[a]	Year	Sales Volumes[a]
1947	703	1949	764	1951	1,125

Source: Data compiled from information in Lehman Brothers, "Burroughs Adding Machine Company: Study of Company and Its Position in the Business Machine Industry," May 19, 1952, Burroughs Papers.
[a] 1946 = 100.

TABLE 17.11
Office Machine Company Sales as a Percentage of
Total Industry Sales, 1947, 1949, 1951

Firm	1947	1949	1951
Burroughs	9.8	10.8	11.3
IBM	20.4	24.0	23.7
Remington Rand	23.0	17.8	20.2
Royal	5.0	5.6	5.4
Underwood	8.1	6.0	6.7
NCR	19.6	22.0	18.8
Addressograph	5.6	5.4	5.1
Smith-Corona	3.0	3.0	2.8
Felt & Tarrant	1.4	1.0	1.2
Marchant	1.8	1.8	2.1
Monroe	2.3	2.6	2.7
Total	100.0	100.0	100.0

Source: Data compiled from table 14, Lehman Brothers, "Burroughs Adding Machine Company: Study of Company and Its Position in the Business Machine Industry," May 19, 1952, unpaginated table, Burroughs Papers.

annual report of the period, 1945–1948, although good, was not without problems. These were caused by readjustment of the U.S. economy to peacetime and by manufacturing capability stretched to the limit at a time when volumes of sales were pushed up rapidly by demand. By 1951, sales momentum in excess of national inflation rates was obvious. For the same three sample years in table 17.11, the percentage of total sales captured by major vendors, illustrates that market share was gained by IBM, NCR, and Burroughs, lost by Remington Rand and major typewriter firms, and remained constant for adding machine vendors. The growth rates in table 17.12, suggest changes; IBM's sales went from a flat base of 100 percent in 1946 to more than 224 percent in 1951. All companies enjoyed strong growth and aggressive rates of expansion.

TABLE 17.12
Office Machine Sales as a Percentage of Growth over Time, 1946–1951

Firm	1946	1947	1949	1951
Burroughs[a]	100	150	202	277
IBM	100	121	153	224
NCR	100	178	216	274
Remington Rand	100	110	93	154
Addressograph	100	154	161	224
Royal Typewriter	100	189	224	316
Smith-Corona	100	150	161	227
Underwood	100	154	135	203
Felt & Tarrant	100	127	100	168
Marchant	100	109	111	200
Monroe	100	161	202	306

[a] This way of viewing growth originated in various competitive analyses in Burroughs Papers.

TABLE 17.13
Total Capital in the Office Equipment
Industry, in Book Value and in 1929 Dollars,
Selected Years, 1904–1948
(dollars in millions)

Year	Book Value	Year	Book Value
1904	85	1929	455
1914	175	1937	438
1919	199	1948	573

Source: U.S. Bureau of the Census, *Historical Statistics*, 412.

Total assets grew, giving vendors the wherewithal to support expansion of traditional product lines and to fuel the kind of R&D and marketing required by the mid-1950s to sell computers without compromising cash flows and profit levels. In table 17.13 I illustrate changes in total capital in this industry over decades to indicate what actually happened in the immediate postwar period. Values in flat dollars (1929) accented the real growth between 1937 and 1948, which reached 24 percent. In table 17.14, I take that macro view down to examples of specific companies in 1949—a year that saw significant transition to more R&D for computerlike projects just before the start of the Korean War. The industry leaders showed up well armed with assets to enter a period of change. The top five were better positioned than others by a wide margin to fund growth. The ratio of assets to sales favored IBM the most:

TABLE 17.14
Assets and Revenues of Office Machine
Companies, 1949 (dollars in millions)

Vendor[a]	Assets	Revenue
IBM[b]	267.34	183.46
Remington Rand	130.85	135.95
NCR	126.07	167.36
Burroughs	64.39	82.46
Underwood	39.96	45.93
L. C. Smith	18.33	23.45
Monroe	15.20	19.98
Marchant	10.01	13.34
Felt & Tarrant	7.89	7.68
Lanston	6.71	3.88
Clary	3.45	5.42

Source: Littlejohn and McClain, "Accounting
Machine Industry," 174, Burroughs Papers.
[a] Data not available on Friden, Victor, and R. C.
Allen.
[b] Excludes the Canadian subsidiary.

$1.46 in assets to support every $1 of sales. Remington Rand and NCR were clearly not proportionately as well positioned. The same was true of Burroughs and Underwood. The latter two had significantly fewer dollars and assets to work with. That reality accounted in part for their strategy of only competing against IBM and Remington Rand in select markets while they challenged smaller firms in others. The approach worked. For example, sales of typewriters, although down in 1948 and 1949, jumped 43 percent in 1950–1951 and came even in the face of growing success by IBM in selling its state-of-the-art electric typewriters introduced in the late 1940s.[9]

By the early 1950s, changes were evident. Production of adding and calculating machines and cash registers in the United States, measured by numbers built or by dollar value, began to decline beginning in 1953. By 1958, production had dropped some 20 percent (see table 17.15). This table is useful for quantifying U.S. volumes because almost all domestic production was consumed within the United States. Foreign sales from Burroughs, for example, were largely supported by production outside the United States. Sales of adding machines peaked in 1956 then began to decline in value. Calculating machines reached their high water mark of the 1950s in 1957, while domestic production of cash registers remained constant, supplemented by volumes from overseas. The Korean War spurred demand for all kinds of information-handling products, whereas the recession of the first half of 1958 slowed sales; by the fourth quarter recovery was evident.[10] Vendors tracked along the

TABLE 17.15

U.S. Production and Sales of Adding and Calculating Machines and Cash Registers, 1953–1958 (dollars in millions)

Year	Adding Machines		Calculating Machines		Cash Registers	
	(No.)	(Dollars)	(No.)	(Dollars)	(No.)	(Dollars)[a]
1953	356,000	89.73	99,717	60.90	101,000	81–91
1954	287,161	81.00	94,206	65.50	109,865	88–99
1955	336,251	89.97	118,675	74.39	116,857	93–105
1956	345,080	94.19	130,914	83.25	102,560	82–92
1957	338,917	92.21	124,419	84.18	87,840	70–79
1958	286,777	67.19	96,971	66.62	81,620	65–75

Source: U.S. Department of Commerce, *World Trade in Adding Macines, Calculators, Cash Registers*, 8.

[a] Estimated. Dollar amounts are retail values.

same time line. In fact, in 1959, sales volumes increased by 7 percent over those of 1958.

A composite picture of sales for all kinds of equipment, including computers, for the early to mid-1950s shows significant growth. Table 17.16 reflects where business came from. In 1953, 18 percent of the value of volumes shipped came from typewriters, roughly 53 percent from computing devices, and some 20 percent from such highly specialized equipment as time-stamp or check-handling machines. By the end of 1958, 60 percent came from computing equipment (not necessarily computers); typewriters contributed another 12.5 percent, down by nearly one-third as percentage of contribution. Tabulating equipment and cash registers combined provided 24 percent of sales in 1953, 19 percent in 1956, and 15 percent in 1958. The big change in relative contributions came from computers, beginning in the mid-1950s with their very high dollar value per unit as compared to smaller, less complex, and less expensive equipment. The $94 million in computer equipment in 1956 represented just over 9 percent of the total volume and, in 1958, had climbed to just over 24 percent. This growth came in a period that saw the total volume of products shipped between 1956 and 1958 rise by nearly one-third. The data suggest that markups were substantial, reflecting the high cost of marketing and distributing some products.[11]

Total receipts by American corporations jumped up by 30 percent in the first two years of the Korean War, whereas income rose on average by 50 percent.[12] A wartime excess profits tax was imposed on American corporations between 1950 and 1954, which motivated companies to plow more funds back into R&D or capital expenditures to avoid paying them to the government as excess profits tax. Money spent on research or bricks and mortar meant firms could declare smaller profits. Payments to stockholders

TABLE 17.16
Office Equipment by Value of Shipments FOB and at Retail List Prices CIF, 1953, 1956, 1958 (dollars in millions)

Type of Equipment	1953 FOB	1953 CIF	1956 FOB	1956 CIF	1958 FOB	1958 CIF
Accounting & bookkeeping	79	127	116	185	104	172
Punch card & cash registers	167	250	187	281	195	292
Coin/currency handling	5	6	5	6	6	8
Adding	57	90	60	94	45	73
Calculating	44	61	56	83	48	68
Rebuilt computing & accounting and cash registers	14	20	16	24	38	56
Electronic computing[a]			94	157	319	532
Stored media DP devices (not card-handling devices)					27	29
Other computing equipment					8	9
Total computing & related machines	366	554	534	830	790	1,239
Total typewriters	127	207	183	296	165	272
Total other office machines[b]	144	222	166	262	142	230
Parts sold separately	58	87	110	165	217	326
Totals	695	1,070	993	1,553	1,314	2,067

Source: John W. Kendrick, *Productivity Trends in the United States* (New York: National Bureau of Economic Research, 1961), 305.

[a] Data for 1953 included in "Total other office machines."

[b] Includes such devices as duplicating machines, dictating machines, check handlers, time-recording and time-stamp devices, and addressing machines.

remained flat. The general response to the new tax largely explains why so many companies remodeled plants, built new ones, and invested substantially in R&D in the early 1950s. A great deal of computer-related research was financed through government contracts, the rest largely through smart tax avoidance. The result of the R&D portion of the tax moves was a large volume of new technologies and products that came onto the market by the mid-1950s.[13] It was no accident or coincidence that, for example, such popular devices as the IBM 650 computer came when they did. Across the entire nation, capital expenditures rose by 50 percent in 1951 and doubled by 1953. Thus a combination of tax incentives, increasing demand for products during the war, and the need for change to remain competitive contributed to speeding up changes in the technological bases of information-handling equipment and sales during the mid-to-late 1950s.

The significant capital expenditures of the early 1950s were a distinct feature of the industry of that period. That major vendors had to adapt to new circumstances was also starkly obvious. Burroughs, for example, enjoyed a 40 percent rise in sales between 1950 and 1951 but paid in taxes the major share of the incremental income. Its taxes went from $10 million in 1950 to $18 million the following year. Management responded in 1952 by expanding plant production and by purchasing Control Instrument Company. Remington Rand felt the same pressures as sales climbed by over 70 percent and taxes multiplied threefold. The pattern was evident at electronics firms, potential rivals in the computer market. RCA, for instance, saw its sales rise by 50 percent between 1950 and 1952 and its taxes by 120 percent.[14] Following the war, the tax rate declined and incentives to sell to the military shrank as the Department of Defense's expenditures of all types went from $44 billion in 1953 to $36 billion in 1955. That decline caused vendors to shift back to commercial markets. It was no coincidence that computers increasingly were produced for business applications in the period 1955–1956.[15]

The final measure of the extent of the office equipment industry is the number of information workers in the United States. Daniel Bell argued that increasing proportions of the American labor force were becoming members of a new economic sector, which he called the information sector. He used that term just like economists employed the phrases agricultural, industrial, and service sectors. Bell intended for his to be the fourth alongside the others in categorizing economic activity.[16] These laborers' primary output was information or knowledge (e.g., teachers, scientists, and office workers). Central to their ability to function was their reliance on aids to data handling, most notably computers and telecommunications but other technologies as well. By his definition, in 1900, some 10.9 percent of the American workforce populated his information worker sector, in 1940, 18.4 percent. In the 1940s it went to 14.1 percent and by 1960 had reached 28.4 percent.[17] What is startling is the percentage of the population involved in this sector for any period, particularly in the midtwentieth century. These workers were prime users of office equipment, and the percentage suggests that the office equipment industry was more influential within the economy than historians and economists had thought. The issue continues to be important today because as late as the start of the 1990s, the number of Americans in offices continued to increase as did their dependence upon information-handling technologies.[18]

There are many ways to look at such issues, but much work has yet to be done to define the function of information workers. However, some have attempted to deliver an answer. Fritz Machlup pioneered work on the problem beginning in the late 1950s and continuing over the next quarter-century. As measured by GNP alone, he estimated that by 1958, 6.5 percent of all American expenditures were being plowed into various types of information-

TABLE 17.17

Total Cost of Computing: Hardware and Personnel Costs in the
United States, 1953, 1956, 1958 (dollars in millions)

	Expense		
Hardware & Personnel	*1953*	*1956*	*1958*
Computing & related machines	554	830	1,239
Other office machines & parts[a]	309	427	556
Total hardware	863	1,257	1,795
Total personnel	1,726	2,514	3,590
Total cost	2,589	3,771	5,385

[a] Typewriters are not included in the above calculations. Personnel
costs were derived by adding personnel costs to retail hardware costs
(CIF) to make an EDP budget reach 100 percent. Hardware made up
one-third of the total. For this rough analysis, salary rates were assumed to have grown at the same pace as hardware's. No attempt was
made to factor actual salary rate changes of the period. The objective
of this table is to validate the magnitude of costs given by other researchers in a manner that might have been used by a manager in the
1950s.

TABLE 17.18

Computing Costs as a Percentage of
the U.S. GNP, 1953, 1956, 1958

Year	*GNP (dollars in billions)*	*Computing Costs[a] (%)*
1953	365.4	0.007
1956	419.2	0.009
1958	444.5	0.012

[a] Calculations were keyed off data in
table 17.17.

handling machines. He concluded that 18.1 percent of the GNP was allocated to R&D across the economy. Machlup thought that communications absorbed another 13.2 percent.[19] He sliced his data by whether expenditures were made by government, business, or consumers. Because office equipment sales were made overwhelmingly only to business and government customers and rarely to private individuals, except for typewriters and a few adding machines, in this period, 58.7 percent of all expenditures came from those sectors of the economy targeted by office equipment suppliers. That suggests even by such segmentation that the proportion of GNP going to information machines might be too high at 6.5 percent but not a great deal less. Machlup's approach also calls out the possibility that the impact of the office appliance industry on the economy has been underestimated.[20]

The inability to be precise about percentages of GNP taken up by office equipment or by its industry is the result of several factors that require further study. First, and also easiest to measure, was how much product was made and sold (see the previous paragraph). However, it was not so easy to define how many products sold in previous years were also operational and thus preserving jobs associated with the industry (e.g., maintenance activity or users). And, what were the ongoing annuity costs for both customers and vendors? These expenditures probably should be calculated into the total cost, an approach that Machlup's work suggests. The industry itself obviously paid less attention to that issue than to future demands for products. A second concern was the cost of using the industry's products. One does not have a good analysis today of what that might have been. In the data-processing industry of the 1960s and 1970s, managers usually found that equipment and software represented one-third of their total expenditures, salaries almost the whole of the other two-thirds.[21] If one applies that formula to the 1940s and 1950s with equipment that was equally labor intensive to use and often employed similar, if not exactly the same, labor-intensive input/output equipment as in the earlier period, then using the data from table 17.16 one can hypothesize that the total value of information handling in the United States might have been quite extensive. An analysis of table 17.17 simply reinforces that notion by suggesting that the cost of information handling, using computing and related machines and not typewriters or other lower-level technology, would have been measurably substantial. It contributed to the volumes suggested by Bell and Machlup. The percentage of the U.S. GNP those expenditures might have been is shown in table 17.18 for selected periods of the 1950s. This is a highly constrained view because ancillary expenses (e.g., office space, electricity, medical benefits) were not included in personnel costs. A note of caution: at best this is a rough cut, but it at least suggests that additional work is needed and that this is not a trivial issue. The industry's participation in the American economy seems understated for the period before 1956 and possibly back to the decade before World War I.

18

Conclusion: The Roles of Marketing, Distribution, and Technology

THE APPROACH in this book has been to identify activities that defined the industry and to call out those that survived to characterize mechanical information processing through the decades. I chose the marketplace perspective. Regardless of decade or technology, product or participants, somebody developed and manufactured a product, sold it, often against competition, and then serviced it. Customers needed to control increasing amounts of information, bought and installed machines to get the job done, and used them until something better came along.

Customers carried out these tasks for many decades before the arrival of the computer. Activities of both vendors and customers were evident as much when the first typewriter sales rep made the initial sale as when Eckert and Mauchly tried to convince the U.S. government to acquire UNIVACs. While one reads this page today, somewhere somebody is building, selling, buying, installing, or using a computer to satisfy some need. Somewhere also, a broken computer is being repaired by a service representative, just as a broken tabulating machine in the 1920s was repaired by a customer engineer from IBM or Powers out on a "service call." This is an industry with patterns of behavior that stretch back a very long time.

The centrality of the buying and selling of products equals or possibly surpasses in importance many other activities within this or any other industry. I have emphasized more what happened at the street level in marketing than what one is used to seeing in a study of the data-processing industry. One normally finds a pure economic analysis of pricing, technology infusion, and other macro issues. What I attempt to show in this study is not that such concerns are irrelevant but that they become realistic only if at a micro level somebody wants, buys, and then uses a product. Trends, pricing, and so forth, then become synonymous as they document such behavior.

Organizations in this industry emerged to manufacture, distribute, and service machines that customers would buy and use; the process was usually very profitable. People became executives if they effectively fulfilled this mission or mastered the politics of their companies. Manufacturing depended on the ability to produce a cost-effective, timely product that satisfied customers. No technology was historically significant until it found a home in the market and was used. It is a useful approach with which to answer the question "When did a technology become significant?" By this gauge, it certainly was not when it was first developed. Television in the 1920s was a historical curiosity; it became historically significant in the 1950s when people started to use it in quantity and were influenced by its technology. Similarly, the development of punched card machines in the 1880s was fascinating but irrelevant to the economics and efficiencies of many customers until the 1900s.

The ability to bring together a number of factors—cost of production and marketing, relative improvement in price performance over previous technologies and methods, and new applications—determined when a technology became relevant to the history of the industry or to the American economy. In an industry as technologically dependent as this one, timing of use becomes a more critical issue for historians to ponder. It certainly is a very useful measure of market acceptance of a particular technology because adoption usually came when a machine was more cost effective than its predecessors, clearly more efficient, usually more reliable, and packaged in a more convenient form.

To a large extent, the history of management has been avoided as a subject more suited to histories of companies where specific examples can be studied. Companies came and went; a few stayed longer, whereas others became great powers. Some, like IBM, were important for a very long time. Invariably, one or a few people in fortuitous circumstances made the difference. Burroughs, Hollerith, Watson, Rand, Powers, and others are examples, and each decade had its share. The "great man" approach to history often has a place in the study of management; in the inception of specific technologies and with occasional visionary work innovators developed and exploited specific devices. Burroughs at home building his first adding machine exemplified an important influencer as did Watson, Sr., making IBM a major force within the industry. More studies of the lives of these people are needed. However, one cannot help but conclude that, generally, patterns of behavior in the industry at large grew out of the creation and operation of organizations made up of many people. Executives and managers fostered conformity, conservative decisions, and specific patterns of behavior among themselves and, consequently, among their employees, which made identifiable common strategies and tactics evident from the turn of the century until the 1950s and beyond.

The industry developed when the need for information-handling equipment increased and when the number of potential users expanded rapidly. From the 1860s through the 1950s, as the economy expanded, industrialization increased, and the percentage of working population moving into offices grew, conditions made it possible to offer products that increased feedback and control. The same happened in Europe, encouraging early development of an international office equipment industry with common business practices worldwide. This industry, built on a large customer base, made it much easier for office appliance firms to market computers, when they arrived, to consumers already used to information-handling hardware.

Marketing and Distribution

The process of marketing and distributing products in this industry changed over the period 1865–1956, but some constants appeared as well. From the days of Remington's earliest typewriters to IBM's broad line of tabulating machines of the 1920s and 1930s to the first commercial computers, inventors and then marketing managers sought to satisfy perceived needs.[1] Invariably, needs were defined first as the requirement to record or manipulate data more rapidly than by previous methods and, second, to store and retrieve that information faster, less expensively, and in more convenient forms than before. Most actual tasks (applications) changed little from preautomation days until around World War II. By the 1940s, more iterative calculations could be done with existing machines. In the beginning (1860–1890), needs emerged from the direct experiences of individuals as they developed products. Burroughs worked at a bank, Hollerith at the Census Bureau, and many different inventors of cash registers in retail operations; engineers in the 1920s and 1930s were frustrated by tedium as they performed increasingly complex calculations on desktop calculators as their discipline became more mathematical.

As organizations emerged to manufacture and distribute products, the process of identifying customer needs became more complicated. At NCR, by the 1890s, sales reps were required to report comments made by customers concerning machine quality, whereas at IBM, by the 1920s, the results of sales calls were being recorded weekly on forms sent to a requirements department. Burroughs constantly polled branch managers, beginning early in the twentieth century. By the 1930s, all major office appliance vendors had requirements departments that queried customers, obtained feedback from marketing representatives, and formulated changes in pricing, practices, and products. Customer surveys and the use of consultants became more prevalent after World War II and, by the mid-1950s, were common across the industry. Watson, Sr., reflected the actions of many generations of executives in his industry by constantly visiting customers during his more than four-decade rule of IBM. He also insisted that his managers do the same. Thus from personal experience to more thorough methods of identifying needs, office equipment vendors were market driven from the beginning in their responses to product development and distribution.

Customers faced the same issues concerning acquisition and dependence on technology much the same way in the 1870s, the 1950s, or 1960s. Whenever presented with a new device or method, they had to (1) determine if it did the job as well or better than the currently accepted technology; (2) determine if they could do the job more cheaply with the new machine; (3) establish if the device would be at least as reliable as the older technology (4) perhaps identify or consider other options; (5) determine if new tasks could be performed that were not possible before. The last point became increasingly important with the development of the computer.[2] Many other questions were asked by customers concerning risks, in what kind of competitive position use of the new equipment would place them, and its ability to enhance service or increase market share. These considerations often were the basis of their decisions as to whether or not they could implement the new technologies.

It was never inevitable that office managers would automate, that the crush of more information would lead to the use of punched cards, accounting machines, or typewriters, or that computers would ever be attractive commercially. Each was not received positively when introduced. There were concerns about the viability of the typewriter and the computer. Predictions about volumes were frequently too low, confidence too limited. Each generation of technology or product had to survive by passing some basic tests put forth by customers much as it does today. Computers did not become commercially viable, for example, until they could do more work for less cost and at least as reliably as punched card equipment. Adding machines replaced earlier models only when they could perform more functions and, thus, increase productivity at less cost per task. When increased volume was an issue, as when the Social Security Administration had to implement New Deal legislation, cost per transaction was still measured as a test of equipment; speed, too, became a benchmark.

Customers almost always made vendors compete against older models or yesterday's technology at least as much as against each other because consumers always had the choice of not changing. Conversion to new methods always offered the risk of failure, hidden costs, and changes to organizations caused by new ways of flowing information through an enterprise. Each decision to move to a new technology called for risk taking. Although many writers leave an impression of inevitability in the move to information-handling machines,[3] the evidence suggests that nothing was further from the truth because customers always had three options: to acquire a proposed technology, use an alternative, or make no changes. The argument, for example, that use of a new technology was essential to be competitive breaks down if a manager did not perceive the advantages of such a new machine. Customer options could also be added to, particularly at the low end, by buying second-hand typewriters, cash registers, adding and calculating machines. Competing technologies were always present in the industry. Accounting or bookkeeping machines were sold against punched card devices; computers proposed to displace tabulating gear; adding machines and calculators were offered against those of another. Finally, manual methods (e.g., more clerks) or different business processes instead of machines had to be considered as rival options. Alternatives were provided by competing vendors that offered the same technology, for instance, the many suppliers of cash registers, typewriters, and simple adding machines. Customers could take their work to service bureaus. With so many options, customers were not shy in asking for features to make products more attractive, less risky, and increasingly productive.

Who were the customers? At the high end, they were usually first government agencies and then large commercial enterprises, such as railroads and insurance companies. All vendors in each period sought large organizations as customers because they could afford to use new technologies earlier than could smaller enterprises to help work out their problems and needed to handle larger amounts of data. Machines invariably were expensive until volumes rose to drive down costs. The $100 typewriter of the 1880s was an expensive machine. The first users of cash registers were large department stores. As costs declined and product lines became more varied, smaller customers could take advantage of equipment. The pattern was the same across all types of products in each period. Even the IBM PC of the early 1980s was initially aimed at large customers; it was not until some five years later that it was sufficiently inexpensive to interest small organizations and individuals.[4] Large customers could buy in bulk too and so were attractive to vendors. They also could mix and match various methods and technologies to optimize cost advantages while lowering the risk of losing a sale. In short, costs and functions helped to dictate which customers would be first and which would be later. It became one of the constants of the industry's history.

Vendors listened to their customers usually very well. For example, most of the changes in punched card products of the twentieth century grew directly out of specific requests from customers. Competition was simply another route by which customer defined their preferences. Printing tabulating equipment was introduced to satisfy auditors in accounting who wanted a documented trail of transactions. IBM's calculating machines of the late 1940s offered additional calculating capacity with punched cards that operated with advanced electronics. That combination caused data to be manipulated in larger and faster amounts but without the risk or cost of using digital computers. Northrop Aviation asked IBM to improve upon IBM's products by lashing various pieces of hardware together to reduce even further the manual steps in the overall process of inputing, processing, and outputing data to and from cards in the late 1940s.[5] That relationship between vendor and customer was evident in each corner of the industry.

Marketing, therefore, began with a response to demands. As customers became more knowledgeable, their requirements had to be met more specifically. As volumes increased, it became easier to justify standardizing features. Many of these changes were attachments or new configurations using known technology and existing components in different ways. Migration of components from one product base to another always took place. The keyboard appeared first on typewriters, then in modified form on cash registers, and later moved to punched card equipment, accounting products, and, finally, to data-entry terminals and microcomputers. The various models of a particular product line also reflected enhancements, corrections of design errors, and additional capacity in almost every product line since the 1880s. The vast majority of changes, however, grew out of requests made by customers. That notion should not be confused with responses to competitive pressure. If, for instance, a tabulating machine vendor produced a better punch, which in turn caused a second provider to bring out a similar or slightly better product, the original impetus was usually from a customer who caused the first provider to enhance a product. That process accounts for the many hundreds of product announcements made across the industry almost each year. To be sure, vendor engineers also thought up improvements, some of which were needed to enhance manufacturing and to maintain products, but the evidence for that linkage is less dramatic than the influence of customers, at least in the proto–information-processing industry.

Service and education went hand in glove from the beginning. During the early days of a new generation of products, performance never met expectations, and suppliers had to be prepared to repair equipment. That need existed as much in the 1870s as in the 1950s or in the 1980s. Mechanical devices required more service than electromechanical ones. With the latter, the problem of service was complicated by the need also to support applications. It was no accident that repair personnel were called "field engineers" and resided across the market in the same communities as salespeople or, in very large installations, on site in a customer's plant or office. Downtime was expensive for customers, who had to continue paying rent and wages to operators who were not using equipment. Thus service was seen quickly by vendors and customers as a way to reduce risks associated with the installation of and growing dependence upon machines.

Closely associated with servicing was the education of customers on how to use products. Sales personnel had to introduce new devices to customers and to show what these could be used for. Instructing users on applications was time consuming. But creating demand through service and education was an imperative feature of this industry's marketing. Demonstrations on how to use equipment fell to the sales rep and remained a constant duty through the first ninety years. Creation of training schools by vendors proved crucial if customers were to use their products and become "loyal" because they lacked knowledge of how to use other vendors' devices in the precomputer era. That remained true after the introduction of the computer too. Felt & Tarrant led the way in education during the early days but almost every other vendor was close behind. They delivered education through salespeople teaching one-on-one or one-on-many sessions on site or at branch offices, or through specially created schools. Recall the problem of typewriter vendors in the beginning: nobody knew how to type! At first, independent organizations took the lead in teaching skills through, for example, the YMCAs and high schools. But it became obvious by the 1880s and early 1890s that vendors had to do the job to sell more products. The more complicated a machine was, the more education was needed. Thus a vendor's "go-to-market" plan had to include selling, service, and education as early as the 1890s; nearly one hundred years later marketing still included the same elements.

Vendors clearly linked creation of demand to education. As lines of products became well understood, that requirement modified. Once most customers knew what an adding machine did, for instance, the need to explain its possible uses diminished. The same held true for typewriters, where the classic sales pitch that sold features and advantages became the norm. By the 1930s, the best understood lines of products included typewriters, small adding and calculating machines, and, to a lesser extent, punched card gear and cash registers. The issue of price competitiveness—as compared to other options customers had—also made new applications possible. The surge in application descriptions published in the 1920s and 1930s hinted at the push for new uses with more cost-effective equipment, a process that remained alive and central to marketing through the 1950s.

Distribution evolved in many ways. During the first five to ten years in the life of a new technology, it was not unusual for the creator personally to attempt marketing and distribution. Hollerith, for instance, personally negotiated directly with various government agencies in the United States and in Europe in the 1890s. At established firms, products were distributed by a direct sales force or by dealers (e.g., cash registers in the 1900s or computers in the 1950s). PCs sold through dealers in the 1980s once again illustrated the process). Less complex equipment was better moved to market through retail outlets, such as dealerships with store fronts. More complex devices required either more training of the marketing representative or the use of highly skilled individuals (perhaps even the creators themselves) to explain them. Cash register and typewriter salespeople were plentiful by the 1890s. Often, selling tabulating equipment required intervention by engineers from IBM's plant at Endicott or from similar facilities run by Powers and, later, Remington Rand.

Marketing that required sales calls on customers was increasingly managed through a network of either direct sales forces or agents. A vendor either recruited and retained a direct sales force that called on customers or allowed retail outlets to sell its products exclusively or as one of many offerings. Retail outlets also employed agents. Outlets were strictly retail or, more frequently, a combination of outbound marketing (sales reps calling on customers) and a showroom facility. Less-complicated products (e.g., type-writers and adding machines) more frequently were distributed through agents and retail outlets. The more complicated the equipment, the greater was the need to use a combination of sales reps, technical support personnel, and service people housed in a local branch office. Although experimentation with distribution went on constantly throughout the entire period and was repeated in the 1980s, the industry found it increasingly necessary to use direct sales forces for its most complex products. As these became increasingly simple, companies shifted to more retail-oriented outlets and redeployed the sales force on new complex items. For example, Burroughs used agent storefronts to sell adding machines but its own sales force for accounting machines by the 1920s, experimented with agent representatives in the 1930s for simpler versions, and relied exclusively on a direct sales force for its largest products in the 1940s and 1950s. IBM sold large, complex systems this way while Remington Rand followed suit by the early 1940s for its most sophisticated products.

By the early 1900s, but before the start of World War I, salespeople were operating out of branches for all types of devices while store fronts in all major U.S. cities frequently offered various manufacturers' equipment at the low end. Tabulating equipment was sold through a few representatives in a very limited number of branch offices, each of which covered a wide geographical area. During the 1920s and 1930s, the number of branch offices of all major vendors combined grew from dozens to hundreds, then to thousands (including retail outlets) by the end of the 1940s, both in the United States and around the world. By the 1950s, these facilities also began to grow in size. For example, the IBM branch office of the 1920s in Washington, D.C., had less than one dozen employees but in the late 1950s was one of several, each with more than twice as many employees. The number of offices and their size grew in response to the expanded local economies and increased numbers of customers. By the 1980s, such facilities frequently had between 75 and 150 employees and shared the metropolitan area with some 10,000 IBM employees. Other vendors experienced similar growth.

Most new companies centralized management control at headquarters in their early years. Corporate facilities often began as a kitchen table, an office, or a corner of a workshop. Humble beginnings continued to the present; for example, Apple Computers of the 1970s operated out of a home garage. But by the 1890s, corporate headquarters were distinct office facilities at initial plant sites (Burroughs, NCR, Remington Rand, and Felt & Tarrant, among others), which remained a pattern for future companies as well (e.g., Underwood, Monroe, and Victor). The function of a vice-president of sales first emerged in the 1890s and early 1900s, and by World War I, regional sales managers were used. By the start of World War II in the United States, as a further refinement, companies sandwiched a district manager between branch sales/service offices and a regional headquarters. IBM and Burroughs each had less than five regional headquarters to cover the United States but more districts. The concept of districts and regions has prevailed in one form or another to the present within the information-processing industry.

Sales reps in the office appliance industry, perhaps more so and earlier than in most other industries, were treated as professional business people by their employers. Patterson at NCR in the 1880s set the pace by making them dress conservatively like customers—a change from the flashy or slovenly look of late nineteenth-century salesmen. Watson ran one of the first classes in American industry on selling fundamentals in the 1890s at NCR and carried such practices to IBM. Both men pioneered the use of quota targets, exclusive territories, 100 Percent Clubs, and other tools aimed at building up the prestige and skills of the profession, and these remained standard practices in the data-processing industry to the present. Yet, at least in the beginning, not all information-handling machine vendors embraced the new thinking about sales. Burroughs's sales reps continued to look and act like their less-admired contemporaries until after World War II. American industry at large, however, by the 1920s began to borrow many ideas about sales management from the office appliance industry. Many of these earlier efforts in the office appliance world were exported to other industries in the early 1900s, however, by alumni of the industry who moved to other kinds of businesses. NCR, for example, was a net exporter of executive talent between the late 1880s and the 1920s, all trained and fired by Patterson. When, during the 1920s, sales management became a subject of considerable study,[6] vendors in the industry embraced the new thinking about selling techniques.

Why were sales reps upgraded to professionals striving for the same degree of self-respect and importance found in accounting or finance? Why did it probably occur sooner in segments of this industry? Although the questions have not been fully examined by historians, there are several possible reasons. First, intelligent marketing managers and executives, such as Patterson and Watson, recognized that customers would buy expensive industrial products that were new if they were shown how to use them and if they had confidence in service (help) after the sale. To accomplish that required salespeople who were more knowledgeable about the products and their customers' business and who would be around to provide support. Second, many complex machines had to be sold to very large organizations at middle manager or executive levels. Executives in the industry came to realize that this could not be done easily by someone who did not come from the same social or educational background as their customers or who did not share the same patterns of dress and life-style. IBM personnels' dark suits reflected this thinking.

Professionalization of the sales force was evident by the early 1900s in some sectors of the office appliance industry and across all segments by the

1920s.[7] Annual reports referred to salespeople; sales manuals spoke of the need for knowing one's customers and products while Watson, for instance, as did his peers, liked to "collect salesmen," making them heroes of their organizations. By the late 1940s, it became increasingly common for sales reps to be college graduates and by the end of the 1950s for them to have technical degrees, a reflection of the need to be able to handle the sale of increasingly complex products that were science-based. There is no evidence to suggest that female sales reps functioned in the industry before the 1960s. Old photographs of graduates from sales schools at Burroughs, NCR, and IBM from the 1890s down through the 1950s, for example, reflected a homogeneous group of white males in dark suits wearing white shirts. Very few were Jewish salesmen; almost all were U.S. citizens; most were Protestant; and all spoke fluent English. Some evidence suggests—at least by the 1920s—that vendors paid attention to pairing marketing representatives of Irish descent, for example, with Irish-American customers in Boston, and so forth. By the 1930s, manuals on selling fundamentals acknowledged this standard practice across many American industries. Sales reps in foreign subsidiaries, as a rule, were local nationals although many of their managers were American.

Analysis by students of business history is insufficient to confirm how important marketing was in product distribution in this century before the introduction of computers. Economists who have worked on the data-processing industry of the post-1955 era suggest that functions of products, manufacturing, and price were more important elements in the acceptance of goods.[8] Those with a marketing bent have a difficult time accepting the notion that "the product sells itself." Typewriters and tabulating machines proved this clearly was not the case. Customers did not flock to vendors to acquire new machines. Certainly, the senior officers of all vendors believed sales reps added significant value. The creation of direct sales forces was an expensive necessity. That manufacturers had to have products in demand is a given; hence, the vendors required feedback from their representatives so that they could develop cost-competitive machines. In short, they had to accomplish distribution with a complex structure of direct salespeople or dealer outlets.

Competition

Products needed intrinsic cost performance and attractive functions to be competitive. Flamm in his study of the computer industry argues that competition in the post-1955 period depended largely on technological innovations. When a vendor introduced a machine based on new technology, it had a momentary competitive advantage. It was during that window of time, say eighteen months or more, that a vendor could sell the product before others copied it or came out with something more cost-effective or functionally superior. Thus Flamm concluded that R&D was at least as important as any other factor that contributed to the success of a product in a high-technology–based industry such as data processing.[9] A machine's attractiveness had to include innovation and improved economies of scale and capture benefits for a vendor in a timely manner. Less-expensive function drove up demand, which customers could take advantage of until the next round of product announcements brought further enhancements.

To a lesser extent, however, the same process could be seen in the office appliance industry before the 1950s. Major technological changes, such as those frequent in the computer business, were less evident or at least slower to appear in the office equipment world. They were more evolutionary. Rivalries caused by important changes in technologies after the advent of the computer were based on a long line of past market battles. In an earlier era that saw less profound changes, rivalry occurred over alternative technologies, pricing, or marketing. Adding machines and calculators, for example, underwent significant changes in technologies most dramatically in the 1880s and 1890s but then stabilized over the next fifty years. Subsequent changes were evolutionary modifications in style, functional enhancements, use of electricity, and new packaging components. Accounting machines evolved the most into standard products in the period 1910–1925 and then remained essentially the same until the introduction of the computer made possible the use of new electronic components. Tabulating equipment stabilized by the late 1930s. Afterward, changes were less fundamental and more apt to be features that added speed and capacity and were introduced in a conservative, gradual manner down to the end of the lives of tabulating products in the early 1960s. Thus, for instance, punched cards changed in size and shape to hold more data (even then only several times), but how they were punched essentially did not change for more than a half-century. Cash registers kept their functions and composition effectively intact through the entire period. In all, competition based on changing technologies, although clearly present, was not as profound as after the arrival of the computer. This pattern of technological evolution reveals the pattern Basalla argues applies to all forms of technology. His notion that diversity exists, "that every novel artifact has an antecedent," and that these reflect economic and cultural realities was clearly evident in the office appliance industry.[10]

Competition depended more on price, which, in turn, was heavily affected by manufacturing efficiencies and less by reduced profit margins or less expensive methods of distribution. Competition was met head-on by introducing new features. Finally, with demand more frequently grossly underestimated by the industry, the individual who turned up first at a customer's doorstep frequently got the sale if normal marketing and selling practices were exercised. Thus the need to cover the market with salespeople was more crucial to a vendor's competitive edge than simply introducing a new device. This was particularly the case once base technologies had stabilized by World War I; the situation did not change until computers were introduced. Given the huge potential, a vendor who grew in proportion as equipment became more reliable and less expensive stood the chance of doing well. This explanation goes far to expose why executives like Watson, with optimistic bents of mind, would feel such an urge to build up sales forces and to train them to realize the potentials of the market.

Price battles did occur; however, they were most frequent at the low end, where customers perceived little or no added value of services (e.g., marketing); at the high end, help was essential. Typewriters, small adding machines, and cash registers, from early on, fit into the low-end category. With larger adding machines and calculators, service proved more important. Differentiation by function was often crucial, whereas price remained a sensitive factor. At the high end, service and function were effective responses to competitive pressures. Reliance on a particular brand of equipment at the high end also proved important because conversion to another base of technology could be more expensive than any price advantage of an alternative product. When IBM wanted its customers to move to computers, it was no accident that it attached to these machines punched equipment compatible with products and cards of the 1930s and 1940s. Such examples of "account control" illustrated street-level actions of what Chandler called "purposeful economic" activity. From almost the first year, control of customer options through technology as well as terms and conditions allowed vendors and users alike to steer an often compatible course that attempted to minimize changes and, consequently, risk. How much influence customers had on the process remains imprecise. However, it must have been substantial given the efforts by vendors to obtain feedback on product functions, reliability, and service.

Histories of industries often focus on the ability of firms to enter and exit a particular industry, often in response to their ability to satisfy customer needs. The issue of entrance and exit concerned the Justice Department, which used the rate of entrance/exit as an indicator of the amount of competitive activity in an industry. Yet across many decades, entrance and success depended more on the complexity of a product set, patent protection in some instances (or lack thereof), and capital requirements than upon some monolithic organization or other factors. It was not an industry simplistically made up of a half-dozen giant organizations acting like well-oiled engines with uniform sets of customers. It was characterized instead by various markets with sectors defined more by product sophistication. With simple devices such as typewriters, vendors came and went—hundreds of them. As complexity increased, the number of vendors who came and went diminished rapidly and early. That was most clearly exemplified by the shakeout with accounting machines. In the late 1950s and throughout the 1960s, the same happened with electronics firms. Market fragmentation ultimately made it difficult to define clearly this industry in any period. It may have had more definition and identity in this book than it had in real life.

Practices

I noted throughout this history the similarities between practices in the early years and those evident in the post-1955 period. An obvious example was the renting and leasing of tabulating then computer equipment with a concerted effort in each period to control the supply of cards and other supplies and services.[11] Sales manuals of the 1920s read very similarly to those of the 1950s, whereas many from the 1970s and 1980s also have the feel of those of a half-century earlier. At the low end, machines were usually sold and service contracts were provided at additional fees. As one moved up the product line in complexity, the option to buy or rent became more prevalent, and at the very high end of accounting or tabulating machinery rental or a lease was normal. These generalizations apply for the entire period back to the 1890s. Because customers were not willing to assume as much risk of obsolescence or failure with more expensive machines as they were with smaller, more stable technologies, they inadvertently encouraged vendors to stabilize quickly the terms and conditions of contracts and to standardize offerings and services.

Vendors also had particular needs that practices helped to satisfy. For example, vendors of small devices needed to recapture capital investments quickly to reinvest in additional machines. They always had to be price competitive, hence their propensity to sell rather than rent. At the high end, a vendor's ability to offer a minimal commitment (rent or lease) made it easier to persuade customers to try a new product because users knew that if it did not work, they could get rid of it quickly. More importantly, a customer could be made dependent on a device (through lease agreements) and then be persuaded to move to a new generation (motivating through new terms and conditions) thus preserving the all-essential cash flow required to fund the rental inventories and expenses associated with service and product development. Customers, once dependent on a particular technology had to rely on their vendors to support effective use and, subsequently, to provide economic incentives, migration aids, and minimized risks to move to new products. That interdependence of one on the other was clearly most evident at the high end. It was the lifeblood of Remington Rand and IBM. It established a pattern of vendor loyalty that has been reinforced in the age of computers for exactly the same reasons.

Close ties were important for other purposes as well. Financing a rental base of equipment was expensive, and few could do it. That ability made it easier for IBM, for example, to compete against rivals that had to sell products to preserve cash flows. IBM and Remington Rand altered prices to account for competitive pressures while they protected the cash flows necessary to support capital investments in rental products.[12] As the risk of commitment rose with reliance on more complex products, it became more difficult for customers to purchase machines, especially if they had never used such equipment before. That factor alone ensured that rental and leasing practices would remain standard with many product offerings into the 1970s. For decades, vendors changed prices, terms, and conditions whenever they could to bring out new products, make old ones obsolete, or meet competitors—not always when customers insisted. Customer price dissatisfaction reflected their inability to cost-justify particular products or led to their insistence upon additional function per dollar. Customer influence on value for function was more indirect or expressed in terms of features compared to various technologies, whereas vendors worried about price extraction for functions offered. For decades, a common practice both in this industry and later in the data-processing era was for vendors to offer more function per price compatible with earlier models (or with migration tools), leading customers to move to newer devices at the end of leases without investing capital in older technologies. That seemed to satisfy both: customers acquired more valuable function and capacity while vendors profited and enhanced cash flows. That pattern was clearly in place by World War I and remained evident into the 1980s.

Although generally, the industry became increasingly capital intensive, movement in and out of suppliers at the low end during the period 1875–1956 suggests that access to sufficient capital was possible. At the high end, capital was needed in substantial amounts but seemed more often than not to be raised through internal funding made possible by high markups on products. Bankruptcy resulting from too much debt was seen more frequently in poorly managed organizations at the low end, particularly with typewriter, cash register, and adding machine manufacturers. No large machine producer went out of business because of capital starvation. Rather, a capital hungry firm would simply be acquired by another more capable of supporting funding requirements and eager to expand into different markets. The reverse was also true: capital rich firms that did not need to plow assets back into the business bought other companies. By the mid-1960s, capital requirements in the computer business had become so great that very few firms could hope to offer integrated systems.[13]

How management was recruited in the industry was not fully understood. Yet this is an important issue because they nurtured a company's culture and carried practices from one firm to another (e.g., Watson from NCR to IBM). In the post-1955 period, managers moved from company to company with great frequency, except at a few places like IBM, which promoted from within its own ranks. In the period 1880–1950, promoting from within increasingly became the norm at NCR, Burroughs, and IBM. I do not know what was normal at Felt & Tarrant, Underwood, Victor, Monroe, or any of the other typewriter and adding machine firms, or at Remington Rand and at Powers. Felt & Tarrant's corporate archives were destroyed in 1988; thus one may never know what its practices were concerning recruitment and retention of management. However, for the industry at large, the very limited evidence suggests that movement was more out of the industry than into it at middle manager or executive levels. From its earliest days until the end of the Patterson era, NCR fired or released executives who then worked in other industries. As the custom of promoting from within took hold by the start of World War II, it became possible for individuals to have full careers within the industry. The limited biographical data that exists on top executives of the pre-1950 period suggests that many, if not most, grew up within one company. That process encouraged slow, evolutionary changes in management practices. In some cases, such as at Burroughs in the 1940s, it proved dangerous when the company was too slow to react to changes in the market. At NCR, the almost fatal decision not to enter the computer market soon enough but to continue to rely instead on its cash register business, clearly was largely the result of a management team long in place and always in one company.

A similar process existed in IBM, where punched card proponents retained power and influence until the very late 1950s. Here the rise of young managers with experience outside IBM (e.g., Watson, Jr., from his days in the military, and many in the Poughkeepsie laboratory) facilitated the move into the computer market.

In the lower ranks, employment continuity also existed and was encouraged. In part, professionalization of sales and service personnel was made possible by retaining employees for full careers. After the end of both world wars, Burroughs, IBM, Powers, NCR, and other high-technology–based firms such as AT&T, went to great lengths to recruit former employees and veterans to staff postwar expansion. Full employment and extensive paternalistic practices were geared toward reducing turnover and retaining employees for twenty-five to forty-five years. Those with long associations at a firm were lionized as heroes through recognition events, mention in company magazines, and Quarter Century Clubs. The office appliance industry was so specialized in its products, marketing, and manufacturing that retention of highly trained employees was crucial if there were to be any serious gains in productivity or retention of competitive posture.

The issue of turnover is important and deserves more study. If turnover was minimal in comparison to other industries, then the body of practices in the office appliance industry can go far to explain the evolutionary nature of product announcements and the effective application of technologies. The overall success of this industry could be attributed to a community of knowledgeable workers and managers burdened and blessed with previous experiences and company traditions. A better understanding of turnover and longevity could

VETERANS OF INTERNATIONAL BUSINESS MACHINES ORGANIZATION

18.1 First members of the IBM Quarter Century Club, 1925. The club was made up of employees who had worked for IBM or its predecessor companies for twenty-five or more years. The club still existed at the beginning of the 1990s (courtesy IBM Archives).

help explain why patterns entrenched by 1910 were still evident in the 1950s and survived into the 1970s.

The emergence of strong corporate cultures is also an important issue because of the role of service, particularly at the high-end product and customer sets. Diverse customers, all dependent on a particular company's products called for high levels of reliable service and responsiveness. It is no accident, for example, that two out of three IBM Basic Beliefs concerned customer service and excellence and have thrived to the present.[14] A corporate culture that effectively caused a firm to be competitive and profitable survived. It also attracted loyal customers.

The office appliance industry was conservative and relied as much on its history as on its future. Figure 18.1 reemphasizes how heritage and tradition were important in the industry early on. This photograph of IBM employees was taken in 1925. Captions below individual photographs states how long these employees had been at IBM or at its predecessor companies. Of the forty-two shown, sixteen had been with the firm thirty or more years; all had served a minimum of twenty-five years. In a history of NCR published by the company in 1984, dozens of short biographies were presented of executives, managers, and other employees with references to their longevity of service in all decades from the turn of the century to the 1980s.[15] Similar references to minimal turnover could be found for major vendors in the industry and for almost any decade of the office appliance or data-processing industries, as in all industries.[16] Even companies with short histories in the post-1956 period had the same focus.[17]

An American Industry

In many ways, the office appliance industry behaved like other industries. Chandler showed that growth came to many American companies after 1920 "by horizontal combination, vertical integration, expansion abroad, and diversification." He argued effectively that initial growth followed a three-pronged investment in manufacturing, marketing, and management, often "through horizontal combination and vertical integration."[18] The experience of companies studied in this book illustrated his observations at work. Companies first had to come to market with attractive products that could be manufactured cost effectively and then sold in volume. Those who accomplished these tasks gained significant competitive advantage and remained in business for decades. These firms, such as IBM, NCR, and Burroughs, defended their investments and market positions with effective management and sound investments. One might argue that the industry had one exception—Powers—that came into it close to World War I and then became as oligopolistic as any of the older entrants. However, in this case, the pattern of product innovation and investment in manufacturing was crucial to its survivability. Its inability to invest sufficiently in effective marketing made it a minor player when compared to IBM, Burroughs, or NCR. If anything, it is an example of a firm that did not make Chandler's three-pronged investment and, hence, suffered the consequences.

One can take an important idea of Chandler's—that first entrants had to invest in distribution—and refine his concept further by arguing that distribution largely meant marketing. It was not enough to use dealers or mail order firms or even agents. Complex products required well-trained salespeople and service personnel, education programs, field offices, and an interactive relationship with customers to refine and enhance products constantly. Marketing was a major, complicated investment to manage. Those who succeeded were very successful; the rest barely survived or left the industry both in Europe and in the United States. Successful vendors were always well down the investment and experience curves ahead of competitors in all crucial activities of a business: R&D, manufacturing, marketing, and management.

The timing of the arrival of major vendors in this industry was the same as for other corporations within the U.S. economy but in different industries. Between 1880 and 1981, like counterparts in many industries, the key long-term players in the office appliance world came into existence: Burroughs, Remington Typewriter, Felt & Tarrant, C-T-R (IBM), NCR, and Underwood. The scale and scope of efforts needed to thrive had appeared with the necessary investments in manufacturing, distribution, and management.[19]

One of the central themes of this book has been the similarities of practices and players from decade to decade, from precomputer periods to the post-1956 era. Chandler saw a similar pattern across American industry: "Indeed, what is striking is how similar the evolution of the new industries in the 1950s and 1960s was to the evolution of those of the 1880s and 1890s, even though the rapidity of technological change in the later period was much greater than it had been before World War II."[20] Clearly practices in the office appliance industry have much to teach about the characteristics of many U.S. industries. It was an industry less unique than one might have thought. It also was always influenced by its environment.

Technological Innovation and Transfer

Prosperity was uniquely supported, however, by distinct technologies. No history or economic survey of the data-processing industry in the period after 1956 has ignored technology's influence.[21] All students of the subject recognize that how technology emerged and was used and priced largely influenced events in this industry. Technology's ebb and flow directly affected the rate of acceptance and then dependence upon products. As technologies became more reliable, easier to use, and less expensive, more of their forms were used in offices and factories. Similar patterns were evident with software and microcomputers in the late twentieth century. In turn, growth in acceptance led to increased volumes of sales, which drove expansion and percentage of contribution to the U.S. GNP. In the early 1990s, it appears that the same process is being repeated in other industrialized sectors of the world much the same as in the United States during the 1920s, 1950s, 1960s, or 1980s.[22]

The role technological innovation played has broad significance—particularly for the period before the arrival of the computer. Increasingly, historians concerned with the rise and fall of nations and empires are concluding that one primary reason that the West became prominent after 1500 instead of the Ming Dynasty, the Mogul Empire, or the Islamic states was its ability and inclination to accept technological change and adopt it quickly.[23] Technology injected into the economy made possible to a large extent the manufacture and delivery of goods of substance and bulk in the West—practical goods that were useful in daily life as opposed to luxury items that characteristically came from the Orient, particularly in the period 1500–1900.[24]

Such a long historical perspective suggests that the application of technology represented a distinct feature of the West, especially the activities of the past two centuries, and offered a source of power and prosperity. The computer and its various related technologies of the post-1945 period were simply part of this much larger mosaic. Yet the creation of these machines also was not an overnight phenomenon; they were simply part of the continuum of technological innovations that had been underway for many decades. That they were linked historically to office appliances is significant in that technological evolution is characteristic of the West. For readers in the late twentieth century, the computer gives meaning and significance to the office appliance industry and to its technologies.

Still unclear is whether technological advances that made the computer possible came from a series of developments that logically built one on the other or evolved in part also because of circumstances and small events that positively encouraged its evolution. It is an issue because in the past two decades an increasing number of economists have been looking at economic behavior not as a neat, almost Newtonian model of activity but more as a series of feedbacks for small events that pushes economic activities in directions that then are predictable. In other words, small chance events early in the history of a technology or, for that matter, an industry, determined the course of major activities and trends.[25] That notion makes sense when applied to the office appliance industry where disparate technological advances and the roles of different vendors twisted and turned and came together in unpredictable ways over a long period of time. Advocates of this new way of looking at economics argue that "technologies typically improve as more people adopt them and firms gain experience that guides further development. This link is a positive-feedback loop; the more people adopt a technology, the more it improves and the more attractive it is for further adoption."[26] Such a process-dependent organic view of economic and technological evolution is a useful perspective for historians of the office appliance and data-processing industries.

That view clarifies the significance of many actions taken in the office appliance industry. It had built a broad base of demand for enhanced computational and information-handling equipment and seized control over the development and distribution of many devices from cash registers and tabulators to computers. Precomputer information-handling devices were more specific, rightful ancestors of the digital processor than electronics. However, electronics contributed too. Although computers have received much attention and their significance constantly has been the object of both exaggerated and prudent discussion, they were part of a much larger response by American society that applied technology to harness scientific knowledge within economically reasonable activities. It came as part of a broad effort, much as it did in the office equipment world. Office machines were special because when they emerged, the population of office workers was growing dramatically and providing the economic justification required to encourage inventors and vendors.[27]

Some characteristics of information-handling technologies were unique, especially in the precomputer era. For example, although generations of technology came rapidly in the computer era, giving vendors with the latest technology a roughly eighteen month marketing advantage over rivals,[28] many of the technological bases of the office appliance industry had been in place for decades. Typewriters, whose technology had stabilized by 1900, were essentially the same until after World War II. Then the only widescale change was electrification. Even that change was not widely adopted by customers until the 1960s. Tabulating and punched card equipment had settled down by about 1915 with thousands of evolutionary changes over the next four decades. Adding machines were essentially in their final form by the end of World War I and remained the same (except for electrication in the interwar period) until the arrival of battery-operated, handheld calculators in the mid-1970s. Although calculating machines came in many forms, their basic structure and purpose had been identified by the late 1930s. They acquired more electronics in the 1930s and 1940s and substantial increases in capacities and throughput only in the late 1940s as they evolved into a direct parent of the computer. The cash register remained basically the same for one century. In fact, many NCR machines built in the pre–World War II era and refurbished during that war, remained in use in small retail firms at the dawn of the 1990s, not just because their brass appearance proved attractive but because they functioned well too.

Consequently, one outstanding feature of the industry before 1950 that one can call out was a collection of products based on innovative technologies that were more stable and less subject to basic change than those of the post-1950 period. That does not deny the thousands of minor changes. R&D from 1900 to the early 1960s largely involved refinement of base technologies that had already been developed in the two decades before 1900 followed by the inclusion of electromechanics and then electronics. The computer's initial creative spurt in the 1930s and 1940s compares to what happened to earlier information-handling equipment in the 1870s and 1880s. But in general terms, the overall process at work before the computer fell approximately into three identifiable periods of technological influence.

The first covered 1865 to roughly 1900 and represented the age during which creative individuals identified the need for specific mechanical aids to calculation and information handling, took advantage of metallurgical progress in the middle decades of the nineteenth century, and responded to the growing demands for specific data-handling methods by constructing such devices as typewriters and punched card equipment. The base patents for these machines were filed in this period as the organizations required to manufacture and distribute them first came into existence. Many of these firms survived in one fashion or another to the present, parlaying first their technical advantages and later their loyal (dependent) customer base. R&D was initially often a one-man process that evolved quickly, as in other industries, into small workshop environments by the end of the century. They, in turn, became precursors of the development laboratories of the 1920s and 1930s.

A second identifiable period extended from about 1900, when typewriters, adding machines, and calculators had acquired many of their common features, to World War II. During this phase, the primary focus of R&D was on enhancing existing products and dependent technologies by adding capacity, efficiencies, and functions. The effort proved effective yet evolutionary. It was effective in responding to market demands as evidenced by successful acceptance of increasing volumes of products. It was evolutionary, even ultraconservative, in that changes generally came in response to customer requests or perceived needs to meet competition. No major breakthroughs in technology appeared in this period comparable to the transistor of the late 1940s or to the chip of the early to mid-1950s within this industry. Electricity, which manufacturers knew how to apply to machinery in the late 1800s, was, however, injected into office equipment during the course of the next century.

The slow approach began to change, however, during World War II. Out of concern for improved electronics and, subsequently, miniaturization of electronic devices, university laboratories, government agencies, and, more often than not, electrical equipment manufacturers, led the charge that substantially changed the study and application of electronics in the general field of information handling. The move to electronics began before the war, yet it took this war to speed up the application of new electronics to information-handling equipment. Wartime circumstances caused information-processing vendors to participate in force. The intermixing of skills and war requirements injected new ideas into the otherwise slow-changing office equipment world and pushed it quickly into the center of much state-of-the-art activity in electronics. A great deal of the R&D history of the immediate postwar period in this industry became a litany of how such technologies were applied to a variety of products, devices that had, in effect, not experienced substantial changes in years.

One might argue that these observations are too generalized or simplistic. The obvious example to attack is the apparently overstated simplicity of the preceding conclusions about the electric typewriter. After all, it had existed since 1900; IBM had its own since the 1930s, and all vendors introduced new electronic versions by the early 1950s. But, using the acid test of when a technology was accepted in quantity and not when someone created it in a laboratory places the electric typewriter in the post–World War II period.

Electronic calculating machines, such as the IBM CPC, followed the same track. To be sure, IBM, Burroughs, Underwood, and all the others moved from mechanical devices of the 1910s and 1920s to more electronically driven units in the 1930s, each capable of faster processing and often with more capacity. However, efficiencies afforded by developments in electronics applied to information-handling devices, which came out of university labs first in the late 1930s, commercial projects (e.g., TV at RCA), and then out of the wartime projects in the early 1940s, made their application practical in office products beginning in the late 1940s and early 1950s. What appears very clear is that transfer of technology from older to newer products came less in response to any ingenuity or effective application within laboratories in the industry than from pressures and experiences pushing from outside, often from customers.

Patent protection has frequently been a subject of interest to historians and economists as a possible influence on the evolution of technology.[29] Patent protection did not really protect computer vendors from others who took advantage of their R&D efforts.[30] The same also held true for the period 1865–1956 in the office appliance world. As with computers later, lengthy legal disputes did not stop competitors from borrowing or slightly modifying someone else's clever effort. Powers tabulating equipment was a direct spinoff of Hollerith's; despite cries of patent violations by the latter, Powers remained a healthy rival in the industry for a long time. Typewriters, originally patented in the last quarter of the nineteenth century, were manufactured by more than 150 vendors by World War I. As with computers, the many incremental changes or advances were difficult for courts to assign as violations of patents. That problem, coupled with the expense and time required to protect patents, rendered ineffective the process for sheltering the benefits of invention for creative originators. Perhaps more important was that the rate of obsolescence was so rapid that patenting did not prove as profitable as inventors and vendors had hoped. The one strategy that worked, but only as a common practice during the period of the computer, was cross-licensing. That office appliance companies tried to protect themselves is not questioned. Recall, for example, how Remington jealously guarded patents by buying and studying copies of every new typewriter manufactured or sold in the United States from the 1870s on. They examined them and then filed suit, if necessary, for breach of patent.[31]

In the office equipment era, inventors exchanged very little information on technical innovations, but in the first years of the computer exchanges were more open. The volume of published articles on base technologies of the precomputer era was limited in comparison to that of the later period.

What was more prevalent and of obvious interest, however, was retroengineering as a method of technology transfer. As Remington acquired other typewriters and dissected them out of concern for patent infringement, its engineers, no doubt, also gathered ideas to improve Remington's own products. Powers building on the machines originated by Hollerith is a classic example of retroengineering. Cash registers were so similar and technologies of the period were so simple that they were easily copied. It was not until products became technologically very sophisticated in the late 1940s that one saw a decline for a while in retroengineering as a tactic for migrating technologies quickly and inexpensively. It again became a tactic in the data-processing world once expertise in such fields as chip design and manufacturing became widely available. Thus, for example, the necessary knowledge to replicate an IBM disk or tape drive in the 1960s and 1970s became available. In short, the "other equipment manufacturer" (OEM) phenomenon beginning in data processing in the mid-1960s had been a way of life in the office equipment world since before 1900.[32]

Technology, Products, and Productivity

Ultimately, technology in most American industries was applied for economic gain. If a technology addressed the needs of the economy, it was adopted. Success was a direct outgrowth of effectivness. Information-handling equipment reflected the broader process of the nineteenth century by substituting technology for direct human labor to improve productivity while controlling costs better. To a large extent, this transfer of work from people to machines was made possible by the generally shared view among managers that technology added value.[33] A whole class of workers, known as managers, came into being in the period and imposed their desire for commercial success on economic activity to give it a purposeful quality.[34] Thus by the end of the 1800s, merging labor and machine—an important task for managers in most industries—was widespread. That process called for R&D and constant improvements in technology-based products.

It was the cautious response of managers in general to improvements in productivity, typically with proven methods and machines, that contributed to the mindset of management in Burroughs, NCR, IBM, and others to modify their offerings to match demands. When the rhythm was disrupted, product enhancement was too. Development of digital computers in the late 1940s and their concurrent availability in the market, generated resistance from potential customers and manufacturers for almost one decade until their worth was clearly justified through improved performance, application, and cost effectiveness. Once established, however, the industry settled down to the unceasing round of changes that characterized the computer business from those early days to the present.[35]

The infusion of new information-handling technologies into the American economy drew fire but generated benefits. Workers were always concerned that automation would eliminate or deskill jobs and make them more poorly paid employees.[36] However, information-handling equipment improved the quality of work and, thereby, the value of an office worker's output. In turn, that created more demand for additional office workers who were better paid and capable of handling larger volumes of activity. The rise of the modern secretary is as much tied to development of the typewriter and other office machines as the invention of the computer is tied to the creation of hundreds of thousands of jobs for programmers.[37]

Future studies of information handling in pre-1956 America will need to focus on the sociological and economic consequences of the office equipment industry's activities. My focus has been on development of the industry itself, not directly on its effects on others. However, as in other industries, between 1865 and the mid-1950s, the industry became, to use Chandler's words, a cluster of firms in which "managerial capitalism had gained ascendancy over family and financial capitalism."[38] Managerial capitalism's common form, recognizable to managers in other industries, illustrated the use of shared values (e.g., market-driven and conscious cost effectiveness), a focus on common concerns about work patterns, and results. The injection of the U.S. government's influence on the economy, haltingly during World War I but with considerable intensity during the depression of the 1930s, affected data processing as it did other industries; that too deserves more time in the study of information-handling technology. The temptation to look at office equipment as a suggestion of a paradigm of twentieth-century industrial behavior is strong but not yet justified. That this technology was important and influential there is no doubt. That it was larger than earlier assumed and, thus, influential on the data-processing industry too, is also now obvious. Ultimately, it was that heritage before the computer that provided the seedbed for many activities in the "age of the computer."

37. Remington Rand card punch, automatic printing tabulator, and sorter at Real-silk Company's payroll department, 1941 (Hagley Museum and Library).

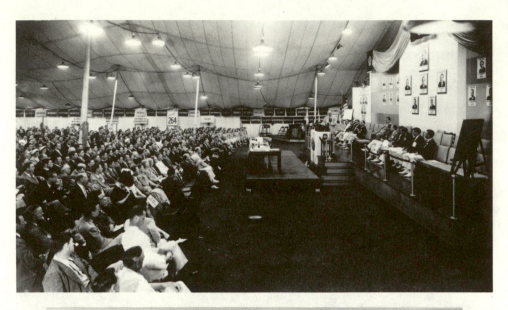

"We just keep him on in case of emergency."

38. "Main Tent" meeting, IBM 100 Percent Club, 1940, Endicott, N.Y. (IBM Archives).

39. The attitude toward computing in the 1930s and 1940s. Note that the equipment is in the accounting department and is headed by a conservative male manager with women clerks (© 1941 *New Yorker*, reprinted with permission).

40. Burroughs manufacturing facility, 1946 (Burroughs Papers, Charles Babbage Institute).

41. Adding machine manufacturing, Burroughs Detroit Plant, 1940s. Notice the "job shop" approach to assembly (Burroughs Papers, Charles Babbage Institute).

42. IBM educational facility, Endicott, N.Y., 1948 (IBM Archives).

Notes

Chapter 1
From Opportunities to Typewriters

1. Recent examples include Robert Levering, Michael Katz, and Milton Moskowitz, *The Computer Entrepreneurs* (New York: New American Library, 1984); Ulric Weil, *Information Systems in the 80's: Products, Markets and Vendors* (Englewood Cliffs, N.J.: Prentice-Hall, 1982); Stephen T. McClellan, *The Coming Computer Industry Shakeout: Winners, Losers, and Survivors* (New York: John Wiley and Sons, 1984); Montgomery Phister, Jr., *Data Processing Technology and Economics* (Bedford, Mass.: Digital Press, 1979). A recent exception is by Egil Juliussen, Portia Isaacson, and Luanne Kruse, *Computer Industry Almanac* (Dallas: Computer Industry Almanac, 1987), which includes information about users and inventors.

2. Of the more than one dozen books on IBM, the most useful for this purpose view the industry through its history: Richard Thomas DeLamarter, *Big Blue: IBM's Use and Abuse of Power* (New York: Dodd, Mead, 1986); Franklin M. Fisher, James W. McKie, and Richard B. Mancke, *IBM and the U.S. Data Processing Industry: An Economic History* (New York: Praeger Publishers, 1983); Nancy Foy, *The Sun Never Sets on IBM* (New York: William Morrow, 1975); Rex Malik, *And Tomorrow the World? Inside IBM* (London: Millington, 1975); William Rodgers, *Think: A Biography of the Watsons and IBM* (New York: Stein and Day, 1969).

3. This perspective is evident in Jeremy Bernstein, *Three Degrees Above Zero: Bell Labs in the Information Age* (New York: Charles Scribner's Sons, 1984); Ithiel de Sola Pool, *Technologies of Freedom* (Cambridge, Mass.: Harvard University Press, 1983); Fred Gruenberger, ed., *Computers and Communications: Toward a Computer Utility* (Englewood Cliffs, N.J.: Prentice-Hall, 1968).

4. René Moreau, *The Computer Comes of Age: The People, the Hardware and the Software* (Cambridge, Mass.: MIT Press, 1984), focused on the evolution of computer generations; David Ritchie, *The Computer Pioneers* (New York: Simon and Schuster, 1986), concentrated on key inventors of mainframe technology as they defined the industry; Joel Shurkin, *Engines of the Mind: A History of the Computer* (New York: W. W. Norton, 1984), also emphasized the evolution of computers as central to the story; and for the latest evolution of electronics see Dirk Hanson, *The New Alchemists: Silicon Valley and the Microelectronics Revolution* (Boston: Little, Brown, 1982).

5. Kenneth Flamm, *Targeting the Computer* (Washington, D.C.: Brookings Institution, 1987); G. Brock, *The U.S. Computer Industry: A Study of Market Power* (Philadelphia: Ballinger, 1975); A. Harmon, *The International Computer Industry* (Cambridge, Mass.: Harvard University Press, 1970); W. J. Lee, ed., *The International Computer Industry* (Washington, D.C.: Applied Library Resources, 1971); J. Soma, *The Computer Industry* (Lexington, Mass.: Lexington Books, 1976).

6. The most thorough expression is by Ernest Brown and Stuart Macdonald, *Revolution in Miniature: The History and Impact of Semiconductor Electronics*, 2d ed.

(Cambridge: Cambridge University Press, 1982), but also useful are Forrest M. Mims III, *Siliconnections* (New York: McGraw-Hill, 1986); P. R. Morris, *A History of the World Semiconductor Industry* (Piscataway, N.J.: IEEE, 1990); and Everett M. Rogers and Judith K. Larsen, *Silicon Valley Fever: Growth of High-Technology Culture* (New York: Basic Books, 1984).

7. Herman H. Goldstine, *The Computer from Pascal to von Neumann* (Princeton, N.J.: Princeton University Press, 1972), Hanson, *New Alchemists*; T. R. Reid, *The Chip: How Two Americans Invented the Microchip and Launched a Revolution* (New York: Simon and Schuster, 1984); and "Microelectronics History Project Begins with Collection Effort," *IEEE Center for the History of Electrical Engineering Newsletter*, no. 3 (June 1983): 1.

8. The most widely read proponent of the idea that data processing is part of a much larger shuffling of information is Fritz Machlup, *The Production and Distribution of Knowledge in the United States* (Princeton, N.J.: Princeton University Press, 1962); and its sequel, idem, *Knowledge: Its Creation, Distribution, and Economic Significance*, 2 vols. (Princeton, N.J.: Princeton University Press, 1980–1982). Useful also for added data is Michael Rubin and Mary Taylor Huber, *The Knowledge Industry in the United States, 1960–1980* (Princeton, N.J.: Princeton University Press, 1986); and Daniel Bell, "The Social Framework of the Information Society," in Michael L. Dertouzos and Joel Moses, eds., *The Computer Age: A Twenty-Year View* (Cambridge, Mass.: MIT Press, 1979), 163–211. The most widely distributed account is by James Martin, *The Wired Society* (Englewood Cliffs, N.J.: Prentice-Hall, 1978), republished by the same press as *Telematic Society: A Challenge for Tomorrow* (1981). JoAnne Yates, *Control Through Communication* (Baltimore: Johns Hopkins University Press, 1989), is the first historian to look at filing systems (all paper) as part of an organizationwide communications process in early twentieth-century American companies.

9. The literature is voluminous, but the only full-length biography of Hollerith is the excellent work, G. D. Austrian, *Herman Hollerith: The Forgotten Giant of Information Processing* (New York: Columbia University Press, 1982). Useful also are most histories of IBM that have sections on Hollerith: Charles J. Bashe, Lyle R. Johnson, John H. Palmer and Emerson H. Pugh, *IBM's Early Computers* (Cambridge, Mass.: MIT Press, 1986), 2–7; Rodgers, *Think*, 69–71; Thomas G. Belden and Marva R. Belden, *The Lengthening Shadow: The Life of Thomas J. Watson* (Boston: Little, Brown, 1962), 107–13; Foy, *Sun Never Sets on IBM*, 21–23. The study that most closely paralleled the theme of this book is Arthur L. Norberg, "High-Technology Calculation in the Early Twentieth Century: Punched Card Machinery in Business and Government," *Technology and Culture* 31, no. 4 (October 1990): 753–79. Norberg also sees the connection between the office appliance and the modern information-processing industry, 756.

10. The case for control has been articulated most forcefully by James R. Beniger, *The Control Revolution: Technological and Economic Origins of the Information Society* (Cambridge, Mass.: Harvard University Press, 1986), whereas the role of purposeful economic activity is best described by Alfred D. Chandler, Jr., *The Visible Hand: The Managerial Revolution in American Business* (Cambridge, Mass.: Harvard University Press, 1977). Chandler's perspective most influenced this book; Beniger's, too, but to a far lesser degree.

11. Walter Buckingham, *Automation: Its Impact on Business and People* (New York: Harper Brothers, 1961), 113.

12. Beniger, *Control Revolution*, 23–26; and for the case that economists have been most guilty of underestimating the complexity of the issues involved see Eli Ginsberg, "The Mechanization of Work," in *The Mechanization of Work* (San Francisco: W. H. Freeman, 1982), 5.

13. The case was most effectively summarized by Chandler, *Visible Hand*, 1–11, 368–70, 498–99.

14. Robert E. Gallman, "Commodity Output, 1839–1899," in Conference on Research and Income and Wealth, *Trends in the American Economy in the Nineteenth Century* (Princeton, N.J.: Princeton University Press, 1960), 13–71; Edwin Frickley, *Production in the United States*, 1860–1914 (Cambridge, Mass.: Harvard University Press, 1947), 64.

15. This argument is summarized by Stephen Salsbury, "The Effect of the Civil War on American Industrial Development," in Ralph Andreano, ed., *The Economic Impact of the American Civil War* (Cambridge, Mass.: Schenkman, 1967), 190–94.

16. Chandler, *Visible Hand*, 498. On the size of the U.S. economy see Simon Kuznets, *Economic Growth of Nations: Total Output and Production Structure* (Cambridge, Mass.: Harvard University Press, 1971), 38–40; and Walt W. Rostow, *The World Economy: History and Prospect* (Austin: University of Texas Press, 1978), 388–93.

17. Kuznets, *Economic Growth of Nations*, 40.

18. Chandler, *Visible Hand*, 498–99.

19. David S. Landes made this an important argument in his masterful study of Europe's economic development, *The Unbound Prometheus: Technological Change and Industrial Development in Western Europe from 1750 to the Present* (Cambridge: Cambridge University Press, 1969), 124–92, 248. Political turmoil also hurt, Francois Crouzet, "Les conséquences économiques de la Révolution: à propos d'un inédit de Sir Francis d'Ivernois," *Annales historiques de la Révolution française* 34 (1962): 182–217; and idem, "Wars, Blockade, and Economic Change in Europe, 1792–1815," *Journal of Economic History* 24 (1964): 567–88.

20. On the supply of labor see Buckingham, *Automation*, 109–130; and for an excellent summary of percentages in agriculture, industry, and service sectors see Beniger, *Control Revolution*, 23–24.

21. Beniger, *Control Revolution*, 24.

22. C. Wright Mills, *White Collar* (New York: Oxford University Press, 1951), 69.

23. For general statistics see Rostow, *World Economy*, 387–93, 782–83; and for other perspectives using similar data see Thomas S. Berry, *Estimated Annual Variations in Gross National Product, 1789–1909* (Richmond, Va.: Boswick Press, 1968); and Jeffrey G. Williamson, "Watersheds and Turning Points: Conjectures on the Long-Term Impact of Civil War Financing," *Journal of Economic History* 34, no. 3 (September 1974): 636–61; Ginsberg, "Mechanization of Work," 5. Farm productivity grew so fast that the decline in manpower on the farm throughout the last decades of the 1800s did not harm the nation's ability to feed a growing population, Wayne D. Rasmussen, "The Mechanization of Agriculture," in *Ginsberg, Mechanization of Work*, 15–27.

24. The biological analogy is developed by Beniger, *Control Revolution*; he also cites other like-thinkers who, like Beniger, see control as "the essential life process," 31–120. Beniger argues that businesses used control to manage distribution, speed, and energy to survive and thrive in the American industrial revolution of the late nineteenth century, 121–290.

25. Chandler, *Visible Hand*, 1.

26. Ibid., 79–205. Close behind railroads were insurance and retail firms, which shared similar problems of distance, size, and control with railroads, Beniger, *Control Revolution*, 291–343; but also see for insurance Morton Keller, *The Life Insurance Enterprises, 1885–1910* (Cambridge, Mass.: Harvard University Press, 1963), and Chandler, *Visible Hand*, 471–72; on retail firms see Daniel J. Boorstin, *The Americans: The Democratic Experience* (New York: Random House, 1973), 101–117.

27. Chandler, *Visible Hand*, 364. Accounting procedures underwent significant changes that led to cost accounting, more gathering of data, and sales analysis, Elliott-Fisher Company, *Bookkeeping by Machinery* (Harrisburg, Pa.: Elliott-Fisher, 1916); and Chandler, *Visible Hand*, 246–47, 445–48, 464–65.

28. Chandler, *Visible Hand*, 365.

29. Alfred D. Chandler, Jr., *Scale and Scope: The Dynamics of Industrial Capitalism* (Cambridge, Mass.: Harvard University Press, 1990), 8.

30. Chandler, *Visible Hand*, 367–68, 375.

31. Mills, *White Collar*, 68.

32. Beniger, *Control Revolution*, 233–34, 282–83, 319–20, 430–34; Yates, *Control through Communication*.

33. Beniger, *Control Revolution*, 13–21, 177, 185, 219–87.

34. Ibid., 282–83, and Beniger's point: "The Industrial Revolution, which brought about the nineteenth-century crisis of control, began with greatly increased use of coal and steam power; the Control Revolution that eventually resulted was achieved by innovation at a most fundamental level of technology—that of information processing and communication" (287).

35. By the late 1800s, Americans were becoming more conscious of statistics. Boorstin, *Americans*, 205, but see also 165–244, "When precise and up-to-date information was available about the *quantities* [Boorstin's italics] of everything, businessmen and consumers could not help thinking quantitatively."

36. James W. Cortada, *Strategic Data Processing: Considerations for Management* (Englewood Cliffs, N.J.: Prentice-Hall, 1984), 15.

37. On Burroughs, John S. Coleman, *The Business Machine* (New York: Newcomen Society, 1949), 14; on Patterson and the Rittys, Samuel Crowther, *John H. Patterson, Pioneer in Industrial Welfare* (New York: Doubleday, Page, 1923); on Sholes and others, George N. Engler, "The Typewriter Industry: The Impact of a Significant Technological Innovation" (Ph.D. diss., University of California at Los Angeles, 1969), 12–18.

38. William Henry Leffingwell, *The Office Appliance Manual* (New York: National Association of Office Appliance Manufacturers, 1926), 284–87; Isaac Marcosson, *Wherever Men Trade* (New York: Dodd, Mead, 1948), 62–63, 109–32; G. Harry Stine, *The Untold Story of the Computer Revolution: Bits, Bytes, Baudes and Brains* (New York: Arbor House, 1985), 45–46.

39. Chandler, *Visible Hand*, 308; William P. Tolley, *Smith-Corona Typewriters and H. W. Smith* (New York: Newcomen Society in North America, 1951), 9; Engler, "Typewriter Industry," 13–25.

40. Austrian, *Hollerith*, 9; Goldstine, *Computer*, 67; Leon Truesdell, *The Development of Punch Card Tabulation in the Bureau of the Census, 1890–1940* (Washington, D.C.: Government Printing Office, 1965), 30–31.

41. Coleman was a senior executive at Burroughs when he wrote about the company, *Business Machine*, 8–9; Boorstin, *Americans*, 204–5; Stine, *Untold Story*, 51–52.

42. Leffingwell, *Office Appliance Manual*, 510–40.

43. Quoted in Stine, *Untold Story*, 47, 49.

44. Quoted from James Bryce, *The American Commonwealth* (1888) as reprinted in Alex Groner, *American Business and Industry* (New York: American Heritage Publishing Company, 1972), 183; these points are corroborated by Robert V. Bruce, *The Launching of Modern American Science, 1846–1876* (Ithaca, N.Y.: Cornell University Press, 1987), 339–56, "The technologists . . . looked to a glorious future" (341).

45. The basic works are M. H. Adler, *The Writing Machine—A History of the Typewriter* (London: George Allen and Unwin, 1973); W. A. Beeching, *Century of the Typewriter* (New York: St. Martin's Press, 1974); and Bruce Bliven, Jr., *The Wonderful Writing Machine* (New York: Random House, 1954). These works have bibliographic references that suggest the magnitude of published interest in the subject.

46. Engler, "Typewriter Industry," 29–32.

47. Margery W. Davies dealt thoroughly with the topic, *Women's Place Is at the Typewriter: Office Work and Office Workers, 1870–1930* (Philadelphia: Temple University Press, 1983).

48. Chandler described the rapid rise of the office appliance industry in the 1880s and 1890s with such phrases as "sudden" and "widespread," growing out of "the cumulative impact of technological innovation." He also recognized that vendors borrowed technological innovations from each other, Chandler, *Scale and Scope*, 71.

49. Engler, "Typewriter Industry," 14–15.

50. Boorstin, *Americans*, 391, 398–99; Beniger, *Control Revolution*, 280–81, 398; Engler, "Typewriter Industry," 11–14.

51. Engler, "Typewriter Industry," 18–25; Donald R. Hoke, *Ingenious Yankees: The Rise of the American System of Manufactures in the Private Sector* (New York: Columbia University Press, 1990), 154–56.

52. Engler, "Typewriter Industry," 23.

53. Ibid.

54. Ibid., 24–25. One of the earliest significant surveys was conducted by the Bureau of Labor Statistics, U. S. Department of Labor, *Industrial Survey in Selected Industries in the United States, 1919* (Washington, D.C.: Government Printing Office, 1920), 487–509.

55. Tolley, *Smith-Corona Typewriters*, 10.

56. Ibid., 9. Tolley states that *The Adventures of Tom Sawyer* (1876) was believed to be the first major American book to be typed. On Twain's attitude see the same publication and Beniger, *Control Revolution*, 281.

57. John A. Zellers, *The Typewriter: A Short History* (New York: Newcomen Society of England, 1948), 14–15.

58. Chandler, *Visible Hand*, 308, 565nn. 42, 43.

59. Ibid., 308–9.

60. Harold U. Faulkner, *Politics, Reform and Expansion, 1890–1900* (New York: Harper and Row, 1959), 141.

61. Because so many decades separated the first typewriters and microcomputers, the earlier experience was probably lost on those of the 1970s and 1980s. Engler, "Typewriter Industry," 28.

62. Vincent E. Giuliano, "The Mechanization of Office Work," in Ginsberg, *The Mechanization of Work*, 77–86.

63. Engler, "Typewriter Industry," 25; for mergers in general in this period see Chandler, *Visible Hand*. On the method of growth by merger see Chandler, *Scale and Scope*, 146, "The continuing growth of the modern industrial enterprise came in four ways—by horizontal combination, vertical integration, expansion abroad, and diversification. Initial growth following the three-pronged investment in manufacturing, marketing, and management came largely through horizontal combination and vertical integration. These strategies were primarily defensive, aimed at protecting that sizable investment."

64. Engler, "Typewriter Industry," 31–32, observed that the success of the Model 5 caused Underwood to lag in developing follow-on products. The firm fell behind "so that by 1938, Royal had the dominant position in the industry." This was a constant danger also faced by vendors of data-processing equipment during the 1960s when Engler wrote these words and increasingly in the 1970s.

65. Ibid., 29–30.

66. Chandler, *Scale and Scope*, argued that mergers and acquisitions at the turn of the century came because "pioneers were plagued by over-capacity and declining throughput. As throughput dropped, costs rose" (71). "The predominant motive behind the majority of mergers was to achieve or maintain market power by transforming existing trade associations into holding companies" (75). One sees later that manipulation of stock prices was also a motive, for example, in the creation of C-T-R by Charles Flint, who Chandler cites as a classic example of the process at work (76, 81). Turnovers in vendors came with existing leaders, rarely from new entrants (91).

67. Tolley, *Smith-Corona Typewriters*, 10. The "systemization" of the early modern office is summarized by Beniger, *Control Revolution*, 393–403, and by Chandler, *Visible Hand*, 277–78, 307–8.

68. Roger Burlingame, *Engines of Democracy* (New York: Charles Scribner's Sons, 1940), 137. Tolley, *Smith-Corona Typewriters*, 10, mentioned the same idea.

69. Boorstin, *Americans*, 398–99.

70. Ibid., 399. On carbon paper see "Carbon Paper after 150 Years," *The Office Magazine* 76 (1972): 124–25; on A. B. Dick see Boorstin, *Americans*, 400.

Chapter 2
Adding and Calculating Machines

1. For a partial list of many such publications see James W. Cortada, *A Bibliographic Guide to the History of Computing, Computers, and the Information Processing Industry* (Westport, Conn.: Greenwood Press, 1990), 20–31, 66–113; modern

surveys include Michael R. Williams, *A History of Computing Technology* (Englewood Cliffs, N.J.: Prentice-Hall, 1985), 48–158; A. Chapuis and E. Droz, *Les automates, figures artificielles d'hommes et d'animaux: histoire et technique* (Neuchatel: Griffon, 1949); S. Lilley, "Machinery in Mathematics: An Historical Survey of Calculating Machines," *Discovery* 6, nos. 5, 6 (1945): 150–56, 182–85; James W. Cortada, *Historical Dictionary of Data Processing: Technology* (Westport, Conn.: Greenwood Press, 1987).

2. For a discussion of issues and problems see James W. Cortada, *An Annotated Bibliography on the History of Data Processing* (Westport, Conn.: Greenwood Press, 1983), xix–xxiv, xxxv–xxxvii.

3. Coleman, *Business Machine*, 8.

4. Leffingwell, *Office Appliance Manual*, 18.

5. Ibid., 17.

6. Quotes from Stine, *Untold Story*, 48–49. The author's grandfather, Jaime Cortada (1872–1940), began his career as a typical nineteenth-century accountant and in old age could still add page-length columns made up of many numbers faster than we could with a mechanical calculator.

7. C. V. Boys, "Calculating Machines," *Journal of the Society of Arts* 34 (March 5, 1886): 376–89; L. R. Dicksee, *Office Machinery* (London: Gee, 1917); M. d'Ocagne, *Le calcul simplifié* (Paris: Gauthier-Villars, 1905), A. Henneman, *Die Technische Entwicklung der Rechenmaschine* (Aachen: Verlag Peter Basten, 1953); H. Sebert, "Rapport fait par M. Sebert, au nem du Comité des Arts Économiques, sur la machine à calculer, dit Arithmomètre inventee par M. Thomas de Bojano, 44 rue de Chateudur, à Paris," *Bulletin de la Societe d'Encouragement pour l'Industrie Nationale* (August 1879): 393–425, and reprinted in the *Bulletin* 132 (1920): 694–720. Bojano was Colmar's son.

8. Williams, *History of Computing Technology*, 150–51; and for a useful set of lists see W. Von Dyck, *Katalog Mathematischer und Mathematisch-physikalisher Modelle Apparate und Instrumente* (Munich: n.p., 1892, 1893); for discussions of major machines see E. M. Horsburgh, ed., *Handbook of the Napier Tercentenary Celebration or Modern Instruments and Methods of Calculation* (Edinburgh: G. Bell and Sons and The Royal Society of Edinburgh, 1914; Los Angeles: Tomash Publishers, 1982), 69–135; for an example of an enhanced machine over the Colmar (ca. 1868) see P. A. Kidwell, "The Webb Adder," *Rittenhouse* 1 (1986): 12–18.

9. Williams, *History of Computing Technology*, 152–53.

10. Ibid., 153–54. To distinguish between adding and calculating machines, discussion of their differences may be found in Leffingwell, *Office Appliance Manual*, 83–86; on the Odhner, *An Illustrated Chronicle of "A Machine to Count On"* (Goteborg, Sweden: Aktielbolaget Original Odhner, 1951); and W. Von Bohl, *Instruments and Machines for Mechanical Calculation* (Russian) (Moscow: n.p., 1906); on Baldwin's machines, J. A. V. Turck, *Origin of Modern Calculating Machines* (Chicago: Western Society of Engineers, 1921); and Cortada, *Historical Dictionary*, 38–39. European developments are in F. Trinks, *Geshichtliche Daten aus der Entwicklung der Rechenmaschinen von Pascal bis zur "Nova-Brunsviga"* (Braunschweig: Grimme, Natalis, 1926).

11. Horsburgh, *Napier Tercentenary*, 84–90; and Trinks, *Entwicklung der Rechenmaschinen*.

12. Beniger, *Control Revolution*, 390–403.

13. J. William Schulze, *The American Office: Its Organization, Management and Records* (New York: Ronald Printing, 1914), 75; Leffingwell, *Office Appliance Manual*, 86–87; Coleman, *Business Machine*; Giuliano, "Mechanization of Office Work," 77–80; Stine, *Untold Story*, 52–56.

14. Williams, *History of Computing Technology*, 155–56; on Felt equipment, "An Improved Calculating Machine," *Scientific American* 59 (1888): 265; C. V. Boys, "The Comptometer," *Nature* 64 (1901): 265–68; and the massive Felt & Tarrant Manufacturing Company book, *Applied Mechanical Arithmetics Practised on the Comptometer* (Chicago: Felt & Tarrant Manufacturing Company, 1914); and the revised edition of 1920.

15. On current developments see C. W. Cooke, *Automata Old and New* (London: Chiswick Press, 1893); A. Galle, *Mathematische Instrumente* (Leipzig: B. G. Teubner, 1912); Horsburgh, *Handbook* (1914) for European developments in general; M. d'Ocagne, *Le calcul simplifié*, 2d ed. (Paris: Gauthier-Villars, 1905); L. Jacob, *Le calcul mécanique* (Paris: Doin, 1911); Von Bohl, *Instruments and Machines*. Later in this chapter, I present additional evidence on the international quality of office machines by reviewing sales of Burroughs and NCR.

16. "Adding Machine," *Scientific American* 53, no. 9 (August 29, 1885): 132, reviews W. J. MacNider's device. On contemporaneous machines see C. V. Boys, "Calculating Machines," *Journal of the Society of Arts* 34 (March 5, 1886): 376–89; "The Burroughs Adding and Listing-Machine," *Engineering* 83 (May 3, 1907): 580–81; "Combined Adding, Listing and Computing Machine," *Industrial Management* 53 suppl. 2 (May 1917); J. Edmondson, "Summary of Lecture on Calculating Machines, Delivered before the Physical Society of London, March 28, 1885," *Philosophical Magazine*, ser. no.5, 20 (July–December 1885): 15–18; H. Genaille, "Sur une nouvelle machine à calculer par Genaille," *Association Française l'Avancement de Science* (1878): 181–82; G. B. Grant, "A New Calculating Machine," *American Journal of Science*, 3d ser. 4, no. 8 (1874): 277–84; E. Krebs, "Die Rechenstäbe und Rechenmaschinen einst und jetzt," *Beitraege zur Geschichte Techn. Ind.* 3 (1911): 147–62; R. Lenz, "Die Rechenmaschinen," *Verein zur Berförderung des Gewerbleisses in Preussen* 85 (1906): 111–38; R. Mehmke and M. d'Ocagne, "Calcul numériques," *Encyclopédie des sciences mathématiques pures et appliquees*, French ed., tome 1, vol. 4, pt. 2 (1908): 196–320; L. Scott, "New Methods of Office Work," *World's Work* 9 (March 1905): 5973–76.

17. On the post–World War I period see L. J. Comrie, "Calculating Machines, Appendix III," in L. R. Connor, ed., *Statistics in Theory and Practice* (London: Pitman, 1938), 349–71; L. Couffignal, *Les machines à calculer, leurs principes, leur evolution* (Paris: Gauthier Villars, 1933); D. R. Hartree, *Calculating Instruments and Machines* (Cambridge: Cambridge University Press, 1947; Cambridge, Mass.: MIT Press, 1984: Urbana: University of Illinois Press, 1949). On the post–World War II period see Stan Augarten, *Bit by Bit: An Illustrated History of Computers* (New York: Ticknor and Fields, 1984); Goldstine, *Computer.*.

18. For the case for deskilling see Harry Braverman, *Labor and Monopoly Capital: The Degradation of Work in the Twentieth Century* (New York: Monthly Review Press, 1974), 315–48.

19. Leffingwell, *Office Appliance Manual*, 80.

20. Ibid., 79. One decade later, Leffingwell wrote, "At first such machinery was

sold to replace human brains, and it was vociferously claimed for each machine that it was 'foolproof.' Those who took the statement too literally and placed 'fools' in charge of the machines got their experience and education together, though at an excessive price" (William H. Leffingwell, *Office Management* [Chicago: A. W. Shaw Company, 1927], 825).

21. Coleman, *Business Machine*, 11–12.

22. Stine, *Untold Story*, 52–53.

23. All quotes from Audit Report, January 9, 1904, by Price, Waterhouse and Co., American Arithmometer Company Records, part of the Burroughs Papers, Charles Babbage Institute (CBI).

24. *Standard and Poors* (1910), 1318.

25. Coleman, *Business Machine*, 12–13.

26. Ibid., 13.

27. Ibid., 9.

28. Erwin W. Thompson, *Book-Keeping by Machinery; A Treatise on Office Economics* (New York: Author, 1906) describes the applications; on insurance uses see C. Walford, "Calculating Machines," *The Insurance Cyclopedia* 1 (1871): 411–25.

29. Schulze, *American Office*, 79.

30. Coleman, *Business Machine*, 18.

31. Ibid., 16.

32. Leffingwell, *Office Appliance Manual*, 60–62.

33. Ibid., 62–63.

34. Schulze, *American Office*, 75.

35. Burroughs Adding Machine Corporation, *Handbook of Instruction* (Detroit: Burroughs Adding Machine Corporation, 1911), 97–98.

36. Schulze, *American Office*, 76–79; Coleman, *Business Machine*, 16. One device called the Vest Pocket arranged data in columns. A user inserted a metal pencil stylus to manipulate numbers. The machine fit into a pocket and was made by the Erie Calculator Company and also by the Pocket Adding Machine Company (Leffingwell, *Office Appliance Manual*, 71).

37. Ray W. Macdonald, *Strategy for Growth: The Story of Burroughs Corporation* (New York: Newcomen Society in North America, 1978), 10.

38. Bureau of Labor Statistics, *Industrial Survey in Selected Industries in the United States, 1919*, 3.

39. Ibid., 3.

40. Ibid., 4.

41. Ibid., 7; NCR, *Celebrating the Future* (Daton: NCR, 1984); Macdonald, *Strategy for Growth*.

42. Bureau of Labor Statistics, *Industrial Survey*, 8.

43. Stine, *Untold Story*, 50.

44. Shurkin, *Engines of the Mind*, 94; "An Improved Calculating Machine," 265; Boys, "Comptometer," 265–68.

45. Williams, *History of Computer Technology*, 155–57; Felt & Tarrant, *Applied Mechanical Arithmetics*.

46. Williams, *History of Computer Technology*, 155–57; Augarten, *Bit by Bit*, 81; Peggy Aldrich Kidwell, "American Scientists and Calculating Machines—From Novelty to Commonplace," *Annals of the History of Computing* 12, no. 1 (1990): 31–40.

47. Trinks, *Entwicklung der Rechenmaschinen*, for a pamphlet-size overview, particularly of Brunsviga; M. d'Ocagne, "Vue d'ensemble sur les machines à calculer," *Bulletin des Sciences Mathématiques* 2d ser., 46 (1922): 102–44, for a solid review of many devices including widely used European systems of the late 1800s; A. Galle, *Mathematische Instrumente*, particularly 23–48 for such offerings as the Thomas, Mercedes-Euklid, Odhner, "Gauss" circular machine, and Millionaire; E. Martin, *Die Rechenmaschinen und ihre Entwicklungs-geschichte* (Pappenhein: n.p., 1925), is a massive source on historical and contemporary devices and uses of European items; W. F. Stanley, *Mathematical Drawing and Measurements Instruments* (London: W. F. Stanley, 1888).

48. Robert H. Gregory and Richard L. Van Horn, *Automatic Data-Processing Systems: Principles and Procedures* (San Francisco: Wadsworth Publishing, 1960), 624–25.

49. Horsburgh, *Napier Tercentenary*, 84–85.

50. Ibid., 104–17; see also citations in chap. 3, n. 61; Boys, "Calculating Machines," 376–89.

51. Chandler, *Scale and Scope*, 201, 275.

52. Ibid., 41–46, 48–54; Fritz Blaich, *Amerikanische Firmen in Deutschland, 1890–1918* (Wiesbaden: F. Steiner, 1984), 41–46, 54–58.

53. Leffingwell, *Office Appliance Manual*, 103.

54. Moreau, *Computer Comes of Age*, 19.

55. Leffingwell, *Office Appliance Manual*, 164.

56. For example, Stine, *Untold Story*, 28–38.

Chapter 3
Hollerith and the Development of Punched Card Tabulation

1. For instance, Shurkin, *Engines of the Mind*, 66–92; Augarten, *Bit by Bit*, 72–74, 175–76; Beniger, *Control Revolution*, 411–23; Goldstine, *Computer*, 65–71; Brian Randell, ed., *The Origins of Digital Computers: Selected Papers* (Berlin: Springer-Verlag, 1982), 127–58; Margaret Harmon, *Stretching Man's Mind: A History of Data Processing* (New York: Mason/Charter, 1975), 97–108; David Ritchie, *The Computer Pioneers* (New York: Simon and Schuster, 1986), 20–21; Stine, *Untold Story*, 39–44; Katharine Davis Fishman, *Computer Establishment* (New York: Harper and Row, 1981), 20–21; Bashe, Johnson, Palmer, and Pugh, *IBM's Early Computers*, 2–7; Christopher Evans, *The Micro Millennium* (New York: Washington Square Press, 1979), 22–24; Charles Eames and Ray Eames, *A Computer Perspective* (Cambridge, Mass.: Harvard University Press, 1973), 21–27.

2. Tabulating Machine Company, *Salesmen's Catalogue* (New York: Tabulating Machine Company, n.d. [1910–1915]), 1; on the card see W. J. Eckert, *Punched Card Methods in Scientific Computation* (New York: Thomas J. Watson Astronomical Computing Bureau, 1940), 4–7.

3. Eckert, *Punched Card Methods*, 7–23; Joseph Levy, *Punched Card Equipment: Principles and Applications* (New York: McGraw-Hill, 1967), 1–20; W. E. Freeman, ed., *Automatic, Mechanical Punching, Counting, Sorting, Tabulating, and Printing Machines* (New York: National Electric Light Association, 1915), for a compendium

of early equipment and for hardware at the sunset of the tabulating period; Robert Casey and James W. Perry, eds., *Punched Cards* (New York: Reinhold Publishing, 1953).

4. A. Barlow, *History and Principles of Weaving by Hand and Power* (London: S. Low, Marsten, Searle and Rivington, 1878); John H. Brown, ed., *Textile Industries of the United States* (Boston: James Lamb, 1911); E. A. Posselt, *The Jacquard Machine Analyzed and Explained* (Philadelphia: Pennsylvania Museum and School of Industrial Art, 1887).

5. C. Ballot, *L'introduction du machinisme dans l'industrie française* (Lille: O. Marquandt, 1923). On Babbage's ideas and work concerning cards, the best introduction is Anthony Hyman, *Charles Babbage: Pioneer of the Computer* (Princeton, N.J.: Princeton University Press, 1982), 166, 168, 183, 245, 254–55, 272, 274–76; the work of Georg Scheutz is conveniently summarized by M. Lindgren and S. Lindquist, "Scheutz's First Difference Engine Rediscovered," *Technology and Culture* 23 (1982): 207–13, and by M. G. Losano, *Scheutz: La macchina alle differenze* (Milan: Etas Libri, 1974); Uta C. Merzbach, *George Scheutz and the First Printing Calculator*, Smithsonian Studies in History and Technology, no. 36 (Washington, D.C.: Smithsonian Institution Press, 1977).

6. Austrian, *Hollerith*, 9; W. R. Merriam, "The Evolution of Modern Census Taking," *Century Magazine* (April 1903): 831–42.

7. Truesdell, *Punch Card Tabulation*, 30–31.

8. Ibid., 31; Goldstine, *Computer*, 68, argued that Billings thought of the idea but Hollerith implemented it.

9. Hollerith described use of his equipment at the Census Bureau, "The Electrical Tabulating Machine," *Journal of the Royal Statistical Society* 57, no. 4 (1894): 678–82. For descriptions of the work in 1890 see Hyman Alterman, *Counting People: The Census in History* (New York: Harcourt, Brace and World, 1969); J. Bertillon, "La statistique à la machine," *La Nature* (September 1, 1894): 218–22; L. d'Auria et al., "The Hollerith Electric Tabulating System," *Journal of the Franklin Institute* 129, no. 4 (April 1890): 300–306, which convinced the Institute to give an award to Hollerith for his contribution; D. Durand, "Counting Our Population by Machine," *Scientific American* 69 (February 12, 1910): 108–10; T. C. Martin, "Counting a Nation by Electricity," *Electrical Engineer* 12, no. 184 (November 11, 1891): 521–30; H. L. Newcomb's useful study, "The Development of Mechanical Methods of Tabulation in the United States," *Transactions of the Fifteenth International Congress on Hygiene and Demography, Washington, September 23–28, 1912*, 6: *Proceedings of Section 9, Demography* (Washington, D.C.: Government Printing Office, 1913), 73–83; R. P. Porter, "The Eleventh Census," *Journal of the American Statistical Society* 2, no. 15 (1891): 321–79; Carroll Wright, *The History and Growth of the United States Census* (Washington, D.C.: Government Printing Office, 1900).

10. On European use of his equipment, Bertillon, "La statistique," 218–222; E. Cheysson, "La machine electrique à recensement," *Journal de la Société de Statistique de Paris* (March 1892): 87–96; H. Rauchberg, "Die Elektrische Zählmaschine und ibre Anwendung insbesondere bei der Osterreichchischen Volkszählung," *Allgemeines Statisches Archiv* 11 (1892): 78–126. Beniger, *Control Revolution*, 419, noted increased use of various types of data-processing technology by government agencies in the United States: state employment service (1890) and a municipal variant (1894),

library cataloging (1901), state automobile registration (1901), federal income tax and Bureau of Labor Statistics (1913), national reserve banking system (1914), Federal Trade Commission (1915).

11. Boorstin, *Americans*, 172–73.

12. Austrian, *Hollerith*, 39–41.

13. Ibid., 17; Bashe, *IBM's Early Computers*, 2–4.

14. Austrian, *Hollerith*, 45–49.

15. Ibid., 47–48.

16. Ibid., 85–87; *New York Sun*, March 23, 1895, 1: "Not less than 100,000,000 cards have been passed through the machines. The last census here used 65,000,000, the Canadian Census took between 4,000,000 and 5,000,000 and the other 30,000,000 are accounted for in Germany and in various individual states."

17. For details on this unique census see Austrian, *Hollerith*, 109–10.

18. Ibid., 115–23, 142–51.

19. Quoted in ibid., 110; for his dealings with the railroads, ibid., 107–41.

20. Ibid., 112.

21. Ibid., 124–41; Beniger, *Control Revolution*, 46–47; Eames and Eames, *Computer Perspective*, 46–47.

22. G. W. Baehne, *Practical Applications of Punched Card Method in Colleges and Universities* (New York: Columbia University Press, 1935), 6; Norberg, "High-Technology Calculation," 766–68.

23. Austrian, *Hollerith*, 200–203; Freeman, *Automatic Machines*, 13.

24. Beniger, *Control Revolution*, 204–5; Austrian, *Hollerith*, 203–5; and on the company during this era see Robert W. Twyman, *History of Marshall Field and Company, 1852–1906* (Philadelphia: University of Pennsylvania Press, 1954).

25. Austrian, *Hollerith*, 203.

26. Boorstin, *Americans*, 211.

27. Beniger, *Control Revolution*, 423.

28. Ibid., 422–423; Austrian, *Hollerith*, 201; Michael Chatfield, *A History of Accounting Thought* (Melbourne, Fla.: Krieger, 1977), 153; Chandler, *Visible Hand*, 465.

29. Freeman, *Automatic Machines*, 55.

30. George Jordan, "A Survey of Punched Card Development" (M.A. thesis, Massachusetts Institute of Technology, 1956), 15–16.

31. Freeman, *Automatic Machines*, 61.

32. Jordan, "Punched Card Development," 16.

33. Schulze, *American Office*, 80.

34. "The Mechanical Accountant," *Engineering* 74 (December 26, 1902): 840–41.

35. John S. Billings, "Mechanical Method Used in Compiling Data of the Eleventh U.S. Census, with Exhibition of a Machine," *Proceedings of the American Association for the Advancement of Science, 40th Meeting, Washington 1891* (Salem: American Association for the Advancement of Science, 1891): 407–9.

36. M. W. Gaines, "Tabulating-Machine Cost-Accounting for Factories of Diversified Products," *Engineering Magazine* 30 (December 1905): 364–73; H. S. McCormack, "Keeping Books by Machine: The Punched Card as a Saver of Brain Energy," *Scientific American* 108 (March 1, 1913): 194–95; "The Mechanized Accountant," *Engineering* 74 (December 26, 1902): 840–41.

37. A. Goddard, "Putting the Payroll on an Automatic Basis," *Scientific American* 123 (September 18, 1920): 275; H. Seward, "Mechanical Aids in Factory-Office Economy," *Engineering Magazine* 27 (July 1904): 605–25; "Wanted: An Electric Nerve-Saver," *Literary Digest* 48 (June 20, 1914): 1484–85.

38. For example, "Tabulating Statistics and Accounts by Machinery," *Electrical Railway Journal* 41 (May 10, 1913): 853–54; and N. Williams, "Les machines à calculer et à classer Hollerith et leur emploi dans la comtabilité des chemins de fer," *Génie Civil* 61 (May 18, 1912): 57.

39. Cortada, *Bibliographic Guide*, 103–7.

40. Austrian, *Hollerith*, 152–67.

41. Ibid.

42. Ibid., 176–78.

43. Ibid., 182.

44. Ibid., 183.

45. Ibid., 249–50.

46. Ibid., 71–72.

47. Ibid., 238–57.

48. Ibid., 257.

49. Ibid., 212–20; Martin Campbell-Kelly, *ICL: A Business and Technical History* (Oxford: Clarendon Press, 1989): 24–46.

50. Robert Sobel, *IBM: Colossus in Transition* (New York: Times Books, 1981): 11–13; Austrian, *Hollerith*, 306–15.

51. Austrian, *Hollerith*, 313; *Commercial and Financial Chronicle* (New York), May 4, 1912, unpaginated.

52. Austrian, *Hollerith*, 335.

53. Chandler, *Scale and Scope*, 36, noted a similar pattern across all of U.S. industry: "Price remained a significant competitive weapon, but these firms competed more forcefully for market share and increased profits by means of functional and strategic efficiency, that is, by carrying out more capably the processes of production and distribution, by improving both product and process through systematic research and development, by locating more suitable sources of supply, by providing more effective marketing services, by product differentiation" and by expanding rapidly into growing markets and out of shrinking ones.

54. Ibid., 169–70, gives an authoritative version of the story. On Pidgin's life see *Dictionary of American Biography* (New York: Charles Scribner's Sons, 1928–1973), 14: 573–74, and *National Cyclopaedia of American Biography* (New York: J. T. White, 1906), 13: 479–80.

55. "Handling of the Census Returns for the Whole United States," *American Machinist* (May 5, 1910): 809–12; Truesdell, *Punched Card Tabulation*, 117–38; Goldstine, *Computer*, 71; Austrian, *Hollerith*, 285–95; Sobel, *IBM*, 21–22.

56. New York Edison was one of the first users of the Powers Tabulator Printer because, finally, a machine printed a record that could be used in managing consumer deposit accounts, Freeman, *Automatic Machines*, 34.

57. Jordan, "Punched Card Development," 11–12, 17; "Handling Census Returns," 809–12; Remington Rand, *Powers Reference Manual* (Buffalo, N.Y.: Remington Rand, 1935) for an overview of the product line late in its life.

58. Austrian, *Hollerith*, 285–305.

59. Ibid., 303; Sobel, *IBM*, 221–22.

60. Sobel, *IBM*, 63.

61. Ibid., 64.

62. Ibid., 23.

63. Ibid., 54–55.

64. Ibid., 55.

65. Ibid., 65; Austrian, *Hollerith*, 330–38.

66. Stine, *Untold Story*, 49. When the story about Gore's machines is told, he taught his clerks how to count cards before inserting them into his machines by listening to the sound as they riffled them under their thumbs.

67. Beniger, *Control Revolution*, 397.

68. Jordan, "Punched Card Development," 13–14; "J. Royden Pierce IBM Engineer Dies Suddenly," *Business Machines* 15, no. 2 (January 12, 1933): 1, (Pierce joined C-T-R when Watson dissolved his company); *The Pierce Automatic Accounting Machines* (Woonsocket, R. I.: Pierce Accounting Machine Co., 1910), a sales brochure describing the machines.

69. Beniger, *Control Revolution*, 390.

70. The other impetus for continued modifications came before World War I when many of the basic patents governing the introduction of the technologies discussed expired. That made it possible for others to enter the fray with enhanced products. One has only to recall the Hollerith-Powers story to appreciate the significance of copyright and patents permits and protection.

Chapter 4
Cash Registers and the National Cash Register Company

1. *Standard and Poors* (1918), 1080.

2. Sobel, *IBM*, 23–33; Stine, *Untold Story*, 44–45.

3. Leffingwell, *Office Appliance Manual*, 283.

4. Ibid., 283–84, 299.

5. Marcosson, *Wherever Men Trade*, 58.

6. Between 1910 and 1930, just over 15 percent of all top U.S. executives were former NCR managers who populated such firms as Remington Arms, Chalmers Motor Car, Delco, General Motors, Chrysler, Burroughs, IBM, Coca-Cola, Addressograph-Multigraph, and Toledo Scale, Stanley C. Allyn, *My Half Century with NCR* (New York: McGraw-Hill, 1967), 26; Marcosson, *Wherever Men Trade*, 127–29; NCR, *1884–1922: The Cash Register Era* (Dayton: NCR, 1984), 9.

7. Key sources are Sobel, *IBM;* Marcosson, *Wherever Men Trade;* Allyn, *My Half Century with NCR;* and NCR, *Celebrating the Future*, a collection of four pamphlets. The closest to historical analysis in depth is T. A. Boyd, *Professional Amateur: The Biography of Charles F. Kettering* (New York: E. P. Dutton, 1957); Crowther, *Patterson*; and Roy W. Johnson and Russell W. Lynch, *The Sales Strategy of John H. Patterson, Founder of the National Cash Register Company* (Chicago: Dartneli Corporation, 1932); Stuart W. Leslie, *Boss Kettering: Wizard of General Motors* (New York: Columbia University Press, 1983).

8. Stine, *Untold Story*, 44–45.

9. Ibid., 45–46; Leffingwell, *Office Appliance Manual*, 284–99.

10. Marcosson, *Wherever Men Trade*, 62; "and removes temptation if the purchase is made by children who are inclined to spend change for soda or sweets on the way home" (62–63).

11. Ibid., 64–68.

12. Ibid., 112.

13. Ibid., 143–44. I have "carried a bag" for IBM and, like NCR's salesmen of old and today's NCR and IBM representatives, took my 100 Percent Clubs seriously, eight as of this writing!

14. Marcosson, *Wherever Men Trade*, 147.

15. Ibid., 137–39; Schulze, *American Office*, 77.

16. Chandler, *Visible Hand*, 402–11.

17. Ibid., 307–8, 564; Stine, *Untold Story*, 80–81; Marcosson, *Wherever Men Trade*, 60–61.

18. Marcosson, *Wherever Men Trade*, 60–61.

19. Quoted in NCR, *Cash Register Era*, 15.

20. Ibid., 15.

21. Sobel, *IBM*, 27.

22. On factory data see *The NCR* 15, no. 22 (November 15, 1902): 849–51; on salesmen, 846–47.

23. NCR, *Cash Register Era*, 2–3; C. T. Fugitt, "Work of the National Cash Register Company," *Caissier's Magazine* 28 (September 1905): 339–59.

24. NCR, *Cash Register Era*, 19.

25. Ibid., 20.

26. Ibid., 21.

27. Ibid., 23–25.

28. Marcosson, *Wherever Men Trade*, 16–19, 95–98.

29. Ibid., 95–96.

30. Ibid., 96–98. In 1894, Detroit cafe owner, Michael Heintz, formed the Heintz Cash Register Company, capitalized at $10,000. He made a register called the "Cuckoo," which first sold for $85. Instead of a bell to ring up sales, a bird popped out like the bird in a cuckoo clock. NCR filed suit against Heintz in August 1895 "for infringement of the Campbell cash drawer patent and secured a permanent injunction which silenced the cuckoo" (98). Only a few of these machines were actually sold to the public.

31. Ibid., 98–100.

32. Marcosson is a useful source for this background despite his pro-NCR bias; ibid, 100–102.

33. Ibid., 104.

34. Ibid., 108.

35. James Bridge, ed., *The Trust: Its Book* (New York: Arno, 1973); *The Federal Antitrust Laws with Summary of Cases Instituted by the United States, 1890–1951* (New York: Commerce Clearing House, 1952), also known by its short title, *Blue Book*; Thomas Conner Henry, *Tricks of the Cash Register Trust* (Winchester, Ky.: Winchester Sun, 1913); W. S. Stevens, "Group of Trusts and Combinations," *Quarterly Journal of Economics* 26 (August 1912): 625–30; Simon N. Whitney, *Antitrust Policies*, vol. 2 (New York: Twentieth Century Fund, 1958).

36. Franklin M. Fisher, John T. McGowan, and John E. Greenwood, *Folded,*

Spindled, and Mutilated: Economic Analysis and U.S. v. IBM (Cambridge, Mass.: MIT Press, 1983), x.

37. Ibid.

38. Ibid., 344.

Chapter 5
Rudiments of an Industry Identified

1. The Spanish-American War (1898) was irrelevant to the process because it lasted only a few months.

2. Evidence does not yet exist to suggest that the Vietnam War contributed as much to data-processing developments as earlier wars. The NASA Space Program and the very large users of computers were very important sources of technological innovation and market demand.

3. Goldstine, *Computer*, 72–83; Kent C. Redmond and Thomas M. Smith, *Project Whirlwind: The History of a Pioneer Computer* (Bedford, Mass.: Digital Press, 1980), 14–28.

4. Representative examples include Paul E. Ceruzzi, *Reckoners: The Prehistory of the Digital Computer, from Relays to the Stored Program Concept, 1935–1945* (Westport, Conn.: Greenwood Press, 1983); Goldstine, *Computer*, 121–236; Nancy Stern, *From ENIAC to UNIVAC: An Appraisal of the Eckert-Mauchly Computers* (Bedford, Mass.: Digital Press, 1981); Eames and Eames, *Computer Perspective*, 128–43.

5. Jordan, "Punched Card Development," 18–20; Chandler, *Scale and Scope*, 32–33.

6. Beniger, *Control Revolution*, 419–20.

7. Austrian, *Hollerith*, 341.

8. Eames and Eames, *Computer Perspective*, 235.

9. U.S. War Department, *The Medical Department of the United States Army in the World War*, vol. 15, *Statistics*, pt. 1, "Army Anthropology" (Washington, D.C.: U.S. War Department, 1921).

10. Stine, *Untold Story*, 73; Edward Roberts, "Tide-predicting Machine," in Horsburgh, *Handbook*, 249–52; Williams, *History of Computing Technology*, 203–5.

11. Stine, *Untold Story*, 76–78.

12. Wright, *White Collar*, 193.

13. Daniel Creamer, Sergie P. Dobrovolsky, and Israel Borenstein, *Capital in Manufacturing and Mining: Its Formation and Financing*, National Bureau of Economic Research Study in Capital Formation and Financing, no. 6 (Princeton, N.J.: Princeton University Press, 1960), A-10. Beniger was one of the first individuals to flag the significance of this kind of data, *Control Revolution*, 398.

14. Beniger, *Control Revolution*, 398.

15. U.S. Department of Commerce, *Foreign Import Duties on Office Appliances* (Washington, D.C.: U.S. Government Printing Office, 1919), 3.

16. Machlup, *Production and Distribution*, 486.

17. *Standard and Poors* (1908–1913).

18. Ibid. (1918), 1339–40.

19. Ibid. (1910), 1318.

20. Ibid. (1912), 1551.

21. Ibid. (1911), 590.

22. Ibid., (1911); 1877–78.

23. For example, Stine *Untold Story*, 46, commented, "With Hollerith's Electric Tabulating Company and Patterson's National Cash Register Company, the computer industry had its first two fledgling firms and was off the ground at the beginning of the twentieth century." I do not mean to single out Stine for special criticism; he was just reflecting conventional wisdom. That wisdom disregarded Burroughs, ignored typewriters, and assumed that activity of any consequence came only after 1900, not before.

24. Marcosson, *Wherever Men Trade*, 178.

25. C. Wright Mills, *White Collar* (New York: Oxford University Press, 1951), 193. Like Stine, for example, Wright underestimated the extent of the new industry when he stated that data-processing equipment was not used extensively until after 1910, ibid., 193. On a comparative basis with earlier decades he was correct but misleading unintentionally because the volumes of the late 1800s were substantial.

26. Leffingwell, *Office Appliance Manual*, 102–27.

27. George Basalla, *The Evolution of Technology* (Cambridge: Cambridge University Press, 1988), 45.

28. Ibid., 91.

29. Ibid., 141.

30. Chandler, *Visible Hand*, 309, 313; Boorstin, *Americans*, 400; Leffingwell, *Office Appliance Manual*, 68.

31. Chandler, *Visible Hand*, 308–10.

Chapter 6
Economic Conditions and the Role of Standardization

1. Robert S. McElvaine, *The Great Depression: America, 1929–1941* (New York: Times Books, 1984), 7–24, 34–39.

2. Chandler, *Visible Hand*, 464–68.

3. Bernstein, *Three Degrees*, 6–9.

4. Wildes and Lindgren, *A Century of Electrical Engineering and Computer Science at MIT*, 82–103, 106–23.

5. Michael Gort, *Diversification and Integration in American Industry* (Princeton, N.J.: Princeton University Press, 1962), 42–45; Chandler, *Visible Hand*, 472–74.

6. U.S. Department of Commerce, Bureau of the Census, *Historical Statistics of the United States: Colonial Times to 1970*, pts. 1, 2 (Washington, D.C.: U.S. Government Printing Office, 1975).

7. Landes, *Unbound Prometheus*, 419–21; B. R. Mitchell, *European Historical Statistics, 1750–1970* (New York: Columbia University Press, 1978), 51–63.

8. Landes, *Unbound Prometheus*, 520–21.

9. I. Bernard Cohen, *Revolution in Science* (Cambridge, Mass.: Harvard University Press, 1985), offers a useful introduction to the problem of "revolutions" with emphasis on scientific revolutions, 6–47 and builds on the seminal work of Thomas S. Kuhn, *The Structure of Scientific Revolutions* (Chicago: University of Chicago Press, 1962); Landes, *Unbound Prometheus*, 193–230; for an economic analysis of nine-

teenth-century issues see W. O. Henderson, *The Industrial Revolution in Europe: Germany, France, Russia, 1815–1914* (Chicago: Quadrangle Books, 1961), 1–7, 65–74.

10. U.S. Bureau of the Census, *Historical Statistics*, 144.

11. On procedures and applications see chapter 8.

12. Beniger, *Control Revolution*, 15–16; Yates, *Control through Communication*.

13. Perley Morse, *Business Machines* (London: n.p., 1932): 6–18.

14. Henry P. Dutton, *Business Organization and Management* (Chicago: A. W. Shaw, 1927), 382–84.

15. For extensive bibliographies see ibid., 535–38; Donald Kirk David, *Retail Store Management Problems* (Chicago: A. W. Shaw, 1922), 1045–50; Norberg, "High-Technology Calculation," 772–75.

16. Morse, *Business Machines*, 67, 71.

17. Ibid., 1.

18. A nice summary and introduction to the literature on control (biological, sociological, economic) can be found in Beniger, *Control Revolution*, but see also Alfred D. Chandler, Jr., "The Large Industrial Corporation and the Making of the Modern American Economy," in Stephen E. Ambrose, ed., *Institutions in Modern America: Innovations in Structure and Process* (Baltimore: Johns Hopkins Press, 1967), 71–101; Manfred Eigen and Ruthild Winkler, *Laws of the Game: How the Principles of Nature Govern Chance*, trans. Robert Kimber and Rita Kimber (New York: Harper and Row, Colophon, 1981); and for a contemporaneous study in the 1920s see George S. Radford, *The Control Quality in Manufacturing* (New York: Ronald, 1922).

19. Morse, *Business Machines*, 2.

20. Ibid., 4.

21. Ibid., 5.

22. For an archtypical example of office products left out of the 1920s in a popular text see Arthur S. Link and William B. Catton, *American Epoch: A History of the United States Since the 1890's* (New York: Alfred A. Knopf, 1967), 249–71, and McElvaine, *Great Depression*, show the old view. Chandler, *Visible Hand*, and Beniger, *Control Revolution*, illustrate recognition of the role of the office products market and the implication for economic influence in the 1920s.

23. Morse, *Business Machines*, 41.

24. Ibid., 61; see also H. G. Schnackel and Henry C. Land, *Accounting by Machine Methods* (New York: Ronald Press, 1929) on effects of such machines on accounting in the 1920s.

25. Chandler, *Visible Hand*, 464–68; a broader view on development and use of information technologies is in William Aspray, ed., *Computing before Computers* (Ames: Iowa State University Press, 1989).

26. Bashe, Johnson, Palmer, and Pugh, *IBM's Early Computers*, 11–12.

27. For an example that linked market demands to actual development of a product (banking equipment) in the late 1920s and early 1930s see Frederick L. Fuller, *My Half Century As an Inventor* (n.p.: privately printed, 1938). Fuller was an outstanding prolific inventor for NCR and IBM for more than fifty years.

28. For example, Stern, *From ENIAC to UNIVAC*, 1–23; Shurkin, *Engines of the Mind*, 93–172; Stine, *Untold Story*, 58–66; Augarten, *Bit by Bit*, 103–7; Williams, *History of Computing Technology*, 271–73.

29. John Vincent Atanasoff, "Advent of Electronic Digital Computing," *Annals of the History of Computing* 6, no. 3 (July 1984): 229–82; Goldstine, *Computer;* Herman Lukoff, *From Dits to Bits: A Personal History of the Electronic Computer* (Portland, Oreg.: Robotics Press, 1979), 28–29; Maurice Wilkes, *Memoirs of a Computer Pioneer* (Cambridge, Mass.: MIT Press, 1985), 25. By World War II, issues concerning national defense also played a major role in the development of equipment for sophisticated applications.

30. The concept of forms also grew out of a late nineteenth and early twentieth-century movement to organize paper files more rationally, which led to 3 × 5 cards, filing cabinets, and so forth. Although no direct evidence links that concept of data organization to mechanical organization of information on machines, the link is obviously there. If for no other reason, the same people who bought filing cabinets also acquired adding and calculating equipment. For a useful account of how indexing and filing systems evolved in the late 1800s and early 1900s see E. R. Hudders, *Indexing and Filing: A Manual of Standard Practice* (New York: Ronald Press, 1920), iii–vi, and for an historian's view, Yates, *Control through Communication.*

Chapter 7
Products, Practices, and Prices

1. H. Arkin, "Development and Principles of the Punched Card Method," in Baehne, *Punched Card Method*, 1–20; L. J. Comrie, *The Hollerith and Powers Tabulating Machines* (London: Privately printed, 1933); C. R. Curtis, *Mechanized Accounting: Being a Review of the Latest Methods of Mechanical Book-keeping, Together with a Survey of the Machines Used* (London: Charles Griffin, 1932), has an excellent review of hardware and applications from Burroughs, NCR, Underwood, Remington Rand, IBM, Campos and others; P. Deveaux, "Present Status of Calculating Machines," *Revue Industrielle* 56 (1926): 113–17, 166–71. Key publications from IBM include International Business Machines Corporation, *The Electric Tabulating and Accounting Machine* (Endicott, N.Y.: IBM, 1925); idem, *A Hollerith Handbook* (Rio de Janeiro, 1934); idem, *Machine Methods of Accounting* (Endicott, N.Y., 1936); and idem, *Managerial Accounting by Machine Method* (Endicott, N.Y., 1939). On Powers and Remington Rand see Remington Rand, *Powers Reference Manual* (Buffalo, N.Y.: Powers Accounting Machine Division, 1935).

2. Bashe, Johnson, Palmer, and Pugh, *IBM's Early Computers*, 1–33.

3. IBM also sold recording clocks for industrial uses and meat and industrial scales. By World War II, these non-DP products had been dropped. On the clocks see Michael O'Malley, *Keeping Watch: A History of American Time* (New York: Viking, 1990), 145–99.

4. This was as true in Europe as in the United States. For details see M. Maul, "Die Elektrischen Lochkarten-Maschinen," *Elektrolechnische Zeitschrift* 48 (1927): 1789–94; E. Beitlich, *Buromaschinenkunde: Maschinenrech-nen, Maschinenbuchhaltung, Vervielfältigungsgeräte* (Hanover: Verlag von Carl Meyer, 1938); Couffignal, *Les machines à calculer*. It is difficult in the 1980s to imagine the enormous variety of equipment made available. For a sense of the responses to customer needs see J. H. McCarthy, *The American Digest of Business Machines: A Compendium of Makes and Models with Specifications and Principles of Operation Described, and Including*

Used Machine Valuations (Chicago: American Exchange Service, 1924), with 640 pages; and the four-volume *The Office Machine Manual: A Loose-Leaf Reference Book on Office Machines and Appliances* (London: Gee, 1938–).

5. "James Wares Bryce," in James W. Cortada, *Historical Dictionary*, 46–48; Randell, *Origins of Digital Computers*, 129; "The Light He Leaves Behind," *Think* (April 1949): 5–6, 30–31; Bashe, Johnson, Palmer, and Pugh, *IBM's Early Computers*, 25–26, 35–36.

6. G. Tauschek, *Die Lochkarten-Buchhaltung-maschinen meines Systems* (Vienna: n.p., 1930); J. W. Negler, "In Memoriam Gustav Tauschek," *Blätter für Technikgeschichte* 26 (1966): 1–14; Randell, *Origins of Digital Computers*, 129.

7. Bashe, Johnson, Palmer, and Pugh, *IBM's Early Computers*, 12–33.

8. R. V. Cradit, "Punched Card Method in Accounting," *Journal of Accountancy* 57 (1934): 272–85. Dozens of articles appeared during the 1920s and 1930s describing uses of punched card equipment, frequently with cost/benefit analysis. Two useful examples that shed light on cost justification are "Accurate Statistics," *Systems and Management Methods* 62 (July 1933): 305–306, which describes savings on clerical expenses, and G. B. Briggs, "Economies in Trust Accounting," *Trust Companies* 64 (May 1937): 551–53, which describes benefits enjoyed by banks in general when using tabulating equipment.

9. Bashe, Johnson, Palmer, and Pugh, *IBM's Early Computers*, 12–20; IBM, *Machine Methods of Accounting*; Jordan, "Punched Card Development," 21.

10. Bashe, Johnson, Palmer, and Pugh, *IBM's Early Computers*, 10–15.

11. Fuller, *Half Century*, 44–51; Austrian, *Hollerith*, 333–34, 335–39; Rodgers, *Think*, 79–81.

12. Bashe, Johnson, Palmer, and Pugh, *IBM's Early Computers*, 16–18. Examples of such are John C. McPherson, "On Mechanical Tabulation of Polynomials," *Annals of Mathematical Statistics* 12 (September 1941): 317–27; a collection of application articles in the sciences (seen as a "leading edge" area for applications) was *Proceedings of the Educational Research Forum* (New York: IBM, August 1940); and on behalf of IBM, W. J. Eckert, *Punched Card Methods*; Watson Scientific Laboratory, *Bibliography: The Use of IBM Machines in Scientific Research, Statistics, and Education* (New York: IBM, 1947), perhaps the first bibliography published on the subject.

13. *Business Week*, October 19, 1935, 10–11.

14. *Literary Digest* 120 (October 26, 1935): 36.

15. James Connolly, *History of Computing in Europe* (New York: IBM World Trade Corporation, 1967), 19–44.

16. Jordan, "Punched Card Development," 22.

17. Sobel, *IBM*, 48–70; Belden and Belden, *Lengthening Shadow*, 88–190; Shurkin, *Engines of the Mind*, 254, 256, 258, 265–66; and for a more realistic assessment, Augarten, *Bit by Bit*, 183.

18. Bashe, Johnson, Palmer, and Pugh, *IBM's Early Computers*, 16–17, 48–50; for the process at work in the late 1950s and early 1960s see Emerson W. Pugh, *Memories That Shaped an Industry: Decisions Leading to IBM System/360* (Cambridge, Mass.: MIT Press, 1984), 248–64ff.

19. Jordan, "Punched Card Development," 22.

20. Fishman, *Computer Establishment*, 35.

21. Quotes from Rodgers, *Think*, 129.

22. *Business Week*, April 6, 1932, 14. The same cites the following expenses: "The government rental of machines (ranging from $300,000 to $400,000 annually) is about $100,000 higher than it would be if the defendants' cards were used."

23. *Business Week*, December 7, 1935, 36 for a contemporaneous summary; Rodgers, *Think*, 129–31.

24. *Business Week*, December 7, 1935, 36; Rodgers, *Think*, 108–10; Belden and Belden, *Lengthening Shadow*, 186–89.

25. Chandler, *Visible Hand*, 375.

26. The literature on IBM's lawsuits with the U.S. government are numerous and often militantly favorable to one side or the other. For a defense of the government's role see DeLamarter, *Big Blue*, and on the 1920s and 1930s, 21–33. For a criticism of the Justice Department see Fisher, McGowen, and Greenwood, *Folded, Spindled, and Mutilated.*

27. *Standard and Poors*-type data are summarized in Jordan, "Punched Card Development," 58.

28. There were also dealers who ran retail shops where one could come in and buy one or more items of a vendor's equipment, new or used. The term *dealer* was not evident in the industry until the 1930s and then first with those who sold typewriters and adding machines. By the 1980s, dealers were also selling microcomputers, such as the IBM PC, Apple, and Compaq.

29. Watson's image of how salespeople should look and act stamped character and definition on his company. For details, Belden and Belden, *Lengthening Shadow*, 124–59.

30. For an historian's version see Sobel, *IBM*, 119; for his own account see Thomas J. Watson, Jr., "The Greatest Capitalist in History," *Fortune* 116, no. 5 (August 31, 1987): 24–35.

31. Based on documents from my personal files. I was a marketing manager in the National Accounts Division Branch Office (December 1983–December 1985) and collected materials on that office's history that dated back to the 1920s.

32. International Business Machines Corporation, *Manual of Business Instruction* (1933): 1, "Reports and Routines" (rev. December 31, 1932).

33. For a recent reprint, Rodgers, *Think*, 114. The original had more verses than reprinted here.

34. Thomas J. Watson, Jr., *A Business and Its Beliefs: The Ideas That Helped Build IBM* (New York: McGraw-Hill, 1963). This book has been distributed routinely to all IBM managers since its publication as part of their initial management training, which possibly makes this one of the most widely read books in the data-processing industry.

35. Ibid., 34.

36. Phrases from Thomas J. Watson, ca. 1921, published as a broadside in which he pushed for more sales: "Double in 1921," courtesy IBM Archives.

37. Because the process has scarcely changed over the past half-century, more recent publications describe the management of salespeople similarly. F. G. "Buck" Rodgers (a senior vice-president of marketing at IBM) and Robert L. Shook, *The IBM Way: Insights into the World's Most Successful Marketing Organization* (New York: Harper and Row, 1986): 181–96; Fisher, McGowan, and Greenwood, *Folded, Spindled, and Mutilated*; Sobel, *IBM*, 28–32, 117, 119, 130–31, 135.

38. NCR, *Cash Register Era*; Sobel, *IBM*, 28–29. The point measurement system

remained in place in the U.S. company until January 1990 when the focus on revenue from all sources became more important than the earlier product orientation.

39. IBM, *Manual of Business Instruction*, 1. On selling techniques of the 1930s see recollections of Thomas J. Watson, Jr., at the time a salesman, *Father Son & Co.*, 78.

40. IBM, *Manual of Business Instruction*, 1.

41. Ibid.

42. Ibid. During the 1930s IBM had an estimated thirty-five hundred customers, which made that kind of approach possible to manage, Thomas J. Watson, Jr., *Father Son & Co.: My Life at IBM and Beyond* (New York: Bantam, 1990): 79.

43. Fisher, McGowan, and Greenwood, *Folded, Spindled, and Mutilated*.

44. Examples of the two extremes are the excellent technical history by Bashe, Johnson, Palmer, and Pugh, *IBM's Early Computers*, and the best history of the firm, Sobel, *IBM*, or the standard for many years, Rodgers, *Think*.

45. A secondhand market for office equipment with industrywide pricing structures already existed. For details see McCarthy, *American Digest*, which is massive; *The Office Machine Manual: A Loose-Leaf Reference Book on Office Machines and Appliances*, 4 vols. (London: Gee, 1938 et seq); and Leffingwell, *Office Appliance Manual*, for just new equipment.

46. IBM, *Manual of Business Instruction*; Tabulating Machine Company, *Salesmen's Catalogue*.

47. Extrapolated from data in Sobel, *IBM*, 84.

Chapter 8
Commercial and Scientific Applications of Punched Card Machines

1. Leffingwell, *Office Appliance Manual*, 179.

2. "Electrical Bookkeeping and Accounting," *American City* 50 (November 1935): 55.

3. Leffingwell, *Office Appliance Manual*, 179.

4. Goddard, "Payroll," 275, 284.

5. For example, "A.B.&A. Introduces Tabulating Machine Checks," *Railway Age* 75 (July 4, 1923): 76–77; M. J. Howell, "Punch Cards for Bills Receivable," ibid. 79 (August 15, 1925): 321–22; G. F. Glacy, "Improved Car Accounting and Statistics at Lower Cost," ibid. 94 (April 15, 1933): 548–52; "Compiling Operating Statistics by Punched Cards," *Railway Review* 79 (October 30, 1926): 647–48; "Fuel Accounting with Punched Cards," ibid. 79 (November 31, 1926): 719–21; the two journals published more than one dozen articles on the subject in the interwar period.

6. J. L. Connover, "Report of Committee on Office Labor Saving Devices," *American Gas Association, Accounting Section*, no. 1 (May 1927): 15–34; "Billing Procedures of the Brooklyn Union Gas Company," *American Gas Journal* 151 (December 1939): 15–17; C. R. Curtis, "Mechanization in Gas Offices," *Gas Journal* 202 (June 4, 1933): 807–9; "Gas Accounts and Records by Punched Cards," Ibid. 227 (April 16, 1939): 395–96; J. H. Kimball and R. M. Segwick, "Tabulating Machines in Customer Accounting," *Journal of the American Water Works Association* 23 (November 1931): 1891–94; Frank Twohy, "Application of Tabulating Equipment in Accounting Procedures," ibid. 28 (November 1936): 1704–11.

7. Typical examples of involved journals were *Management Engineering, Ameri-*

can Machinist, Automobile Engineering, Engineer, Industrial Management, Chemical Age, Rubber Age, Management and Administration, Textile World, Food Industries, American Business, Factory and Industrial Management, and *Electrical Engineering.*

8. Leffingwell, *Office Appliance Manual,* 180; Sidney Ratner, James H. Soltow, and Richard Sylla, *The Evolution of the American Economy: Growth, Welfare, and Decision Making* (New York: Basic Books, 1979): 505–10.

9. A. W. Bosworth, "Advances in Trust Accounting and Control," *Trust Companies* 62 (January 1936): 25–32; G. B. Briggs, "Economies in Trust Accounting," ibid. 64 (May 1937): 551–53; I. I. Sperling, "Reducing Routine to Minutes," *Banking* 30 (May 1938): 66–68; W. J. Weig, "Punched Card Accounting for Mortgages," ibid. 29 (January 1937): 28.

10. H. C. Little, "Time Saving Sales and Quota Record," *American Business* 8 (January 1938): 32ff.

11. P. M. Atkins, "Industrial Cost Accounting for Executives," *American Machinist* 59 (October 18, 1923): 591–94; R. P. Perry, "General Accounting with Bookkeeping Machines," *Electric Railway Journal* 61 (March 10, 1923): 413–14; E. W. Workman, "Cost Accounting by Machinery, The Hollerith System," *Engineering and Industrial Management* 6 (September 1921): 314–18; R. Y. Cradit, "Punched Cards Method," 272–85; L. E. Vannais, "Punched Card Accounting From the Audit Viewpoint," *Journal of Accountancy* 70 (September 1940): 200–217; and Ibid. 70 (October 1940): 339–56.

12. Cradit, "Punched Cards Method"; C. R. Curtis, "Mechanization in Gas Offices," *Gas Journal* 202 (June 14, 1933): 807–9, W. V. Davidson, Jr., "How A Wholesaler Became Efficient," *Food Industries* 9 (March 1937): 120–23; W. J. Graham, "Distribution Methods by Hand and Machine," *Journal of Accountancy* 53 (March 1932): 171–85.

13. W. J. Graham, *Cost Accounting and Office Equipment* (Chicago: American Technical Society, 1929); International Business Machines, *Hollerith Handbook;* idem, *Machine Methods of Accounting;* idem, *Managerial Accounting;* Gail A. Mills, *Accounting Manual for Colleges* (Princeton, N.J.: Princeton University Press, 1937); many books on business management, such as those cited in this chapter, have chapters devoted to the subject. Two widely distributed examples, however, were Schnackel and Lang, *Accounting by Machine Methods,* reflecting thinking of the 1920s, and J. Brooks Heckert, *Accounting Systems: Design and Installation* (New York: Ronald Press, 1936).

14. Morse, *Business Machines,* 78.

15. Ibid., 19–20, 24.

16. Ibid., 21. Washington, D.C. high-school curriculums commonly included a six-week course on calculating machines, stenciling, mimeographing, and electric adding machines with thirty to thirty-five students per class. Other courses ran for four weeks. Similar programs existed at the High School of Commerce, Springfield, Massachusetts, at the New Haven Commercial High School, and at the John Adams High School in Cleveland, Ohio, ibid., 21–22.

17. "Cities Are Adopting Modern Office Practice," *American City* 51 (June 1936): 101.

18. "Accurate Statistics," 305–6.

19. "Billing Procedures," 15–17.

20. A. W. Bosworth, "Advances in Trust Accounting," 25–32; G. B. Briggs, "Economies in Trust Accounting," 551–53.

21. R. H. Butz, "Punched Cards Speed Stock Control," *Food Industries* 8 (December 1936): 631; "Cards Tell Facts," *Systems and Management Methods* 62 (August 1933): 357; Davidson, "Wholesaler," 120–23.

22. For example, C. W. Dean, "Gates Rubber Company's New Budgetary Control System," *American Business* 7 (May 1937): 34–35ff.

23. G. A. Gardner, "Improving Operation of Tabulating Machine Installations," *NACA Bulletin* 21 (December 15, 1939): 481–90, on Schenley Distillery Corporation.

24. D. H. Linton, "How We Make a Market Survey," *American Gas Journal* 146 (March 1937): 18–20.

25. "Mechanical Method Provides Accurate Control of Warehouse Stocks," *Systems* 62 (December 1933): 560–61; "Rock Island Goes Modern in Material Accounting," *Railway Age* 106 (June 10, 1939): 976–84.

26. W. B. Cragg, "How Census Data Is Tabulated," *Credit Monthly* 32 (August 1930): 48–49; "Our Machine-Made Census," *Literary Digest* 64 (February 28, 1920): 26; J. A. Stewart, "Electricity and the Census," *Scientific American* 122 (January 31, 1920): 109. For a history of the 1920 and 1930 counts see Truesdell, *Punch Card Tabulation*, 139–94. The most useful account is by Norberg, "High-Technology Calculation," 775–78.

27. Morse, *Business Machines*, 156.

28. "Electrical Bookkeeping and Accounting," 55–56.

29. Contemporaneous literature is listed in U.S. Department of Labor, *Automatic Technology and Its Implications: A Selected Annotated Bibliography*, bulletin no. 1198, Bureau of Labor Statistics (Washington, D.C.: Government Printing Office, 1956).

30. There was one small exception to the otherwise widespread pattern of developing equipment for commercial and government users. In 1937, IBM announced the 805 Test Scoring Machine, a result of work with Columbia University and the original developer of the device, Reynold B. Johnson; see Bashe, Johnson, Palmer, and Pugh, *IBM's Early Computers*, 275.

31. The debate over the U.S. government's role was recently studied in Kenneth Flamm, *Targeting the Computer.*

32. For a comparison of device types for scientific and engineering applications, Baehne, *Punched Card Method;* V. Johns, "On the Mechanical Handling of Statistics," *American Mathematical Monthly* 33 (1926): 494–502; Wendell A. Milliman, "Mechanical Multiplication by the Use of Tabulating Machines," *Transactions of the Actuarial Society of America*, pt. 2, 35 (October 1934): 253–64.

33. Bashe, Johnson, Palmer, and Pugh, *IBM's Early Computers*, 32.

34. L. J. Comrie, "The Application of the Hollerith Tabulating Machine to Brown's Tables of the Moon," *Monthly Notices*, Royal Astronomical Society 92, no. 7 (1932): 694–707.

35. Goldstine, *Computer*, 72–83, 127–39.

36. Bashe, Johnson, Palmer, and Pugh, *IBM's Early Computers*, 22; H. R. J. Grosch, "Harmonic Analysis by the Use of Progressive Digiting," in IBM, eds., *Proceedings of the IBM Research Forum* (Endicott, N.Y.: IBM, 1946): 81–84.

37. "The Application of Commercial Calculating Machines to Scientific Computing," *Mathematical Tables and Other Aids to Computation* 2 (1946): 149–59; "Calcu-

lating Machines, Appendix III," in L. R. Connor, ed., *Statistics in Theory and Practice* (London: Pitman, 1938): 42–51; Leslie J. Comrie, *The Hollerith and Powers Tabulating Machine* (London: Privately printed, 1933); "Inverse Interpolation and Scientific Application of the National Accounting Machine," *Supplement to the Journal of the Royal Statistical Society* 3, no. 2 (1936): 87–114; "Modern Babbage Machines," *Bulletin, Office Machinery Users Association, Ltd.* (London, 1932): 1–29; "Recent Progress in Scientific Computing," *Journal of Scientific Instruments* 21 (August 1944): 129–35.

38. C. W. Snedecor, "Uses of Punched Card Equipment in Mathematics," *American Mathematical Monthly* 35 (1928): 161–69; Jack W. Dunlap, "The Computation of Means, Standard Deviations, and Correlations by the Tabulator When the Numbers Are Both Positive and Negative," *Proceedings of the Educational Research Forum* (New York: IBM, 1940): 16–19; Paul S. Dwyer, "Summary of Problems in the Computation of Statistical Constants with Tabulator and Sorting Machines," ibid., 20–28; and Paul S. Dwyer and Alan D. Meacham, "The Preparation of Correlation Tables on Tabulator Equipment with Digit Selection," *Journal of the American Statistical Association* 32 (1937): 654–62.

39. For details see B. V. Bowden, ed., *Faster Than Thought* (London: Sir Isaac Pitman, 1953), 24–26.

40. Williams, *History of Computing Technology*, 240, 254, 259, 301, 384, and on Moore School, 211, 266.

41. W. J. Eckert, "Facilities of the Watson Scientific Computing Laboratory," in IBM, eds., *Proceedings of the IBM Research Forum*, 75–80; and his best-known work, Eckert, *Punched Card Methods*. On the laboratory see J. F. Brennan, *The IBM Watson Laboratory at Columbia University: A History* (Armonk, N.Y.: IBM, 1971).

42. Bashe, Johnson, Palmer, and Pugh, *IBM's Early Computers*, 24.

43. E. C. Bower, "On Subdividing Tables," *Lick Observatory Bulletin* 16, no. 455 (November 1933): 143–44; L. J. Comrie, "The Application of Hollerith Equipment to an Agricultural Investigation," *Supplement to the Journal of the Royal Statistical Society* 4, no. 2 (1937): 210–24.

44. On ballistics the best source remains Goldstine, *Computer*, 72–83, and on astronomy, 27–30, 108–10.

45. Lukoff, *Dits to Bits*, xii; Andrew Hodges, *Alan Turing: The Enigma* (New York: Simon and Schuster, 1983); 93–109; Williams, *History of Computing Technology*, 206–8, 240–41.

46. Bashe, Johnson, Palmer, and Pugh, *IBM's Early Computers*, 25; Goldstine, *Computer*,

Chapter 9
International Trade in Punched Card Machines

1. James Connolly, *History of Computing*, 10–14, has written the only detailed account covering the precomputer era in Europe.

2. Ibid., 15–18; Campbell-Kelly, *ICL*, 47–57, 62–66.

3. Several examples of Watson names for susidiaries are Watson Business Machines (Japan), Watson Java (Netherlands East Indies), followed by Watson Mexico, Watson Italy, and so forth.

4. Connolly, *History of Computing*, 19–20.

5. Ibid.

6. IBM owned 90 percent of DEHOMAG; BTM was owned 100 percent by British interests but had licensing and royalty agreements with IBM. The agreements were canceled in 1949, pitting IBM as a competitor against BTM.

7. Connolly, *History of Computing*, 24–25.

8. Ibid., 25.

9. Ibid., 28.

10. Sobel, *IBM*, 135.

11. Jacques Vernay, "IBM France," *Annals of the History of Computing* 11, no. 4 (1989): 299–311.

12. Comrie, *Hollerith and Powers Tabulating Machines*, a forty-eight page booklet; Deveaux, "Calculating Machines," 113–17, 166–71.

13. For a sense of the market's concerns and interests see Beitlich, *Buromaschinenkunde*; R. Berger, "Die Lochkartenmaschine," *Z.V.D.I.* 72 (1928): 1799–1807; Curtis, *Mechanized Accountancy*.

14. Connolly, *History of Computing*, 133. IBM did the same in Japan where it manufactured for the entire Asian market, Robert Sobel, *IBM vs. Japan: The Struggle for the Future* (New York: Stein and Day, 1986), 115. On French activities, Pierre E. Mounier-Kuhn, "Bull: A World-Wide Company Born in Europe," *Annals of the History of Computing* 11, no. 4 (1989): 279–97.

15. Although long gone from IBM publications by the 1970s, the phrase survived as a faded sign on the side of the IBM building at 590 Madison Ave., New York, one-time corporate headquarters. The building and its painted sign were replaced by a new IBM building in the 1980s.

16. Campbell-Kelly, *ICL*, 52.

17. Ibid.

18. Ibid., 72, and for the 1930s, 73–102.

Chapter 10
The Great Depression in the United States

1. Christopher Lasch, "Technology and Its Critics: The Degradation of the Practical Arts," in Steven E. Goldberg and Charles R. Strain, eds., *Technological Change and the Transformation of America* (Carbondale: Southern Illinois University Press, 1987), 79–90; David F. Noble, *Forces of Production* (New York: Oxford University Press, 1986), 191–92.

2. James Fallows, "America's Changing Economic Landscape," *Atlantic Monthly* 251 (1985): 47–68. Efficiencies can also go too far. After the U.S. stock market collapsed momentarily in October 1987, computerized trading using microcomputers was blamed as a major cause of the problem; a slight dip in prices triggered wholesale sales, which, in turn, drove down prices too quickly for humans to react.

3. Ratner, Soltow, and Sylla, *Evolution of the American Economy*, 402.

4. That represented a decline of 15 percent. Burroughs went down in the same period by 38 percent, which suggests the kinds of swings experienced by others in the industry.

5. SSA's activities to implement the Social Security Act of 1935 were considered the largest bookkeeping applications of its day. It kept records on more than 26 million

Americans. For that activity SSA rented 120,000 square feet of factory space in Baltimore that could hold the weight of 425 card punch and sorting machines. IBM equipment processed 500,000 cards daily. IBM developed the Type 077 sorter for the project. For details see Stine, *Untold Story*, 91–93.

6. Sobel, *IBM*, 71.

7. Augarten, *Bit by Bit*, 183.

8. Sobel, *IBM*, 78.

9. "Call For Business Machines," *Business Week*, January 25, 1935, 16.

10. Howard Florence, "A New Era for Business Machines," *Review of Reviews* 89 (January 1934): 30–33.

11. Augarten, *Bit by Bit*, 183–84.

12. Florence, "New Era for Business Machines," 33.

13. Campbell-Kelly, *ICL*, 77ff.

Chapter 11
IBM and Powers/Remington Rand

1. Augarten, *Bit by Bit*, 183.

2. Belden and Belden, *Lengthening Shadow*, 3, 314.

3. Malik, *Tomorrow the World?* ix–xvi; DeLamarter, *Big Blue*, 1–3, 11–26.

4. Fisher, Mackie, and Manche, *IBM and the U.S. Data Processing Industry*, 11–14, 24–25.

5. Rodgers and Shook, *IBM Way*, 67–94.

6. The two most balanced views on the firm are Sobel, *IBM*, and Rodgers, *Think*. Both recognized that a complex of factors was at work and set the company within historical perspective.

7. Michael E. Porter, *Competitive Advantage: Creating and Sustaining Superior Performance* (New York: Free Press, 1985), xvi; Thomas J. Peters and Robert H. Waterman, Jr., *In Search of Excellence: Lessons from America's Best-Run Companies* (New York: Harper and Row, 1982), 89–327.

8. On his marketing plans see Connolly, *History of Computing*, 16, 37; Rodgers, *IBM*, 84, 91.

9. Sobel, *IBM*, 23–69; Rodgers, *Think*, 15–79; Belden and Belden, *Lengthening Shadow*, 33–58, 125–59.

10. Sobel, *IBM*, 70–92.

11. Based on IBM's sales manuals from the period.

12. See pp. 118–27.

13. Frederick Hart and Co. to O. E. Braitmayer, December 22, 1922, Domestic Box 1, Manufacturing, Inventory, Shipment (1918–1954), IBM Archives.

14. Rodgers, *Think*, 130.

15. James W. Cortada, *Historical Dictionary*, 235–41.

16. Laurence H. Sloan and Associates, *Two Cycles of Corporation Profits, 1922–1933 1934–19XX* (New York: Harper and Brothers, 1936), 411–14; Saul Engelbourg, *International Business Machines: A Business History* (New York: Arno Press, 1976), 128–30.

17. All quotes drawn from Sobel, *IBM*, 87–88.

18. Ibid., 88.

19. Austrian, *Hollerith*, 267–76, 289–90.

20. Sobel, *IBM*, 72; Augarten, *Bit by Bit*, 182, 183.

21. The process continued, and in 1955, Remington Rand merged with Sperry Corporation, itself the product of many mergers. The new entity was best remembered for the UNIVAC computers of the 1950s.

22. *Moody's Industrials*, 1938, 2992.

23. Augarten, *Bit by Bit*, 183.

24. Fishman, *Computer Establishment*, 44–47.

Chapter 12
Other Accounting Machines and Their Uses

1. U.S. Bureau of the Census, *Historical Statistics*, 421.

2. Morse, *Business Machines*, 34.

3. One of the most useful publications for the earlier part of the interwar period was McCarthy, *American Digest;* the already cited Office Equipment Catalogue, Inc., *Office Equipment Catalogue* (vintage 1920s), and *The Office Machine Manual*.

4. Leffingwell, *Office Appliance Manual*, 128.

5. Eugene J. Benge, *Cutting Clerical Costs* (New York: McGraw-Hill, 1931); Comrie, "Calculating Machines," 349–71; Harold D. Fasnacht, *How to Use Business Machines; A Brief Introductory Course* (New York: Gregg Publishing, 1947); *Modernes Rechnen* (Zurich: Heinrich Daemen, 1930) are examples of literature in which uses of the technology are described.

6. Leffingwell, *Office Appliance Manual*, 128–63.

7. Ibid., 164–79.

8. Ibid., 102–27, 180–201, 283–99, 374–98, 405–50, 510–40.

9. Edward Littlejohn and C. J. McClain, "The Accounting Machine Industry: A Study in Competition," (Burroughs, June 1950, Typescript), 70–75, Burroughs Papers. The study was done in anticipation of antitrust action against Burroughs by the U.S. Justice Department.

10. I extrapolated the ratio by dividing rental prices into purchase prices of randomly selected equipment and then checked for reasonableness by performing the same calculation with revenues and profits for Burroughs for the interwar period.

11. Littlejohn and McClain, "Accounting Machine Industry," 40–45.

12. Ibid., 45.

13. For a useful description see Leffingwell, *Office Appliance Manual*, 55–81.

14. Harry Jerome, *Mechanization in Industry* (New York: National Bureau of Economic Research, 1934), 172.

15. "Adding Machines" (ca. 1949, Typescript), 2, Burroughs Papers.

16. Ibid., 6; and Littlejohn and McClain, "Accounting Machine Industry."

17. "Adding Machines."

18. Leffingwell, *Office Appliance Manual*, 55–81; Benge, *Cutting Clerical Costs*, 170–73.

19. Williams, *History of Computing Technology*, 213–64 and for the technology upon which commercial devices were originally based, 152–57.

20. Turck, *Origin*.

21. Leffingwell, *Office Appliance Manual*, 83.

22. Ibid., 90.

23. Goldstine, *Computer;* Stern, *From ENIAC to UNIVAC*, 37–38, 56; L. J. Comrie, "On the Application of the Brunsvig-Dupla Calculating Machine to Double Summation with Finite Differences," *Monthly Notices, Royal Astronomical Society* 88, no. 5 (March 1928): 447–59; L. Couffignal, "Sur un probleme d'analyse mecanique abstraite," *Comptes Rendus de la Academie des Sciences de Paris* 206 (1938): 1336–1338.

24. "Call for Business Machines," 16; Leffingwell, *Office Appliance Manual*.

25. Leffingwell, *Office Appliance Manual*, 17–54.

26. Littlejohn and McClain, "Accounting Machine Industry," 122.

27. Ibid.

28. Ibid., 125; Goldstine, *Computer*, 115–225.

29. Littlejohn and McClain, "Accounting Machine Industry," 131.

30. Ibid., 132.

31. Ibid., 133.

Chapter 13
Vendors, Practices, and Results

1. *Office Equipment Catalogue*, unpaginated.

2. Ibid.

3. Ibid.

4. Frank Baldwin was still alive and active in the 1920s.

5. *Office Equipment Catalogue*.

6. Ibid. Trials are the classic "puppy dog close" for sales reps: take the puppy home and try him for thirty days; if you don't like the little fella, bring him back for a cash refund. What child would allow his parents to do that?

7. Ibid.

8. Ibid.

9. Ibid.

10. Ibid.

11. Ibid.

12. Burroughs, *Decisions in Force*, February 1919, 1, Burroughs Papers.

13. Ibid., February 1921, ix.

14. Ibid., x–xi.

15. C. D. Stevens to Field Force, May 1, 1913, Burroughs Papers.

16. E. D. Shaw to Field Force, September 27, 1920, Burroughs Papers.

17. L. V. Britt to Field Force, July 1, 1921, Burroughs Papers.

18. L. V. Britt to Home Office Sales Department, May 15, 1931, Burroughs Papers.

19. "It's In the Bag!!!" memorandum to Home Office Sales Department, November 7, 1933, Burroughs Papers.

20. Ray R. Eppert to Home Office Sales Department, February 12, 1936, Burroughs Papers.

21. Sobel, *IBM*, 75.

22. The percentages were derived by dividing profits by revenues—the classic return on investment (ROI) formula.

23. Augarten, *Bit by Bit*, 183.

24. Macdonald, *Strategy for Growth*, 11–12.

25. "The General Nature and Size of the United States Business Machines Industry," (November 1951, Typescript) Burroughs Papers (see table XIV, unpaginated, for details).

26. Ibid., 3.

27. Macdonald, *Strategy for Growth*, 11.

28. See Burroughs, *Annual Report*, random years, 1920s–1930s, for listings.

29. Burroughs, *Annual Report*, 1925, 1.

30. Ibid., 1929, 1.

31. Ibid., 1931, 1.

32. Ibid., 1932, 1.

33. Ibid., 1939, 1.

34. Civil war in Spain and internal political and economic turmoil in the Soviet Union can explain away most of the reason for lost sales while Burroughs's problem in Germany awaits additional historical investigation.

35. Burroughs, *Annual Report*, 1939, 4.

36. NCR, *1923–1951*. For an introduction to the kind of technology that was injected into NCR's traditional customer base see Malcolm McNair and Eleanor May, *The American Department Store, 1920–1960* (Boston: Harvard Business School, 1963).

37. Ibid., 1.

38. Ibid., 12.

39. *Office Equipment Catalogue;* Leffingwell, *Office Appliance Manual*, 283–99.

40. Allyn, *My Half Century at NCR*, 55.

41. NCR, *1923–1951*, 2.

42. Augarten, *Bit by Bit*, 182.

43. NCR, *1923–1951*, 20.

44. Ibid., 21.

45. Ibid., 24.

46. Ibid., 25–26.

47. Ibid., 28.

48. Ibid., 19.

49. *60 Jahre Brunsviga* (Braunschweig: Brunsviga-Maschinenwerke, Grimme, Natalis & Co., 1931); *Brunsviga-Sonderheft 1936* (Braunscweig: Brunsviga-Maschinenwerke, Grimme, Natalis & Co., 1936).

50. Results of this work were reviewed in contemporaneous publications. For example, Charles Harmann, *Uber Elektrische Rechenmaschinen* (Neu-Babelsberg: Privately printed, 1932[?]); W. Lind, "Getreibe der Addiermaschinen," *Zeitgesch Vereinigung Deutschen Eng Engenierwesen* 75 (1931): 201–5; and idem, "Getriebe der Multipliziermaschinen," ibid., 985–90; W. Meyer Zur Capellen, *Mathematische Instrumente* (Leipzig: Akademische Verlogsgesellschaft, 1949), 53–122.

51. N. Apraxine, "Machine à calculer mue électriquement," *Comptes Rendus de la Academie Sciences de Paris* 195 (November 1932), 857–58.

52. NCR, *1923–1951*, 25.

53. Morse, *Business Machines*, 34.

54. Ibid., 34.

55. Ibid., 35.

56. Ibid., 34.

57. Mills, *White Collar*, 195.

58. Ibid., 5.

Chapter 14
Economics, Government Controls, and Applications

1. Examples are Stern, *From ENIAC to UNIVAC*. Goldstine, *Computer;* Williams, *History of Computing Technology*. The bibliography on specific World War II computing projects is extensive and focuses primarily on code breaking. See Ralph Bennet, *Ultra in the West* (London: Hutchinson, 1979); Jozef Garlinski, *The Enigma War* (New York: Charles Scribner's Sons, 1979); I. J. Good, "Early Work on Computers at Bletchley," *Annals of the History of Computing* 1, no. 1 (July 1979): 38–48; David Kahn, *The Code Breakers* (New York: Macmillan, 1967); Mina Rees, "The Mathematical Sciences and World War II," *American Mathematical Monthly* 87, no. 8 (October 1980): 607–21.

2. Stern, *From ENIAC to UNIVAC*, 45.

3. For a detailed history of those relations see Kenneth Flamm, *Creating the Computer* (Washington, D.C.: Brookings Institution, 1988)..

4. Ratner, Soltow, and Sylla, *Evolution of the American Economy*, 401–3.

5. Belden and Belden, *Lengthening Shadow*, 210; NCR, *1923–1951*, 31–33; "Norden Bombsight" file, Burroughs Papers.

6. "Export Summary Report, Burroughs Corporation, June 1946," 1–3, Burroughs Papers.

7. Ibid., 1.

8. Ibid., 2–3.

9. For a description of the process, ibid., 30–33.

10. War Production Board, "History of the Administration of Regulations of the Office Machine and Typewriter Industries, 1942–1945," (August 1945, Report): 1, copy in Burroughs Papers (hereafter cited as WPB).

11. Ibid., 3.

12. Ibid., 7.

13. Ibid., 9.

14. Ibid., fig. in app. 5, xxvii.

15. Ibid., xxvii.

16. Ibid., 12.

17. Ibid., 13.

18. Flamm, *Creating the Computer*, describes relations just before World War II, 29–36.

19. Arthur Sanders, "Section II Addendum Administration of Regulations of Office Machine and Typewriter Industries in 1944," WPB, May 1945, Report: 1, copy in Burroughs Papers.

20. Ibid., 3.

21. Ibid., 29.

22. Ibid., 30.

23. Richard W. Murphy, "Section III Addendum Administration of Regulations of

Office Machine and Typewriter Industries in 1945" WPB, August 1945, Report, 2, copy in Burroughs Papers.

24. Ibid., 2.

25. E. F. Neubecker, "Price Controls," December 18, 1946, 1–5, Burroughs Papers.

26. Ibid., 14.

27. E. F. Neubecker, "Production and Sales," January 10, 1947, 36, Burroughs Papers.

28. Ibid., 40, 54–55.

29. Mills, *White Collar*, 190–98; Georgina M. Smith, *Office Automation and White Collar Employment* (New Brunswick, N.J.: Institute of Management and Labor Relations, Rutgers the State University, n.d. [1960?]), 5.

30. E. F. Critchlow, "Measurement and Prediction of Aircraft Vibration by Punched Card Systems," *S.A.E. Journal* 52 (August 1944): 368–79; "Punched Card Machines and Studies of Flutter and Vibration in Planes," *Journal of the Civil Aeronautics Administration* 7 (January 15, 1946): 2ff.

31. "Daily Production Material Control Cuts Inventory and Speeds Planning," *American Machinist* 88 (August 3, 1944): 94–96.

32. D. J. Egan, "It's All in the Cards," *Bus Transportation* 23 (November 1944): 48–51.

33. "Government Moves to Stabilize Office Salaries," *American Business* 13 (July 1943): 17–18.

34. "Handling Partial Payments on Cash Splits with Mark Sensing Tabulating Cards," *American Gas Association Monthly* 26 (October 1944): 418–19.

35. International Business Machines Corporation, *War Accounting Service* (Endicott, N.Y.: IBM, 1943).

36. J. C. McNeill, "Machine Methods Promote Efficiency in Mine Accounting," *Coal Age* 50 (November 1945): 109–14.

37. J. C. McPherson, "Mathematical Operations with Punched Cards," *Journal of the American Statistical Association* 37 (June 1942): 275–81.

38. E. L. Moore, "Paperwork for Smooth Flow and Close Control," *Factory Management* 103 (October 1945): 134–38.

39. Cyrus Tanner, "Talent Tabulator," *Personnel Journal* 23 (April 1945): 375–77.

40. Belden and Belden, *Lengthening Shadow*, 209; Engelbourg, *International Business Machines*, 299–300.

41. Jordan, "of Punched Card Development," 52.

42. Flamm, *Creating the Computer*, 35–36; David Kahn, *The Codebreakers: The Story of Secret Writing* (London: Weidenfield and Nicolson, 1967, 1974): 300ff, 332–33.

43. Wildes and Lindgren, *Century*, 213–17.

44. Goldstine, *Computer*, 127–56; Stern, *From ENIAC to UNIVAC*, 9–10.

45. See memoirs of a U.S. Navy employee, Robert Atha, "Bombe! 'I Could Hardly Believe It'," *Cryptologia* 9, no. 4 (October 1985): 332–36; those of one at Bletchley Park, P. Calvocoressi, "The Secrets of Enigma," *The Listener* 97, no. 2492 (January 20, 1977): 70–71; idem, no. 2493 (January 27, 1977): 112–14; idem, no. 2494 (February 3, 1977): 135–37; and idem, "The Ultra Secrets of Station X," *Sunday*

Times, November 24, 1974, 33–34; Good, "Computers at Bletchley," 38–48, also offers memoirs; the major study of the British is F. H. Hinsley, *British Intelligence in the Second World War* 3 vols. to date (London: H.M.S.O., 1979–1984); on Poland's role, Wladyslaw Kozaczuk, *Enigma: How the German Cipher Was Broken and How It Was Read by the Allies in World War II*, ed. and trans. Christopher Kasparek (Frederick, Md.: University Publishers of America, 1984).

46. W. W. Chandler, "The Installation and Maintenance of Colossus," *Annals of the History of Computing* 5, no. 3 (July 1983): 260–62; Allen W. M. Coombs, "The Making of Colossus," ibid. 5, no. 3 (July 1983): 253–59; Thomas H. Flowers, "The Design of Colossus," ibid. 5, no. 3 (July 1983): 239–52; Brian Randell, "The CO-LOSSUS," in N. Metropolis et al., eds., *A History of Computing in the Twentieth Century: A Collection of Essays* (New York: Academic Press, 1980): 47–92.

47. Flamm, *Creating the Computer*, 39–40.

48. Ibid., 41 n. 34. Belden and Belden, *Lengthening Shadow*, 218.

49. Ceruzzi, *Reckoners*, 43–72; Bashe, Johnson, Palmer, and Pugh, *IBM's Early Computers*, 25–26, 29–32, 47, 48, 316–17, 319–20.

50. Goldstine, *Computer*, 203.

51. Main thesis of Flamm, *Creating the Computer*, 29–41.

52. Simon H. Lavington, *Early British Computers* (Maynard, Mass.: Digital Press, 1980), 8–12, 23–30, 44–47.

Chapter 15
The Role of Major Vendors, 1939–1946

1. Burroughs Corporation, *1941 Annual Report*, 1.

2. Burroughs Corporation, *1942 Annual Report*, 1.

3. Macdonald, *Strategy for Growth*, 12.

4. Burroughs Corporation, *1943 Annual Report*, 1.

5. G. E. Leitch to L. V. Britt, October 3, 1945, "Norden Bombsight" files, Burroughs Papers.

6. Goldman, Sachs and Co., "Burroughs Adding Machine Company," (August 28, 1947, Report), 4–6, Burroughs Papers.

7. Ibid., 6.

8. Burroughs Corporation, *Annual Report*(s): *1941*, 1; *1942*, 1; *1943*, 1.

9. Neubecker, "Production and Sales," 15. Three spot authorizations were made for additional production of cash registers during the first quarter of 1945: NCR for six thousand, Allen Calculating for one hundred per quarter, McCaskey Register for one thousand, Sanders, "Section II Addendum," 5.

10. NCR, *1923–1953*, 31.

11. Ibid., 32–33.

12. Allyn, *My Half Century with NCR*, 69.

13. Marcosson, *Wherever Men Trade*, 191.

14. NCR, *1923–1951*, 34–35.

15. Quoted from *NCR Factory News* in Ibid., 38.

16. Ibid., 34.

17. Ibid., 38.

18. Marcosson, *Wherever Men Trade*, 150.

19. NCR, *1923–1951*, 38.

20. Marcosson, *Wherever Men Trade*, 158, 175.

21. NCR, *1923–1951*, 39.

22. Marcosson, *Wherever Men Trade*, 72.

23. Sobel, *IBM*, 105; Engelbourg, *International Business Machines*, 300–301.

24. Data from plaque with IBM's awards, IBM Archives.

25. Sobel, *IBM*, 104–5.

26. Fishman, *Computer Establishment*, 36; Sobel, *IBM*, 103, believed that IBM's population grew by only 50 percent.

27. Bashe, Johnson, Palmer, and Pugh, *IBM's Early Computers*, 21.

28. Belden and Belden, *Lengthening Shadow*, 210–11. IBM equipment was also used to track prisoners in Nazi concentration camps. Machines used for that purpose are now in the Holocaust Museum in Washington, D.C.

29. Editors of *Think, Think Magazine's Diary of U.S. Participation in World War II* (New York: IBM, 1946), 314.

30. Bashe, Johnson, Palmer, and Pugh, *IBM's Early Computers*, 26–27, 30.

31. Neubecker, "Production and Sales," 17–19.

32. Sanders, "Section II Addendum," app. 1-a, unpaginated.

33. Ibid.

34. Ibid.

35. Ibid.

36. Littlejohn and McClain, "Accounting Machine Industry," 24.

37. Ibid., 27.

38. Sanders, "History of the Administration of Regulations of the Office Machine and Typewriter Industries," 43.

39. The best study on the role of government that most completely summarizes opinions of historians on the topic is Flamm, *Creating the Computer*.

Chapter 16
Industry Structures, Vendors, and Practices, 1945–1956

1. Ratner, Soltow, and Sylla, *Evolution of the American Economy*, 401–38.

2. U.S. Department of Commerce, *Historical Statistics*, 139.

3. Ratner, Soltow, and Sylla, *The Evolution of the American Economy*, 479.

4. U.S. Department of Commerce, *Historical Statistics*, 73.

5. Ibid., 75.

6. Ibid., 77.

7. Foy, *Sun Never Sets on IBM*, 15–47.

8. U.S. Federal Trade Commission, *Report of the Federal Trade Commission on the Concentration of Productive Facilities* (Washington, D.C.: Government Printing Office, 1948): 41.

9. Ibid., 42.

10. Littlejohn and McClain, "Accounting Machine Industry," 6.

11. Engler, "Typewriter Industry," 156–58; but also see comments by John Zellers, *The Typewriter: A Short History* (New York: Newcomen Society of England, 1948). a vice-president of Remington Rand.

12. They were Swift and Clary.

13. Littlejohn and McClain, "Accounting Machine Industry," 17.

14. Ibid., 25.

15. For a description of the importance to IBM of tabulating marketing in the late 1940s see William W. Simmons and Richard B. Elsberry, *Inside IBM: The Watson Years. A Personal Memoir* (Bryn Mawr, Pa.: Dorrance and Co., 1988), 17–34.

16. Littlejohn and McClain, "Accounting Machine Industry," 29–30.

17. NCR, 38–45, NCR, *1952–1984: The Computer Era* (Dayton: NCR, 1984) 1, 4–6.

18. Simmons, *Inside IBM*, 17–34.

19. Census of Manufacturers data (1947, 1949) as presented in Littlejohn and McClain, "The Accounting Machine Industry," 142.

20. IBM, *Manual of IBM Punched Card Accounting Machines and Auxiliary Equipment* (New York: IBM, ca. 1956, with pages dating to early 1950s); on 650 see the section "IBM Punched Card Multiplying, Dividing and Calculating Machines," 23–25, where it was described as "a numerical, stored-program, data-processing machine," 23.

21. Littlejohn and McClain, "Accounting Machine Industry," 155, 157; Edwin Darby, *It All Adds Up: The Growth of Victor Comptometer Corporation* (Chicago: Victor Comptometer Corporation, 1968), 99–107.

22. As an IBM salesman in the Data Processing Division in 1979, I found an intact data center belonging to Worthington Pump Corporation at a foundry in New Jersey, which was completely stocked with punched card equipment from the 1940s and 1950s, proof that even decades later, computers had not fully displaced all tabulating technology. The entire data center's equipment was replaced with one IBM 8100 system that submitted work over a telephone line to the company's state-of-the-art IBM 4341 computer at the main data center.

23. Sobel, *IBM*, 131–32.

24. Foy, *Sun Never Sets on IBM*, 40–47; Connolly, *History of Computing*, 47.

25. Sobel, *IBM*, 197.

26. Ibid., 198–203.

27. Ibid., 107.

28. Watson, "Greatest Capitalist in History," 24–35, but also see a perspective by a highly influential management consultant and professor, Peter F. Drucker, "Thomas Watson's Principles of Modern Management," *Esquire* (December 1983): 194–202, which discusses both father and son. For Watson, Jr.'s account of relations with his father in this period see Watson, *Father Son & Co.*, 208–13, 220–26, 251–52. Many employees thought Watson, Sr., was still very much in command; see Herbert R. J. Grosch, *Computer: Bit Slices from Life* (Novato, Calif.: Third Millennium Books, 1991), 6–7.

29. Sobel, *IBM*, 142–44; Fisher, McKie, and Mancke, *IBM*, 34–35.

30. Watson, *Father Son & Co.*, 216.

31. Ibid., 218.

32. Ibid., first quote, 268; second quote, 270; and for Watson's view of the case, 268–71.

33. William F. Sharpe, *The Economics of Computers* (New York: Columbia University Press, 1969): 248–52.

34. Sobel, *IBM*, 144–47.

35. Ibid., for problems of definition by an historian, 138–41; by a team of economists see Fisher, McGowan, and Greenwood, *Folded, Spindled and Mutilated*, 43–97.

36. L. Beman, "IBM's Travails in Lilliput," *Fortune* 88 (November 1973): 148–50; R. P. Bigelow, "U.S. Versus IBM: An Exercise in Futility," *Abacus* 1, no. 2 (1984): 42–55; International Data Corporation, *IBM and the Courts: A Six Year Journal* (Waltham, Mass.: International Data Corporation, March 1975).

37. Phister, *Data Processing Technology and Economics*, 253–59, 263.

38. *Historical Dictionary*, 235–41.

39. Arthur D. Little, Inc. and White, Weld and Co. Research Department, *The Electronic Data Processing Industry* (New York: White, Weld and Co., 1956) for a sense of the times.

40. Yet within one year, IBM had more computers installed or on order than did Sperry Rand. The combination of the two older firms remained, however, a formidable rival to IBM. In the early 1960s, it was still second to IBM. Although it slipped through the 1970s and 1980s, over the summer of 1986 it merged with Burroughs Corporation to form Unisys, again making it the second largest vendor in the industry. Cortada, *Historical Dictionary*, 240–41.

41. *Poors' Register of Directors and Executives*, 1950; it also lists numbers of employees for all office appliance firms. Of some 31 firms listed, total employee population approached 149,000. As a point of interest, IBM had worldwide in 1946 more than 1,000 salesmen, of which 850 made quota, Watson, *Father Son & Co.*, 148.

42. Data drawn from table XIV, Lehman Brothers, "Burroughs Adding Machine Company: Study of Company and Its Position in the Business Machine Industry," Typescript, unpaginated table, copy in Burroughs Papers.

43. Phister, *Data Processing Technology and Economics*, 291. These declined to $864 million the following year and in 1958 increased to $990 million. These figures ranged from $1.17 billion in 1960 to $1.75 billion in 1969. By the early 1960s, some 50 percent of all Sperry-Rand revenues were from computer products, enough to keep UNIVAC in second place during the 1950s and very early 1960 (44–45).

44. Marcosson, *Wherever Men Trade*, 148–49, 150–51.

45. NCR, *1923–1951*, 46.

46. Allyn, *My Half Century with NCR*, 158.

47. Ibid.

48. NCR, *1952–1984*, 3–5.

49. Ibid., 5.

50. NCR, *1923–1951*, 41.

51. Ibid., 39–40.

52. Ibid., 44.

53. Phister, *Data Processing Technology and Economics*, 291.

54. Ibid.

55. Lehman Brothers, "Burroughs Adding Machine Company," table XIV, unpaginated.

56. Ibid., table XV, unpaginated.

57. Macdonald, *Strategy for Growth*, 13; Goldman, Sachs and Co., *Burroughs Adding Machine Company* (New York: Goldman, Sachs and Co., August 28, 1947), 1, copy in Burroughs Papers.

58. Burroughs, *Annual Report 1947*, last sheet, unpaginated.

59. Burroughs, *Annual Report 1946*, 17.

60. Burroughs, *Annual Report 1947*, 5.

61. Ibid., 9.

62. Ibid., 11.

63. Burroughs, *Annual Report 1948*, 4.

64. Ibid., 8.

65. Macdonald, *Strategy for Growth*, 15.

66. Fisher, McKie, and Manke, *IBM*, 46.

67. Quoted in ibid., 82.

68. Ibid., 82–85, for Burroughs's activities.

69. IBM, NCR, Remington Rand, Addressograph, Royal, Smith-Corona, Underwood, Felt & Tarrant, Marchant, and Monroe.

70. Data drawn from Lehman Brothers, "Burroughs Adding Machine Company," table XIV, unpaginated.

71. Ibid.

72. Phister, *Data Processing Technology and Economics*, 291.

73. Ibid., 293.

74. Ratner, Soltow, and Sylla, *Evolution of the American Economy*, 415–17.

75. Fisher, McGowan, and Greenwood, *Folded, Spindled, and Mutilated*, 344–46.

76. DeLamarter, *Big Blue*. Sample reviews: *Choice* 24 (June 1987): 1588; *Library Journal* 112 (March 15, 1987): 28; *New York Times Book Reviews* 91 (November 23, 1986): 13; *SciTech Book Notes* 11 (January 1987): 3.

77. Littlejohn and McClain to Coleman, June 30, 1950, Burroughs Papers.

78. Littlejohn and McClain, "Accounting Machine Industry," 69.

79. Russell B. McNeill, "The Lease as a Marketing Tool," *Harvard Business Review* (Summer 1944): 423–25.

80. For background on the issues, *Federal Antitrust Laws;* W. S. Stevens, "Trusts and Combinations," 625–30; Simon N. Whitney, *Antitrust Policies*, vol. 2 (New York: Twentieth Century Fund, 1958); Fisher, McGowan, and Greenwood, *Folded, Spindled, and Mutilated.*

81. Fisher, McGowan, and Greenwood, *Folded, Spindled, and Mutilated*, 341–52.

82. Sobel, *IBM*, 254–76.

Chapter 17
Business Volumes

1. Connolly, *History of Computing*, 46–48.

2. Ibid., 55.

3. Ibid., E-18.

4. Moreau, *Computer Comes of Age*, 25, 63, 64; Foy, *Sun Never Sets on IBM*, 23–24; Connolly, *History of Computing*, E-19-E-23. On IBM see Jacques Vernay, *Chroniques de la compagnie IBM France* (Paris: IBM France, 1988), and idem, "IBM France," *Annals of the History of Computing* 11, no. 4 (1989): 299–311; also useful for Machines Bull is H. Cahen, *La compagnie des Machines Bull, ses machines, leur application à la facturation de la Biscuiterie Alsacienne* (Paris: École Superieure de

Commerce, 1955). See also Stephen Christian Lutze, "The Formation of the International Computer Industry, 1945–1960" (M.A. thesis, University of California, Santa Barbara, 1979).

5. U.S. Department of Commerce, *World Trade in Typewriters, 1948–1958* (Washington, D.C.: Government Printing Office, 1959).

6. U.S. Department of Commerce, U.S. Business and Defense Services Administration, *World Trade in Adding Machines, Calculators, Cash Registers, 1953–1959* (Washington, D.C.: Government Printing Office, 1960), 4.

7. Ibid., 6.

8. Firms used were Burroughs, IBM, NCR, Remington Rand, Addressograph, Royal Typewriter, Smith-Corona, Underwood, Felt & Tarrant, Marchant, and Monroe.

9. Lutze, "International Computer Industry," 89, for statistics on typewriter sales.

10. U.S. Department of Commerce, *World Trade in Adding Machines, Calculators, Cash Registers*, 7–8.

11. The same pattern perdured with large computers in the 1960s and 1970s, Fisher, McGowan, and Greenwood, *Folded, Spindled, and Mutilated*, 219–69; and for an opposing view DeLamarter, *Big Blue*, 77, 91–92, but also 47–52 for the 1950s; and on the period generally, Sharpe, *Economics of Computers*, 61–93.

12. U.S. Department of Commerce, *Historical Statistics*, 1109.

13. Lutze, "International Computer Industry," 89–90.

14. Ibid., 90, annual reports cited.

15. John M. Carroll, "Electronic Computers for the Businessman," *Electronics* 28 (June 1955): 122–31; "New Tools for Managers Catch on Fast," *Business Week*, February 12, 1955, 88; "Sale of Computers to Business Hits a New Stride, Makers Say," ibid., September 24, 1955, 146.

16. Daniel Bell, "Social Framework," 163–211.

17. Ibid., 186.

18. Shoshana Zuboff, *In the Age of the Smart Machine: The Future of Work and Power* (New York: Basic Books, 1988): 415–22ff.

19. Machlup, *Production and Distribution*, 360–61. He updated his work in idem, *Knowledge*.

20. Machlup's three books. For a creative, useful study of the implications of technology on workers see Zuboff, *Age of the Smart Machine*.

21. I have explored the issues in Cortada, *Strategic Data Processing*, 37–46, 94–107, 191–92. For discussion of costs more contemporaneous to the 1950s see Gregory and Van Horn, *Automatic Data-Processing Systems*, 414–44, which includes additional bibliography on the topic.

Chapter 18
Conclusion: The Roles of Marketing, Distribution, and Technology

1. All the early inventors focused on what they perceived as needs, not demand. Not until a class of products existed could one speak of market demand because potential customers were not requesting specific products, such as typewriters or tabulating machines, as a rule, until they were invented.

2. For example, C. West Churchman, Russell L. Ackoff, and E. Leonard Arnoff,

Introduction to Operations Research (New York: John Wiley and Sons, 1957); Workshop for Management, *Proceedings of the Eighth Annual Systems Meeting* (New York: Systems and Procedures Association of America, Management Magazines, 1956).

3. For an example see Beniger, *Control Revolution*.

4. Zuboff, *Age of the Smart Machine*.

5. Bashe, Johnson, Palmer, and Pugh, *IBM's Early Computers*, 69–71.

6. Neil Rackham, *SPIN Selling* (New York: McGraw-Hill, 1988), ix, includes examples of selling in the computer world of the 1980s.

7. Ibid., 139–41.

8. Flamm, *Creating the Computer*, 217–24; Sharpe, *Economics of Computers*, 131–34, 375–80; Fisher, McGowan, and Greenwood, *Folded, Spindled, and Mutilated*.

9. Flamm, *Creating the Computer*, 203–234.

10. Basalla, *Evolution of Technology*, 208–9.

11. This was true at least until the Consent Decree of 1956 led IBM to reduce its dominance in card sales.

12. See chap. 6.

13. For a useful discussion of how capital requirements became an entry barrier see Gerald W. Brock, *U.S. Computer Industry*, 55–68.

14. Zuboff, *Age of the Smart Machine*, 107–13. On IBM's Basic Beliefs see Watson, Jr., *Business and Its Beliefs*. The basis of my thinking about corporate culture comes from a study with many examples drawn from the data processing world, Terrence E. Deal and Allan A. Kennedy, *Corporate Cultures: The Rites and Rituals of Corporate Life* (Reading, Mass.: Addison-Wesley, 1982).

15. NCR, *Celebrating the Future*, all four pamphlets.

16. I am collecting biographies of IBM executives as they retire. Of the five hundred in my possession, all stress longevity of service and involve careers of more than twenty years, most of careers of more than twenty-five years. They are proof of the emphasis on continuity of employment as a virtue.

17. For example, Claude Baum, *The System Builders; The Story of SCD* (Santa Monica, Ca.: Systems Development Corporation, 1981); Computer Sciences Corporation, *CSC News* 15, no. 3 (April 1984): 1–32, dedicated to the history of CSC (1959–1984); Dataproducts Corporation, *The First 20 Years of Dataproducts* (Woodland Hills, Calif.: Dataproducts Corporation, 1982); Hewlett-Packard Company, *Hewlett-Packard: A Company History* (Palo Alto, Calif.: Hewlett-Packard, 1983); Glynnis Thompson Kaye, ed., *A Revolution in Progress: A History of Intel to Date* (Santa Clara: Intel Corporation, 1984); Sandy Lanzarotta, "Datamation—The Early Days," *Datamation* 28, no. 10 (September 1982): 157–60.

18. Chandler, *Scale and Scope*, 146.

19. Ibid., 84, 89.

20. Ibid., 610. I was completing this book at about the same time Chandler was his and thus did not have the opportunity to benefit fully from his latest thinking until after I had reached my conclusions. Thus I believe the evidence from the office appliance industry stands on its own as a ringing confirmation of his ideas. For that reason, I concluded that the office appliance industry can be instructive about other industries per se, not merely other "high-tech" ones.

21. Although Beniger, *Control Revolution*, is an excellent example of the concern, see also Nancy Dorfman, *Innovation in the Computer and Semiconductor Industries* (New York: Ballinger, 1987).

22. William F. Finan and Annette M. LaMond, "Sustaining U.S. Competitiveness in Micro-Electronics: The Challenge to U.S. Policy," in Bruce R. Scott and George C. Lodge, eds., *U.S. Competitiveness in the World Economy* (Boston: Harvard Business School Press, 1985), 144–75; McClellan, *Computer Industry Shakeout*; Tom Forester, *High-Tech Society* (Cambridge, Mass.: MIT Press, 1987), 17–49.

23. For a good summary see Paul Kennedy, *The Rise and Fall of the Great Powers* (New York: Random House, 1987), 3–30.

24. C. C. Cipolla ed., *The Economic Decline of Empires* (London: Methuen, 1970); Joseph Needham, *The Grand Titration: Science and Society in East and West* (London: Allen and Unwin, 1969); E. L. Jones, *The European Miracle: Environments, Economies and Geopolitics in the History of Europe and Asia* (Cambridge: Cambridge University Press, 1981) to mention three of dozens of recent studies.

25. W. Brian Arthur Yu. M. Ermoliev, and Yu. M Kaniouski, "Path-Dependent Processes and the Emergence of Macro-Structure," *European Journal of Operational Research* 30 (1987): 294–303; W. Brian Arthur, "Competing Technologies, Increasing Returns, and Lock-in by Historical Events," *Economic Journal* 99, no. 394 (March 1989): 116–31; Philip W. Anderson, Kenneth J. Arrow, and David Pines, *The Economy as an Evolving Complex System: Proceedings of the Evolutionary Paths of the Global Economy Workshop, held September 1987 in Santa Fe, New Mexico* (Reading, Mass.: Addison-Wesley, 1988).

26. W. Brian Arthur, "Positive Feedbacks in the Economy," *Scientific American* 262, no. 2 (February 1990): 98; the article is a good introduction to the new economic theories, (92–99).

27. Beniger, *Control Revolution*; Albert Borgman, *Technology and the Character of Contemporary Life* (Chicago: University of Chicago Press, 1984), and Daniel Boorstin, *The Republic of Technology* (New York: Harper and Row, 1978) are two good background studies but also Herbert G. Gutman, *Work, Culture and Society in Industrializing America* (New York: Vintage Books, 1976).

28. Flamm, *Creating the Computer*, 217.

29. C. T. Taylor and A. A. Silberston, *The Economic Impact of the Patent System: A Study of the British Experience* (Cambridge: Cambridge University Press, 1973), is a model study that needs to be replicated for the United States.

30. Flamm, *Creating the Computer*, 219.

31. Telephone conversation with Dave Sheridan, February 6, 1989. Sheridan retired from what is now called Unisys in 1981. His last position was director of advertising, and he spent his career at Remington Rand and its successor firm.

32. For discussion of OEM activities in different periods see Fisher, McKie, and Mencke, *IBM*.

33. Robert Rotenberg, "Community, Time and the Technical Order," in Steven E. Goldberg and Charles R. Strain, *Technological Change*, 133–44.

34. Chandler, *Visible Hand*.

35. I have surveyed the industry in Cortada, "An Introduction to the History of the Data Processing Industry," in Cortada *Historical Dictionary of Data Processing*, 1–44.

36. For a sense of the issue see Rotenberg, "Community, Time and the Technical Order."

37. Zuboff, *Age of the Smart Machine*, 115–16.

38. Chandler, *Visible Hand*, 493.

Index

A. B. Dick Company: birth of, 23–24; in World War II, 196

Abbott Coin Counter, 224

Académie des Sciences, 27

Accountancy: demand for adding machines, 166; early uses of adding machines, 32, 35–36; in late 1800s, 26–27; role and function of accountants (1920s), 101–2; use of Hollerith equipment (1900–1917) in, 50–52: in 1920s–1930s, 92

Accountants, printing tabulators and, 132

Accounting machines: from NCR (1923–1930s), 178–80; prices of, 125; uses and types, 159–62; vendors (1941) of, 217

Add-Index, 178

Adder Machine Company, finances (1910–1913) of, 85–86

Adding machines: become viable, 267; early uses of, 32; in Europe, 181–82, 247–55; initial demand for, 26; marketing of, 162–63, 171–86; non-U.S. sales of, 37–39; number built, 163–64; production of (1950s), 258–59; railroads use, 9; sales analysis with, 50; significance of, 25–26; speed of acceptance compared to cash registers, 65; technology of, 26; uses and types, 162–67; vendors, in 1920s, 98–99, 101; vendors, in 1941, 217

Addler, 21

Addressing machines, 161

Addressograph-Multigraph Corporation (Addressograph Company), 147, 161, 197

Advertising, at NCR (1800s–early 1900s), 69

AEG, 21

Africa, cash registers in, 64

Agents: in Europe (1920s–1930s), 139; role in marketing (1920s–1930s), 119

Aiken, Howard, role of, 203–4

Air mail, 98

Allen-Wales Adding Machine Company, 217; acquired by NCR (1943), 212

Allies, U.S. purchases for, 191–92

Allison, J. W., role at NCR, 73

Allyn, Stanley C., 178, 236, 238; role of, 196

American Astronomical Society, Columbia University and, 135–36

American Cash Register Company, NCR suit against, 77

American City, on use of accounting machines, 130–31

American Gas Journal, on data processing, 129

American Sheet and Tin Plate, as Hollerith customer, 54

American Steel and Wire, uses Victor machines, 172

American Telephone and Telegraph Company (AT&T), 83, creates Bell Laboratories, 94; Hollerith's equipment, 51; legal problems with U.S. Justice Department, 4, 75, 222; World War I and, 82

American Writing Machine Company, 17

Analysis machines. *See* Punched card equipment

Antitrust activities, 4; NCR and, 74–78; in 1930s, 116–18; in 1945–56, 242–46. *See also* International Business Machines Corporation; Remington Rand Corporation

Apple Computers, 271

Applications, commercial (1920s–1930s), 92; in Europe, 42–43, 138; machines for, 160–70; military uses, 189, 201–5; nature of, 266; punched card uses, 49–52, 128–36

Argentina, NCR in, 73

Arithema, established (1947), 248

Arithmometer: described, 28; sold, 41

Arithmometer Company, 13; history of, 32–36

Armour and Company, uses Victor machines, 172

Asia: office applications (late 1940s), 224; post-1945 activities in, 247, 250

Astronomers, punched card needs of, 134–35

Astronomy, at Columbia University, 135–36

Auditing Machine Company, 5

Australian Exposition (1887), uses NCR cash registers, 73